Currents of Unrest

OTHER BOOKS BY ORRIN E. KLAPP

Social Types: Process, Structure and Ethos (1971)

Collective Search for Identity (1969)

Symbolic Leaders: Public Dramas and Public Men (1964)

Heroes, Villains, and Fools: The Changing American Character (1962)

Ritual and Cult: A Sociological Interpretation (1956)

Currents of Unrest

An Introduction to Collective Behavior

ORRIN E. KLAPP
California State University, San Diego

Holt, Rinehart and Winston, Inc.
*New York   Chicago   San Francisco   Atlanta
Dallas   Montreal   Toronto   London   Sydney*

Copyright © 1972 by Holt, Rinehart and Winston, Inc.
Library of Congress Catalog Card Number: 76–189252
ISBN: 0–03–085305–2
Printed in the United States of America
2 3 4 5   038   9 8 7 6 5 4 3 2 1

Preface

This book deals with what is commonly called mass or collective behavior such as exhibited by crowds, emotional contagions, rumors, fads, fashions, audience vicarious experience, hero worship, and elementary collectivities and movements. While the margins of this field are not necessarily sharp, the focus of the book is on *anonymous interpersonal interactions*—communications that come from an unidentified source, from a network not clearly defined, or from people one does not control and with whom one has no personal relationship. Because such communication flows largely unwittingly among persons who do not know one another, it is difficult to trace, study, or even be aware of its impact. It is hard to control because, unlike mass media, its sources, channels, and gatekeepers are unknown.

One kind of such communication consists of emotional contagions, discussed in Chapters 3 (crowds) and 6. Another consists of stories, songs, sayings, catchwords—verbal messages of a repeatable sort coming from everywhere and nowhere, treated in Chapter 8. There is a more subtle kind of anonymous interpersonal communication called vicarious experience, which consists of taking roles of (identification with) other people, one that is not in the least inhibited by the fact that the models happen to be strangers (accuracy is, of course, another thing). This type occurs all the time in daily life, as in fashion; but it is most conspicuous in audience dreaming while viewing dramas, and in the orientation of fans to popular heroes.

It is true that for all the main forms of anonymous interpersonal communication (contagion, rumor, vicarious learning, and fashion), we usually do not know where the messages come from, who influenced the person who influenced us, or by what channel they came. The impact of interaction among uncounted numbers of people who pass each other on the street or who meet briefly in daily life gives rise to the currents that we propose to study.

Such communications create a sense of "we" among strangers and unite people in vague collectivities and shifting alignments. In the last analysis, they are what make a mass society *masslike*, as contrasted with the status relations of an oral system, discussed in Chapter 8. Such communications do not follow established networks nor do they have manifest and authorized functions. Nevertheless, they "spill over" into the mass consciousness, and therefore tension theory is required to help explain them.

Now well we know that the more masslike a society is, the more it has certain kinds of problems—commonly called by names like unrest, hysteria, alienation, powerlessness, anomie. Thus, to analyze phenomena of collective behavior is at the same time to analyze communication and diagnose ills of mass society. It is impossible to write a meaningful account of collective behavior such as that of protest, riots, and movements without an exploration, even an indictment, of conditions that are stressful, tension-producing, and which ought to be remedied if possible. One need not make a value judgment to study a thing scientifically; but the fact remains that many of the phenomena are symptoms of social malaise, and society would be better off if it had far fewer of them.

This means, from a pedagogical point of view, that it is more natural—and probably more interesting—that collective behavior be treated as a matter of human concern in relation to the strains that give rise to such behavior rather than as "pure" sociologic phenomena, at least in an introductory course. This is the perspective I have taken, and for this reason the book may be useful in courses that deal with social problems and communication.

On the theoretical side, there is a matter that should be pointed to here: the use of metaphors and models that do not fit well together. This, as I would like to explain, reflects the state of theory as it appears to me, and is an effort to grasp a reality that is more complex than the models (the story of the blind men and the elephant will perhaps come to mind here).

The two main types of inconsistent metaphors are those, on the one hand, that express the idea of a system, such as tension and "safety valves," and, on the other hand, a free-flowing process or "river" that is not "functional" within a system but which is seeking outlet to an unspecified destination. The "counterculture" is an example. The truth, I believe, is that our society is engaged in a pursuit of meaning which will go considerably beyond what present planners, legislators, and even reformers have in mind. That, indeed, is the central theme of this book—that collective behavior at its deeper levels is concerned with the pursuit of meaning and identity.

It seems hardly likely that one can have both at the same time—a system that is preserving itself with some oscillations, and a river that is going somewhere, no one knows quite where. Yet, at this time I see no way of making sense of collective behavior without using both models, however inharmonious. Sometimes a "wave" or "pendulum" metaphor seems appropriate; at other times novelty and emergence seem to be the thing.

The fact that systems theory and terms like feedback and entropy are only beginning to be applied to collective behavior gives us no way of telling yet how far one can go with such models. It might be said, for example, that there is a kind of equilibrium, sometimes disturbed by pendulum swings, in modern society between forces making for alienation and forces making for "we." On the other hand, symbolic interactionists such as Blumer are justified in pointing out that mechanical analogies cannot be applied to phenomena like communication and social integration and function without distorting human reality.

Somewhere between are metaphors, such as incubation and ferment—which are basically biological—expressing systemic forms to be realized from a prototype or seed, while at the same time signifying open-ended evolution of new forms in natural selection (free flow).

There is more to be said about this problem. Perhaps we may be excused for not trying to settle the question and go ahead with inconsistent metaphors, perhaps heartened by the precedent of wave-and-particle energy theory in physics. Mixed metaphors in such a situation, then, reflect necessity and not just carelessness.

Somewhat the same holds for the ancient controversy over instincts (or whatever one may call biological determinants) as they express themselves in institutions and collective behavior. Since this argument still boils fiercely among scholars, why try to calm it down by arbitrarily deciding that Freud or Dewey was wrong? Until it is settled, animal collective behavior is relevant; and that is why we have included Chapter 4, whether it proves the difference or the similarities between animals and humans.

The main relevance to the student is that, in this world of "future shock," "countercultures," and ever more rapid change, institutions and establishments tell us where we have been, but it is the study of collective behavior that is going to tell us where we are going.

The whole development of social movements is beyond the scope of this book—a separate course usually being devoted to this subject. Our study here treats only the grounds of unrest, contagions (anonymous interpersonal communication), and seeding of collectivities from which movements develop. A single case is treated in Chapter 11, the "countercultural" movement, as an example of a meaning-seeking movement, which responds to spiritual emptiness, formalism, and banality in a system. That modern society suffers from such a malaise seems plain enough, but this condition is not a new phenomenon, for other periods and cultures have had it in different terms. Meaning-seeking movements are harder to understand than practical ones because they begin by a strange (what Weber calls charismatic) experience leading them to reject the premises of a system in which they emerge; but *their* premises can be seen clearly only after the groping is over, that is, when their positive affirmations are established in ritual, names, creeds, and myths.

The study of collective behavior was started by thinkers like LeBon, Durkheim, Tarde, Simmel, Weber, and Freud. But Americans Edward A. Ross, and Robert E. Park and his students, especially Herbert Blumer, were the ones who really put "collective behavior" into business as a recognized area of sociology. This book tries to follow in that tradition.

I gratefully acknowledge the advice of colleagues who have been kind enough to read portions of the manuscript: Herbert Blumer, Walter Buckley, Shelly Chandler, Mohammed El-Assal, Lawrence J. Fogel, Joseph R. Gusfield, Richard D. Jones, Tamotsu Shibutani, and Anselm L. Strauss.

San Diego, Calif.   O. E. K.
March 1972

Contents

PART I

Elementary Collective Behavior

CHAPTER 1

Collective Identity
and Social Entropy

We begin this book by exploring the meaning of togetherness
—a rare, a vanishing, a nostalgic commodity. When stabi-
lized, it is ethnic identity; when evanescent, it is the "we"
feeling of crowds, or, perhaps, of encounter groups. Somewhere between each state are various degrees of collective
identity, sometimes referred to as morale or reference-group

orientation. Absolute zero of collective identity would be total alienation.

Collective identity provides a background for the study of collective behavior. It seems plain that in collective behavior and social movements people are negotiating *collectivity* of one kind or another, from anonymous crowds to the most durable collective identity. Collective identity is a major reason for getting together with people; for some it is a whole world, for others it is a world lost.

Who Are "We"?

People who have a clear sense of themselves as a people and as a group distinct from others may be said to live in a world of collective identity. For example, the Navajo call themselves "The People," to which no one belongs who cannot speak their language and trace connections with their relatives (Kluckhohn and Leighton, 1947:183–231; Leighton and Leighton, 1944:22–23). Gypsies, too, have a fierce pride, and secretiveness protects them from too much contact with outsiders; a non-Gypsy finds it impossible to penetrate their tight little world of "we" (Yoors, 1967:81; Webb, 1960:19–21). So it is with Cretans, or Arabs, or any tribe or small community that has lived a long time without too much contact with outsiders. Redfield said that in very close-knit groups, one finds a kind of group personality:

> The unity and distinctiveness of the little community is felt by everyone who is brought up in it . . . the people . . . know each of the other members of that community as part of one another . . . as belonging together: The "we" that each inhabitant uses recognizes the separateness of that band or village from all others. (Redfield, 1960: 9–10.)

The point is that there is no way to enter such tight little worlds unless one shares in the people's image of "we." To know the culture, even to speak the language and be accepted as a "friend," is not enough. When an outsider finally made it into a Gypsy company, it was only after years of association as a boy (Yoors, 1967: 81).

Such a world of collective identity is, of course, unlike that of most Americans. Mobile pluralism makes it hard to sustain, even to experience, a social world with restricted boundaries. This reflects the fact—perhaps intensified in America—that for the past hundred years the trend of modern societies has been to weaken local "we" feeling, not as deliberate policy but mostly as a side effect of "progress" and modernization. The modern man is psychologically mobile (Lerner, 1959); his hallmarks are individualism and independence of close ties, among other things (Kahl, 1968:18–21). In short, modern man has, for practical purposes at least, escaped his "we" group—if, indeed, he had any. Earlier sociologists called this the movement from "natural" (Gemeinschaft) to "rational" (Gesellschaft) groups (Tonnies, 1940) or primary to secondary groups (Cooley, 1909; Park and Burgess, 1924). Sociologists pointed out that loss of morale might be the price paid if primary groups were destroyed or neglected (Mayo, 1933; Roethlisberger, 1941; Nisbet, 1953:246).

What takes the place of "we" in a modern, mobile, pluralistic society is *reference groups*. These are groups with which a person *compares* himself, or to whose norms he *refers* for personal guidance. It is not necessary to *belong* to reference groups, which can be in conflict, and a person may change from one viewpoint to another (Merton, 1968:279–334). The limits of a reference group are not set by whom a person knows, but by what M. and C. Sherif (1964:184) called the *self-radius*: "where he sets his sights . . . his personal goals." So, it is clear that self-radius may extend to life styles in mass media and other groups in which a person has no membership. A person may have many more self-references than collective identities as shared concepts and reciprocal relationships. The point is that the individual *chooses* reference groups and is not necessarily chosen by them; he does not have to interact with the members in order to prove and discover that he shares the same collective identity. A person may make superficial (reference) claims to a group identity by mere verbal assertions, names, argot, self-reference, dress, even pose, none of which has a basis in membership. Suppose, for example, that he wants to adopt the style of "show people," or declare himself a Buddhist. No reciprocal response from the group is necessary. So we see that a mass society might be a great fluff of identity claims based on reference, without possessing the characteristic of what we call collective identity.

Perhaps the main point is that collective identity is not just a shared concept or reference to a group norm, but a net, or *system*. As a leading theorist James G. Miller said—

> Living systems at the group level and above maintain their cohesion by . . . memories; by messages signaling the interlocking relationships among their units; by common purposes and goals; by common rewards, payoffs, or gratifications; or by common punishments by boundary-maintaining processes for actions leading to dissolution of the system. . . . Information flows over a channel or network are necessary to integrate a system, unless all components were pre-programmed by information stored in them at an earlier time. (Miller, 1965:375.)

If this is so, then mere reference of *A*, *B*, *C* to the same norm or symbol cannot give them a collective identity unless sufficient *system* exists among their relationships for them to continue to act jointly, share goals and rewards, recognize one another, keep in communication, build common memories, and maintain boundaries. In this sense, transitory "we" feeling in crowds and other anonymous collectivities, fashions, and much reference-group behavior fall short of collective identity, because there just isn't enough system underlying them. The minimum requirement seems to be a *closed feedback loop* of messages among members so that they can develop and maintain a collective identity over time.

Where such a system exists, it is possible to build an identification with others that is more than transitory or merely a reference. When a person has a well-developed "we," his personal identity is composed of two parts: the "I," "me" (ego, self-images) and the "we," or concepts of self-as-belonging, including one's place as member or memory of interactions with others (who have corresponding "we" feelings), and appropriate responses such as loyalty. A person may have a strong "I" and a weak "we," or vice versa, though normally they go together. Needless to say, many relationships and organizations in modern life—the market, bureaucracy, society as a total system—are weak in "we." Figure 1.1 may make plainer the part played by "we" as a social bond.

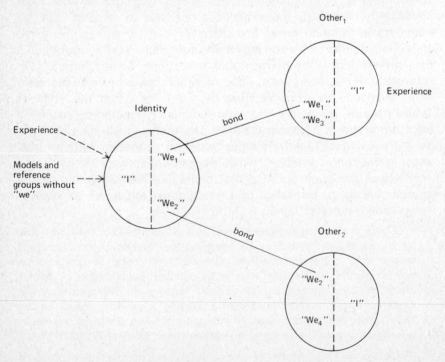

FIGURE 1.1.   Identity and "we" feeling.

How Collective Identity Grows and Is Kept Alive

What is the origin of collective identity? Inputs from group experience and history provide the information that can be fed back to make collective identity. Illustrations may be found under the general headings of *history*, *ritual*, and *interaction*.

First, it seems plain that events such as the landing of the spaceship Apollo and planting of an American flag on the moon, or the defeat of Napoleon by Wellington, can become landmarks of national identity. What Jew can forget Masada, a rock on which, in the year 73 C.E., a band of Jewish zealots—960 men, women, and children—defied a Roman army, and then died at their own hands rather than surrender? In the opposite way, a burden of guilt was suffered by many Germans after World War II, when they discovered what had been going on in the concentration camps. So historical events make their contribution to collective identity. Deutsch said that the growth of national consciousness occurs by the attachment of "secondary symbols" of nationality to information that otherwise might not unite or might even divide the people. Symbols such as names, flags, and heroes must be added to highlight whatever interdependence and ethnic distinctness there may be (Deutsch, 1953:144–152). Merritt (1966) identified such a period in the emergence of American national consciousness during the American Revolution. *Separation*, whether chosen, (as in the case of the Mormons) or imposed (as in the case of ghettos) is an important experience for establishing collective identity, since it not only sharpens boundaries but also creates a barrier against communication of "noise" from other groups (Deutsch, 1953:149). *Conflict*, of course, sharpens the sense of collective identity: depicting the outsider as a villain and drawing the ingroup closer in loyalty and common cause. There are even cases when a group that feels a threat to its identity will seek deviants to sharpen its own boundaries, as in the persecution of "witches" by New England Puritans in the seventeenth century (Erikson, 1966:155–156). Spicer stresses continued opposition as a factor in forming cultural identity systems (1971).

A major source of feedback for group identity is the role of heroes and leaders as *group superselves*, who embody on a larger scale—through acts, style, or personality traits—what the group believes and wishes itself to be. This type of feedback was exemplified by leaders like Churchill, Nassar, Dayan, Sukarno, and De Gaulle, of whom a study concluded that his contribution to the grandeur and pride of the French was a "style without much substance" (S. and I. Hoffman, 1968). This is, perhaps, a little hard on De Gaulle, but the point is that a dramatic role or style may make more contribution to collective identity than will practical achievement. In the group superself, people realize what they think they *ought to be* in the light of their ethos; their hero is not a modal personality but an ideal by means of which people can realize themselves imaginatively and heroically. His task is not to act as an average man but to fulfill the collective identity. Like Odysseus at the prow of his ship, he provides a journey for all who ride with him (Klapp, 1969:211–256.)

All the trappings of history, including any fiction and legend that has been produced, are fed back to group awareness by means of *ceremony* and *ritual*. We readily see that festivals like Christmas, Easter, July Fourth, Thanksgiving, and Yom Kippur repeat events of great significance not only to inform people of what happened but also to remind them of who they are. A similar function is performed by ritual drama, such as repetition of the *Ramayana* in South Asia, or a reunion of a Scottish clan in its ancient castle to hail the chief, dance to bagpipes, and drink from the horn. All such ritual feeds back to the group some essential part of the collective identity. Because events of the day, called news, continually put new roles into this feedback, public drama needs to be continually studied as a crucible for the forming of collective identity (Klapp, 1964a).

Beneath ritual and historical experience there is the importance of continuous *interaction*, both verbal and nonverbal (nondiscursive), which assures people in countless ways, in daily life, and in primary groups that they understand one another, are concerned about one another, share similar "we" concepts, and so on. Expressive gestures must maintain the right feeling-tone in interaction. There should be sufficient spontaneity and "peak" experiences (Maslow, 1962) to make it fun as well as reassuring to be together. Such things being investigated in the area of kinesics (Birdwhistell, 1970), therapeutic communication (Matson and Montagu, 1967; Jourard, 1964; Rogers, 1961), and small group interaction (Bales, 1950) need not concern us in detail here.

To see collective identity in its systemic aspect, however, we shall gain by considering a feedback model of a communication net, by which morale and other feelings of collective identity are generated. To have any idea at all of how groups grow a collective identity, we must suppose that they have an adequate feedback system, including reliable channels and a favorable balance of messages having to do with "we." Until he met Friday, Robinson Crusoe was in a predicament because he lacked such feedback; his "we" was fading—hence his meaning system—and he needed a new input.

It is possible to construct a systemic model of a net of communication needed by a group, large or small, to achieve and preserve a collective identity over time, including turnover of generations. The basic functions, whether performed by one or several members, are *A* the actor, agent, or executive who acts upon (transduces group output to) the external environment; *B* the receptor, gatekeeper, innovator, or news carrier, who brings most outside news into the group; *C* the teller or chronicler, who relays and records information for the group; *D* the creative interpreter, artist, or poet, who embellishes and constructs works of art or myths and theories; and *E* the custodian of norms and tradition, who acts as historian, arbiter, umpire, ritualist, or protocol expert who holds the keys, so to speak, to group memory. Figure 1.2 represents these functions.

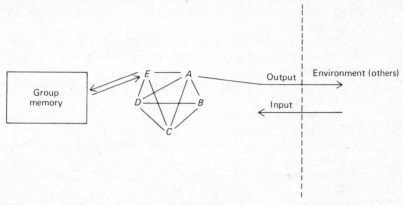

FIGURE 1.2. Feedback model of collective identity.

Group memory is crucial. Deutsch held that group identity and autonomy (the ability to make independent decisions and govern oneself) depend on it: "The selfhood of any social system" depends upon an open flow of feedback of information to memory; without this, self-determination is lost and the group becomes passive and loses its power of self-steering, like a drifting ship. It is essential, however, that "we" symbols attach themselves to primary items of information moving through the channels so they can be stored in group memory as "ours." Thus, "every self-governing system must . . . remake its own memories and inner structure as it acts" (Deutsch, 1953:146, 152; 1966:221).

A number of hypotheses flow from such a model, many of which are well supported by experience. Some of these are:

1. *A well-developed collective identity normally has the other things that go with it, such as morale and cohesiveness; and conversely for poorly developed collective identity.*
2. *Collective identity is stronger, the more speedy, accurate, and trustworthy is the communication net (including gossip):*

    a. General exchange of information.

    b. Specialized functions (gatekeeper, artist, etc.).

3. *A well-developed collective identity has good feedback, especially with regard to*

    a. "We"-related information (see 4 below).

    b. Payoffs from the system in response to members' contributions.

    c. Interpersonal interaction (see below).

    d. Building up and referring to group memory.

4. *Collective identity will be stronger, the more "we"-related information there is; for example:*

    a. The better and more favorable is the information *from the environment about the collectivity* ("we," "our," etc.), such as feedback about group efforts and success.

    b. The more favorable internal information there is *about the group from members* (testimonials, statements of feelings such as pride and loyalty, etc.).

    c. The more, and more favorably, an *individual hears about himself* from members as belonging, succeeding according to group norms, being honored, etc.

    d. The more effective are ritual and ceremony reviving and reinforcing group memory:

        1) Regularity and frequency.

        2) Emotional effectiveness.

    e. The more satisfying is the role of "our" leader or group superself (including martyrs):

        1) Direct interaction.

        2) Dramatic (vicarious) role.

    f. The more nondiscursive communication (gestures, kinesics, expressions, etc.) supports "we."

5. *The relation of the collectivity to its "we" is homeostatic—in several ways; for example:*

    a. Threats or information adverse to "we" will be followed by reactions to strengthen and defend it.

    b. Because a group wants favorable feedback to its "we," it tends to listen to its own side rather than the other (commonly called ethnocentrism). Hence it

        1) Rejects criticism and negative information as "disloyality," "insult."

        2) Opens itself to flattery and self-homage.

        3) Fails to see itseif as acting immorally (Niebuhr, 1932).

6. *Interfering with the above communication circuits and homeostasis weakens collective identity and related variables of solidarity, especially*

    a. Gaps and interruptions too long (for example, "news from home"), so group memory fades.

    b. Overload of information that is not "we"-related in proportion to that which is "we"-relevant (Chapter 9).

    c. Overload of monological information in proportion to dialogical (oral, interactional) (Chapter 9).

d. Deterioration of crucial feedback cycles within group, especially
   1) Interpersonal, discursive, and nondiscursive (for example, loss of trust, affection, concern).
   2) Responsiveness of leaders to members, and vice versa (for example, loss of trust, alienation, too much social distance).

These hypotheses do not exhaust the subject but merely give an idea of the kinds of things we should look at when we ask what builds, or weakens, solidarity. "We"-related information is the key. Information not so related should not be expected to have much effect on morale; for example, the U.S. Strategic Bombing Survey during World War II found that over half of the people in bombed cities of Germany experienced intense fear without lowering morale. We would interpret this as meaning that the fear of bombs did not damage the group image; for example, they did not lose trust in one another or confidence in leadership.

Dimensions of Collective Identity

Let us briefly distinguish some dimensions of what is commonly called togetherness, assuming that collective identity is like the hub of a wheel and the spokes are its elements. We use this model even though we recognize that, with the possible exception of cohesiveness, there is considerable disagreement in the definition of terms (Zetterberg, 1958).

Where collective identity is strong, we should expect group will and output, commitment to a collective goal—that is, *morale*—to be high. When people are so committed to a task that they are willing to sacrifice themselves for it, they practice what is usually called martyrdom or fanaticism, as in the Japanese *kamikaze* (suicide) attacks during World War II (Inoguchi et al., 1958:149–150). But, whether or not they go to such extremes, morale is capable of producing results so remarkable that it effects a seeming miracle. Such was the "Road of One Hundred Days," built by the men, women, and children of a tiny village in Greece, without tools other than pick and shovel—an "impossible" road from their mountain village to the highway. The resulting "miracle" of collective will was believed by the villagers to be due to God's help. As it happened, it was filmed by the United States Information Agency and became one of its most effective village development films in the Middle East and Latin America. The effect of this display of morale was to stimulate the collective identities of other groups who tried to do the same ("if they, why not we?"). Many cases of extraordinary work output due to high morale have been reported in industry (J. V. Clark, 1962).

When a collective identity is strong, there is likely to be close *consensus*, not only in attitudes and concepts but also in such things as status order and the roles played by members. An important part of consensus is moral integration, the agreement of members that social relations are "right" (Angell, 1958:8–9). When consensus prevails, cooperation, conformity, and ease of communication are maximal (M. and C. Sherif, 1964:93; Klapp, 1957; Scheff, 1967).

With maximal effective conditions, one may also assume *cohesiveness*, the tendency of collectivities to stick together, prefer their own company, and maintain tight boundaries. Sometimes cohesiveness is the attractiveness of the group to its members or the resultant of forces that keep a member in a group (Festinger et al., 1950:164; J. H. Davis, 1969:78; Libo, 1953). Deutsch measured cohesion by the ability of groups to transmit information with smaller or larger losses or distortions—that is, their efficiency in internal communication (Deutsch, 1966:150). It seems plain that loyalty to a collective identity is one of the main things that makes groups stick together, like one another, and defend their boundaries.

Synergy (Cattel, 1957) refers to a momentary, extraordinary burst of energy, more than the sum of individual outputs, an "all-together-now" surplus of effort or payoff, presumably due to a catalysis in interaction, as in "brainstorming." Such an output is especially likely when the "we" feeling is high.

The other end of such a spectrum is *alienation*, a lack of cohesiveness and feelings about collective identity. A totally alienated society would be a society of strangers, lacking morale and even mutual concern, not far from the view of things given us by Beckett (1967:15–18) in his pictures of the homeless man who has no sense of belonging to anything or anyone.

Most persons in a mass society are poised between strong collective identity and pure alienation, in a world of shifting relationships and reference groups, toward most of which they show no firm commitment. Various dimensions of alienation have been identified: powerlessness, meaninglessness, normlessness, isolation, and self-estrangement (Seeman, 1959); also, ethnic self-hatred, a group disliking itself (Lewin, 1948:186–201). Tests allow a person to estimate his own alienation by responding to items such as: I do not vote in national elections, do not enjoy TV, think most married people lead trapped lives, could just as easily live in another society, think most politicians are more interested in themselves than in the public's welfare, agree "most people live lives of quiet desperation" (Nettler, 1957). *Anomie* refers more to how world conditions affect one and not so much to the feeling of being left out; for example: "Everything is so uncertain these days"; "what is lacking in the world today is the old kind of friendship"; "everything is in such a state of disorder, it's hard for a person to know where he stands" (McClosky and Schaar, 1965). Some sociologists use the term *entropy* for social disorder (Buckley, 1967; Monane, 1967; Nisbet, 1970:55).

On such a spectrum, we may suppose that modern, mobile, pluralistic societies are in an intermediate position, with larger (national, corporate, community) identities relatively weak and blurred and with most of the real morale in smaller groups whose boundaries permit sharper collective identity.

Opening and Closing

Opening and closing are functions in all living things. The sea anemone in a tide pool extends and retracts its green tentacles. Some animals withdraw into shells for protection or rest. Hibernation is a seasonal closure after exploring the environment to eat, mate, and rear young. The Old Testament says:

> To everything there is a season. . . . A time to keep and a time to cast away . . . a time to keep silence, and a time to speak. (Ecclesiastes 3:1–7.)

The Sabbath is a traditional weekly closure against worldliness. The pupil of the eye dilates when the light is dim and contracts when it is bright. Youth is a time of risk, and old age is one of caution, saving, and stock taking. The child crawls, reaches, tastes, eats, cries, but then curls up to rest, disregarding noises around him. From these examples we see that what we call aliveness—resilience, adaptability—is not continual intake of food, resources, information; nor is it any constant policy—it is instinctive and sensitive alternation of action and inaction, phases of openness and closure or acceptance and rejection. The mind attends alertly and then becomes oblivious to signals, shutting them out somewhat like pulling down a window shade. The artist retiring to a workshop, or a religious hermit lost in meditation, is another kind of closure to what society has to offer. Thus, it would be a mistake to suppose that an open society is like a clam incessantly siphoning all the sludge in the bottom of a bay. The natural pattern is alternation, and the more alive a system is, the more alertly it does both.

Opening and closing is a sign of homeostasis, a process that assures self-preservation by using as feedback information about the effects of one's own actions in order to achieve equilibrium. Against what is the struggle of self-preservation, except disorder and death—in broader terms entropy? All living systems must at some point resist too much entropy. The game of life is to defeat entropy, by closing too much out and encoding information into order.*

Closure is reflected in society as *ingrouping* at many levels—towns, neighborhoods, ethnic groups, parties, cults, families, cliques, gangs, colonies, communes—tightening up their intakes, closing ranks to outsiders, increasing redundancy, emphasizing boundaries. However, closure is no more a constant function than is opening. Rather, there is an oscillation, like a pulse or the tides. A closed system oscillates near the upper limits of collective identity (morale, etc.). The open (mobile, pluralistic) system oscillates in a middle range, trading a higher intake of entropy (noise, etc.) for creativity in adapting to new conditions. It is dedicated to the proposition that the gain in information from leaving the gate open (telling secrets and exchanging knowledge) will, in the long run, be greater than the disorder created by outsiders trooping in. However, the price is that it verges now and then on crisis from too much entropy. For example, an open system easily suffers information overload (Chapter 9).

So, in opening and closing, we see a basic biosocial process that is an important context for collective behavior: On the one hand, we have peaks of communication, agitation, movements, when fads spread easily and new styles come in; everyone seems to want to know and try everything. On the other hand, there are troughs of "conservatism," "isolationism," "prejudice." How can one predict the success of a movement without taking account of such tides?

Entropy in Communication

A major cause of oscillation toward closure is presumed to be too much entropy in communication—a systemic strain (to be discussed in Chapters 6, 7, and 9).

Many problems need to be solved about entropy in communication, but it may help the student to think in such terms of strains generating collective behavior. One might think of a kind of "information pollution," consisting of such things as overload of noise and irrelevant information; lack of relational information (which establishes meaning) versus that which comes in bits; lack of identifying information that makes one more aware of oneself or of "we"; decay of oral circuits in media systems, leading to loss

---

* This view, unifying living and social processes under one rubric—communication—is known as information theory. According to information theory, entropy is the other "side" (reciprocal) of information; that is, information is negative entropy (Shannon and Weaver, 1949; Wiener, 1948; Brillouin, 1949; Raymond, 1950). A concise summary of information theory is given by Attneave (1959).

of personal feedback and status-related information, as well as of gatekeepers to screen signals for relevance (Chapter 8); one-way-ness of messages, leading to a sense of powerlessness, apathy, frustration, or lack of trust; malfunction of silent (nondiscursive) language, largely in the area of gestures and roles; or overload of "bad news," falsity of information, banality, semantic corruption, or any other content that confuses information and destroys trust.

Past a point, entropy in communication of a mobile, pluralistic, mechanized society presumably generates cognitive dissonance (Festinger, 1957), alienation, meaninglessness, and identity problems (Klapp, 1969).

Claims of Collective Identity

By the 1970s there were signs in America of a swing, whether as main current or eddy, toward ingrouping: ethnic separatism and revivalism; the "melting pot" in disrepute (Glazer and Moynihan, 1963); cultism and communalism. The president of Columbia University noted on campus:

> the rapid growth of sensitive alienated groups, each pressing for a special identity. . . . Not to seek acceptance or assimilation but to close ranks with your own kind . . . (McGill, 1970).

And on the national level, these signs seemed paralleled by such things as fears of military encirclement and trade protectionism.

In suburbia, too, one found "pseudo-community," "a belief in emotional cohesion and shared values" that had "little to do with . . . actual social experiences." Rather, it was a "purified" or "mythical" image that, however unreal, led residents to display prejudice toward newcomers, especially of different ethnic stock (Sennett, 1970a:36–38). Likewise, community resentment of "freakish" types was visible everywhere in America. In other words, the claims of collective identity were running high.

In this light we may view the picture of a "temporary society" in the world of tomorrow projected by Bennis and Slater (1968:73–74), in which relationships will be transitory, systems will be temporarily organized around problems, and the individual will be separated "from those permanent groups that provide him with ready-made values and traits and from which he derives his identity." We must imagine interchangeable people in quick and intense relationships in which personal ambiguity, alienation, and meaninglessness will be part of the price as modern nations become temporary societies (Bennis and Slater, 1968:124).

Is a society without "we" possible? In light of the considerations discussed in this chapter, it is doubtful. First, a totally open temporary society would violate the homeostatic requirements of social order, including redundancy, and be overwhelmed by entropy. Though it achieved its technical tasks, it would be an enervating place in which to live; one simply would not care enough about the people around him; the "we" feeling and responsibility would dry up, and identities would dissolve like writing in the sand. It seems safe to presume that collective identity in some form would assert its claims before such a gloomy extreme was reached—though this does not imply that one would like all the forms that the claims of collective identity might take (Fromm, 1941; Hoffer, 1951; Nisbet, 1953). Most of the phenomena of collective behavior are a testimony of the ingrouping and regrouping processes of a society yet very much alive and vigorously searching to preserve its viability.

It is this state of an ongoing society that is illustrated in the subsequent chapters. After finishing the book, the student is advised to reread this chapter.

CHAPTER 2

What Is
Collective Behavior?

The field we are about to study is disorderly, colorful, and
ill-defined, often referred to as "mass psychology" or "crowd
behavior"—the spontaneous collectivities and social movements that emerge from the unrest of an urban, or mass,
society. As historians and newsmen see this field, it is
inherently exciting and colorful, because it is connected with

momentous events: crises, disasters, upheavals—society in turmoil as mobs run riot and loot and as political regimes fall. Reid's *Twenty Days That Shook the World*, or Trotsky's history of the Russian Revolution, or Carlyle's history of the French Revolution, give the flavor of such events. Participants have an even more exciting view of collective behavior—for them it can be dangerous if not tragic, since many social contagions take the form of panics, stampedes, and witch hunts, which have by no means gone out of style since the times of the Massachusetts Bay Puritans. With the currents of mistrust flowing in our society, it is not altogether fanciful for anyone to imagine that he might wake up some morning to find himself a scapegoat. To speculators, on the other hand, the risk is not so much personal as it is a chance for profit or loss from swings of popular enthusiasm, as we see them in the fads of bubble gum, Beatles recordings, or miniskirts. Bernard Baruch, the famous financier and adviser to American presidents, said that he had saved millions of dollars by a study of crowd psychology. Charles Mackay (1932) described vividly some of the speculative fevers and "bubbles," such as the tulip mania, which taught Baruch this lesson. In a political sense, it might also be said that demagogues are speculators in human fate, since their "market" is crowd response and their "capital" is hatred.

Audiences see yet another side of collective behavior, since to them it is a show, melodramatic or comic. We see such a side in Frederick Lewis Allen's *Only Yesterday* (1946), which tells not only of stockmarket panics and Red scares but also of fads such as goldfish swallowing, Charleston and Black Bottom dances, Mah Jong, Boop-a-Doop, and flagpole sitting, in one exciting and fairly happy decade of American life, the 1920s.

To psychologists and philosophers, who are concerned with understanding human life, collective behavior offers yet another view—the puzzling and irrational extremes (for example, strange cults) to which people go. The prime question here is: What meaning can be found in such behavior; why do people act as they do?

Finally, from the political point of view of the ordinary citizen, collective behavior offers two faces: To conservatives it is a threat of rebellion and anarchy; to radicals it is an opportunity for change and reform made possible by the weakening of old forms.

Three links in the development chain of collective behavior are the subjects of study in this chapter:

1. Origin in unrest
2. Anonymous interpersonal communication
3. Formation of collectivities

Origin in Unrest

A miniskirted Roman catholic nun with hair to her shoulders indicted along with three Catholic priests, a former priest, and a Pakistani, for plotting to kidnap the presidential assistant for national security affairs and to blow up the heating systems of federal buildings in Washington.

With 182 protest gatherings, marches, and boycotts in one year, demonstrations are called a "way of life" in the nation's Capitol (1970). Slogans at DuPont Circle say, "America has gone to pot," "Burn flags, not people."

Radical movements burgeoning, dissenters becoming politicized; an officer says of inmates in a California correctional institution, "They have a sense of politics they never had before. Before they were a thief or a murderer, but now they're revolutionaries."

Expressive movements also, such as rock festivals.

"Peace of mind" search through religion, hippyism, "dropping acid"; an occultic boom of major proportions.

Widening gaps between "left," "right," ethnic groups, youth, and elders; presidential commissions to study and report on the state of affairs in America.

To call these events *unrest* may seem a ludicrous understatement, but this is the name used in common speech and sociology for a state of affairs in which:

1. People are restless, tense, and disturbed.

2. Feelings are expressed in overt behavior (signs) that can stimulate other people.

3. Actions in fact become contagious. Blumer said—

When people have impulses, desires or dispositions which cannot be satisfied by the existing forms of living they are in a state of unrest. Their experience is one of feeling an urge to act but of being balked . . . consequently . . . discomfort, frustration, insecurity, and usually alienation or loneliness. This inner tension, in the absence of regulated means for its release, will express itself usually through random and uncoordinated activity. . . . In . . . social unrest, restlessness has a reciprocal character, i.e., its display awakens a similar condition of restlessness on the part of others, and there occurs mutual reinforcement of this state as individuals interact with each other. (Blumer, 1946: 226.)

4. Unrest is the starting point for collective behavior in the special sense understood by sociologists. Swanson said—

Elementary collective processes begin when people discover that they must do something together but do not know exactly what it is that they must do and are not organized to do it. . . . Continued work has . . . made us aware that social unrest is ubiquitous and so, therefore, are the collective processes built upon it. The spectacular outbursts associated with great public issues are only a tiny fraction. . . . The career of every organization . . . includes frequent . . . periods of renewel, revival, or reaffirmation. (Swanson, 1970:126, 129.)

But how can people be shaken from their settled ways so that they will leave the grooves of custom, habit, and organization? It seems that there must be sufficient tension from within and/or crisis from without to accomplish the change. An example would be the "halo effect" of neighborliness and good will among strangers, observed shortly after disasters (see Chapter 6).

"Contagion" is the term used here to denote the spread of waves of urgent feeling and imagery by symbolic communication, among people who, having already been unsettled, are disposed to engage in "collective behavior."

By implication of this definition, as we shall see below, all collective behavior is emergent to some degree—groping for goals, forms, means, and meanings. So, the particular directions it will take will depend only in part on conditions such as pre-existing beliefs, symbols, and culture. In other words, one cannot simply project from the past to the future in predicting the emergent and free-flowing part of collective behavior. That's what makes forecasts interesting, but also difficult.

The theoretical sequence of events that trigger collective behavior may be outlined as follows:

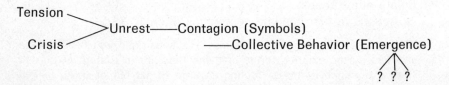

Tension

>Unrest——Contagion (Symbols)

Crisis   ——Collective Behavior (Emergence)

? ? ?

Anonymous Interpersonal Communication

Anonymous interpersonal communication gathers under one umbrella a variety of processes usually treated separately: crowd suggestion and imitation; faddism; unwitting convergence of norms (Sherif, 1936); social unrest; hysterias and other emotional contagions; rumors; vicarious experience (role taking or identification); and popular "we" feeling and morale. Such communications consist of messages coming to us from anywhere and everywhere—we cannot say from whom, or by what network, or whether they are decisions in our own minds. Mass media are not the main factors in such communication, though they may constitute a source or provide a link.

If messages come to us from anonymous senders, obviously the sources cannot be scrutinized, no one source is identifiable and accountable, and the sender is not responsive to appropriate feedback. This explains why the public, however excited, is not always guided by a distinguishable leadership. Mandates of the public will are then ambiguous and fickle, and society seems headless and blind—spooks and fantasies supply its images; fads, its inventions; moods, its conscience. In this welter of distorted and discordant communications, democracy falters and is subject to attack by its critics.

Two major social conditions leading to irresponsibility in communication are anonymity and one-wayness. Both are in large measure true of what we call collective behavior (not, of course, to rule out mass communication and bureaucracy).

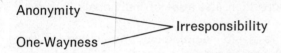

Anonymity
One-Wayness
Irresponsibility

Anonymity occurs when signals come from strangers, or opinion leaders and gatekeepers are unknown, or sources of propaganda are unidentified. To some extent, anonymity also occurs when the person who delivers a message is unwilling or unable to disclose his real feelings (hence, unknown as a real person).

One-wayness occurs when the one who gives the signal is not available to respond to further inquiry and verification, or the one who sends a message is not sympathetic to the receptor. One-wayness occurs when conditions of communication do not allow prompt answering in true dialogue.

An indirect (and reasonable) product of irresponsibility in communication is mistrust. So, if you are a sender, try to avoid increasing mistrust by irresponsible communication.

When messages come to you that are anonymous and/or one-way in their networks, beware! Take care to search out the grounds for whatever action you take. One task might be to try to trace a chain of responsible communication. The other alternative is to gather your own information and think for yourself.

What would be required to make the chains of communication in our society responsible at every point?

In short, whatever we least like in the idea of *massness* is caused by irresponsibility—in the last analysis, unresponsiveness and personal unaccountability—of communication. When such communication enters bureaucracy, however organized, it, too, becomes headless and departs from its ideal of rationality. This is why the loss of oral culture and its responsible gatekeepers is so serious (Chapter 8).

So far, the description of the process of collective behavior indicates that *anonymous interpersonal communications* arise from *unrest* in a *mass* setting. We shall now study how these factors involve people in *collectivities* from which new behavior and meanings emerge.

Collectivities

From anonymous interpersonal communications come waves of suggestion, resonances of mass behavior such as fashion and "we" feeling, and formation of collectivities that involve people in new relationships and awarenesses of each other. *Collectivity* is the term used by sociologists to designate the point at which part of a mass interacts and becomes more than just a lot of individuals, however temporarily.

We recognize here the basic sociological proposition of the reality of the group, namely, that over and above the individuals who make them up, collectivities exist (Warriner, 1956). In other words, though individuals may remain the same, collectivities can vary. For example, in a given collection of individuals we might find several collectivities at successive times and even at the same time: family group, work force, regiment, athletic team, church congregation, fraternal organization, businessmen's association, public faction, hero-following, political party, and—because they are all together in one place—a crowd. While the crowd may be the only visible group, all these other groups exist, too. However, the groups one cannot see, but which are present in the individual's mind, are customarily called reference groups (M. and C. Sherif, 1964). The same collection of individuals, then, can be a congeries of different but overlapping groups. In sorting all this out, the following crucial questions need to be answered: (1) What kinds of interactions go on among which of these individuals? (2) What kinds of consensus —in terms of culture, "we" feeling, and morale—do they share? People who possess a common culture and interact together can quickly form "we" feeling and morale for many goals, and hence form many collectivities. (Refer to Fig. 2.1.) In this sense the group is more than the individuals who make it up, and the whole is more than the sum of its parts.

This explanation leads us to accept the possibility of sociology as distinct from biology, psychology, and the physical sciences. Le Bon (1895), in his classic study of the crowd, was the first actually to show this psychologically. Whatever else he failed to do in his pioneering study, he convinced people that a crowd had greater

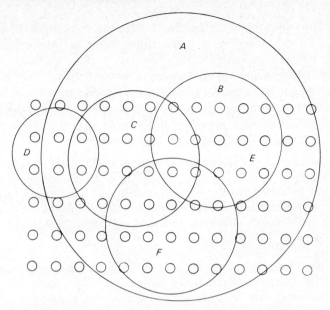

FIGURE 2.1. Individuals the same but collectivities vary.

significance than a mere collection of individuals. He showed that, under conditions of crowd suggestibility, a group "mentality" comes into being, one that cannot be predicted from knowledge of the character of the individuals making up the crowd. Thus, he improved on earlier organismic theorists such as Hobbes, Spencer, and Comte, who claimed there was a supraindividual unity in the group, by showing that crowd mentality was based on an interactive or communicative bond. Thus, Le Bon deserves great credit for founding social psychology. The full development of this idea to encompass not only the crowd but all of society as a body comprising "social facts" that cannot be explained by reference to individuals was achieved by Durkheim (1895). For example, one cannot explain the wearing or taking off of hats in church by any individual need; this act would be called for only in a society that has certain concepts of the sacred and appropriate behavior toward the church. The social fact has a moral quality that is impossible for any individual, however ethical, to create.

A social fact is to be recognized by the power of external coercion which it exercises or is capable of exercising over individuals, and the presence of this power may be recognized in its turn either by the existence of some specific sanction or by the resistance offered against every individual effort that tends to violate it. . . . The constraint is easy to ascertain when it expresses itself externally by some direct reaction of society, as is the case in law, morals, beliefs, customs, and even fashion. (Durkheim, 1895.)

What Durkheim said, of course, is that the consensus of society was established prior to any individual, and is supported by a collective effort.

Le Bon claimed that even the crowd's ideas have such a moral character. But it is necessary to go beyond this to a more special meaning of the term *collective*, which applies not to the established order but to new forms of interaction that emerge from—in a sense, spill from—this order. Blumer said—

> While most of the collective behavior of human beings exists in the form of regulated group activity, there is a great deal which is not under the influence of rules or understandings. . . . In these instances, the collective behavior arises spontaneously and is not due to pre-established understandings or traditions. (Blumer, 1939.)

Turner and Killian said—

> By agreement the term "collectivity" can be used to refer to that kind of group characterized by the spontaneous development of norms and organization which contradict or reinforce the norms and organization of the society. Collective behavior is the study of the behavior of collectivities. (Turner and Killian, 1957:3–4.)

This quality of emergence, or spontaneity, is perhaps the chief characteristic that distinguishes "collective" from organized or institutionalized behavior.

Thus, the Woodstock Rock Festival of the summer of 1969 might be considered a perfect example of collective behavior. It was a mammoth concert of electrically amplified rock music staged near the little community of Woodstock, New York. Judging by previous experience with such festivals, police and townspeople were expecting the worst. Past experiences had been riotous orgies of angry teenagers letting go tensions in the ecstasy of the deafening music and battling with whoever interfered. The crowds exhausted available supplies and reduced the neighborhood to a shambles. But this concert did not conform to what had apparently been institutionalized as the pattern for such affairs. There was, even worse than expected, a phenomenal traffic jam stopping cars for miles around the area. Four hundred thousand youths came, estimated by *Time* to be the largest crowd of people ever assembled. But the extraordinary thing was that there was no trouble. The kids cooperated and took care of themselves. Consideration and good will reigned. True, psychedelic drug use was rampant, but police did not (dare to?) interfere. A peculiar euphoric mood developed—whether due to "pot" or the music, or a unique combination of both was not clear. But the happy mood of the youth enveloped the police, too. Charmed, they gave way to sentimental expressions like "a swell bunch of kids." This idyllic mood shared by police and "rebels" was not the only thing that suggested that something more than a "happening" had happened. *Time* commented that the really significant development was that the rock movement, and in a broader sense youth itself, had acquired a new collective self-awareness. It was the first time that so many rock fans had gathered in one place. They felt the strength and a deeper sense of their togetherness and mission as a movement. Many observers agreed that something new had happened and that more change was ahead. For instance, Harold Taylor, former president of Sarah Lawrence College, remarked that the Woodstock Festival was setting an example for a new kind of life, for the shaping of a world movement of young people. *Time* hailed it as "History's Biggest Happening," and saw in it a cultural revolution, the making of a new hippie, hedonistic ethic; people are "finally getting together" (*Time*, Aug. 8, 1969:32–33.)

Is this not similar to a seemingly different phenomenon, called by sociologists the "halo effect," or emergence of a "fund of good will," in disaster? Loomis said—

> Various studies of disaster . . . show that at a certain point after a social organization has been stricken, there develops a level of integration and communication of sentiment unknown to members before. It has been called the "halo effect" and usually occurs at a predictable stage in the sequence of events after the intense rescue and salvage activities. Members who, in pre-disaster days, were relatively isolated and insulated from each other, come out of their shells, take part in a meaningful enterprise, cooperate in rescue work, help to rebuild, and find in the work that they have an increased understanding of and liking for one another. A fund of good will is begotten. During this period, actors communicate sentiments which produce community or system morale, making the community an end in and of itself. Perhaps some would say that a therapeutic community emerges. It is related to —perhaps the same thing as—expressive ceremonies and ritual following arduous task endeavor. . . . Revolutionaries, skilled in the use of violence and disruption, bring havoc to existing social systems. . . . One aim is . . . the euphoria which comes from weathering a crisis with companions. . . . In short, I hypothesize that revolutionaries use disruption precisely to create the halo effect, or fund of good will, for one another which they can share as insiders—insiders since, having produced it, they were there when the disaster occurred and . . . were there in every one of the sequential steps which built up to a "we" feeling of an intensity never known before by many members of the target system. (Loomis, 1967:887.)

Seemingly, then, different things—a rock festival, a tornado, and a violent revolution—can have similar results in new feelings and meanings among people who have not felt such relationships before.

These examples illustrate another feature of collective behavior, namely, that it does not occur in villages, tribes, or other groups who have familiar relationships, but in rather intense interactions with strangers, in circumstances that thrust them into relations with others unknown to them and remove their support from known groups. Such circumstances of intense involvement with strangers can release impulses under the cloak of anonymity, and can generate transient and often spurious "we" feelings and sharing of sentiments. Such temporary "we" feeling might be seen in a stadium crowd watching a game, the enthusiastic reception of a hero, a riot resulting from rumors that "we" are being attacked by "them." Such spontaneity is not the kind that is attained in a primary group where people realize themselves by their knowledge of each other; rather, it is the spontaneity of "letting go" with people of whom one knows very little, if anything. The one exception to this rule of anonymity is that collective behavior can occur in a group that we thought we knew and could depend upon, but which in crisis broke down and left us in strange relationships with people who were no longer predictable in terms of their normal roles. Such behavior might be seen, for example, in the panic of a military unit or a disaster in a small town.

It is this relatively intense involvement with strangers that gives behavior what Blumer calls the "sense of the collective" as a "sense of transcending power when one identifies himself with a large group or participates wittingly in a large group enterprise" (Blumer, 1957:128–130). Thus, a person gets a sense of participation in something big, involving strangers in new relationships, going somewhere. His relationship with these strangers is impersonal, whether there is circular reaction, chainlike transmission (as in rumors), one-way communication (as in broadcasting), or two-way communication without dialogical interplay.

A third distinctive mark of collective behavior in the special sense is the interaction that provides reinforcing forms by which an individual gains added control, pressure, and suggestions from others, all of which add to his motivation and feedback to them. This effect can occur in organized groups such as tribal dances and corroborees. It occurs also in the informal jazz institution known as the "jam session" (Cameron, 1963:118–130) and in rock music. But, again, the important thing is the emergent quality, the tendency of reinforcing interaction to spill out and over existing lines, involving and disturbing others who were not previously committed.

This does not inhibit the general tendency of collective action to become more organized as time passes: Actions repeated become habits and expectations; expressive gestures become ritualized; consensus is reached through interaction; norms are formulated and rules laid down; plans are made for future action; structure is built, whether bureaucratic or traditional; culture is transmitted to the young and to new recruits; and better arguments (ideology) are invented for the whole group. But, however structured and rational a social system may become, reinforcing interaction always has the power to spill out anew.

A fourth characteristic of collective behavior is contagion, its tendency to spread by suggestion and imitation to others, as seen in panics, rumors, and fads. The spread of the miniskirt and the Beatle haircut, for example, did not require intense interaction with other people; the mere appearance of these styles was enough to cause a rush in the clothing markets; within a week after the Beatles' American debut, 20,000 wigs per week were being sold in New York.

This takes us to the problem of rationality. Most writers from Le Bon's time to the present have presumed that collective behavior represents the darker end of the spectrum of rationality. The very phrase "crowd mindedness" connotes this. This label almost condemns a faddist as a person having poor judgment. At the very moment that this page was being written, a student demonstration was going by the office window—a procession blowing whistles, banging pots and metal wastebaskets, with the last participant capering in bare feet and blowing pipes. No placard or slogan was visible. No one seemed to know what it was about. A student, sent out to investigate, came back with the word that the demonstration was merely "disruptive." Whatever meaning there was, to the bystander at least, was inaccessible. Rational or irrational? We are baffled by inability to even find the message. But even granting the presumption that this was a deliberate demonstration, there is some justification for classing it as collective behavior, not only because of impulsiveness and spontaneity previously discussed, but because the messages of collective behavior tend to be like this in their beginning—inexpressible, mystical, and difficult to describe, explain, or recall. What does Boop-boop-de-doop mean? Historians now have little more success than people of the 1920s in explaining it. So it seems justifiable to characterize collective behavior as less, rather than more, rational, if only for the reason that something emergent is at first imperfectly understood and symbolized. If by rationality we mean being clear about values and goals, calculating consequences, adapting means (tools, tactics, strategies) to ends, rank-ordering priorities, disciplining oneself to adhere to a plan, and using feedback from results to modify one's course, then it is feasible to arrange human behavior from less to more rational—for example, from "impulse" buying to consulting a consumer's guide before purchase, from a gold rush to planned development of resources, from a crowd outburst to a Supreme Court decision.

Some writers question the applicability of the criterion of rationality to collective behavior (Turner and Killian, 1957:16–17), while others apply game theory to it (R. W. Brown, 1969). The main objection to the criterion seems to be that everyone tends to find his own view (however reached) as reasonable, and those with which he disagrees as unreasonable. Anything of which a culture approves, even the most bigoted belief or prejudice, is usually regarded as reasonable. This is a serious difficulty. But to leave the matter there—that "rationality" is merely what you feel is right or depends on which side you are on—would be to abandon Socrates and all he represented, namely, that there really is something called rationality which can be determined by a test such as the dialectic. Nor does this depend upon whether we happen to agree with a certain side or opinion. A military move by an enemy may be something of which we disapprove very much, yet we have no trouble in conceding that it is rational. The criterion, of course, must be the *method* by which the decision is reached, not its results, since winning horses and successful policies can be selected on the bases of impulse and prejudice. It may not always be easy to tell scientifically whether behavior is rational, but to abandon the game would be of a piece with giving up the concept in philosophy, education, and law—the aim of which is usually conceived to make men in private and public affairs somewhat more rational. What this implies, then, is that collective behavior, by its very nature, is rather "against" rational philosophy, education, and government, and is on the side of what Max Weber called charisma. Or, in Freudian terms, collective behavior is on the side of id and superego versus ego. The Freudian concept of rationalization sufficiently concedes the difficulties and pitfalls of the concept. Nevertheless, one rule will help in many cases to decide whether behavior is rational: the absence of "if . . . then . . ." reasoning as a necessary antecedent—namely, that the occurrence of the event does not *depend* on prior calculation, planning, or deliberation. (See Chapter 3.)

So now we see our field as behavior together that is to a high degree (1) emergent, (2) with strangers, (3) reinforcing, (4) contagious, and (5) nonrational, occurring in collectivities that are intermediate between organized groups with cultures and a sheer mass. (See Fig. 2.2.) This kind of collective behavior is governed by the content, pattern, duration, and characteristics of the network of interaction.

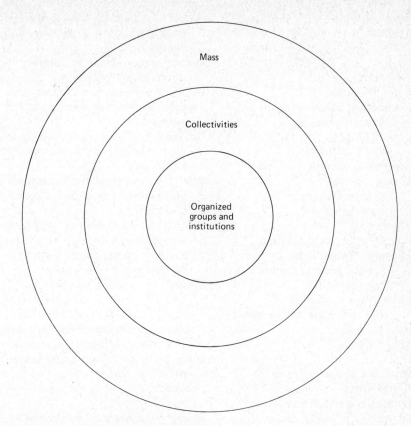

FIGURE 2.2. Field of collective behavior.

A sheer mass, then, is considered as the source from which collectivities emerge. It is theoretically considered (rather like absolute zero in physics, where there is no interaction of particles) as a free-flowing pool of people, in any numbers from a few to millions, where social interaction is minimal, where response to others is almost entirely physical—as, for example, when you share a room with people but not much else, or when you enter a large department store and push through a crowd, hardly seeing the people who are there for purposes similar but unrelated to yours. A famous photograph in the New York Museum of Modern Art shows a man reading a newspaper as he steps by—almost over—a prostrate man on the subway steps. The ironic title is "His Brother's Keeper." This typifies mass response.

Here are some kinds of collectivities and behavior that fall in the region between mass on the one hand and social organization and culture on the other:

Crowd behavior
mob
riot
panic
expressive
Milling of cattle:
collective behavior of
animals showing
inability to rise to
symbolic level
Collective outbursts
"Wildcat" strikes,
demonstrations
Social contagions
hysterias
persecution, scapegoating
popular crazes, fads,
rushes, booms, manias,
popular moods
Popular heroes, celebrities,
and their fans, followings
Poses, poseurs
Style rebellion
Cults
Emergence of social types
Cultural drifts
New fashions and their meaning
Early stages of social movements

Rumor and gossip: how it travels,
grows, and what it does in community or public
Public opinion as it is forming in
interaction, discussion
Symbolic leaders: how they emerge;
their impact and meaning to the
public
Dramatic public events that have
deep, perhaps nonrational, meaning to public
"We" feeling and morale, emergence
of, in relation to sense of collective identity
Safety-valve mechanisms: systemic
arrangements that act to damp
or divert what might otherwise
be destructive outbursts
Strains in systems which lead to
certain kinds of outbursts (for
example, frustration, rebellion)
Crisis as experienced collectively
(for example, disasters, anomie)
Loss of meaning in institutions,
ritual, or human interaction
Feedback cycles in collective behavior
Ritual, responses of audiences to,
meaning of
Self-abandonment, collective experience of
Conversion to new points of view in
group situations

From these considerations, it is plain why there are difficulties in the study of behavior—why, indeed, it will probably never be a laboratory science. Its nonrationality means that it is difficult to explain or even describe in meaningful terms, especially in early stages of development. Observers have the problem of always being confounded by their own projections and rationalizations, as is the case with psychiatry. Because collective behavior often occurs suddenly and unexpectedly, one cannot usually set up observations in advance, as astronomers do for an eclipse of the moon. It is usually all over before you can see it; or, if you do observe, you will have trouble sorting out the stages. You can go into crowds, hoping to see collective behavior, but nothing will happen; at another time you will be so excited that you forget to take out your notebook, and will remember very little of what happens. Of course one can deliberately go to places where movements are likely to be simmering, such as Hyde Park Corner or an "angry voices" coffee house or book shop. And research teams can rush to disasters to catch them in their later stages. Another research difficulty, of course, besides inconvenience, is the sheer danger of participant observation.

Finally, a peculiarity of the field is that experimentation is virtually impossible, the main reason being that it is irresponsible to create, perhaps even to simulate, such things as rumors, mobs, and panics. The alternative is systematic comparative illustration (Smelser, 1962:386), taking note of such things as covariation and the presence or absence of factors, to determine what is necessary. So, we have the disadvantage of a subject that is even less amenable to experiment than is medicine, and worse off than astronomy because it not only cannot manipulate events but also cannot even observe precisely what these events are. The difficulties are felt most keenly when one tries to talk about the meaning of collective behavior.

The Meaning of Collective Behavior

We may conclude, then, that collective behavior, though it breaks out irrationally, is not meaningless, that it is not like a transient hiccup or convulsion. Even in its early stages, it has an unwitting goal, though somewhat nebulous, which is rather like that of a man who is restless and hungry but doesn't know for what. In retrospect, we look back at a time like the "Golden Twenties" and say, "how funny, odd, foolish, tragic, etc.!" *Now* we know better, having had a chance to see what came of it. What was that generation up to? Was it just expressing tensions, having "fun" in activities that went by names such as ballyhoo and high jinks? Or was it seeking solutions without knowing it, such as a new status for women, or dramatizing superiority of Wasps over ethnic newcomers, as Gusfield (1963) has interpreted the temperance movement? Especially with regard to fads, we would do well to take a long view and liken those activities to arrows shot at a target, which only now and then hit the bull's-eye of a new taste, style, or institution. In a long-run analysis, this should be viewed as a process of societal selection, in which the parties may have no inkling of participation (Klapp, 1964a:26–65). In this sense, then, the meaning of collective behavior is found in its objective, much as one might say the goal of eohippus in evolution was the horse. On this premise, if we could only understand it, we can define collective behavior as an unrealized historical potentiality, the voice of the future. But we don't know what it is announcing now. The needs are too inchoate, the ideas are not yet rationalized (mystiques whose time has "not yet come"), too strange to be recognized in their fully significant future form. The tendency to mock or suppress distorts them so they are not allowed their full expression. A poem by Doris Peel well expresses this situation:

Who Waits To Be Heard

Lurking in the wings
is somebody else.

Not the recognized performer
out in front:
with his lines
  all written for him,
scene by scene, and every
inflection, gesture, stance
fixed from the start.

There is somebody else
(not listed at all)

inchoate, urgent
who without a voice
  is crying—crying—
"*But that isn't it!*
        That isn't what
I mean in the least!"

If he were to escape
  from where he's hid,

if he were to bolt
onto the lighted stage
and blurt out
  whatever it is

how the house would shake
from gallery to pit!
And this lulled audience,
nodding in rows,

Oh to what fierce news
would it suddenly awake?

(Doris Peel, *Christian Science
Monitor*, September 27, 1969.)

The problem is this: Which of the "voices" waiting in the wings are crazy, criminal, obscene; and which are creative, constructive, liberating? The old meaning rarely gives a clue. As we well know, some joked about Hitler, not seeing what was coming; and they joked about Jesus, too.

We have the vantage point now to assess the Hitler era, for the facts are in and history has judged. In the early years of the Great

Depression, the Nazis were only a minority party in conflict with others, struggling for a voice and a role, not taken seriously in Germany, let alone the world at large. In the post-depression years, say from 1933 to 1936, there was growing enthusiasm for Hitler in Germany, paralleled by a small but growing concern outside—at least a few got the message! By 1937 the German enthusiasm for Hitler had turned to fanaticism, which carried Germany into war. By then, fear was the dominant mood of the rest of the world; almost everyone got the message. But even up to 1939, many Americans, including some prominent ones, were attracted to Hitlerism. The turning point was, perhaps, the English publication of *Mein Kampf* in 1939, followed by the invasion of Poland. From D-Day on was the time of disillusionment and awakening to horror for Germany, paralleled by triumph for the Allies (1944–1945). The postwar generation of Germany entered a period of guilt, accompanied by war-crime trials conducted rather self-righteously by the Allies, which persisted for at least two decades. So, the meaning of a message that began with a crackpot minority and ended with a totalitarian regime and world war is now fairly complete.

Without pressing the above analogy, and keeping in mind differences of national character, we may ask: What is happening in America now? Again we are in the dark; waves of something are spreading; people are being mocked and fought; there is a reaction of "law and order." Amid the babel of ideologies that confuse as much as reveal the issue, have been voices of a vague, almost mystical, kind. Thus, Jimi Hendrix, a rock music "demigod" of the late 1960s, regarded himself as a "messenger" for a new era and he felt it was his mission to usher it in:

> Music is going to break the way. There'll be a day when houses will be made of diamonds and emeralds which won't have any value anymore and they'd last longer in a rainstorm than a wooden house. Bullets'll be fairy tales. There'll be a renaissance from bad to completely clear and pure and good—from lost to found. The everyday mud world we're living in today compared to the spiritual world is like a parasite compared to the ocean. . . . One way to approach the spiritual side is facing the truth. People who make a lot of money—they get sadder and sadder because deep down they feel they hurt. So they go and buy a prostitute on Saturday and go to church on Sunday and pray down on the ground in a little salt box, hearing another man who has the same problems preach—and the collection plate keeps going around and around. . . . Atmospheres are going to come through music because music is in a spiritual thing of its own. It's like the waves of the ocean. . . . It is the biggest thing electrifying the earth. . . . I can explain everything better through music. You hypnotize people to where they go right back to their natural state which is pure positive—like in childhood when you got natural. . . . And when you get people at that

weakest point, you can preach into the subconscious what we want to
say. That's why the name "electric church" flashes in and out. . . . I
had very strange feelings that I was here for something and I was
going to get a chance to be heard. I got the guitar together because
that was all I had. I used to be really lonely. (*Life*, Oct. 3, 1969:74.)

And we see a groping on the part of university students for
something, a reaching out into the same realm that Hendrix was
exploring, in the course offerings of an experimental college (free,
without credit) in 1969: Witchcraft; Mysticism; Liberation: male
and female; Apollo and Dionysius—order and revolution; Making
of a Counterculture; Communication and Interpersonal Relationships;
Communal Living; Pursuit of Awareness; An Introduction to Scientology; You're a Woman, So What?; Communication Blocks; Zen;
The Tao and Zen of Human Encounter; Yoga for Beginners Like Us;
Workshop in Nonviolence; Herman Hesse; Basic Principles of Ob-
jectivism; Avante Garde Theology; Confrontation and Encounter;
Women's Liberation: A Creative Process; A Reflective Approach to
Hair Care . . . Your Image of Yourself, Others' Image of You; The
Opening of the Way, An Ethic for Radical Politics. Here, again, as
with popular entertainers, we see a groping by people who are not
aware of being part of a social movement. The goals remain in
doubt because so many of the explorations, like fads, will miss the
mark and die. Yet, it was perhaps possible to say that, in its
beginning, the movement was toward greater self-expression and
realization than was possible in the more conventional channels of
education and work (Klapp, 1969).

Though in early stages of social movements and most collective
behavior we are not in a position to tell precisely what a movement
seeks, we can say something in general about what it moves
toward. First, there is little doubt that much collective behavior
has a *goal of expression*, a release or catharsis of feelings, an
emotional realization that is distinct from whatever practical purposes it may have. Second, there is a consensual goal of bringing
strangers into *common understandings*, and finding or forming adequate *symbols*. This symbolization becomes progressively rational
as movements develop ideologies. Third, there is little doubt that
much collective behavior, especially of the expressive kind, has
functions for the self, or *identity*. It offers a chance to "let go," to
escape from oneself, and perhaps to find a new identity in an
emergent interaction.

Behind this statement of general goals of collective behavior are
four basic assumptions: (1) Humans do things individually and
collectively, the purpose of which they are not aware, as amply
shown by Freud; (2) humans are rational by preference, and will
rationalize and systematize their symbols if they have a chance;

(3) all groups need consensus and will tend to seek and support it rather than disperse and create a situation where there is no consensus at all (anomie); and (4), all humans seek to realize (express, validate, find, lose to find, redeem) themselves, that is, have identity needs which they satisfy through group processes. These assumptions would be enough to put a mass into motion in ways that would lead to collective behavior, but they are not enough to tell us what forms the behavior would take.

Conclusion

In this chapter we have explored what is meant when we say that collective behavior is an *emergent process.* Such a characterization means that it is not only an unexpected and difficult process to predict, but also that it is a creative process of the deepest theoretical and practical importance. We will not be too wrong if we think of it as the birth or cradle of society, a process of genesis occurring in times of change and accompanying the breakdown and upheaval of old forms. Other metaphors are appropriate and helpful: Collective behavior is the "incubator" that keeps ideas warm until their time has come; the "seedbed" that sprouts and germinates changes; the "hotbed" for social ferment; the melting of the ice of old institutions into freshets of movements; a dam breaking, or a river overflowing and finding a new course. A particularly likely metaphor is that of waves coming higher on the beach with the incoming tide. This fits well, for example, the way in which agitation progressively makes new things conceivable and politically possible, and the way we get used to, and finally enthusiastically adopt, new fashions that at first seemed slightly ridiculous.

Finally, among the metaphors, we should recognize the deep connection noted between collective behavior and religion, since Le Bon first said that the crowd makes its heroes and its gods. Durkheim followed this up by trying to explain religion as a product of collective excitement. And students have related collective behavior to the fervor of totalitarian movements. Eric Hoffer (1951: 166), for example, called the fanaticism of social movements—less with approval than with dread—"a miraculous instrument for raising societies and nations from the dead—an instrument of resurrection."

Yet, for all this emphasis on emergence, we should not forget that collective behavior is also concerned with reasserting the old order, that some of its expressions are countermovements reflecting the deep need for consensus and the security that it offers. Even the metaphor of waves on the beach does not deny the principle of balance, of return to equilibrium. Indeed, a principal concern of this book is to harmonize the claims of equilibrium theory, seeing collective behavior as being often a safety-valve process, with the view of collective behavior as an open, free-flowing river. From the systemic point of view, collective behavior is a kind of spillover caused by strains and imbalances within institutions, working either to rebalance or change the system. The free-process view, on the other hand, is not oriented toward what collective behavior may do for systems; rather, it depicts all human behavior as a continual construction and reconstruction of meanings, which may or may not be consensual. It seems rather artificial and forced, for example, to relate all that goes on in fads, leisure activities, casual crowds, and vicarious experience to some kind of function or relation to a system, even a very "open" one. So, in this book, we shall accept both points of view—as does modern systems theory—stressing equilibrium or free-flowing metaphors when they seem to fit. Part II will deal with the systemic aspect of collective behavior, and Part III will emphasize symbol making and seeking.

CHAPTER 3

Crowd Behavior

Probably there were important similarities among the mobs who stoned St. Stephen, who stormed the Bastille, who lynched Blacks in the South, and who emerged among both spectators and police at the Democratic National Convention in Chicago in 1968. The crowd is protean and perennial. If our assumptions are correct, there has been no basic change in it since human history began. In our theory, the crowd is an amorphous collectivity that falls in that "in-between" region, outside organization, where relations take fluid form. We expect the crowd to be relatively unaffected by its organizational context, just as we can say that ice melts in much the same way, regardless of the shape of the container and other circumstances. In other words, according to the definition we have adopted, to say that collective behavior does not change is truer than to say this of institutions. Indeed, it would be rather depressing to believe that to understand what was going on in collective behavior now, one would have to read the latest newspaper and could not use observations made a year, or a decade, or a century ago. The goal of sociology is to seek for recurring regularities; and, fortunately, the crowd offers much in this regard. Presumably we could compare crowds, not only from different eras but also from different cultures. Of course contexts vary and have their influence. This is where history, political and economic analysis, and the rest of sociology come in.

The crowd, then, is the prototype of collective behavior, and it is appropriate that we should begin with it so that we have the advantage of the light it throws on the rest of the phenomena in this field. Le Bon's classic, for all practical purposes, inaugurated the study of collective behavior; and the problem he posed still stands as the central one we should be concerned with, namely, the nature of the process and mentality that makes the crowd different from other groups:

> The most striking peculiarity presented by a psychological crowd is the following: Whoever be the individuals that compose it, however like or unlike be their mode of life, their occupations, their character, or their intelligence, the fact that they have been transformed into a crowd puts them in possession of a sort of collective mind which makes them feel, think, and act in a manner quite different from that in which each individual of them would feel, think, and act were he in a state of isolation. There are certain ideas and feelings which do not come into being, or do not transform themselves into acts except in the case of individuals forming a crowd. (Le Bon, 1895, 1960:27.)

While the "group mind" hypothesis is no longer much in favor, our attention still focuses on the crowd process and what it produces.

But the crowd has a bad reputation. Not only does it have a distinctive character, but something about its dynamics seems to produce results more often regarded as bad than good. Indeed, the French Revolution, as well as Le Bon, helped much to inaugurate the study of collective behavior because it showed in a shocking way the excesses of mob mentality, and started the individualists of the Enlightenment in thinking that there was more to group decision than a rational contract. Perhaps it is only a bias in favor of rationality that causes us to see good judgment and fairness so often threatened by crowd decisions. The trial of "war criminals" in Cuba in 1959, following Fidel Castro's triumph, gave a shocking example of the intrusion of crowd spirit into judicial process. The trial was held in Havana's Sports Palace, under floodlights, before 15,000 spectators screaming "kill him!" when they saw someone they didn't like. There was no jury; a three-man tribunal, ruling by majority, sat as judge and jury, and often as prosecutor too. Hearsay evidence was admissible. Outside, 600,000 Cubans demonstrated in a lynch fever, pantomiming with mock gibbets the fate of those within. *Life* summed it up as a Roman circus held by Castro for his public, "Hate Holds Court in Cuba." The point here, of course, is not that hatred was manifested toward the defendants, but that the crowd multiplied the hatred manyfold and exerted an irresistible pressure against any who might have been disposed to defend the victims. Such displays seem to justify the view of those who feel that crowds are much more bloodthirsty and evil than individuals severally can be, such as Canetti (1962), who gives numerous examples to show the crowd's insensate lust for power, and views history as a history of combating crowds. A similar thesis, that collectivities multiply and sanction the worst tendencies of men, is maintained by Niebuhr (1932), though his focus is on the nation. Conversely, there is a tendency to regard as heroes those able to stand against crowd pressures—provided the observers are not in the crowd. Such a view is shown in John F. Kennedy's *Profiles in Courage* (1956).

But we shall get a more balanced view by going back to the beginning, so to speak, and considering crowd development from its most elementary stages.

The Crowd Process

A more moderate view is to see the crowd as the most elementary group—the "amoeba" of sociology. As Park and Burgess pointed out, the crowd is a transitory group, with no history or future.

> [It] has no tradition. It has no point of reference in its own past to which its members can refer for guidance. It has therefore neither symbols, ceremonies, rites nor ritual; it imposes no obligations and creates no loyalties. (Park and Burgess, 1924:790.)

It does not normally have "we" feeling, "at least until it comes in contact and in conflict with some other crowd or mob." It acts with "a minimum of organization or with no organization at all, except what has been called by Le Bon psychological organization."

The crowd's action pattern is "extremely fragile and ephemeral" and what division of labor there is is without clearly defined roles (Park, 1955:15, 128). Hence, the crowd is structureless; it is fluid and has no boundaries. It is cultureless and passes nothing of its own through a continuous line of successors. Anybody can join a crowd; there are no entrance requirements, no status obligations—the crowd takes them as they come. It forms its own consensus and structure on the spot; and, since it starts "from scratch," it has to work fast. Typically, its individuals are a heterogeneous lot, with nothing in common except the fact of being together when the crowd begins to form.

"Nothing in common," however, needs to be qualified by the following statement by Blumer:

> Any instance of joint action, whether newly formed or long established, has necessarily arisen out of a background of previous actions of the participants. A new kind of joint action never comes into existence apart from such a background. The participants . . . always bring to that formation the world of objects, the sets of meanings, and the schemes of interpretation that they already possess. . . . One is on treacherous and empirically invalid grounds if he thinks that any given form of joint action can be sliced off from its historical linkage, as if its makeup and character arose out of the air through spontaneous generation instead of growing out of what went before. (Blumer, 1969a: 20.)

The crowd, in other words, has nothing in common of *its* own, though members may have much to draw upon from a common background by which to form a crowd consensus.

Anyone can start a crowd. The simplest procedure would be to do something startling that would cause people to draw together to look, such as scream or have a fit. A favorite exercise is to stand on a crowded street, looking fixedly upward at a window; the usual experience is that others gather and look up too, forming for a moment a crowd held by an object of attention. At such a point, people have left the mass and have entered a relationship with one another, if only to focus on a common object of attention. The next step, however, usually follows quickly—some interaction takes place, such as asking a question. Interaction, of course, includes a whole range of gestures, facial expressions, noises, and activities beyond speech, which have communicative effect. Anyone who has ever sat in an empty theater watching a movie becomes aware of how much of the crowd interaction he has counted on for his enjoyment of the film; the absence of laughter and the more or less subliminal sounds of rustling, whispering, opening candy wrappers, coughing, and fidgeting, usually have a distinct effect upon his enjoyment of the show. Reinforcement of laughter in comic shows is especially important. Thus, a person in a crowd is influenced and sustained by innumerable stimuli, most of which he may not be fully aware. But all of these, especially when a crowd is boisterous, are having some effect on his mood.

The third element in the formation of an elementary crowd is a common mood. This mood can be sensed even when one does not share it. Park said—

> Every occasion, be it a funeral or a wedding, has its characteristic atmosphere. Every gathering, even if it is no more than a crowd on the street, is dominated by some sentiment. One is more likely to notice this mood, perhaps, when one cannot share it. In that case, whether it be a sad or a happy occasion, one is repelled and inevitably seeks more congenial company. (Park 1955:135.)

For example, the reader is invited to compare the differences in mood among a Christmas shopping crowd, people listening to a nightclub comedian, an audience of Billy Graham, and a thousand GI's waiting for a personal appearance of Brigitte Bardot. The individual enters such a scene and usually catches some of the spirit, for most crowd moods are developed from common attitudes. On the other hand, the experience of being "alone in a crowd" shows that normal people can maintain their aloofness from the crowd mood, at least at elementary levels, if the people and attitudes are uncongenial.

A fourth element of the simple crowd is communication of some ideas or images, if only stereotypes, that are understood by all, even when the mood is not strongly developed. The definition of the situation and the clichés of speakers and performers are part of this common understanding. But Le Bon made much of the point, and it is still valid, that crowd ideas are common denominators, simple notions, that can be shared by all—two plus two but not E equals Mc squared. Le Bon described crowd ideas as simple, rather like lantern-slide images, succeeding one another without logical connection. The point is well taken; any performer knows that logic is not an important characteristic of the flow of crowd thought and shifts of attention. Because of this, Le Bon (1895; 1960) reasoned that men of education act like imbeciles together when they form a crowd. "In crowds it is stupidity and not mother-wit that is accumulated." Added to this basic simple-mindedness is the fact, as Le Bon thought, that these ideas are received by an individual immersed in a crowd with an almost hypnotic suggestibility. On this point, again, there is no reason to deny the truth of Le Bon's observation, if one confines it to highly emotional crowds.

In some cases, the basic elements in forming a simple crowd seem to be: (1) an object sufficiently interesting to focus attention,

(2) interaction among the members, (3) a common mood resulting from interaction, and (4) simple ideas or images shared by all by virtue of the experience in this crowd.

Thus, a type of consensus is the basis of crowd unity; but I hasten to add that, even where ideas are discussed, much of the crowd consensus is nonrational. This results more from the kind of interaction than the content of issues or ideas shared. The following example of a collective decision by some college seniors will illustrate the characteristics of a crowdlike transaction as contrasted with a more rational decision made only moments before by the same group. The seniors had gathered in the Greek Bowl to rehearse their graduation that afternoon. The president of the class explained to them that if they were willing to graduate without having their names called, it would save at least forty minutes in the hot sun. It had been the custom up to that time for each graduate to have his name called, cross the stage, and receive his diploma personally from the president of the college. But, as the president remarked, it was going to be warm that afternoon. There was some discussion; then the class voted to speed up the ceremony by eliminating the calling of names.

At this point, a senior rose angrily from one of the upper seats and pitched his folding chair down the steps into the arena where the orchestra was seated, narrowly missing the kettle drum. He said, "I've waited four years for this, and I'll be damned if I'm going to graduate without having my name called!" Then he stalked out.

There was a moment of stunned silence. Then one of the students made another motion, to have names called after all; it was passed unanimously.

A wave of feeling produced by the gesture of the student, who should now be considered the crowd leader, had made them all realize that it was more important to be honored personally at graduation than to save a little time in the hot sun and that this is what such ceremonies were for. It was a victory for sentimentalists. Those who may have objected were not heard from. Such a unanimous wave of decision, stimulated by emotional gestures, is typical of the crowd process. No more rational is uproarious laughter, applause, hissing and booing, or throwing either bouquets or missiles. Such decisions can be judged to be nonrational on the basis of four criteria: (1) that they are rapid and do not allow time for careful thought, (2) that they are emotional and impulsive rather than based on rules of procedure such as logic, (3) that they are intuitive and unwitting without consciousness of deciding, and (4) that they are unanimous and do not allow criticism and consideration of various points of view. Such faults, from the logical standpoint, are plainly in the procedure, not in the content, of the thought. It is quite possible that the second decision of the seniors, though hasty, emotional, and unanimous, was better in the sense of expressing what the students really wanted. Our criterion of rationality, then, focuses on the process by which the crowd communicates and decides rather than on the simplicity, inaccuracy, or other faults of the ideas *per se.*

Yet the example just cited gives little evidence of *circular interaction*, which most sociologists hold is the central process of the excited crowd. Most interactions flow along from one thing to another; they do not build up at one point. Dialogue from almost any play will serve as an illustration.

MARTHA: THEY'RE MY BIG TEETH!
GEORGE: Some of them . . . some of them.
MARTHA: I've got more teeth than you've got.
GEORGE: Two more.
MARTHA: Well, two more's a lot more.
GEORGE: I suppose it is. I suppose it's pretty remarkable . . . considering how old you are.
MARTHA: YOU CUT THAT OUT! (*Pause*) You're not so young yourself.
GEORGE: (*With boyish pleasure . . . a chant*) I'm six years younger than you are. . . . I always have been and I always will be.
MARTHA: (*Glumly*) Well . . . you're going bald.
GEORGE: So are you. (*Pause . . . they both laugh*) Hello, honey.
MARTHA: Hello. C'mon over here and give your Mommy a big sloppy kiss. (Albee, 1962:14–15.)

Circular interaction is caught in a reinforcing feedback loop. Parties continuously reinforce each other by escalating mutual displays of anger, laughter, crying, derision, shouting, and so on. Normally, when a person speaks too loudly, we answer quietly and try to hush him. But when response is circular, feedback becomes positive and we answer more loudly. When reinforcement comes from many people, the effect can be very powerful. Blumer compares the circular interaction of crowds with the milling of cattle that can lead to a stampede:

> The inter-stimulation assumes a circular form in which individuals reflect one another's states of feeling and in so doing intensify this feeling. It is well evidenced in the transmission of feelings and moods among people who are in a state of excitement. One sees the process clearly amidst cattle in a state of alarm. The expression of fear through bellowing, breathing, and movements of the body, induces the same feeling in the case of other cattle who, as they in turn express their alarm, intensify this emotional state in one another. It is through such a process . . . that there arises among cattle a general condition of intense fear and excitement, as in . . . a stampede. (Blumer, 1946:224.)

A typical example of human milling leading to a stampede would be a fire panic in an auditorium. Perhaps a woman in the audience whispers audibly to her companion, "Do you smell smoke?" Her companion answers, "No. Do you think there is a fire?" The lady on the other side hears the word "fire" and looks alarmed, asking "Is there a fire?" The first two ladies now see her scared look and, being alarmed by it, look scared themselves. This frightens the third lady even more, and now all their scared looks are being observed by others in the audience. A little smoke or some triggering stimulus, such as a raised voice, can bring on a condition in which many people are scared, watching each other, looking for exits, rising—in brief, frightening each other by their own behavior more than by the signs of the external situation. Running could precipitate a stampede.

Blumer also pointed out an important thing, namely, that the reason for this locking feedback is that automatic, conditioned response rather than interpretative interaction tends to make people different.

This distinction, however, should not cause us to lose sight of the fact that circular interaction is a *symbolic transaction*, not just an intensification of feeling but a change in the terms of reference, conceptions of things about which emotion is felt. Images in crowd excitement become more turgid, rich, vivid, dramatic, and imperious. To say that these new conceptions are vastly more sentimental is putting it mildly. The mood created would be impossible for one individual to sustain or even to imagine by himself. Statements like these are little windows into the world of the excited crowd:

> I shivered, and as I glanced again at the Armenian, darting his eyes from one quarter to another in suppressed panic, I felt my pity slip from me. I began to exult, like a hunter who has found a wild animal in a trap . . . "Kill the damn thief! Kill the damn dago!" the crowd was yelling. It thrilled! (A. Johnson, 1918.)

> I don't know what got into me. I seized a staff, improvised a banner by tying a piece of the school colors onto it, and led a chanting, raving snake dance of students onto the playing field. Then the most incredible thing of all: a student was standing by watching the dance. I knocked his hat off, yelling "Salute the flag!" He looked abashed, did not challenge me but kept his hat off, and soon joined the dance. Where this idea of saluting the flag came from I have not the slightest idea. It is totally unlike my regular self. (Unpublished document)

These examples are meant to illustrate that there is a change not only in feeling but also in the way things are interpreted and symbolized—indeed, that there is creation of symbols in collective excitement. In other words, the fact that a response is interpretative and symbolic does not rule out its being coercive.

Thus, by generating an image of what it wants to do, and by circular interaction a heightening of emotion—a surplus that will spill over—the crowd readies itself for a higher level of activity. But, in order to trigger this activity, it must release its members from their regular status obligations, giving them freedom to act in unrestrained and unaccountable ways. This is presumed to occur through rapport and the resulting loss of self-awareness. Rapport is usually defined as an intimate, harmonious relationship. In hypnosis, it is withdrawing attention from the environment and responding only to commands from the hypnotist. In crowds, we may describe rapport as a tendency to be totally absorbed in collective interaction and highly suggestible to what others are doing. A crowd, as some have said, is wrapped up in itself and oblivious to the world outside. But one cannot be absorbed in what others are suggesting without losing consciousness of oneself, and ceasing to be concerned with whether one is living up to a role or an ethical standard. Hence, one gains the freedom to act in unrestrained ways that cannot be predicted from one's ordinary roles and statuses.

Outbursts of excited crowd action, then, depend upon what moods and images have been developed. A *mob* is a hostile crowd acting concertedly toward a goal, which is usually that of inflicting violence on somebody. A *riot*, on the other hand, is a free-for-all of crowds and individuals in violent conflict, in which there may be "sides" but in which the activity as a whole is not concerted. A crowd *panic* is a precipitous flight in which coordination breaks down and individuals act for themselves without concern for others. Contrasted with these crowds that are going somewhere is the *expressive crowd*, which ordinarily goes nowhere and does "nothing" except "let off steam" by shouting, dancing, or other activities, which, by using up much energy and releasing tensions, gives the members an experience of catharsis. As Blumer said, the height of the expressive crowd is collective ecstasy in which individuals are carried into exalted states and experience feelings that they have never had before. While a cheering crowd at a sports event is a good enough example of an expressive crowd, a religious revival is a better example of collective ecstasy. To get a better idea of this, read how an eyewitness describes one of the most prodigious revivals ever to occur on the American continent, in 1801, in Bourbon County, Kentucky:

> At a distance the sound was all roar and confusion, like Niagara, 15,000 men, women and children at the camp meetings; Baptist, Methodist and Presbyterian preachers all shouting at once to their own

audiences. People were singing, praying, or "crying for mercy in the most piteous accents." At one time, at least 500 were swept down, overcome by religious frenzy, the "slain of the Lord" taken with the "falling exercise," some lying unconscious, others shouting and screaming; others rolled and tumbled in the mud clutching their knees, others were stricken by the "jerks," in which caps and bonnets would fly off and the loose hair of women "would crack almost as loud as a wagoner's whip"; others were afflicted by the "holy laugh," or would run on all fours and bark. (R. Wallace, 1955.)

This orgy lasted six days and nights, and set off a great wave of revivalism in America.

Doubtless, such fervency requires a great deal of "old-fashioned" religious piety; yet much the same thing goes on today, as told by an eyewitness of nightly revivals in Los Angeles. This account shows more clearly what kind of incitement and circular interaction bring on the ecstatic crowd response.

The tabernacle is filled with men, women, youth, and children, mostly white but with a sprinkling of Negroes. About ten men are sitting on the platform holding Bibles. They are well dressed, and look rather like a chamber of commerce. But Brother Fuller is unmistakably the leader. He stands in front in his shirt sleeves. His voice is hoarse from shouting. He begins by talking about the threats to his church from outsiders, mainly city interference. He asks the crowd, "Am I the leader?" They cry, "Yes!" His sermon theme is that the devil is in our midst. It is not the communists that are wrong with America, but compromising church members. "Come on! It's getting awful quiet!" he screeches. A woman responds by standing up, raising and shaking her hands. The crowd shouts. The preacher says, "No devil's gonna come in this church and keep you from shoutin'!" One of the men on the platform then stands up, comes forward, and with eyes closed gives a frenzied rapid fire sermon, with shouts. The crowd answers, "Amen! Halleluyah!" continuously. The white-shirted leader calls to the crowd, "You can run, dance, or shout or do anything you want to in this place. . . . I don't care whether you're Baptist or what. You must be *born again*. There's not gonna be a stall up there (referring to Heaven)." He weeps before the crowd as he tells them what his ministry means to him, the tears running down his face. Then comes a mass "tuning in on God." They all rise, raise their hands in the air, while the minister with raised hands prays for the holy spirit. He calls, "Do you want God again?" They cry, "Yes!" He prays some more.

He calls for those who feel the spirit to come up for healing. They come up in a line, and give a description of symptoms or testimonial of faith. The preacher takes a firm grip on the back of each one's head, with hand on his forehead, prays, then gives a sudden jerk. He sends them staggering and jerking across the stage. (Mostly women jerk, some raise their hands. Children and men walk more calmly, one boy shakes his head and blinks.) A Negro testifies that his umbilical hernia is healed. Others praise the Lord for cures. Then the crowd, with the help of piano and electric guitar, sings "Lord, I believe." The minister then asks the crowd to all join hands and sing.

Then evangelist R. C., the "fireball" from Chattanooga, Tennessee, comes on. As he speaks, the fire from heaven seems to descend upon the audience. Men, women and children begin dancing with jerks. Women begin speaking in tongues. A youth dances for a long time by himself, eyes closed, bent sideways. A girl about twenty years old stands in the aisle beside me, her eyes closed, teeth chattering, and talking to herself in a high voice. A woman gets up with a shriek and rushes out. People stand and give impromptu sermons and testimonials. The evangelists sing and beat on little drums with cymbals. One little girl about eight years old watches the scene with open-mouthed wonder. The children begin imitating. Now the climax is reached. The whole crowd flows down in front to meet with the evangelists, singing, praying, crying, hands raised, embracing, receiving holy touches. Women fall unconscious, stretched out on the floor, trembling and twitching. Miracles, miracles, miracles seem to be in the air, according to all kinds of testimonies. Some women are so excited they can't control themselves, and return to their seats with difficulty, like a sailor clutching a rope against heavy seas. (Unpublished document)

This meeting unquestionably produced something the members would have been unable to do for themselves. The difficulty is in sorting out hysteria from whatever genuine religious experiences the crowd may have been feeling.

There is no reason to suppose that there is anything peculiarly religious about collective ecstasy as such. It is also achieved in secular group experiences, such as tribal and folk dances, and jazz jam sessions (Cameron, 1963). That sports audiences sometimes attain heights of collective ecstasy is shown by the following account of audience response to the winning of the World Series by the New York Mets, Shea Stadium, 1969. By all accounts, the audience, both in the stadium and elsewhere, experienced an explosion of excitement and joy that has seldom been matched. Strangers embraced. Construction workers cheered from high amid the girders of new buildings. Cars stopped in traffic were rocked by passersby. Wall Street was ankle deep in a snowstorm of paper. But it was on the playing field, after the final game, where the most remarkable manifestations of collective ecstasy took place. Fans rushed out into the field to collect any souvenir they could get hold of, such as bits of "magic sod" where there were footprints of the Mets. A woman said—

I have a shopping bag full of sod from the infield of Shea Stadium. On hands and knees I pulled it up right after the Mets won the World Series. The getting of the sod was an unlawful but joyous thing. And even the law was on my side for awhile—as evidenced by the police-

man who helped me off the fence that separated me from the infield and spectator stand when I headed for the sod. . . . The policeman brought a chair to help me off. "We have to have some," my son said. "It's magic." To him, the sod stands for underdogs who win. . . . "It stands for every man's chance." . . . Every man's chance it was—for the sod—once we got onto the field. In the pulling, I felt a little funny. Down on hands and knees, ripping that nice grass up. I felt more comfortable when I saw a very dignified gentleman doing the same. . . . The thousands of fingers pulling the sod also pulled out telephones from dugouts, chairs from seats, pieces from tarp. Fingers tore at foam rubber from the bullpen and feet kicked off pieces of the backfield fence. Some overambitious fingers and shoulders tried to make a souvenir out of the batting practice cage. This was on wheels. They got it out of the gate. Then the police came and wheeled the property . . . back to its place. . . . I was still on my hands and knees, pulling up sod when an officer came and ordered me to get up and go. . . . Reluctantly we left— most of us holding our sod with the cautious manner reserved for newborn babies. Firecrackers were going off. Orange flares were being ignited. The organ was booming "Goodnight, Ladies." . . . The important thing was that the Mets had won the World Series. The second most important thing was that each of us being shuffled into subway turnstiles had a hunk or bag or suitcase or armful of sod. "Just touch it for magic anytime," my son said. . . . A woman with white hair and an armload of sod said: "I'm going to plant mine. I am going to put a fence around it. I won't let anyone walk on it. It has the Mets' footsteps on it." (Patricia McCormack, "Mother, Son on Knees Gather in Magic Sod," UPI, *San Diego Union*, Oct. 17, 1969.)
 . . . Pearl Bailey, who sang the national anthem, was embracing a piece of sod as she entered the New York clubhouse to congratulate the team.

This example illustrates two points: the character of secular crowd ecstasy, and how it attaches to objects that become symbols having cultic value. Le Bon said: "Crowds unconsciously accord a mysterious power to the political formula or the victorious leader that for the moment arouses their enthusiasm. . . . All their beliefs have a religious form. The hero acclaimed by a crowd is a veritable god for that crowd" (Le Bon, 1895, 1960:73–74).

So much for the effort to identify the main elements of the crowd process. To summarize, an elementary crowd possesses at least four things in common: (1) a common object of interest and attention, (2) interaction, (3) a mood of its own, (4) shared images or ideas arising from the situation. The last two items comprise minimal crowd consensus. A crowd develops to "higher" levels of activity and excitement by additional elements, which are presented without implying that they are necessarily in a temporal sequence. The truth is that there has not been enough observation of crowds to settle the question of what follows what. Some of these probably act continuously: (5) increased rate and intensity of stimulation (including triggers along the way); (6) shift in imagery to more vivid, excited, dramatic terms; (7) locking into a circular interaction of positive feedback on one theme, with quick escalation; (8) a state of rapport, with total absorption in mutual stimulation and high suggestibility; (9) loss of self-consciousness and control in rapport; (10) collective outburst action proceeding on the basis of the mood and imagery generated.

Conditions of Crowd Development

The question of causation—which conditions are necessary and sufficient, and in what order—for crowd development is obviously one for which we do not have sufficient answers. As already noted, the stages have not been sufficiently observed, and experimentation —the main source of causal knowledge—is largely precluded. Experiments done with small groups do not come very close to realistic conditions; see, for example, Festinger et al. (1952), Sherif and Harvey (1952), and Swanson (1953). A "value-added" sequence of stages of collective outbursts has been suggested by Smelser (1962: 13), but scholars are not agreed (Quarantelli and Hundley, 1969), and the matter may still be regarded as open.

Let us therefore compare some crowd outbursts—mainly riots— that came off, and some that did not come off, and attempt to identify the elements that rather obviously were necessary or were observed to have produced effects, without implying that the factors are sufficient or in the right order. They will be treated under the following headings: (1) common attitudes, (2) tension, (3) mood, (4) imagery, (5) triggers, (6) circular interaction.

1. Common Attitudes

It is fairly evident that a collection of people are not going to develop a common mood, or even be drawn together in the first place, without a stock of common attitudes. Individuals from widely different cultures would have difficulty forming even an elementary crowd because they could not share the same situation or respond to each other's meaningful gestures. Therefore, interaction would remain at the biological (natural sign) level, with possibility that even such gestures as smiles and yells would be misinterpreted. Indeed, it is perhaps not overstating the case to say that humans would have about as much luck interacting with chimpanzees as with humans of totally different culture. We bear in mind that even the most elementary crowd situation presumes stereotyped definitions and some meaningful communication. This does not deny that new images and moods develop, but only holds that there has to be a stock of conditioned responses, common attitudes, and meanings to start with. E. Faris said this long ago when he was investigating imitation; we do not quickly imitate anything unless predisposed:

> White men have been aroused to extremes of emotion quite surprising to themselves when in a mob attacking Negroes. . . . I can find no record of a Negro being swept into the contagion of a mob of white people attacking a member of his own race. . . . Imitation in crowd behavior is limited to the release of attitudes or tendencies already existing and which are not new. (E. Faris, 1937:76–77.)

Thus, enthusiastic crowds that one sees in sports arenas, churches, or political rallies have a large stock of common sentiments with which to work. It is quite possible, of course, that an audience can split into two crowds if there are two kinds of opposing consensus. But a quite heterogeneous audience, as entertainers know, is hard to play to and arouse. There is simply not a large enough consensus with which to start.

The following example of a riot of wrestling fans at Madison Square Garden illustrates the advantage of homogeneity as well as several other conditions of crowd development. Late in the evening, a "tag match" ended with a decision in favor of the "heroes," after the "villains" had indulged in the approved number of gouges, groin kicks, fouls, and body slams. Even after the decision, they continued to be "bad sports" attacking the "heroes." At this point, one of the "heroes" made a discovery that changed his definition of the situation: he found real blood on his face, not the red fluid from the pill that wrestlers carry in their mouth to imitate bleeding. Worse, it was his own blood. Enraged, he seized one of the "villains" and began knocking his head against a ring post. This produced more real blood. The audience of 13,000 fans, which had been lively up to this time, throwing paper cups into the ring, now became more energetic.

> "Stimulated by what was probably the first honest competition they had ever seen, some hundreds surged forward toward the ring." Chairs were broken up for use as weapons, fruit and bottles were thrown down from the gallery, a cry of "Get the Bruiser!" went up. "The first fan to penetrate the middle of the ring was a man somewhat incongruously equipped for combat: he was wearing an Army jacket and brandished a furled umbrella. Another fan broke a chair and thus obtained a sharp pointed stick. Bearing this lance, he charged. . . . The Garden was a pandemonium. A dozen scuffles and fights took place in the jammed aisles. . . . Bruiser Afflis, the main target of the crowd's wrath, had resolved to fight to the last fan. As customers charged toward him up the short steps or crawled through the ropes, he methodically picked them up and threw them out of the ring, like a farmer digging potatoes. . . . Rocca finally tired of bashing Graham's head, and the behemoths turned to watch Afflis with professional inter-

est. After a moment they began to help him throw back customers. Finally the city police arrived to help the special police and the 101 ushers and ticket takers who had pitched in to help. (Brean, 1957.)

A crowd of avid fight fans may be presumed to have attitudes highly disposing them to riot. Moreover, their mood had been heightened by about three hours of vicarious conflict and circular interaction. It was easy, therefore, for a trigger to set off such a crowd. The trigger in this case seems to have been the perception of real blood and genuine fighting, which destroyed the conventional definition of the situation as make-believe, and excited people by the sense that something real was happening. Presumably, also, the vicarious experience of the drama and prolonged circular interaction, with behavior largely restrained, had heightened the tension level of the crowd so that it was easy to set it into action by a suitable trigger. What kind of action would have resulted if the crowd had been, instead of avid fans, a random collection of businessmen, or, say, The League of Women Voters, one can only conjecture; but it is understatement to say that such a riot would have been less likely.

2. Tension

Tension, as well as common attitudes, is something that crowds bring with them to a situation. We must presume that tension level, even though not easy to observe, has much to do with the explosion of crowds into action. This applies obviously to interracial riots. It probably also helps to explain those youthful outbursts that go beyond "high spirits" to destructiveness. The following riot lacks an obvious issue and, by its irrationality, its "spilling over" character seems to require an explanation in terms of tension.

More than a thousand Princeton University students went on a rampage on the campus and in town . . . mobs of shouting students, moving in one main body and in split-off bands . . . inflicted considerable property damage during their three-hour spree. The students set fires, tried to overturn a two-car train, tore up iron fences, ripped off house screens and sent a one-ton air compressor crashing into a lamp post. The homes of both the school's president and the state's Governor were targets . . . the outburst started abruptly with a barrage of cherry bombs . . . and it spread swiftly. . . . Within thirty minutes more than one thousand students spilled from the campus and went first to Nassau Street, where they burned bus-stop benches and a bicycle rack in front of a restaurant. The next stop was the track line for a commuter shuttle train, linking Princeton with the Pennsylvania Railroad. The students started a bonfire on the tracks, broke several windows in the station and tried—but failed—to turn over a two-car train. Dr. Goheen's residence was the next target. The students tore down a forty-five foot section of an iron fence around his property and trampled flowers and bushes. The undergraduates also lobbed cherry bombs onto the lawn of the residence of Governor Richard J. Hughes and then trampled a fence and hedges at a day school next door, where they also bent a flagpole. From there roving bands of students spread out against many targets. They paraded through the ballroom of Westminster Choir College, about half a mile from the Princeton campus, and tossed fireworks as a formal dance was ending. They staged a panty raid at the women's dormitory of the college. Some students overturned garbage cans and tore screens from homes on their yelling treks back to campus. Others knocked down a contractor's wooden fence at Woodrow Hall. One group of students spotted the one-ton air compressor and pushed it over the crest of a hill. As the compressor sped wildly down the road, motorists were forced to veer their cars out of the way. Finally the compressor rolled off the road and smashed into a lamp post. By 1:30 this morning the students had returned to their rooms. . . .

Dr. Robert G. Goheen, president of Princeton University, made it emphatic . . . in an angry statement that "high spirits" would not be accepted as an excuse for the rioting. He described the outbreak as "the worst I've seen . . . their conduct cannot be brushed aside by 'spring madness,' 'boys will be boys,' or any such euphemism. This riot was a shocking display of individual and collective hooliganism on the part of young men who have no possible justification for sinking into it." The University's president called the riot a "surrender to raw mass impulse." (*New York Times*, May 8, 1963.)

The diffuse and shifting pattern of this riot minimizes the plausibility of a political explanation and favors a tension interpretation. We know that tension, unlike specific attitudes, can spill from one thing to another; psychologists call this "displacement." Tension can lead to many kinds of behavior that are difficult to explain; for example, crying from happiness, or a voice rising to a very high pitch. Tension —which we may think of as an inner pressure that is hard to release, but when released lets go with considerable vehemence in unexpected ways—results from inner conflicts and personal stresses that are not our business to explore here. However, it is permissible to note that many tensions come from background experiences that continue to disturb individuals by memories and persisting attitudes.

Many such background disturbances are traceable to what sociologists call *systemic strains*. For example, maladjustments of roles, failure of institutional functions, conflict of reference groups, and rapid social changes put many individuals into tension and stress which cannot be explained by individual psychology. In the case of university students, well-known systemic strains are produced by final examinations, the "impersonality" of bureaucratic procedures, lack of concern of teachers for students, and various administrative errors, which have been eloquently pointed out by the "New Left" rebellions of the late 1960s.

Smelser (1962) thoroughly explored strain as a dimension of collective behavior; it will be treated further in Chapter 5. For our purposes, the contribution of tension to crowd behavior is what is important here.

Four hypotheses, especially, should be stated: (1) Tension is retained or stored in some manner within individuals, as the result of various experiences; (2) tension builds up and thereby becomes more likely to be expressed in action; (3) while an individual can have an outburst all by himself, prior tension gives circular interaction something to build upon—a head start, as it were, toward collective outburst behavior; (4) because it "spills," tension can contribute to the development of new crowd goals.

3. Mood

As already pointed out, crowds are characterized by distinctive moods, which help to determine what they are likely to do. Therefore, mood management and development are an important part of the conditions of crowd behavior. Leaders try to control and develop certain kinds of moods in order to get the results they want; for example, a performer facing an audience tries to sense the "house," and if it is apathetic, he attempts to overcome its mood by "warming" tactics. The mood sets a range of what is appropriate and possible. In the case of the wrestling-audience crowd, previously cited, the mood of joy of combat plainly made the outcome more likely; on the other hand, with the Princeton students, the lack of knowledge of their mood made the rampage surprising to those who were out of touch with it. Students in the crowd on campus that evening, sensing the mood, might have been able to say what was about to happen. The point here is that the mood is something that develops in the crowd, and is not simply an expression of common attitudes. Beyond knowing all of the common attitudes of people, it is necessary to know which ones are being aroused at the moment and combined into a certain mood. To use an analogy, if attitudes were notes of the scale, then a mood would be a melody. No amount of knowledge of individual notes can predict a melody. Neither can prediction be helped by the fact that crowd moods can change, therefore change the range of what is possible and likely.

Even though there is not sufficient knowledge of crowd moods, it is possible to advance several hypotheses:

(a) A crowd mood is developed more from collective interaction than from acts of leaders, who more or less have to operate within the crowd mood.

(b) The mood that has been developed sets a range of what is possible and probable in crowd behavior at that time.

(c) The crowd mood is a product of common attitudes, but the combination is unique and not simply predictable from knowledge of the attitudes.

(d) Imagery helps to set the crowd mood; therefore, manipulation of imagery gives some control over crowd mood.

4. Imagery

Common images are obviously an important part of crowd consensus, for without them the crowd would be unable to develop goals. When rioting crowds rushed off to attack distant objectives, when Christians of the eleventh century listened to Pope Urban II and took off on a crusade, these actions were precipitated by vivid images formed in the crowds, portraying new ventures they had not thought of before. Crowd images apparently develop in interaction along with the mood. There is no advantage, except analytically, in separating them. Leaders, by their input into communication, doubtless contribute to crowd imagery; but there is no reason to suppose that such imagery is entirely controlled by leaders or is simply created by them. Rumors make a large contribution to crowd imagery, coming from no one knows where. A crowd can also see apparitions or hallucinations.

> CAIRO. Twelve persons were trampled to death . . . when thousands tried to force their way into the Archangel Michael's Church. . . . The twelve victims, eleven of them children, were killed and thirty persons injured . . . as thousands flocked to the church following reports a colored figure of the Virgin appeared on a plain glass window near the altar about four feet from the ground. One bystander said: "It looked like the Bible's description of the day of judgment." Said another: "Barefoot women, some carrying their babies, rushed onto the streets. Many stumbled, and crawled, and were trampled on by others." Eyewitnesses said the color disappeared after about two minutes, leaving only a shadowy outline on the glass, which later disappeared. . . . Police have now cordoned off the area around the church and a special municipal committee is charging twenty-four cents for an entrance fee. The committee also has placed some 5,000 chairs around the area. (*International Herald-Tribune*, May 21, 1968.)

Imagery obviously gives focus and content to the crowd's mood; therefore it has more predictive value than merely knowing how people feel. Imagery can be determined from rumors, catchwords, placards, excited demonstrations, and other communicative behavior in the crowd at the time. If these are followed closely, one should be able to keep track of the crowd mood.

The principal hypotheses to be stated here are that (a) the crowd does not act toward a distant goal without forming an image; (b) the image determines the general pattern of collective action; (c) communications that create vivid images are especially effective in moving and controlling crowds. Thus, it is well known that leaders who are most successful at manipulating crowds are masters at self-dramatization and by their words or actions create vivid images that everyone can see and be thrilled by. Any number of popular heroes and leaders have illustrated this; it was also demonstrated by the college student who threw the chair at graduation rehearsal. (d) Many instances of such leadership tactics strongly imply that drama is a better medium of creating crowd images than matter-of-fact communication and persuasion. (e) Although vividness is an obvious advantage in crowd imagery, it does not follow that this is true of rational clarity. We cite not only the well-known advantage of rhetoric over logic (epitomized for intellectuals by the trial of Socrates), but the fact that many crowd ideas seem to be quite mystical. We note, for example, the underdog, or "Cinderella," theme that was prominent in the crowd attitude toward the victory of the New York Mets. There was also a mystique in the fans' thinking about the Mets as being "hot," "magical," and therefore unstoppable. Such matters are exceedingly difficult to explain, but seem to communicate in crowds very quickly.

5. Triggers

By triggers we mean the various stimuli, including acts of leaders, that precipitate crowd action or new stages of feeling at various points in the development process. As already implied in discussing attitudes (paragraph 1 above), triggers work only when there is a predisposition. Further, the "strength" of a trigger is not a matter of physical force, but rather of the vigor of stimulation and efficiency of communication (versus noise, excessive redundancy, fatigue, and so on). It is quite plain that at times a whisper can be more exciting than a shout. Drama and music use diminuendo, significant pauses. Even silence can be terrifying. More important, perhaps, is the fact that whatever strength there may be in a trigger depends upon the tension level (paragraph 2 above). If tension is high enough, action will not wait but will search for a trigger; indeed, it is debatable whether triggers are needed at all in some outbursts. Yet, we recognize that in most cases a crowd's development proceeds by stimulation coming from outside, ranging from the rhetorical thunder of leaders to trifling accidents.

The following example from the famous Watts riot, Los Angeles, 1966, shows how a minor incident, where there is a high tension level and milling occurs, can set off a disastrous racial explosion.

A motorcycle policeman tried to give a ticket to a speeding motorist. The stop was made in a neighborhood which happened to be Negro, and the two occupants of the car also turned out to be Negro. The policeman talked to the driver on the sidewalk, "sparring verbally in a cautious but friendly way," before 25 or 30 people who had streamed from nearby apartments and sidewalks. Some were sipping from beer cans. They were "good-natured and rather amused" at what seemed rather a comedy. The officer was "the picture of police-textbook propriety." He noticed, however, that the driver was drunk, and, having given him a field sobriety test, informed him he was under arrest. The driver took this good-naturedly (as he said later, "I was joking with the officer—I mean, we was getting along.") Soon a transport car arrived in answer to the patrolman's radio call, to take him to the station. The crowd was growing, but they were still joking and laughing. Then came the minor event, which was the first trigger of the Watts riot. It happened that the mother of the driver was in the neighborhood and had come to the scene. Her presence produced a change in the alchemy. She rebuked her son for being drunk, but his reaction to her was quite unexpected: he "whirled away from his mother and screamed" obscenities at the cops, declaring they were not going to take him to jail. The spectators had become sullen. By the time police had put handcuffs on the driver, the crowd attitude had turned to "openly hostile." The police backed off and put in a call for help. When two more officers arrived, they forced the driver into the car, and in the process struck him with a night stick. At this point the mother jumped on an officer's back, and they were forced to handcuff her and put her in the car with her son. Then something happened which seems to have been the second trigger. The driver tried to get out of the patrol car, and a policeman shoved him back in, using his knee to get his legs into the vehicle. It appeared to many in the crowd that the officer had not only kicked the boy but slammed the door on his feet. A woman called out: "Why did you have to do that? That boy's already handcuffed and bleeding. You didn't have to do that." At this point was raised for the first time the cry of "police brutality." "By now the mob was a wounded animal, waiting for just one more aggravation." An "angry babble" was going on all around, and the policemen saw people with rocks and pop bottles in their hands. Now came the third, critical, trigger from a girl who stepped out of the crowd and spat at the officers. When they apprehended her, she is reported to have shouted "Take your hands off me, you s.o.b. white cop—turn me loose! I haven't done anything!" The officers grabbed her and began pulling her out into the street. The girl said she did not resist, but recalled her hair curlers shaking out and falling to the pavement. Then the crowd began a tug of war with the police, pulling the girl one way and then the other. It happened that the girl, who was a barber, was wearing a loose-fitting blue barber's smock which looked like a maternity dress. Protests went up, "Look how they're treating a pregnant woman!" At this point the mob headed for the police with shouts of "Let's get them cops!" "This is the end for you, white man!" The police station wagon was forced to back out, do a U-turn and then leave with the mob chasing it, "people running after us—yelling, screaming. They began throwing anything they could get their hands on. Bottles and rocks were bouncing off the back of the station wagon." Above the uproar the could hear a young man shrieking, "Burn, baby, burn!" (Cohen and Murphy, 1966.)

This example shows three triggers precipitating a riot—coming almost accidentally from people who became crowd leaders—by their disturbed or provocative behavior. It also shows crowd imagery coming from perception (misinterpretation) of the triggers (police brutality, mistreating pregnant woman). These images helped to change the definition of the situation and became the basis of rumors that brought more people into the crowd. The example also shows the milling process, which brought people into a hostile escalation—particularly the tug of war—and served as an audience-participation device, putting the milling on a physical as well as a verbal and gestural basis.

The case shows that dramatic power or extreme provocation is not necessary in gestures when there is a high tension level. It may take an Aimee Semple McPherson or a Billy Graham to arouse an ordinary audience from the street, but when tension is high, little things are big sparks that set off explosion. Nevertheless, there was natural drama in these triggers of the Watts riot; the audience was enjoying the show, and only after a change in the pattern—a dramatic conversion (Klapp, 1964a:148–175)—did the mood become ugly. The occurrence of what in melodramatic terms would be called a "dirty deed" created a vivid image of the cops as villains and quite displaced the comic view with which the episode had begun. Thus, we have an example of how drama can shift the imagery of a crowd and turn it into a mob (compare the mob image of the Armenian described by Johnson, 1918; see page 44).

6. Circular Interaction

Even if people are tense and excited, even if provocations occur, even if they give vent to their feeling in individual outbursts, it may be hypothesized that people will not be moved into *crowd* action unless circular interaction builds to the point of rapport and loss of self-awareness. Most of the previous examples of active crowds (with the exception of the graduating college seniors) had ample opportunity for circular interaction: several hours in a stadium, the call-and-response of a revival meeting; the Watts crowd's tug of war with police. Several kinds of interaction seem likely to become circular: repeated expressive behavior, such as cheering and stamping; call-and-answer responses between a leader and an audience; rhythmic action and stimulation, which sets up in the organism a periodicity or resonance that intensifies subsequent re-

sponses to the repeated stimulus (Sarvis, 1933; Verveer et al., 1933);
confrontations in which parties face one another competitively or
defiantly; and audience-participation devices.

Figure 3.1 shows an extremely simplified model of the feedback
pattern of an escalating encounter between a crowd and another
party, which becomes more polarized as the loop is repeated.

The central hypothesis here, of course, is that if circular interaction can be prevented, crowd outburst action will not occur. Many
of the practical measures to control a crowd, whether to warm it
up or cool it off, are based on this hypothesis. For example, the
standard police tactic is to "keep them moving," that is, don't let
them congregate and begin milling. Conversely, those who want to
stir up a crowd, such as entertainers seeking to build an enthusiastic audience, hire a *claque*, whose fervent tributes can sometimes
excite applause from an audience that isn't particularly enjoying
the show. Likewise, a cheering section at a college football game
uses every possible device to stir up circular interaction.

Another rule for those who wish to prevent circular interaction
is to avoid close-packed gatherings or any circumstances that allow
people in a crowd to stimulate each other unduly. Conversely, separating the crowd into small groups or dispersing it over large
grounds minimizes the chance of circular interaction. Another tactic
is distraction, aiming to break the chain of crowd ideas and destroy a
common focus. Sometimes joking or playing music will switch a
subject and ease tension. Likewise, stimuli from all points of the
compass (such as shots, floodlights, loudspeaker sounds, balloons
released, leaflets and souvenirs falling) might be used to distract
a crowd and destroy its focus.

On the other hand, aggressive acts, confrontations, lineups behind barricades, and injudicious arrests antagonize and solidify a
crowd. Therefore, common practice by law enforcement officers is
to remove crowd leaders quietly (if at all) and discreetly, with
minimum force. It is much preferable, of course, if one knows who
they are, to prevent their showing up in the first place. In general,
since the urban riots of 1967 and the subsequent disturbances
among university students, authorities and administrators are recognizing the necessity of avoiding an escalating response, searching
for lines of action that make it unnecessary or impossible to find
something to defy. The "don'ts" in this matter include: taking an
authoritarian posture, drawing lines between "us" and "you" or
"them," making victims (Watts Riot), and dramatizing issues that
might be left on a low-key basis. Rumor control is another dimension
of the hypothesis of avoiding active crowds by preventing milling.
Many communities, for example, now have telephone answering
services where people can immediately get authoritative information

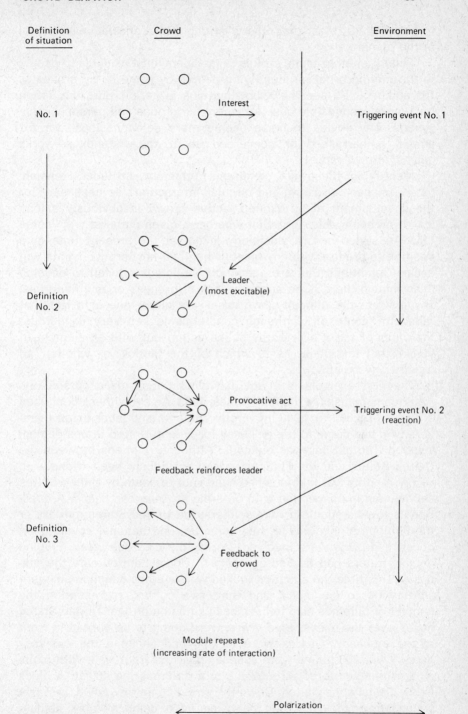

FIGURE 3.1.   Escalation process.

to help belie a rumor that otherwise might have incalculable effects in the community.

Finally, another tactic strikes at the anonymity available to people in the milling process. Identifying people by name or by groups in the audience ("I see the X bowling club is here") puts the action on a more responsible basis of reference groups and personal reputations. Any device to make people more self-conscious—for example, embarrassed or concerned about their standing—works against crowd rapport.

Identifying these six conditions (common attitudes, tension, mood, imagery, triggers, and circular interaction) as necessary for the development of an excited, active crowd is obviously a long way from being able to predict whether a given outburst will "come off." As stated before, sociology is not at the present time in a position to predict with any nicety when and how crowd events will occur. Conditions that are seemingly sufficient can fail to develop even though there is no apparent lack of process or raw materials. To illustrate the difficulty, two cases are cited: one of a riot that failed to "come off" although conditions looked very dangerous; the other of a riot averted by police action but with an element of "luck" that left doubt as to which of the tactics, or whether all together, were effective.

The first example is a riot that almost took place outside the American embassy in the Philippines, 1965. An eyewitness described a crowd of 3,000 to 4,000 university students and labor union members who had come to the embassy for an anti-United States demonstration. The outlook was ominous. Although relations between the United States and the Philippines had previously been friendly, in recent months two Filipinos had been shot to death by United States servicemen in connection with pilfering at American bases. A question as to who should try the soldiers, the United States military or the Philippine government, had come up, and national sovereignty, honor, and pride were involved. During the previous week, Filipino demonstrators had burned an effigy of Uncle Sam outside the embassy. This time the situation looked worse, since communists were said to be in command, and thirty-two coffins, representing the number of Filipinos said to have been killed on or near United States bases over the past twelve years, were going to be burned in front of the embassy. Guards were locking and chaining the embassy gates. Over 200 police were spaced along the front wall, with plainclothesmen scattered through the crowd across the street. A block away, fire engines waited. Down the street came the crowd, first five young men on bicycles, then the main army of demonstrators, holding high in the torchlight signs reading "Go home white monkey," "U.S. imperialists," and also some less inflammatory, such as "abrogate parity," and "Blast off, Blair! (the ambassador)." Another banner said "U.S. businessman—Drakula in the Philippines." Fiery speeches began coming from the sound truck, demanding that the United States stop maltreatment of Filipinos. But, said the observer—

> There was little response. In fact, it was quiet enough for us to hear the tinkling bells of vendors' carts in the grassy area behind us. They were peddling ice cream, corn on the cob, peanut crunch, soft drinks. The police, who had been keeping the spectators back on the curb, relaxed and some people wandered forward to get a better look at the speakers.
>
> Now came the high point of the rally, the burning of Uncle Sam in effigy. Uncle Sam was brought forward, a ten foot high cardboard figure in red, white and blue with Juan de la Cruz, the Filipino common man, hanging by the neck from his hands. . . . He made a brief but lively blaze. A pretty young Filipino girl turned to my wife and said happily, "This is my first demonstration." (Graves, 1965.)

The twelve coffins, however, were not burned, apparently because of a protest by the Catholic Church against the mockery of a sacrament. But the speeches went on and on.

> When one speaker said straight out that the U.S. bases should be got rid of altogether, he was booed by the spectators. "Nobody wants *that*," exclaimed a woman who just finished telling me she had once been beaten with an umbrella by an American. . . . When people were drifting away . . . a young man . . . said, "The reason it is so quiet is that there isn't any real anti-American feeling. There are just some things we want changed." . . . When the demonstration finally ended, the anti-U.S. marchers carefully picked up all their discarded signs and placards and poles to use them for firewood, leaving the street clean. (Graves, 1965.)

The impending riot did not come off, though most experts thought the signs looked bad enough. True mob mood and imagery did not develop, in spite of good communication and plenty of opportunities for milling and an apparently serious provocation prior to the demonstration. Apparently it never reached boiling temperature; that is, interaction in the crowd itself did not become reciprocal and intense enough to drown out even the sound of vendors. The crowd remained at low pitch and did not respond to appeals of speakers or the supposedly inflammatory gesture of burning in effigy, which, to a real mob, might have signaled a destructive outburst. Finally, with prudence they saved their materials for future use.

Looking back at the factors already discussed, some questions may be asked as to what kind of information about this crowd would have been more useful in predicting its behavior.

1. In the light of United States-Philippine relations, were there actually anti-American attitudes strong enough to cause Filipinos to wish to separate from the United States, and were they sufficient to be a basis for a riot?
2. Obviously, tension was inadequate. Would careful tension measurement have shown that it had not been built up enough, perhaps by news treatment or lack of time, for prior milling and rumor to do its work?
3. Plainly, the mood (judging by signs such as "abrogate parity") was lukewarm, and did not respond to triggers from the speakers or to the burning ceremony.
4. Likewise for imagery. Remarks cited did not show that images had become vivid or that there was focus on any goal other than what they were already doing.
5. The response to triggers was rather like that of wet tinder to a lit match.
6. Circular interaction, such as intensified yelling or call-and-answer responses, apparently did not develop. Was military restraint (absence of provocative behavior), or perhaps fear of hidden forces, a factor in preventing milling?

It is interesting to speculate how the Watts crowd would have acted in parallel circumstances. This example, though it gives clues as to why the riot did not occur, fails to tell us what perhaps only observers at hand with adequate measuring instruments could have told. The presumption is that common attitudes and tensions—the raw materials needed to start a crowd action—were insufficient. The example does, however, perhaps make us more aware of the kinds of things we should know about if we are to predict crowd behavior.

The other example of a riot that didn't happen comes from two sociologists (Shellow and Roemer, 1969) who had the fortune to be called in for advice by police in order to plan supervision of a scheduled motorcycle race in Maryland, 1965, at which disorderly groups such as "Hell's Angels" were expected to arrive in force. The problem was not only the coming presence of these undesirables, but the possibility that the sheer influx of outsiders for an activity that was not particularly welcome might create serious friction with the "locals." There was concern, then, that existing sources of strain could generate hostile "we" feeling among groups in the area, perhaps provoked by ineffective control efforts by the authorities. Also, a fair number of motorcyclists attending were expected to be Blacks, which added the possibility of racial conflict. The inadequacy of facilities for even a modest crowd of motorcyclists not seeking trouble was sure to produce a strain that would increase tension. Moreover, attitudes were known to exist which would favor hostilities, including the animosity of locals toward all motorcyclists, stereotyped as "hoodlums" and "wild ones"; an existing sense of persecution by all motorcyclists that they were unfairly treated as result of such stereotypes; "Hell's Angels" and similar groups spoiling for a fight as an opportunity for glory and ready to provide riot leadership; and a tough attitude of police likely to be provocative and lead to escalation of violence. Judging by what had happened at recent similar events, the outlook was grim.

The sociologists set four major goals to guide advice to police: (1) advance planning and coordination; (2) avoid polarization between authorities and motorcyclists by convincing police that motorcyclists "are not essentially different from other citizens" and that "indiscriminate harsh treatment of all motorcyclists would confirm the latter's sense of persecution"; also to draw local motorcyclists into cooperation with police and weaken their sense of solidarity with the "hoodlums" by arousing concern for the "deteriorating image of motorcycling"; (3) provide adequate facilities to contain the crowd, inhibit milling, and allow them an area where they could do pretty much as they pleased without spilling over into other areas; (4) continually monitor, check rumors, and keep abreast of events.

The weekend as it developed did indeed bring together a dangerous crowd, including a liberal supply of "Hell's Angels," "Pagans," and similar groups ready for trouble. Although there was much sporadic violence, and several riots loomed, police were able to contain and dissipate them successfully by a combination of sufficient ready force and a fairness and neutrality that avoided antagonizing crowds unduly. Tactics actually used included the following: allowing the motorcyclists a field to camp in, even though they had entered it illegally; neutral and impartial law enforcement, treating motorcyclists just as they would any motorist; a continuous unobtrusive observation with an elaborate communication system. When a riot did break out, police cars arrived promptly and fanned out in a half-circle, presenting the crowd with an array of flashing red lights and thus distracting as well as intimidating the crowd. Another riot in a tavern was averted by a low-key encounter in which the police sergeant talked in a manner that reduced tension. In several other confrontations, "Hell's Angel's" were faced down by a prompt display of well-equipped riot squads. The whole thing came off in such a way that police felt that the control effort had been a success, although they had spent from $6,000 to $10,000.

The sociologists agreed that, without the extra planning and expense, the hoodlum element sooner or later would have burst out of the camping area and become mob creators. They attributed the general success of the police policy to four factors: (1) a police policy of strength and fairness, without antagonizing motorcyclists but convincing them that overwhelming force was available on a moment's notice; (2) not interfering with the motorcyclists' camping and drag racing on private property, with result that they were segregated from the larger crowd they might have had among the track spectators, and were kept busy with activities among themselves, such as drinking, dragging, and showing off, without annoying other citizens; (3) a continuous flow of intelligence; and (4) "plain and simple good luck" such as a factional dispute between the "short haired" locals and rowdies, which precluded an alliance between them; and the fact that, for reasons known best to themselves, when it was necessary to clear the field, most of the rowdies left the county entirely. Another piece of luck was that the failure to provide camping facilities, as promised in the race publicity, did not have more serious consequences than it did in providing the racers with a real grievance. Finally, the sociologists noted that the registry included motorcycle tag numbers and this fact might have destroyed the anonymity that is such an important factor in crowd outbursts (Shellow and Roemer, 1969).

This motorcycle crowd, then, was apparently a more dangerous one than others we have considered (wrestling audience, Princeton students, Filipinos at the embassy), in terms of attitudes and tensions predisposing to hostility, and in these respects was more like the Watts rioters. Police action, fortified by tactics aimed at avoiding triggering and milling and combined with prompt but unprovocative force, in good measure succeeded; this contrasts with the failure of the tactics used by the Los Angeles police. No judgment is made here, either as to general causes of riots or police tactics, but such cases call our attention to the factors that should be studied. Even the "success" in the motorcycle case is of limited value for drawing conclusions, for the use of police force—even a show of force—obscures the other factors that may be operating. In a sense, any *use* of force is a failure of control. True riot control would be based on psychological principles rather than the time-honored method of main force. The real trick would be to blow the fuse of a riot psychologically, without using any force at all.

However, these remarks about psychological control of crowds apply only to true crowds. Janowitz (1969), for example, noted a change in race riot patterns in the United States from communal (characterized by ethnic "we" feeling) to commodity rioting, to urban guerilla tactics. We could not expect psychological tactics to have much effect on a disciplined force of trained guerilas. Take, for example, the demonstrators during the trial of the "Chicago Eight," 1969, who used tactics resembling mob action superficially but which actually were disciplined "banzai" attacks, which observers described in these terms:

I was in my apartment reading a magazine when I first heard the shouts of the demonstrators. I looked out a back window and saw what must have been a dozen helmeted protesters run wildly down the street —screaming and shouting and striking wooden sticks against building sides. . . . I was just standing here when they came swarming around the corner from everywhere. They were yelling and screaming like madmen. They broke into small groups and jumped on top of all these cars. They used wooden clubs to smash out the windows. The whole thing was deliberate and swift—like an army attack. Then they scrambled off the cars and ran to the next street. . . . They snake-danced by the street—and all of a sudden, without any warning, a gang of them came running toward the building, throwing things, smashing windows with clubs. (Halverson, 1969.)

Such actions clearly have little place in our analysis of crowd behavior.

Mentality of Crowds

We may now reconsider the somewhat harried question of the rationality of crowds. Looking at the examples considered in this chapter, it seems hard to deny that in this matter Le Bon was right: There is a substantial loss of rationality when collective decision becomes crowdlike. Common opinion seems confirmed: Being "caught up" in a crowd does seriously distort the judgment of individuals. Such a power has been misused by demagogues, well stated by Huxley (1958). The classic experiments by Asch (1952) show the tyranny of the majority. Yet, we should be careful not to exaggerate this power, since it has often been observed that people can be in crowds without being moved by them (Turner, 1969:101). One reason for this, as noted before, could be lack of common attitudes. But the question here is not so much the power of the crowd as the rationality of its decisions.

In what ways is the crowd less rational than, say, a committee or a problem-solving group (Shaw, 1932)? It may be faulted on three counts: (1) the process itself; that is, conditions minimize or preclude logical operations such as weighing of evidence, counterargument, resolving contradictions, formal inference; (2) its images and symbolization, which tend to be rhetorical, melodramatic, metaphorical, stereotyped, and so on; (3) the things people do as a result of crowd processes, namely, act impulsively and capriciously, and show a lack of responsibility and accountability.

What happens in crowd decision? Sociologists agree that it is not just a quick contagion, circular or not, but includes emergence of social norms (Turner, 1969:100). All agree that some kind of shift of perspective occurs, in which a crowd sees a situation differently.

The question is, what happens in this shift? There is a breakdown of conventional assumptions such as "business as usual," or "this isn't real, it's only a show." A different perspective emerges fairly rapidly, as in an escalation from confrontation to defiance, or as in the case of the graduating seniors changing their minds about having their names called, or as in a blaming process (Bucher, 1957; Kilpatrick, 1957; Veltfort and Lee, 1943), or as a "dirty deed" that causes crowd outlook to become melodramatic; or as a dramatic conversion (Klapp, 1964a:Chap. 6).

Many of these changes are shifts to perspectives already established. Let this not rule out the possibility of true novelty, emergence of a perspective that is quite new—that is, never before entertained by the group as a whole, such as a new mood which is like a new melody played on the old scale and the same strings—or perhaps a quite new "voice" waiting in the wings and now getting its chance, as illustrated by the Peel poem cited in Chapter 1. Also, the psychoanalytic view holds that in collective behavior, "unconscious" impulses freely expressed may be those ordinarily suppressed; that is, id forces become stronger as ego controls weaken (Martin, 1920; Strecker, 1940). It is difficult to gainsay this view, which opens the door to both greater variability and irrationality. However reached, the crowd becomes totally involved for a time in its new perspective, and then returns to "normal" perception. In normal perspective, it is usual to be at least a little apologetic, perhaps to regret the foolishness of actions in the crowd; and in some cases memory of what one did may be imperfect.

This view of the nonrationality of crowd decision does not rule out ideas. Rather, it asserts that the crowd does not think ideas that are clear and distinct, so prized by Locke, but images that are rich in sentiment, vivid, melodramatic, but intellectually murky. A good term for such ideas is *mystique*. These are collective representations, in the terminology of Durkheim; but, along with old collective representations, such as of prejudice and patriotism, they are new, inchoate norms, resisting rational characterization because they have not yet been adequately symbolized. The term *mystique* may be defined as a concept that is hard to explain at the discursive level except by metaphorical symbolization and ritual. The poet Kazantzakis told of his difficulty in expressing by a single adjective how he felt, and in so doing he gave a pretty good description of the difficulty people have in verbalizing mystiques:

> I love adjectives, but not simply as decorations. I feel the necessity of expressing my emotion from all sides, spherically; and because my emotion is never simple, never positive or negative only, but both together and something even more, it is impossible for me to restrict myself to one adjective. One adjective, whatever it might be, would

cripple my emotion, and I am obliged, in order to remain faithful to my emotion and not betray it, to invite another adjective often opposed to the previous one, always with a different meaning, in order that I may see the noun from its other equally lawful and existent side. Only thus, by besieging a meaning from all sides, may I conquer it, that is, may I express it. (Kazantzakis, 1958:xxxii.)

Both poets and demagogues appeal to such reservoirs of sentiment below the conscious level. The crowd, too, opens up these domains of mystique and allows people to enter, to enjoy togetherness. Crowd-mindedness offers "instant we" feeling in terms of such mystiques, and we see people enjoying them temporarily at sports events and more deeply at religious revivals. Such mystiques, operating in politics, make the public crowdlike. Symbolic leaders, as they will be discussed in a later chapter, evoke and create mystiques. The paranoid style (Hofstadter, 1966) is a mystique that allows innumerable events to be linked with a sense of conspiracy. Even catchwords ("un-American," "fifty-four forty or fight," "boop-boop-de-doop," "we love you Mets") are not so superficial as some think them to be, but are momentarily satisfactory symbols of deep underground sentiments not subject to logical analysis, especially after their supporting mood has evaporated. We see such symbols as rather like the iceberg, which has figured so largely in psychoanalytic theory—one-eighth above the water, seven-eighths beneath. Such mystiques act just the way unconscious wishes are supposed to act; for example, the "underdog," or "Cinderella," expectation of the Mets' victory in 1969 was a general feeling of "it just had to be," a kind of self-fulfilling prophecy. Compare the Truman victory in the presidential race of 1948 (Klapp, 1964a:150–155). Where mystiques are involved, connotation always exceeds denotation; logic cannot delineate the whole except by introducing contradictions at the same time. But, being normative, mystiques are not fully unconscious in Freudian terms; rather, they are at an intermediate level between the unconscious and rational thought, as indicated by Figure 3.2.

For such reasons, crowd behavior is not a blind, instinctive release, or a "letting go," but a highly normative transaction that makes descriptions like the following (from an older study of race riots) seem quaintly unrealistic: "In the race riot mob, no rules apply, no fair play. No ethics of any kind have meaning except the crude ones of the human-pack, even more brutal than the wolf-pack." (Lee and Humphrey, 1943:103.)

According to this explanation of crowd mentality, it seems clear that it is not just a contagion, reinforced by collective interaction, but entrance into a realm of ideas that are conscious but not easily verbalized, that makes crowd behavior nonrational. Obviously, this

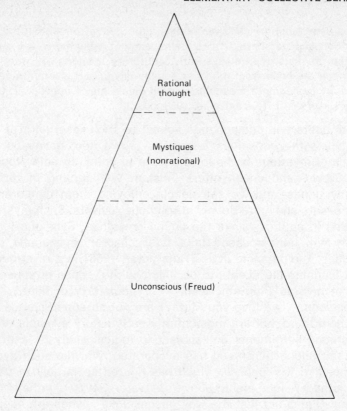

FIGURE 3.2. Levels of collective rationality.

is not a criticism of crowd ideas themselves, many of which are "good" and some of which are terribly important. But, nevertheless, it is a consensus of mystique, which poetry and ritual have better means of managing than science and logic.

In the next chapter the question is approached from another point of view—not how far crowds fall below rationality but how far they rise above animal collective behavior. By contrast with flock and herd behavior of lower animals, we can better appreciate what is involved in the human symbolic transaction as it occurs in collective behavior.

CHAPTER 4

Animal Collective Behavior

To attempt to study human collective behavior without looking at that of animals would be like building a house without
a foundation. If our behavioral development is superior to
that of animals, we shall see it more clearly by the comparison. If our collective behavior is dependent on the same
mechanisms as that of lower animals, we should base our

study on them.

The similarities are intriguing, but some writers have overempha-
sized them. The monkey stereotype (monkey-see-monkey-do), for
example, has been pushed too far. Clarence Day, in *This Simian
World*, gave a strictly humorous treatment of human chattering and
imitativeness, but it was quite off base zoologically, for humans go
beyond all other animals in chattering and copying one another.
There was nothing gained by calling us "simians." A serious, but
nevertheless amusing, book by Desmond Morris (1967a) depicts
man as a bad-tempered, naked ape with small teeth (though over-
large in other appendages), in danger of self-extinction when his
instinctive aggressiveness is augmented by technology. Though
many quarreled with the anthropology, this unflattering picture by an
ethologist had a chastening effect on human pride. Some writers,
such as Trotter (1917) and more lately Lorenz (1966) and Canetti
(1962) have overdrawn the herd, or pack, instinct as the source of
human trouble. Such pictures, hopefully the evidence will prove,
put us down too far on the animalistic behavior scale.

Nevertheless, it would be a mistake to give man too much imaginary superiority, with tinsel wings by which, like Icarus, to fly too
high. We should find a reasonable balance between animal and
angel, slime and the sublime. If man belongs with the animals, he
is still the star performer in the zoo. How is he different? Does the
difference hold even when he is venting his emotions in a mob? Or
are these the times when the pack and the herd instincts assert
themselves, when inherent flocking mechanisms go into play, communication sinks to animal signs, and the consensus of the human
crowd is not greatly different from that of the animal crowd? Let us
look at the parallels and see what kind of case we can make for
the similarity or the difference.

Monkey Hill

Baboons are markedly gregarious and offer more examples of
collective behavior than do chimpanzees, gorillas, and orang-utangs.
"Monkey Hill" was the scene of some pioneering observations by
Zuckerman (1932) of what seemed at the time a reasonably natural
approximation in captivity of the life of a colony. While a normal
social order of dominance and harems seemed to obtain, boredom
also seemed prominent and every now and then the Hill seethed with
excitement as contagious fighting broke out. Several kinds of riots
were observed. One began with the cry of a small baboon for
protection when being bullied. His squeal of terror brought adults
rushing to the scene, threatening and attacking one another, while
the young animal scampered away. Another riot occasion was often

a display of dominance by one male over another; others would rush in to join the less dominant animal, and it would sometimes spread throughout the colony, with family parties joining the fight, thus polarizing factions of the community so that the battle front no longer centered around the quarrel of the two males. A third occasion for rioting was the effort of an overlord to protect his harem from interlopers, drawing in outsiders in the same contagious way. Fourth were riots from crowding at feeding.

Finally, there were "sexual fights," which occurred seldom but were severe: The atmosphere would suddenly change and every male appeared to be trying "at the peril of life, to secure a female in an attack on a harem" (Zuckerman, 1932:252). Such fights could involve most of the colony, and could kill as many as thirty female baboons who happened to be the center of the issue. Such alarming outbursts of aggression quickly drew attention to the misery of crowding baboons into confines without the range of their natural habitat. Zuckerman (1932:217) noted that, because they were confined and unable to escape, baboons were probably able to carry their fights much further than in the wild. Moreover, appeasement gestures (such as submission or offering to groom) did not work as they normally do. Something was causing aggression to go too far, and was interfering with an instinct that worked all right in the natural state. Field studies, for example, showed no such sexual fighting among Chacmas baboons. The abnormalities of "Monkey Hill" were generally attributed to the tensions of overcrowding and too low a proportion of females (which was in part produced by the deaths in sexual fighting). Murraytown, a natural open-colony sanctuary for woolly monkeys, remedied this difficulty. Free to "roam the whole of Cornwall" if they wished, they did not leave but stayed in their territory and defended it. Disputes were resolved by peaceful means, rarely by serious fighting (Williams, 1968:28, 32).

Increased aggression from crowding brings up the question of territoriality (Ardrey, 1966, 1970). Many animals become instinctively aggressive when their home territory is encroached. Territoriality often becomes especially strong when mating bonds are formed. For example, rats in a large enclosure "which provided them with completely natural living conditions . . . became really aggressive only when they began to settle and take possession of territories. At the same time, pair formation started" (Lorenz, 1966:152). At this point, life became very difficult for unmated rats without home territories; the mated pair managed to kill all the unpaired rats in two or three weeks. However, within the rat pack there is usually no real fighting. The notorious "rat pack" response occurs only when a strange rat enters clan territory. Then a "quick news system" functions by "mood transmission" and soon begins—

one of the most horrible and repulsive things which can be observed in animals. The strange rat may run around for minutes . . . without having any idea of the terrible fate awaiting it . . . till finally the stranger comes close enough to one of them for it to get wind of the intruder. The information is transmitted like an electric shock . . . by a sharp, shrill, satanic cry which is taken up by all members of the tribe . . . with their eyes bulging from their sockets, their hair standing on end, the rats set out on the rat hunt. They are so angry that if two of them meet they bite each other. . . . On the day of persecution of the strange rat all the members of the clan are irritable and suspicious. Evidently the members . . . recognize each other by the clan smell, like bees and other insects. . . . The strange rat . . . is slowly torn to pieces by its fellows. Only rarely does one see an animal in such desperation and panic, so conscious of the inevitability of a terrible death, as a rat which is about to be slain by rats. It ceases to defend itself. (Lorenz, 1966:154–157.)

Ethologists regard territorialism as a "basic characteristic of non-human primate groupings" with striking analogies in human behavior (C. R. Carpenter, in Southwick, 1963:37). Lorenz applied it to urban crowding and, by implication, to human outbursts:

Every inhabitant of a modern city is familiar with the surfeit of social relationships and responsibilities and knows the disturbing feeling of not being as pleased as he ought to be at the visit of a friend, even if he is genuinely fond of him and has not seen him for a long time. . . . That crowding increases the propensity to aggressive behavior has long been known and demonstrated experimentally. . . . (Lorenz, 1966:244.)

Lorenz adds the disturbing observation:

Man's social organization is very similar to that of rats, which, like humans, are social and peaceful beings within their clans, but veritable devils toward all fellow members of their species not belonging to their own community. If . . . [an observer] knew of the explosive rise in human populations, the ever-increasing destructiveness of weapons, and the division of mankind into a few political camps, he would not expect the future of humanity to be more rosy than that of several hostile clans of rats on a ship almost devoid of food. (Lorenz, 1966:229.)

Two forms of instinctive animal collective behavior noted by Lorenz are most relevant for comparison with human crowds. One is the "mobbing" pattern just illustrated in rats. This is a group counteroffensive against an enemy: Birds will mob an owl; crows, a cat; geese, a human; zebras, a leopard; and cattle, wolves. The other relevant instinctive response is "close herding" as a protection against predators; for example, African buffalo make it difficult to separate a single animal in order to attack it. These are basic flocking reactions (Lorenz, 1966:23, 137).

Of course close flocking precludes much internal aggression within the flock. This brings us to another disturbing relationship noted by Lorenz and other ethologists: that it is in those animal societies where there are the strongest bonds of affection that we find the strongest aggressive urges toward other bands of the same species. Love and aggressiveness toward one's own kind are two sides of the same coin. Lorenz puts the case in a striking way: that the price of the social bond is aggression against the outsider. Geese and ducks, for example, show their love—so to speak—by a cere-monial attack, offering to drive off and thrash a rival. This is a bio-logically fixed ritual that signifies at the same time, the control of aggression and formation or strengthening of a social bond. "Re-direction of the attack is evolution's most ingenious expedient for guiding aggression into harmless channels" (Lorenz, 1966:54–75). In this way, social cohesion is purchased by what we might call scapegoating. Thus, among baboons, it is noted that a battle within the band gradually develops into a fight between bands as aggression is redirected against outsiders (Kummer, 1968:105–106); and the formation of friendship and mating ties is expressed in sublimated aggression ritual among woolly monkeys (Williams, 1968:156).

So, from ethology we get several principles that may help in explaining behavior of human crowds: the tendency to flock (mass densely) together when threat is felt; the "mobbing" response; and affirming or strengthening group unity by aggression against outsiders.

Anthropologists have not been slow to attack these claims, which seem to imply that instinct is more important than culture in what humans do. They deny, for example, that small cohesive groups are instinctively aggressive. As evidence, they point out tribes like the Arapesh of New Guinea, the Lepchas of Sikkim in the Himalayas, and the Pygmies of the Congo, which are gentle people with no habits or even concept of war against their fellow man (Gorer, in Ashley-Montagu, 1968:34). Also, some ethologists have become un-comfortable with the idea of territorial aggression as applied to man, noting that clear territoriality is absent among some of the higher primates, such as certain monkeys (*Cercopithecus*, *Macacus*), baboons (*Papio*, *Theropithecus*), chimpanzees, and gorillas (John Hurrell Crook, in Ashley-Montagu, 1968:168).

An alternative theory (which does not necessarily rule out instinct) explains at the cultural and symbolic level this widespread phenomenon of the purchase of group solidarity by aggression against outsiders. Conflict is not merely a disruptive process; it also contributes a great deal to group unity (Coser, 1956). Such func-tions, however, occur at the cultural level—for example, symbols and ceremonies such as sorcery—rather than at the biological level.

The contribution to group unity is no less great, but no modification of genes is involved. Sumner (1906) was probably the first to introduce this cultural theory in the idea that the "mores make anything right" for the ingroup, such as cannibalism and lynching, even when rational ethics interpret the behavior as evil. Mores are essentially habits that grow up as means to group survival. An important later statement of this idea was by R. Niebuhr (1932): that groups create their own morality, and that demands for absolute loyalty, as in patriotism, flout ethics; men individually may be moral, but collectively they are immoral. A sociological theory that accounts for these facts, yet does not require an instinct of aggression, might be stated as follows: Humans have an inherent need to belong, to feel closely together. (It is not necessary to debate whether this comes from instinct or from the experience of the primary group.) Making heroes and defining enemies are both symbolic processes that help people to feel more together in a threatening world.* Hero and villain images are built by symbolic processes such as art, drama, and story telling. Idealizing heroes, whose acts show perfect loyalty ("I have but one life to give for my country"), make people feel more closely and securely together. Depicting the enemy as being "so bad we have to stick together" also serves group unity. The worse the enemy is painted, the more important the social bond becomes. Psychologists would call this tendency the displacement of hostility by means of scapegoat symbols. The point is that instinctive processes, beyond a need for togetherness, need not be invoked. According to this interpretation, if another group encroaches, it threatens group *identity* (as a sense of who we are), not instinctive "territoriality." However, as already said, this is no proof that instinct and symbolic processes of group unity might not be working together.

The preceding discussion illustrates the kind of contribution that study of animals may make to the understanding of human crowd aggression. Let us now look at the social coordination of animal flocks, to see how they work together and whether this throws any light on how human crowds act together.

Social Coordination

Some of the most astounding examples of collective coordination come from the lower reaches of the animal kingdom. We are familiar with the complex colonies of the bees and the termites,

* Symbolic processes generating "we" feeling were discussed in Chapter 1.

which have a division of labor that seems more complex and more trouble-free than that of humans. We may, however, look closely at a few examples of such coordination, ranging from that of insects to that of primates, to see clearly the character of such coordination.

A striking example is described by the French naturalist Fabre (1916) of the social behavior of the Pine caterpillar, which is typically found traveling in processions that may measure up to thirty feet in length. This insect is perhaps the world's champion follower, since the strongest desire of each, even stronger than the desire for food, is to follow another caterpillar, which in turn is looking for another caterpillar to follow. "The Pine Caterpillar is more sheep-like than sheep. Where the first goes all the others go, in a regular string, with not an empty space between" (Fabre, 1916:58). Whoever happens to be the leader lays down a path of silk that others follow, each adding to it. One day Fabre had an opportunity to do an experiment. He saw a procession crossing his garden and finally climb the side of a large tub. Reaching the top rim, the procession began marching around it. Soon the circle was closed, and at that point Fabre rubbed away the other caterpillars, leaving the ones on top in an uninterrupted circular procession. His question, then, was what will they do? "Will they walk endlessly round and round until their strength finally gives out?" They kept it up all that day, passing the time when normally they would eat. A "branch stands green and tempting not a hand's breadth away. To reach it they need but go down; and the poor wretches, foolish slaves of their ribbon, cannot do so." Fabre visited them again at dawn. They were pursuing their path with machinelike obstinacy. The following morning they were still stoutly marching around, without a sign of discouragement. The third morning, and the fourth morning the same. On the fifth morning "a certain disorder becomes manifest. Weariness increases the confusion. The crippled, who refuse to go on, are many." But the march continued. On the sixth day, some caterpillars in the procession sporadically broke away, to explore gropingly, then returned to their place in the procession. It was not until two days later—the eighth day of the experiment—that the caterpillars came down, singly and in small groups, breaking the magic chain that had held them. (Fabre, 1916:71–89.)

We may compare another example of the extraordinary loyalty of insects to their collective enterprises, this time of aggressive behavior that might, by a stretch of imagination, be likened to its human counterpart, the notorious army ants of Africa whose marching columns arouse fear in all other animals of the jungle—including man. Hardly bigger than our red wood ants, they advance at about the speed of a soldier on the double, making a column about an inch wide:

> There is nothing to fear as long as one leaves 20 to 30 centimeters between one's feet and the edge of the procession. If one neglects this . . . the workers often swing around and attack one in the rear.

For seven hours they have been passing. The sand has been worn down into a gully by millions of tiny feet. Along the sides of the path are stationed the soldiers, with mandibles fiercely outstretched, shielding the workers in the ranks:

> One party of workers carries the young larvae and all stages of the brood. Another party goes hunting: they climb a tree and occupy it completely, down to the smallest twig. All the inhabitants of the leaves and branches retreat before these inexorable aggressors and finally drop to the ground, where more ants are waiting to tear them to pieces. . . .

The army ants have no fixed nest. They make only temporary camps and move on when food is eaten up. Their terrifying raids are stimulated by the queen's oestrus cycle. On such occasions, the ants suddenly increase their activity, then burst out upon the warpath. (Chauvin, 1968:115–117.)

Another famous example of animal collective coordination comes from the lemming, a rodent found in Scandinavian countries, whose frenzied migrations have been likened to stampedes that sometimes destroy human crowds. A kind of madness seems to come over them every three or four years. They multiply excessively, come out into the open daylight, outrun their habitat, and start to migrate. Such a mass movement is rather like that of the locusts of Africa, except that migrating lemmings keep out of close touch with each other, getting into big masses only when faced by an obstacle such as a river, viaduct, or ditch. Then they will throw themselves into the water in mad imitation of fellows who have gone before, until millions have followed and the ditch is filled with bodies. Or they will swim out to sea until they are all drowned. They:

> . . . swim straight forward and scale all obstacles in their path, such as a boat, which can become so loaded with them that it sinks [a lemming is hardly bigger than a mouse]. They will venture out to sea . . . "a steamship going at full speed . . . had to pass through a veritable soup of lemmings swimming away in the waves with their innumerable little heads puncturing the surface as far as the eye could see." At these times the lemming, usually so timid, is not afraid to be seen in the middle of towns, even in the houses of men, whom it will even sometimes attack. (Chauvin, 1968:149; the inner quotation is from Laurent.)

Such swarming, unlike that of the army ant, has no apparent adaptive value. It seems to be a mechanism that operates without even the excuse of overcrowding, which the baboons had for their outbursts, though ecological factors may be found to explain it as a way of restoring natural balance. We have sufficient illustration, at any rate, of how blindly instinct works, how mechanical it is compared to the freedom and fluidity of human crowds, and how little it seems to depend upon circular interaction to motivate even something that resembles a stampede.

As we move up the evolutionary scale, we cannot pass the herd, to which human collective behavior has been so often compared. The organization of a cow herd is reported to be very simple. The relationship among animals depends, above all, on age and weight; these seem to govern dominance in a "peck order." When a strange cow is introduced into the herd, she is smelled and possibly threatened by the other cows, but in no way disturbs the peck order; she takes her place at the bottom. Besides dominance, there is the flocking mechanism:

> Cows . . . do everything together: they all feed at the same time, they all ruminate together; but if a single wire fence separates the herd into two parts each of them becomes independent and one section may ruminate whilst the other crops the grass. (Chauvin, 1968: 234.)

Only two things seem to upset this simple order: oestrus; and calving, when the cow leaves the herd for three days, then rejoins it. However, a number of signals are cues for this coordination. The communication of cattle has been analyzed by a naturalist who followed a herd on horseback for some 2,000 hours of observation. Emotion is not expressed in facial expressions (which to humans seem blank) but in inclination of the head and horns in relation to the neck. These indicators of mood are "at once recognized by the rest of the herd," and humans can get to know them, too. Smells, especially of the hindquarters, are also of great importance. In vocal expression, eleven different tones of mooing and lowing were distinguished, including a call that summons the herd, a threatening bellow toward a rival, the call of a cow to her calf, and a "call to play" in which calves chase one another. Supplementing vocalizations are gestures, such as scraping the soil with a forefoot, rubbing neck and side of head on ground, and rubbing trees with horns—all of which seem to have threat significance in the presence of a rival. Finally, contacts have a part in communication, such as the licking of shoulders of another; or contacts of forehead and horns, which seem to be a game and do not develop into a fight (Chauvin, 1968: 234). Such communication, especially when emphasizing touch, is capable of becoming circular (milling) when cattle are confined, building up tension that can lead to stampede if there is an opening for movement. But the general picture of herd coordination is of a rigidity and mechanicalness that seem more like that of insects than of humans.

Finally, we return to the baboon troop, which seems in its movements superficially like a human crowd:

> When one first sees a troop of baboons, it appears to have little order, but this is a superficial impression. The basic structure of the troop is most apparent when a large troop moves away from the safety of trees and out onto open plains. As the troop moves the less dominant adult males and perhaps a large juvenile or two occupy the van. Females and more of the older juveniles follow, and in the center of the troop are the females with infants, the young juveniles and the most dominant males. The back of the troop is a mirror image of its front, with less dominant males at the rear. Thus, without any fixed or formal order, the arrangement of the troop is such that the females and young are protected at the center. No matter from what direction a predator approaches the troop, it must first encounter the adult males.
>
> One day we saw two dogs run barking at a troop. The females and juveniles hurried, but the males continued to walk slowly. In a moment an irregular group of some 20 adult males was interposed between the dogs and the rest of the troop. When a male turned on the dogs, they ran off. (Washburn and DeVore, in Southwick, 1963:100–101.)

Here we see that the disorder is only an illusion, and that an extraordinary coordination of a fluid pattern keeps the troop ready for attack—a deployment that would do credit to a human military detachment.

The baboon troop is important for our study, for it is the best we have as an example of a higher primate collectivity to compare to that of man. Its movements, leadership, and even collective decisions have been carefully observed; so we may follow it, looking for parallels with the human crowd. The "pseudopods" that flow from the baboon troop might be thought to resemble, say, a human crowd flowing into a field or a train station. There is a flow in it that resembles a "bandwagon effect" when the majority swings undecided individuals into a collective decision. There is also a tentative exploratory process, resembling a crowd trying to reach a collective decision, as would-be leaders stick their necks out (A. K. Cohen, 1955) in a milling process. Pseudopods "are sent out and drawn in again until finally one . . . grows longer and longer and the rest of the troop flows into it" to form a column leaving in a quick march (Kummer, 1968:12). Kummer's account allows us to look closely at this collective decision:

> . . . a pseudopod or runner takes about ten to thirty minutes to form. It starts when a male leaves the troop proper and sits down some three to ten meters beyond the troop's periphery. In a short time other males

follow suit, sitting down 2 to 5 meters next to him. All these males have their backs to the troop. In this way a male front is formed. The area behind this front is taken up by their females and other one-male units. Usually the units shift as clear entities; when they halt, their females sit behind their males centerwards. The pseudopod is further developed by units from the center moving ahead of the foremost males. In this way the males of an advancing pseudopod front are often exchanged. . . . An actual departure will occur when unit after unit at the center of the troop walk toward the pseudopod. If enough animals in the center are walking at the same time, the pseudopod's front too rises, goes ahead, and the troop departs. (Kummer, 1968:138–139.)

Such a decision looks like a "bandwagon" effect in which the motion of the majority is the prevailing factor, but we see that it can be abruptly canceled by the determined action of one "old red-faced male" who stands up in the middle of the troop and marches decisively in a different direction from that in which everybody seemed about to go. The apes respond to this new leader with contact grunts and follow him in increasing numbers; within a few seconds the entire troop moves, leaving the original starter (the "crowd leader") far in the rear and unable to catch up with the lead (Kummer, 1968: 139). The old ape "neither pauses nor looks back nor presents to any of his neighbors." The swinging of his hind region seems a sufficient notification to everyone. This example shows, of course, how little like a crowd decision the baboon troop movement really is, in spite of its development of pseudopods. The crowd type of leadership, in which anonymous members start a trend, is valid only if the real leaders follow.

But leadership of the baboon troop is not quite so simple as this picture of old male leadership implies. Actually, what typically happens is the cooperation of a two-male team of leaders, which is one of the "most fascinating phenomena in the social organization of the hamadryas." The typical pattern is for an older and younger male to form a partnership, dividing leadership and protection of their females and young between them. The marching pattern is one male, followed by the females and young, with the other male bringing up the rear. The male in front is the one who has initiated that particular move; but the direction of march results from a compromise of the two leaders, who adjust their positions to one another as they march. Kummer gives us an example of how this extraordinary leadership cooperation works. The first move is made by the younger leader (Circum), who goes to the older (Pater) and exchanges glances. Then he starts off to the north, followed by all the animals. They go to the water hole in the following order: Circum, his females, all the young, Pater's females, Pater. Thus, the older leader puts his stamp of approval on the move initiated by the younger leader. The next example shows how it goes when the younger leader is not supported by the older:

> Circum rises and slowly goes to the north, turning back to the troop several times. His females follow him; some even passing him as they search for food. . . .
> Pater who was sitting southmost, rises and begins to move in the opposite direction, to the south. Within three seconds, all of the females and young follow him; finally, even Circum. (Kummer, 1968.)

Thus, a "protocol" operates in the leadership of the baboon collectivity: (1) the younger male usually initiates a move; (2) but his advances are only "proposals" in which the decision is completed by the older partner; (3) females can influence the decision by following—"throwing their weight" toward—one male; but (4) the general tendency of females with young is to seek the center (helping hold the unit together); and (5) nonvocal signals coordinate the movements (exchanges of glances, initiatory movements, "notifying" gestures in which one male approaches another seated and looks in his face, and the established taking-leave courtesy in which an approacher "turns abruptly and presents his 'anal field' followed by a hasty retreat, this ritual alerting the neighbor that 'the spatial relationship between him and the active partner is about to change in a way which is important for the cohesion of the party"). (Kummer, 1968:125–130.) Though this leadership protocol is the most important single mechanism of collective decision, a mass-action principle—roughly comparable to the "bandwagon" effect—is also involved:

> Although adult males, in proportion to their statuses, determine group movements, a large number of low order individuals, i.e., females and young, may have a summed effect which outweighs the effects of the positions and the movements of males. Thus, generally males, even in the lead, coordinate their behavior with the center of the mass of the whole group. (Carpenter, 1964:381.)

We have now looked at several examples of animal collective coordination, ranging from insects to higher primates. Certain conclusions seem justified:

1. Animal collective coordination and "decision" are largely if not altogether determined by instinctive mechanisms.
2. Complexity of coordination, while impressive among baboons, does not increase greatly—if at all—from the level of social insects; there has been no evolutionary "gain" in instinctive coordination.
3. In view of unsettled controversy, it is not justifiable to categorically rule out the possibility that such mechanisms (as flocking) may operate in human groups.

4. Obviously, much more than instinctive action is working by way of symbolic process at the human level, even in crowds, and surely in the enormous coordination of organized human groups.

The point seems obvious that humans achieve by laborious teaching and drill—and their own folly—what animals do by inherited responses. Some anthropologists, such as Margaret Mead, go so far as to deny that there is any instinct operating in human collective behavior at all:

Do you think human beings en masse have a lemming-like instinct?
DR. MEAD: No.
SENATOR PELL: You do not?
DR. MEAD: But I also think that they *do not have a protection against behaving as if they had lemming instincts. . . . We only behave in groups in the way you are speaking of in states of panic or riot*, which, after all, are not our normal state. We go into danger much more because of the *inertia* of elected or appointed *officials*, for whom it is safer to do nothing at all. It is *such persons who do the harm* in an organized society and not group or mass behavior.
SENATOR PELL: Thank you.   (M. Mead, 1969a.)

Communication and Imitation

People have tried hard to find something among apes which justifies their reputation for being imitative, and even harder (judging by efforts like those of the Kelloggs, 1933) to see if they could speak. Zuckerman says—

The layman believes that monkeys and apes are very good imitators —by which he usually means that they reflect the actions of individuals they may observe. In actual fact it is uncertain whether they do imitate in this manner, or indeed whether they are better mimics than dogs. . . . Imitation, implying social modification of behavior, may . . . mean no more than that the experience of one monkey or ape within a group may be shared by all its fellows. (Zuckerman, 1932:164, 171.)

Yet, such behavior is important in our search for animal parallels to hun.an collective behavior, for it is the basis of contagion. We may restrict the notion of "collective" to behavior that is communicative or imitative. For example, animals flocking to a water hole because they are thirsty are not acting collectively, but they are when responding to a cry of distress or howling in a "battle" with another group (of howler monkeys; Southwick, 1963:187). Thus, any behavior capable of being generalized through a troop, herd, or flock by means of communication or imitation is defined as collective rather than parallel response to a situation. The question very much concerns play, for here is where much of so-called ape imitation occurs. Gorillas, for example, copy one another in their play, throwing water, swinging on ropes, playing with water, and pounding their chests at one another. But examples of true imitation—if by this one means learning to do something as the result of watching another—are hard to come by. A careful observer says of mountain gorillas:

> There seemed to be considerable imitator-imitatee relationships between the two gorillas when their moods and behavior were properly synchronized. However, the problem is raised of what is meant by imitated behavior. Acts which are merely initiated by the activity of another animal are not acts of imitation. The following examples are those in which the behavior of one animal set off similar behavior in another . . . although the behavior stimulated is already a part of the action system of the second animal. This . . . may be called *copying* as contrasted with true imitation. One of the gorillas would begin to dash water from the pool and the other one would follow suit. It is reported that the animals would copy a rhythm of locomotion as set by their keeper, but I was unable to verify this. Furthermore, simple forms of behavior such as playing with objects, swinging ropes or rings are copied from one animal by another. If Mbongo had the opportunity to let water run from a hose into his mouth and Ingagi saw him, immediately Ingagi would chase Mbongo away and take the water in his own mouth. In this instance there is a striving for a common incentive which requires similar behavior patterns. (Carpenter, 1964:117.)

Nevertheless, Carpenter did find communication in the copying, for example, of chest beating, which "seemed to signify a challenge" to wrestle. It also seemed to be a form of display: "He would perform some feat . . . and immediately afterwards beat his chest . . . when he seemed particularly anxious to attract the attention of a person" (Carpenter, 1964:115). This, as such examples show, is about as close as subhumans come to communicating with each other by imitative gestures. Most copying lacks the message character of gorilla chest beating. Nevertheless, chimpanzee play is more varied and lively, and may contain a higher proportion of imitative acts (as contrasted with mechanical copying): They are attracted by objects thrown into the enclosure, carry bags, wear baskets on their heads, carry pipes in their mouths, tinker with old watches, play with toads, carry each other on their backs like a jockey, "dance" by somersaults, and entice each other to play (Zuckerman, 1932:258–262). But probably the most striking examples of learning by imitation are found in "acculturative" behavior among Japanese monkeys, which bears some comparison with human fads; for example, a candy-eating habit formed by one monkey spread to 51 percent of the troop in a year and a half, and another group was observed to take up washing sweet potatoes in water before eating them, after one monkey had tried it (Southwick, 1963:72, 88).

We now have a basis for comparison of true imitation with the instinctive "ritual" behavior of lower animals, which seemed to be highly symbolic; for example, the "inciting" ceremony of female ducks, which consists of a mock attack on another couple, followed by retreat; or the famed "dance" of cranes, whose symbolism, said Lorenz, "tempts us to translate it into human language." A bird rears up before another, unfolds its wings, points its beak threateningly as though in imminent attack; the next moment he turns about and, still with spread wings, directs a fake attack "on any substitute object, preferably a nearby crane which is not a friend, or even on a harmless goose or on a piece of wood . . ." seeming to say as clearly as human words, "I am big and threatening, but not toward you— toward the other" (Lorenz, 1966:55, 168–169). Such a ritualized sequence, however meaningful it may be to humans, can be credited as an instinctive mechanism, less imitative than a gorilla's chest beating, and not collective as it has been defined here—incapable of being spread (as could a human dance step) among the group.

It is on the question of communication by signs and how far animals approach language that the most important comparison between animal and human collective behavior hinges. For language is the most efficient means of spreading any mental state contagiously.

There is no question that the animal world is full of communication. Birds call to one another, mosquitoes give "love calls" by buzzing, bees "dance" to give signals to other bees about the direction and distance of food. There is general agreement, however, that such patterns of signaling are stereotyped and innate in each species, so that the newly hatched member needs no experience to respond to it properly (Von Frisch, 1955, 1962). Granting the effectiveness of this kind of communication, but taking account of the insect "brain," which is hardly more than a cluster of ganglia, one cannot grant that it is symbolic in the way that humans (perhaps also apes and dolphins to some extent) communicate. True, bird calls are modifiable and imitative, especially those of the mocking bird, parrot, and raven. This is a very small gain, however, when one sees that a parrot, for all his facility in mimicry, uses "words" without conversational give-and-take or sense of the appropriateness of the situation (saying "damn!," for example, when the preacher visits). Imitation of human sounds, then, while it may gain responses from humans, is not presumed to have any corresponding meaning to the animal that utters them. It falls in the same category with the conditioned salivation of the dog at the ringing of a bell.

Returning to the communication that animals use among themselves, we find a good supply of vocal gestures that are highly
communicative. Baboons, for example, have a "language" with over
a dozen distinct sounds. The bark is a greeting, but it is also a signal
of alarm which spreads excitement; the troop's attention is riveted
on the barker, and they sit and watch for a vocal or motor signal.
The leader baboon tastes a farmer's vegetables and, if it is safe,
he calls the troop waiting for his signal. If the farmer comes out
dressed in women's clothes, with a gun hidden under his dress,
the baboons are not fooled; they hoot and bark at him from safety.
Besides the bark, other sounds include a laugh of pleasure, a grunt
of well-being and satisfaction, kek-kek for "ouch," scream for severe
pain, moaning and lamentation, and lip smacking for affection. Nonvocal gestures of threat are made by raising the brows, hand flicking,
slapping the ground, jumping up and down with mouth open, yawn-
ing, and grinding of the teeth. (It is recommended, therefore, that
humans do not smile or laugh showing their teeth at apes, since it
is interpreted as a threat and makes them nervous.) "Baboonese"
has been learned by humans, and at least in one case helped a
keeper to talk his way out of a cage when threatened by an enraged
baboon (MacDonald, 1965:42–47, 103). Rallying cries have a distinct
relation to baboon "rioting," especially the terror squeal of the
young, the high-pitched screech of a female, the rage cry of the male,
and deep-throated barks heard in the wild state when a troop is
scattering or an enemy is approaching, which seem to help the reunion of the scattered troop (Zuckerman, 1932:251–264).

Another view of primate communication is given by the signals
used by New World monkeys. Touching and offering to groom is a
generally friendly signal. Rubbing the hind quarters or chest on a
tree branch or other object in the environment is a highly important
olfactory signal for establishing a territory and mutual identification. Visual gestures include facial expressions (protruding lips,
baring teeth, partly closing eyes); postures and body movements
(swaying and head-down postures of alarm, aggressive tail lashing);
pilo-erection (raising of the hair of head, body, and tail); and a
variety of acoustic signals, in two groups: high-pitched sounds
(squeaks, whistles, trills, screams), and low-pitched sounds (grunts,
barks, moans). Threat patterns such as tail lashing not only spare an
individual's having to fight, but induce mobbing responses by com-
panions and thus help save the individual from predators (M. Moynihan, 1967:236–266).

Such examples of "monkey talk" should be sufficient to give us
a picture of the considerable capacity of apes for communication,
yet leave open the question to what extent this is language comparable to that of humans. A statement by an ethologist (Carpenter,

1964:356–357) will serve to summarize some of the important limitations of ape communication. One is that ape communication is more fixed and specific than that of humans; that is, it takes place "only when the organisms have been fittingly related" by heredity, maturation, common reactions to ecological factors, and conditioning. In other words, there is a smaller chance that individuals can "get together" by communication if not specifically adapted for it in the first place. Another limitation of ape communication is that "responses are made to and become . . . a part of the immediate situation," and lack the human capacity to refer to things that are far away in time and space. A third limitation is that, apes "lack the capacity to learn a very wide range of motor responses which can be used symbolically, the repertory being fixed by heredity." Finally, they "have only limited capacity to characterize, represent or abstract perceived situations" (Carpenter, 1964:356–357). A further consideration is the enormous size and the grammatical and syntactical complexity of human language, a matter that has been investigated extensively by Lindesmith and Strauss (1968). The key point is that humans are able to improvise, stock, and use in versatile ways large numbers of *conventional symbols*, as contrasted with natural signs, which are a vehicle for both memory of what they know and for passing it on as a social heritage.

The immediate consequence of this is absence of any body of consensus (common understandings) in animal cooperation comparable to that of humans. Animals work "together but not in common" (Lindesmith and Strauss, 1968:76–78). Park said that human participation in a common purpose and a common life is rendered possible by—

> a fund of common symbols and meanings. The lower animals have neither words nor symbols; nothing, for them, has what we may describe as meaning. The lower animals have, in the words of Durkheim, no "collective representations." They do not organize processions and carry banners; they sing, and sometmes, we are told, even dance, but they do not celebrate; they acquire habits which are sometimes transmitted as a kind of social tradition, but they have no customs, and for them nothing is either sacred or lawful. Man . . . lives . . . through his imagination, in the minds of other men, who share with him not merely their possessions, but their hopes and their dreams. (Park, 1927.)

Conclusion

We have considered various examples of animal collective behavior which have some similarity to what goes on among humans. We considered "rioting" of apes and rats in conditions of confinement, which some have compared to those of humans crowded in ghettos. We noted instinctive flocking, mobbing, and aggression in defense of home territory, along with the thesis of Lorenz that the security of the social bond is somehow purchased in evolution by redirecting aggression from members of the group outward toward an enemy. We then considered the rather remarkable social coordination of animals, ranging from insects to baboons, which seems to be based largely—if not altogether—on instinctive responses that occur almost automatically, without learning or anything resembling deliberate decision. Such instinctive coordination, however, though beautifully reliable and automatic, does not help baboons much more, if at all, than it does the social insects. Something else has to happen in the evolutionary process if higher levels of coordination are to be achieved.

In the matter of communication we found that apes are not very good imitators; nor do they live up to their reputation or give humans any serious competition in this regard. Moreover, the sign language of apes, as well as the lower animals, is found to be richer than superficial observation might reveal, but it is fixed and rather limited in scope, and quite inadequate to allow apes to develop a substantial stock of consensus or culture.

It is concluded, then, that animal collective behavior is determined largely by instinct, triggered by natural signs in appropriate situations, but that humans are capable of doing much more than instinctive responses to signs, able to use true language and a large store of ideas as common understandings. All this consensus would not be needed, nor could it find a function, in relatively simple transactions such as crowds and spontaneous outbursts. Nevertheless, we can expect a substantial flow of symbolic communication— say of sentiments, stereotypes, and mystiques—as long as humans are capable of responding symbolically at all and stress has not reduced them to aphasia or stupor.

However, granted that humans are usually symbolic, it is another thing to say that they are never instinctive. From the comparisons we have made with the collective behavior of lower animals, and considering the persisting controversy among scholars, it is not justifiable to rule out the possibility that underlying mechanisms of flocking, mobbing, "mass principle" (bandwagon), aggression displacement, or territorial defense operate in appropriate conditions, such as in overcrowding or intrusion of strangers into territory. This should be considered as even more possible when strain increases tension and reduces the effectiveness of normal symbolic communication, rules, and institutional functioning. The safest position is that both levels—symbolic and instinctive—may be operating in human collective behavior, but that symbolic processes usually govern. Sorting out these influences, of course, is difficult. Yet, it is probably generally true that, however close to the ground a human crowd flies, it is still, by symbols, far above the level of the animal herd in its greater capacity for imitation of a wide range of behaviors and communicating ideas too complex to be handled by natural signs.

Distinguishing these levels should not be allowed to create the misapprehension that the animal group is less organized than the human crowd. As we have seen, the baboon troop is coordinated by a highly organized protocol of leadership. If baboons act crowdlike, as in the "riot" of "Monkey Hill," they are departing from their normal instinctive coordination just as much as humans in a riot depart from their normal institutional coordination. Therefore, even though it might be true that humans revert to the instinctive level in crowds, it does not follow that they would have a free flight into instinctive abandon. They could be locked into mechanisms as tightly restrictive as those governing apes. As we have vividly seen in the case of insects, instinct is not freedom.

It is plausible that a human crowd, if it could somehow be deprived of speech and consequent higher mental functions, would allow us to see what was going on at the level of the animal crowd. There is no way of doing this, but an animal ethologist (Jones, 1967) did the next best thing by looking for parallels between human and subhuman collective behavior in nursery school children (three to five years of age) who were barely into the language realm and still presumably relying much on biological nature. Subgroups formed, but he found no sign of defended territory nor was there clear evidence of peck-order patterns so familiar among lower animals. Fights did, however, occur over property, in which the beating movement was the commonest expression:

> It is an overarm blow with the palm side of the lightly clenched fist. The arm is sharply bent at the elbow and raised to a vertical position then brought down with great force on the opponent, hitting any part of him that gets in the way. Biting seems . . . more commonly done by girls than by boys. These attacks are often preceded and accompanied by fixating the opponent and what looks like a frown with lowering of the brow . . . and no conspicuous modification of the mouth expression. Often the child shouts "no," or "let go," with a characteristic tone, low pitch and hard explosive quality. . . . When there are signs, such as stepping back . . . that something is inhibiting the attack, the mouth expression changes and the child shows a "fierce" expression with lower teeth bared and the corner of the mouth drawn down. (Jones, in Morris, 1967b:354–355.)

He found rough-and-tumble play patterns "almost identical" with those of rhesus monkeys, including running and chasing, wrestling, jumping up and down, beating at each other with the hand without hitting, laughing, falling down, and throwing themselves into soft places.

> There seems to be a common facial expression in this play . . . seen when a child is about to be chased by another and stands slightly crouched, side-on to the chaser and looking . . . with this "mischievous" expression, an open-mouthed smile with the teeth covered, which morphologically resembles the "playface" of *Macaca* and *Pan*. (Jones, in Morris, 1967b:357–358.)

But language supplements also intruded. Words were used to ensure group cohesion (for example, "Come on"). And rough-and-tumble play developed rather promptly into formalized games like "tag" and "cowboys and Indians." Group play included manipulative construction together, and also imaginative role-playing games like fireman (Jones, in Morris, 1967b).

The writer's own observations of nursery school collective behavior show—even without language—imitation, and coordination unlikely to be seen among apes: for example, three girls carrying a board, one on each end and one holding in the middle; competitive hanging of four boys from parallel bars; three boys shoveling sand at one another; a crowd gathering quickly, showing curiosity around a child who has a toy animal, who chases another boy with the toy animal saying, "Grrrr!" while the crowd disperses; five boys jumping imitatively and competitively on a board between boxes; ten children working together at a table silently with materials; all gathering around a phonograph and clapping hands on legs in time to music, imitating teacher's gesture. We can only imagine how startled we would be to see apes doing much of this sort of thing. Clearly, the "game is up" and imagination, conceptualization, and language have carried the nursery school far beyond the animal crowd. All these examples give us little more than a glimpse of the instinctive level— where much of the evidence is negative, such as the absence of clear territoriality and peck order. The biological level of human behavior, at all ages after speech begins, remains obscured by the symbolic factor. Games with rules, dramatic play acting, bluffing, threatening or insulting by significant gestures, casting blame, all take us deeply into symbolic transactions and emphasize the gulf between the animal and the human level.

A key question, then, is the point at which symbolic transactions terminate—if they ever terminate—in human interactions. If symbolic transactions were to cease—that is, people were to stop interpreting, constructing, and symbolizing situations—then it might be possible to see a collectivity operating "merely" at the instinctive level. But it seems impossible to find a group of normal humans in which this occurs. The question of what happens in a symbolic moratorium remains open.

In conclusion, the position that collective behavior occurs outside institutional structure by no means implies that it is nonsymbolic. We can only say that symbolic transactions become more fluid outside institutional structures. Norms, mores, sentiments, and all manner of cultural symbolism probably continue to operate, but in a more freely flowing way. We can see that there are certain kinds of symbolic transactions, such as drama and dialogue, which are rich in emergent possibilities. It is here, rather than to animal instinct, that we should look for the emergent qualities of human collective behavior.

In Chapter 5 we shall look at what is involved in a symbolic transaction as sociologists treat it.

CHAPTER 5

Symbolic Transactions

A cat and a cow in the same meadow are nevertheless in different worlds, said George H. Mead (1934). Could this be less true for humans, who build symbolic jungles and (as painters like Rousseau and Brueghel show) are capable of finding extravagant monsters in them? We are fabricating a pseudo-environment by modern communication, "a thicket of unreality which stands between us and the facts of life" (Boorstin, 1962:3). The first uncomfortable, general awareness of this process in America came from Lippman (1922), who referred to it as the making of stereotypes. Lippman showed that psychological and social forces transform the largely unseen environment into "pictures in our heads" (1922). But a rather rationalistic perspective made most researchers regard stereotypes as merely faults of cognition and perception—inaccurate modeling—rather than part of a symbolic process making society (Klapp, 1962:7–24).

Durkheim's theory (1895) of collective representations, which had so much to do with founding sociology, left unanswered the question of how one goes about constructing the collective representations on which society is based. Answers to this question have been supplied by subsequent thinkers in many fields—philosophy, psychology, sociology, anthropology, linguistics, communication, literature—who have elaborated the view that man not only constructs objects but also builds his own symbolic world. These worlds vary (or are indemonstrably identical) for each individual and cultural group. Yet, a frame of reference that is *collectively constructed* allows members to coordinate their behavior in ways which would never be possible without such common understandings.

Humans are continually constructing images of the present, images of the future, and images of the past—and tying them together and sharing them by symbols. This is the reality to which they respond. In brief, reality is what you make of it.

This common world is variously called culture, consensus, language, depending upon which aspect one wishes to emphasize. Activities that build and rebuild it are called symbolic transactions.

Our concern here is in reviewing theories of symbolic transactions to see what is involved in them, and to learn how they might enter that free-flow phase of interaction that we call collective behavior.

Thus, if grandfather and grandson or teacher and student live in different worlds, the question is: What symbolic transactions have been going on that they did not share?

Constructed Reality

The first important formulation of the idea that communication makes society was by Cooley (1909), who argued that communication is "the mechanism through which human relations exist and develop—all the symbols of the mind. . . . In a sense all objects and actions are symbols of the mind"—and this includes people. Society grows by extension of the "social consciousness," which is a "cooperative activity of many minds." The group is not only an extension of the member's consciousness, it is part of his personality. "We" and "I," society and the individual are aspects of the same thing. The process that makes it all is communication. Were tradition to be the main process of communication, there would be little change. But modern society grows by extending its public consciousness; ideas come from everywhere, and no small part of this is that "influences . . . come in sidewise and fashion rules over custom." The revolution in communication makes "a new world for us" (Cooley, 1909:10, 35, 61, 65, 339). Cooley's well-known theory of the "looking glass self" showed clearly how the individual was remaking himself by feedback from the same process that was making society. There could not be a clearer statement that symbolic transactions construct the reality that is the social world.

The competing view in American sociology came from Sumner (1906), who saw folkways and mores growing up by habit ("use and wont" rather than rational decision) and meeting the test of success in "societal selection." In other words, Sumner's theory involved an evolutionary process rather than development through communication; yet, for collective behavior, great interest attaches to his idea of societal selection as a mechanism of fashion, and of the "crescive" growth of institutions without rational decision (which we today would say indicated unwitting or nonrational symbolic transactions).

The symbolic transaction theory received its greatest impetus— indeed, was put into business—by George H. Mead (1934, 1938), whose sweeping theory explained two things especially important for understanding the creation of social order by symbolic process. One was that humans do not simply respond to their environment, but construct it by a complex ongoing "act" that is exploratory and pragmatic. An "object" is no more than the subjective residue (image, meaning, attitude) by which the individual guides his action. Failure of the act causes the object to break down and be reconstituted in further exploratory activity. The object, insofar as it has any constancy, is a "collapsed act," which (if we may add a metaphor that Mead did not use) is like a folding umbrella one carries around for future use. The other especially important idea that Mead developed for symbolic transaction theory was that of the significant symbol. A symbol is made, not by an individual decision, but by the response of others to a gesture which was originally meaningless. That is, the uttering of a sound, raising of eyebrows, or waving a hand could mean nothing to the individual who used this gesture until others responded to it and thus assigned a meaning. The individual, then, must not only observe others, but must also communicate with them sufficiently to see how his act seems to them. When he is able to look at his own gesture from their point of view, it has become significant. Mead called this "taking the attitude of the other," which, when done toward a symbol, he called *significance*. The meaning of an act is another's act performed in the imagination. This idea is extremely important, for it is at the same time the mechanism of symbol, thought, role taking, self, and society as an order constructed of such symbols.

> Where the response of the other person is called out and becomes a stimulus to control his action, then he has the meaning of the other person's act in his own experience. That is the general mechanism of what we term "thought," for in order that thought may exist there must be symbols, vocal gestures generally, which arouse in the individual himself the response which he is calling out in the other, and such that from the point of view of that response he is able to direct his later conduct. It involves not only communication in the sense in which birds and animals communicate with each other, but also an arousal in the individual himself of the response which he is calling out in the other individual, a taking of the role of the other, a tendency to act as the other person acts. One participates in the same process the other person is carrying out and controls his action with reference to that participation. It is that which constitutes the meaning of an object, namely, the common response in one's self as well as in the other person, which becomes, in turn, a stimulus to one's self. (G. Mead, 1934:73–74.)

> That which makes society possible is such common responses. . . . What goes to make up the organized self is the organization of the attitudes which are common to the group. . . . Through a process of taking the different roles that all the others furnish he comes to get the attitude of the members of the community. . . . Whole series of such common responses in the community in which we live are what we term "institutions." (G. Mead, 1934:161–162, 261.)

Thus the symbolic transaction creates mind, self, society, and the world of objects. Mead (1934:240) denied this process to lower animals, and also held that "in the mob we have a reversion to the society of a herd of cattle"—a question left open to argument.

From such writings emerged the point of view in sociology now known as *symbolic interactionism*. Symbolic interactionism not only regards the social order as constructed, but also considers the entire social process, within and outside institutions, as an emergent transaction. It denies that institutions imply a coercive or determinative control over transactions now going on. Blumer said—

> Most of the situations encountered by people in a given society are defined or "structured" by them in the same way. . . . These common definitions enable people to act alike. The common repetitive behavior . . . should not mislead the student into believing that no process of interpretation is in play; on the contrary . . . the actions . . . are

constructed . . . through a process of interpretation. Since ready-made and commonly accepted definitions are at hand, little strain is placed on people in guiding and organizing their acts. However, many other situations may not be defined in a single way . . . in this event, their lines of action do not fit together readily and collective action is blocked. Interpretations have to be developed and effective accommodation . . . worked out. In the case of such "undefined" situations, it is necessary to trace and study the emerging process of definition which is brought into play. . . . To catch the process, the student must take the role of the acting unit whose behavior he is studying. . . . Interpretations of new situations are not predetermined by conditions antecedent to the situations but depend on what is taken into account and assessed in the actual situations in which behavior is formed. (Blumer, 1962: 187–188, 191.)

Such lines of theory, interacting with other strands of European and American theory, gave rise to the conception of an entire symbolic world—the only world that humans know—constructed by symbolic transactions. Given this perspective, it is preferable to see collective behavior as not outside but within the transactions by which the social order is recreated; that is, every outburst, every fad, every crusade, every movement has something to do with the reconstruction of the symbolic world.

Symbolic Worlds

So we have the general picture of man as the maker of his world and of himself through symbols, *animal symbolicum*. As Cassirer (1944) said:

No longer in a merely physical universe, man lives in a symbolic universe. Language, myth, art, and religion are parts of this universe. They are the varied threads which weave the symbolic net, the tangled web of human experience. . . . No longer can man confront reality immediately; he cannot see it, as it were, face to face. . . . Instead of dealing with the things themselves man is in a sense constantly conversing with himself. He has so enveloped himself in linguistic forms, in artistic images, in mythical symbols or religious rites that he cannot see or know anything except by the interposition of this artificial medium. . . . Man does not live in a world of hard facts, or according to his immediate needs and desires. He lives rather in the midst of imaginary emotions, in hopes and fears, in illusions and disillusions, in his fantasies and dreams. (Cassirer, 1944:43.)

Sapir (1949) also saw the cultural world as the product of sociolinguistic processes:

Language is a guide to "social reality" . . . it powerfully conditions all our thinking . . . human beings do not live in the objective world alone, nor alone in the world of social activity as ordinarily understood, but are very much at the mercy of the particular language which has become the medium of expression. It is quite an illusion to imagine that one adjusts to reality essentially without the use of language and that language is merely an incidental means of solving specific problems of communication or reflection. The fact of the matter is that the "real world" is to a large extent unconsciously built up on the language habits of the group. No two languages are ever sufficiently similar to be considered as representing the same social reality. The world in which different societies live are distinct worlds, not merely the same world with different labels attached. . . . Culture defines for every society the world in which it lives. (Sapir, 1949:68–69, 122.)

Such views allow us to see that culture, language, conception, and perception are inextricably intertwined; and that a change in any one implies a change in the others. This relationship has been explored thoroughly by Lindesmith and Strauss (1968). From the sociolinguistic side, another famous exponent of this view is Benjamin Whorf (1967), who holds that even the laws of logic are not the same from one symbolic world to another; that nature itself changes, since it depends upon grammatical and linguistic categories from English to Hopi to Chinese to Choctaw. Such a view of culture may seem to imply that man is caught in perspectives from which he cannot escape because of inflexible categories of language, myth, religion, custom, and so on. But this is far from the case. It merely calls attention to the fact that changing one's mind is not a mere matter of shifting one's point of view but of a symbolic process in which meanings must be changed. It forces us to ask, even in crowd behavior, what symbols are being used or formed?

Another common use of the term "world" in sociology shows how relevant it is to processes of collective behavior. The term "social world" is used to refer to areas in cities where distinctive culture and argots grow up, along with social types that thrive in this particular environment. For example, Zorbaugh described the curious types of people in the urban slum who inhabit the "Rialto of the Half-World," of which the "street of forgotten men" is the axis:

> By day or by night, it is a street of queer and exiled types, a street whose people are in the city but not of it—the hobo, the radical, the squawker and the stickup man, the panhandler and the prostitute, the dopey, the jazz hound, the golddigger, and the charity girl. To all these denizens of the half-world North Clark is Main Street. (Zorbaugh, 1929: 106.)

Such a neighborhood is not a mere locality; it is a "state of mind" with a culture, lingo, and universe of discourse all of its own; outsiders do not understand. Even nextdoor neighbors may be complete strangers unless they share the same meaning worlds. There are innumerable social worlds, said Shibutani (1962), in an urban area; some are small and concentrated, others are dispersed—cults, Bohemians, underworld groups, ethnic minorities, and so on; each knows that "outsiders do not share their values." Some are exclusive, have secret languages, and demand loyalty of their participants.

> Each social world is a universe of regularized mutual response, an arena in which there is some kind of organization that facilitates anticipating the behavior of others. Each social world, then, is a culture area, the boundaries of which are set neither by territory nor formal group membership, but by the limits of effective communication. A social world is an orderly arena which serves as a stage on which each participant can carve out a career. There are special norms of conduct, a set of values, a prestige ladder, and a common outlook toward life—a *Weltanschauung*. In each world there evolves a different historical orientation, selectively emphasizing past events of special interest. Common memories are built up and reinforced within the limited communication network. (Shibutani, 1962:136–137.)

Shibutani sees these worlds as offering an "amazing variety of standards" by which Americans live, allowing people to develop a number of different perspectives, depending upon which communication networks they participate in; "the particular combination of social worlds differs from person to person" (Shibutani, 1962:138–139).

From such considerations, we can see that the growth of social worlds, with their perspectives and argots, is an enormously important process of emergent collective behavior, which goes on almost without anyone noticing it until sightseeing companies find it profitable to send buses to certain areas to look at the "hippies" or such. Wherever "types" and lingos are emerging, new worlds—and perhaps new styles for future man—also are being shaped.

A point of great interest is that, whether isolated cultures or crowded urban populations, such worlds do not interpenetrate and dissolve by mixing; rather they are like oil and water. People can pass the cultural barriers, go from world to world, *if* they know the language. Side by side in modern society we see such diverse cultures as "street people," hippies, acid rock, and the psychedelic culture; New Left and Radical Right; "soul brothers" and "whiteys"; surfers, easy riders, Hell's Angels, drug users, homosexuals, violent gangs, and so on. There is hardly more difference between the Navajo and White than between hippie and "straight," "soul" and "white." Likewise, we see the "generation gap," a new youth world with its own lingo generated right under the noses of parents living in the old world. Such things show that the world-building process is as active today as it ever was with old cultures, perhaps going even faster. But there is some doubt that we are moving toward "one world"; the supposed homogenization of culture by mass communication is partly a myth.

A major difference is that the old worlds were built by oral tradition and gossip (Redfield, 1947); thus, Blumenthal (1932) in *Small Town Stuff* showed a town buzzing with self-oriented gossip. How strange and constricted these little worlds are can be seen by reading novels like Sinclair Lewis, *Main Street*; Sherwood Anderson, *Winesburg, Ohio*; or William Faulkner's south. New worlds are built by a larger proportion of mass communication in the form of printed information, television, recordings (like Jimi Hendrix, The Beatles, Mothers of Invention), and films (like "Alice's Restaurant," "Easy Rider," 1969). Small interacting groups select content from such things, according to their interests, and build them into different worlds. In this sense, the supposed uniformization of culture by mass communication is partly a myth.

But, of course, it isn't all myth. The standardization of technology is far too important a factor in the world's building process. Part of the part that isn't myth is the fact that technology is fabricating a set of images and kinds of experience that crowd out the native imaginative processes by which people invest their *own* worlds with meaning. Boorstin (1962) called this a pseudo-environment. Heidegger (1962) put his finger on a point that strikes most deeply at man's capacity to generate his own meaning (McLuhan's panegyrics not withstanding), namely, that "calculative" thinking (inherent to technology) drives out "pondering" or meditative thinking. Likewise, Marcuse (1964) sees repressiveness, a restriction of mental life ("happy consciousness"), in the very abundance of technology. Against this backdrop, the response of hippielike (mind-expanding) groups in the late 1960s seemed an effort to reactivate natural meaning-creating processes—paradoxically by chemical (psychedelic) and electronic priming. The psychedelic experience enabled hippies to claim to have something that "straight" society did not (which was true); so, they could "put down" straight society as lacking in meaning. A linguistic gap separated the "tuned in" and "turned on" from the "turned off" and the "straight." We shall take up this theme again in Chapter 9, "Meaning Gap." It is important here merely to note various ways in which symbolic transactions can make up a "world"—or fail to do so.

Thus, we see alienated groups actively building their worlds (subcultures) within, and rather in defiance of, the standard imposed culture: Madison Avenue's consumption values of a capitalistic society (advertising keeps alive the dream of happiness for Americans, but some unbelievers are repudiating this dream: "tell it like it is"); "straight" morality and religion in official views and codes; and the "pseudo-events" that so dismayed Boorstin (countered by a

"credibility gap" and retreat of alienated groups into their introverted worlds of music, psychedelics, sports, religion, and so on).
Alienated groups do this by a kind of gravitational process, as individuals with similar orientation come together, forming argots by
trying to talk about what interests *them*, creating a universe of
discourse known only to themselves, selecting facts and images as
"relevant" input, building an ethos and cult of their own, and setting
up a shield of lingo, pose, and "put on" between themselves and
outsiders, which is as effective a screen as that which separates
Hopi Indians from White tourists who come on the reservation to
try to snap pictures of tabooed ceremonies.

The idea of societies constructing their own reality takes on a
larger sweep when exposed to theories like that of Weber (1946), in
which the development of science as well as the growth of bureaucratic and legal institutions are part of a vast process of rationalization by which man constructs a set of matter-of-fact rules that
governs not only the universe but himself. This process is viewed
as a kind of dialectic between the nonrational force of charisma,
which stirs humans to great enthusiasms, and the more efficient
constructions of rationality, which displace mysticism and mystery
from life in favor of calculability (Weber, 1946). Along this same line
evolved the theory of ideologies and utopias as world views pro-
jecting the interests of groups, "which never succeed *de facto* in
the realization of their projected contents." Masking and unmasking
of ideologies by conflicting groups goes on; but the process of
illusion (reality transcendence) perpetually goes on:

> It is always the dominant group which is in full accord with the
> existing order that determines what is to be regarded as utopian,
> while the ascendant group which is in conflict with things as they are
> is the one that determines what is ideological. (Mannheim, 1936:175,
> 183.)

Modern sociologists take such views quite seriously, and con-
tend that the entire social order is constructing its own reality by
both rational and nonrational processes, that at no point can we
assume man to be responding to "things as they simply are," un-
contaminated by social reality. The most thoroughgoing account of
how man constructs his world symbolically as part of the process
of institutionalization is perhaps given by Berger and Luckmann
(1966), following Schutz (1967). Their theoretical model of institutionalization is based on Schutz's fundamental principle that all
meaning is reflective; that is, we cannot know the meaning of what
we have done or what has happened until we look back at it in reflection (a view closely paralleling that of pragmatists like G. H.
Mead, 1934, and John Dewey, 1922).

The idea of social construction of reality (that people not only make social structure but the reality—meaning—that goes with it) is only an implication of the symbolic world point of view: All that we call reality is some kind of meaning; all meaning, as retrospection, is created by memory and its processes of symbolization. Every object that a human responds to is a symbolic construction, made by designations, references, and definitions that are inherently an interaction (or feedback) from others. When the interaction is with others, we call it conversation; when with ourselves, we call it thinking. In this sense, nothing known to man in the common world can be properly called "individual."

Let us take for an example the child of a tribal hunter learning how to track game. The clues he follows are not made just by animals, but are signs interpreted and taught by others: the older man who points out the clues while teaching him the arts of tracking, weapon making, and so forth; language classifications; initiations (rites of passage) of the hunter; and the supernatural totemic order that coexists with the game and the people who eat it. Thus, from the beginning, the natural world is socially defined and the jungle is a social place—no less so than the jungles of polite society that Proust described.

Berger and Luckmann's (1966) analysis of this world-defining process starts from "scratch," that is, two people hypothetically meeting for the first time. It all begins when either of them forms a concept of the other, a "typification." However A and B interact, A will conceptualize or typify B as he watches him perform. He will also attribute motives to B. If and when B does it again, A repeats both typifications, of act and motive. Soon he is able to say, "Aha, there he goes again." After taking account of such patterns, A and B can begin to play roles in relation to each other. When they have both performed similar actions, they are able to exchange roles. For example, one might say, "He pitches hay and I stack it; but we could easily take each other's place because we both know how to pitch and stack hay." Moreover, each would have a pretty good idea of how the other felt doing it. So, a collection of roles as typified and mutually understandable actions develops, which they share. The behavior of both becomes more predictable. "There he goes again" becomes "there we go again."

Thus, widening spheres of common routines with division of labor make possible a social order; "a social world is in construction." Then comes the stage of passing it on to newcomers. As children are taught the typifications, the social arrangements become a "historical institution." Historicity is accompanied by objectivity: "The institutions that have been crystallized . . . are existing over and beyond the individuals" who embody them at the moment; they have "a reality of their own." As time goes on, the institutional world "thickens" and "hardens" for everyone: "This is how these things are done." It seems as natural as the physical world. It was that way before the member was born and will be that way after he is dead. Not to understand it in no way lessens its reality. (Berger and Luckmann, 1966:53–57.)

The relationship between man the maker and the world he makes is not, however, constant but "dialectical." He interacts with himself and with others about this given world in changing ways. Those parts of it which he "internalizes" are most important for him, and this varies with person and relationship. Tacked onto this primary objectivity is ideology, a "second-order" objectivation that legitimates the existing order, that is, makes it plausible by explaining and justifying it as part of a "symbolic universe." (Berger and Luckmann, 1966:85–89.)

By such processes, whole cosmologies, including the more esoteric religious and mystical conceptions, become real within their respective cultures. Let us apply it to something so strange and deviant as "pot" smoking, which was first analyzed sociologically by Howard Becker (1963). Individuals come together who have had no prior psychedelic experience. They pass around what seems to be a cigarette, and the world changes in indescribable ways, becoming distorted, intensified, and enchanted. A person feels that he floats rather than walks. Music is inexplicably gripping. Little things, to which one would ordinarily pay no attention, become fascinating. Afterwards, the people are told that they were "high." They try to describe in words how this feeling was different from intoxication by alcohol: "groovy," a "kick," "way out," "out of this world," "too much." By such words, which mean little enough to an outsider, the high state becomes an object of common reference, and soon is a standard rather than a peculiar experience. New smokers are taught to expect to have certain experiences. Smokers, as they join the culture, act toward each other in special ways—by speech, mannerisms, and roles—as sharers of a culture.

An ethos and world of references thus emerges which are real for insiders, however unknown and unreal they may be for outsiders. Newcomers are introduced to this world as a set of facts. So much for what Berger and Luckmann call *primary objectivation*. Further moves, to legalize marijuana, to test and certify its consequences, to make it part of pharmacology, would belong to the secondary stage of objectivation: justifying a strange and ineffable experience by fitting it into a rational world scheme. While there is no guaranty that psychedelic experience could thus be fully objectivized, there is nothing about marijuana intoxication *inherently* more difficult to validate than prophecy and mysticism, which are accepted as real in many cultures.

What we have done so far is try to establish a general picture of the social world as a humanly made symbolic reality. Now let us look at some of the particular ways in which reality is reconstructed by symbolic transactions within and outside institutional settings.

Symbolic Transactions within Institutional Settings

Social construction of reality never stops. Not only is ideology being generated by the voices of legitimizers and protesters, but all kinds of meanings are also being created largely at the subrational level in day-to-day transactions within institutions. The transactional process is inherently morphogenic, according to Buckley (1967:160), that is, out of it continually emerge new structures. By *transaction* is meant a rather open symbolic interaction in which values or meanings are not all known in advance; parties enter them expecting that something will be achieved (perhaps by bargaining, dialectic, or carrying off roles). Transactions may proceed by stages, each stage making possible something not predictable from the preceding stage. A look at a few transactions within institutions will give us more of a feeling for the emergence going on within the apparently established social order.

The institutional world might be likened to a game played according to rules, or a drama in which people act according to expected roles. Both metaphors are simultaneously valid. At the same time, another metaphor applies, hardening or the accumulation of a crust. That is, the working world is threatened by clichés and routines that deaden spontaneity and produce boredom. Hence, there is a continual battle or dialectic of impulse erupting against habit (a point recognized by major theorists such as Dewey, Weber, Freud, and the existentialists). Students are not the last to recognize this situation. These three metaphors present a picture of a continual flow of reinterpretation, improvisation, and reconstruction of meanings, even in the most disciplined institution—especially if consensual processes are allowed to work, people can get together and share viewpoints. In other words, no game, however strict the rules, is ever played the same way twice, especially when there is a feeling of rebellion against a crust; therefore we expect a continual flow of new meaning. Consequently, the notion of rigidity in social organization is only an illusion—perhaps an expression of conflict between two norms, both of which have emerged.

The game or drama is carried on by cues, which tell a person what the scene is, what rules apply, and how to treat people in terms of their role and status. Symbols of rank, for example, help a person establish his place in a social hierarchy and get appropriate responses from others. Thus, the army officer with bars expects a salute from one with chevrons; the boss who owns a Buick expects his employees not to "upstage" him with a Cadillac. Encroachments on other people's status symbols are resented because the social order, like a game, must go on and be played by certain rules, and to encroach on another's status symbols is like an actor's swiping another's costume from the theater dressing room. The game "stays on the tracks" so long as parties are knowledgeable, able, and willing to use the cues.

The institution, like the show, must go on by dramatic enactment, which Goffman (1958) has analyzed so well. Professionals, such as doctors and nurses, work together as dramatic teams, much as would actors in a theater, to manage a scene and the impression it makes on an audience, which might be the patient, his family, other professionals, or even the general public. To be successful, an institutional performer must not only do his job but also give signs (such as professional assurance or "bedside manner") that help his act to dramatic realization. How this turns out, rather than merely what is technically done, determines the meaning of the institutional activity. In a larger sense, the entire institutional world is a series of such dramas, more or less successful.

A properly managed scene stays "on the track." If it gets off the track, people engage in symbolic negotiations to "account" for it and themselves (Lyman and Scott, 1970). When people are unwilling or unable to keep it on the track, we begin to talk about deviance. As long as you improvise within the limits of the role (expectation) and things go "according to Hoyle," endless freedom is possible: In this sense, new things are emerging all the time, even in the tightest organization. A "troublemaker," however, upsets bureaucracy. Various societal strains that give rise to deviance—cause people to go beyond role limits—need not concern us here (Merton, 1968:185–248; A. Cohen, 1966:76). A person may be unable to act "normally" even if he tries. Ernest Becker (1962) says that reality hangs by the "fragile thread," a mere dramatic assumption that depends on the ability to carry off a role. Neurotics and psychotics fail, so their reality collapses. However, if such difficult people can get together and interact to create new roles and meanings acceptable among themselves, a collectivity deviance occurs (A. Cohen, 1966:22).

Within tolerable limits, however, important differences and variations of construction go on. The "working consensus" (Goffman, 1958) may be quite different from the real situation; for example, parties might be very dishonest while maintaining a front that everyone is operating on the highest standards. As long as there is general agreement not to challenge the working consensus, almost anything is possible. Rather similar in tolerance for variability is Goode's (1960) theory that relationships are achieved by role "bargains" in which people neither get nor give what they expect, and in which considerable dissensus and strain are normal. Strauss and colleagues (1963) have well described the *"negotiated order"* that results from endless variations of role bargaining and working consensus in the bureaucratic setting (Strauss et al., 1963; Schatzman and Bucher, 1964).

Even dying is a "structural process" that emerges from interactions and which could not be predicted from knowledge of the natural event itself or of hospital structure (Glaser and Strauss, 1965, 1968). The process of psychiatric diagnosis provides a good example of how doctors together construct an "illness," more or less arbitrarily, in a tactical game with institutional rules (Daniels, 1969). Thus, a whole informal, *subrosa* organization can grow up under the noses of officials in forms such as group control of "rate busters" (Homans, 1950:60); a black market (Clinard, 1952); or the "underside" of institutional life, exploitative relationships, communication systems, "conning," group and personal territories, covert ways of evading rules, and so on (Goffman, 1961). Sumner called this *crescive* development, and sociologists have shown how it comes about and how important it is.

Organizations have tried to capitalize on this development, as it were, capture the creative process and put it to work by, for example, "brainstorming" methods of group decision or encounter groups that use novel devices (attack therapy, holding hands, nude encounter, all yelling a person's name) to shake people loose from old understandings (clichés) and into spontaneity and insight into themselves and others through feedback. Psychodrama (Moreno, 1953) is developed as a therapeutic technique for producing "surplus reality," a "new and more extensive experience of reality" in "spontaneity theater," which aims at a release similar to the frenzy of primitive mystery religions (Greenberg, 1969).

At this point we turn to an aspect of primitive society of great significance for understanding collective behavior. As we know, primitive societies use ceremonies to maintain social vitality by making the juices of emotion flow more freely. Sociologists say this strengthens collective sentiments (Durkheim, 1915). Rites of passage, such as graduations, weddings, fraternity initiations, religious confirmations, bar mitzvahs, puberty rites, all make individuals feel more significant by emphasizing their steps of status change (Van Gennep, 1909). We can see more clearly how all this works by looking at an example from the life of a tribal people, the Ndembu of Zambia, described by Victor Turner (1967). In the "relatively simple and monotonous existence of these hunters," he was astonished to find contrasting "colorful symbolism of . . . religious life. . . . a vast and complicated system of ceremonial practices." These included life-crisis rituals (passage), such as initiations and funerals, and ceremonies to propitiate ghosts and prevent afflictions which might come from failing to win their favor. Appropriate ceremonies were performed in hunting cults for men, fertility cults for women, and curative cults for both sexes, all involving mysteries (V. Turner, 1967:2–26). One of the most interesting of their ceremonies was one in which the chief and his wife get insulted. This occurs during the installation rites of the new chief. The chief-elect, clad in nothing but a ragged waist cloth, and his wife are called to enter a special shelter just after sundown. They sit there crouched in shame or modesty while being washed with medicines. Then a ceremony called "The Reviling of the Chief-Elect" begins. A headman cuts the underside of the chief's arm and puts medicine into the incision. Then the chief and his wife are forced to sit on the mat. The headman lectures them as follows:

> "Be silent! You are a mean and selfish fool, one who is bad tempered! You do not love your fellows, you are only angry with them! Meanness and theft are all you have! Yet here we have called you and we say that you must succeed to the chieftainship. Put away meanness, put aside anger, give up adulterous intercourse . . . we have granted you chieftainship. You must eat with your fellow men, you must live well with them. . . . Today you are born as a new chief. You must know the people. . . . You must give up your selfish ways, you must welcome everyone, you are the chief!". (V. Turner, 1969:100–102.)

After this lesson, anyone who has been wronged by the chief has the privilege of reviling him and expressing resentment as fully as desired. The chief sits with bowed head, "the pattern of all patience." The headman splashes him with medicine and bumps him insultingly with his buttocks from time to time. During the prolonged ordeal, the chief is not allowed to go to sleep. Other important men manhandle both him and his wife, and make them do lowly tasks such as fetching wood (V. Turner, 1969:100–102).

After this, the chief is installed with all pomp and ceremony. What is the significance of the chief and his wife being dressed identically in ragged clothes, stripping them of their former status, and making them symbolically sexless and anonymous? Turner's interpretation is that it is a return to a state of "liminality," or threshold to status. In liminality, people possess nothing; they have no status, property, insignia, or anything to distinguish them from others who are also about to be initiated. "It is as though they are being . . . ground down to a uniform condition to be fashioned anew

. . ." (V. Turner, 1969:95). Something like this happens to "boots" in the Marine Corps. But such stripping is not all loss. There is a great gain in a return to a "generic bond" of fellowship and equality among men, which Turner calls "communitas." When men are released from the more or less artificial distinctions of social structure, their bond with their fellow man is revitalized by the experience of communitas. They are flooded with new and unusual feelings. Spontaneous communitas is very similar to what hippies today would call "a happening." In Martin Buber's terms, it is a return to "genuine mutuality," the "essential We" (V. Turner, 1969:132, 136–137).

> Spontaneous communitas has something "magical" about it. Subjectively there is in it the feeling of endless power. But this power . . . is no substitute for lucid thought and sustained will. On the other hand, structural action swiftly becomes arid and mechanical if those involved in it are not periodically immersed in the regenerative abyss of communitas. (V. Turner, 1969:139.)

Thus, it is a great satisfaction for people to be reminded that they share a fundamental togetherness—offsetting differences of rank, which are revealed as artificial by this reminder—and that there is something more real than the "crust" of routine and custom. But, beyond that, return to liminality is something very similar to the anonymity of crowd relationships and the spontaneous "we" that they often generate. Likewise, periods of great mass movements and revolutions can be likened to immersion in communitas and rebirth (Hoffer, 1951). So, in liminal ceremonies we have something going on in organization very similar to spontaneous collective behavior; "spontaneity theater" in psychodrama and encounter in T-groups seem to be aspects of the same thing.

We can conclude, then, that emergence of new forms and meanings by symbolic transactions within the institutional setting goes on continually and never quits. Outside, such processes simply flow more freely.

Symbolic Transactions Likely To Be Operating in Collective Behavior

Most of the symbolic processes occurring in institutions are also occurring outside, flowing more freely. For example, the status symbols of institutions are used more freely in the mass setting in what we call the fashion race and faddism. But here, out from under the watchful eye of the boss and one's neighbors, a furious competition for status symbols confuses the rank order of social classes (Klapp, 1969:73–115). Fashion leadership operates by waves of imitative change, which are only partly (or belatedly) conscious participation. G. H. Mead (1934) describes the emergence of meaning in fashion within a flow of unwitting imitation:

> In speech definite changes take place that nobody is aware of at all. . . . Without any conscious direction . . . change is going on all the time. Take a person's attitude toward a new fashion. It may at first be one of objection. After awhile he gets to the point of thinking of himself in this changed fashion, noticing the clothes in the window and seeing himself in them. The change has taken place in him without his being aware of it. There is, then, a process by means of which the individual in interaction with others inevitably becomes like others in doing the same thing, without that process appearing in what we term consciousness. We become conscious of the process when we do definitely take the attitude of the others, and this situation must be distinguished from the previous one. Perhaps one says that he does not care to dress in a certain fashion, but prefers to be different; then he is taking the attitude of others toward himself into his own conduct. . . . It is this . . . process of using his self-consciousness which gives him the attitude of self-assertion or the attitude of devotion to the community. He has become, then, a definite self. In such a case of self-assertion there is an entirely different situation from that of the member of the pack. . . . (G. Mead, 1934:193–194.)

Thus, Mead not only analyzes the meaning-creating process of fashion as a way of giving new meaning to one's self, but distinguishes it from the imitation of pack behavior by such a difference. (See Chapter 4.) Beyond the unwitting waves of fashion change is something else that people are not aware of: a process of style search, or societal selection, in which a few innovate experimentally and then the emulation of others brings about a test of the style for living, in competition with other styles. We shall deal with this in Chapter 11.

Another aspect of the free flow of competition for status symbols in the mass setting is the challenge to status prestige and authority from charismatic leaders (heroes, celebrities, popular favorites, demagogues, and so on), whose irrational authority, said Max Weber (1946), continually brings new patterns of meaning into public affairs—and into institutions. It is here we see that the public drama carries on dramatic transactions on a broader and freer scale than the more tightly managed ones within institutions. News media are endlessly generating events (such as the Kennedy assassinations, Democratic Convention in Chicago in 1968) of which there is little if any management, though public relations strategies may have tried to control them. The disorderly flow of events in the public drama produces ever-changing alignments of audiences in relation to heroes and villains, and provokes changing definitions of the situation. This introduces a politics of drama, or status politics, as distinguished from power politics; or, as Thurman Arnold (1935, 1937) put it, politics has the double task of getting things done and moralizing it ritually. Thus, Gusfield (1963:176) showed that the temperance movement was more than a law-making effort; it was a "ritual of prestige enhancement" for rural Protestant Americans who sought "public designation of respectability" versus immigrant groups who drank. Likewise, today the radical right is seeking to project a world view of a "communist conspiracy," with themselves as defenders and crusaders—"Paul Reveres" waking up the Republic with alarums (Klapp, 1969:262).

In the public drama, symbolic leaders emerge with new identities as entertainers or public figures evolving from crowd feedback; and images are made and remade by such things as type violations and dramatic conversions (Klapp, 1964a). Thus, in the public sphere, drama cannot be so tightly managed as within institutions; it breaks forth, and when it does, people continually reconstruct reality.

Likewise, the crescive growth of a "negotiated order" within institutions is paralleled in the mass setting by freer, improvisatory "swinging" arrangements unhampered by bureaucratic rules. Thus, the "rock" festivals outside institutional settings already mentioned, the "free universities" with "groovy" curricula, and the hippie "crash pads" as loosely run hostels. The Free Clinic of Los Angeles grew up as a hippie health center, a "sort of an establishment for disenfranchised youth," as a psychologist, one of the founders, put it. Though staffed by volunteers and serving people unwilling to use establishment facilities, it became such a success that the Los Angeles County Health Department copied it in a center in Hollywood in 1969. So, a social order is being negotiated more freely outside the institutional setting.

Similarly, institutions devoted to return to liminality and communitas, such as tribal initiations, seem to be paralleled by consensual processes seen in the mass setting, especially in crisis. A "halo" effect of spontaneous growth of "we" feeling seems to occur in disasters (Loomis, 1967). Rumors continually supply new definitions of reality and social support in crises of communication and institutions (Shibutani, 1966:170–176). As we learned before, crowds, especially ecstatic ones, provide an experience approaching the return to liminality and communitas, although through interaction quickly generate new definitions of situations. Thus, it seems probable that even in anomie—short of total stoppage of communication —creation of a new world and order never stops.

Experiments with small groups throw some light on how social reality emerges or is recreated when consensus is minimal. In experiments with a "minimal social situation," two persons were put in separate rooms, unaware of each other's presence. They were told to press buttons, not knowing that it would have an effect on the other's button-pushing (fate-control, i.e., of the reward or punishment outcomes of the other's actions; or behavioral control, a lesser degree of influence from pressing a button that merely made it possible for the other to receive *either* a reward or punishment, but not determining which). Without knowing that they were interacting, subjects arrived at patterns that benefitted both by generating more rewards and fewer punishments (Kelley et al., 1962; Rabinowitz et al., 1966). Thus, even in such a discouraging situation some kind of "collective structure is emerging" (Weick, 1969:49).

Of course, without knowledge that another exists, it is hard to say that there is a social relationship in the well-known definition of Max Weber (1946): "a probability . . . that there will be, in some meaningfully understandable sense, a course of social action." But we should lean toward, rather than away from, the idea that humans can construct meanings even in apparently meaningless situations. Especially interesting for us is McHugh's (1968) study of how people define "anomic" situations. Here the discouraging situation set up for subjects was a conversation with a computer designed to give anomic responses to questions by random (50:50) yes or no, or by all yes or all no. The machine might, for example, give the subject a baffling series of no's, leaving him no alternative of any kind. McHugh found that in such anomic encounters, "situations continue to be definable and significant, and are not jumbles of senseless chaos. . . . When order is overcast by disruption . . . past and future procedures of definition give way to consideration of the immediate locale." That is, subjects stopped relating their interpretations to the past and future, and concentrated on different points of view toward present possibilities. On the other hand, in conditions of "order," definitions are made by looking at the present in the light of varying views of the past and the future. McHugh called these two basic types of construction of meaning: in the present, "relativity"; and in past, present, and future, "emergence." "Anomie is not devoid of meaning. Relativity appears quite regularly. . . . Anomie is not social death." (McHugh, 1968:99, 107, 121, 136.)

These are not crowd situations, of course; but they suggest that a crowd would have plenty to go on were it to "start from scratch" in a situation of minimal meaning and consensus. There is no reason to suppose that interpretations of the situation would not quickly emerge and be shared by interaction. Existing ideas, norms, sentiments, rumors, stereotypes are "money in the bank" in giving the crowd capital to work with in building its emergent definitions. Thus, Dewey's (1922) conception of the crowd breaking down habitually into emotion and response to immediate stimuli hardly does justice to the ability of the crowd to construct new meanings:

The crowd and mob express a disintegration of habits which releases impulse and renders persons susceptible to immediate stimuli, rather than such a functioning of habits as is found in the mind of a club or . . . political party. Leaders . . . may . . . resort to stimuli which will break through the crust of ordinary custom and release impulses on such a scale as to create a mob psychology. . . . A political democracy exhibits an overriding of thought . . . that is, thought is submerged in habit. In the crowd and mob, it is submerged in undefined emotion. . . . The introduction of many novel stimuli creates occasions where habits afford no ballast. Hence great waves of emotion easily sweep through masses. (Dewey, 1922:60–61.)

The word "undefined" seems to imply that the crowd is in a blur of emotion without clear meaning. Perhaps research on the quick formation of imagery in crowds will throw more light on this.

Conclusion

This chapter has tried to show what sociologists mean by saying that the social world is continually being created by symbolic transactions. Public information, education, and ideology building create the world; meanings emerge in day-to-day transactions as objects and situations are defined by individuals and groups, the outcomes of which are not known in advance. Thus, man makes his world, and in so doing makes and remakes himself. Collective behavior seems to offer some of the best opportunities for dramatic changes of definition in freely flowing transactions.

No hard-and-fast line separates institutions and collective behavior with regard to creating new definitions. It is just that the flow is freer when unhampered by bureaucratic rules and detailed "scripts," as in the public drama, the wild elaboration of rumors, or the faddish spread of status symbols. Therefore, we should never assume that the world is being made primarily within institutions. The symbolic drifts, contagions, and momentary meanings of even brief collectivities (outbursts, demonstrations, "happenings," crowd sympathy, and "we" feeling) may be far more significant indicators for telling us where the "action" is and what it consists of.

We shall not, however, know what is going on in collective behavior without analyzing meanings, without realizing what worlds are seen and projected. The growth of symbols, perspectives, and styles should be followed. Also, processes like outbursts and group catharsis should not be looked at just as an emotional "letting go," a kind of relief from pressure, but a meaningful movement—a letting go made possible by new images and perspectives, which had to be formed before the outburst or catharsis could occur. Similarly, "strains" on people from a situation or system should be not looked on as just pressures but as tensions *about images*, meanings, and symbols, such as disillusionment, disappointment, suspicion, which always require a definition (of what? about what? from what? to what?).

Thus, we see that symbolic transaction is the "name of the game" as humans play it, wherever they play it. There is no situation, we presume, where defining the situation stops, as long as thought and communication can occur. Our concern, however, is not with the institutional setting but with those in which transactions occur and meanings emerge more freely; where, having this free-flowing character—whether by contagion, circular interaction, rumor, dramatic definition, dialogue, or some other kind of encounter—something is happening that isn't simply predictable from the institutional structure. Much of this happens, of course, when institutions break down; and, though free flow is omnipresent, it is most clearly seen in crises. The hypothesis is, however, that if defined as a free-flowing symbolic transaction, collective behavior goes on inside and outside institutions. The proper analogy (bearing in mind that it is a symbolic process) seems to be that of a river or stream that flows through institutional structures and even more freely outside them. Such a metaphor allows also the possibility that symbolic transactions could be "dammed up" in such a way as to create a pressure which could break forth as outbursts in reaction to strains of the system. Another fluid metaphor that seems appropriate to collective behavior is that of the freezing and unfreezing of social systems.

Such things, however, are left to Chapter 6, which considers collective behavior as somehow connected with the redress of imbalances in social systems. In that sense, the tensions released and the consensus formed in free-flowing transactions are somewhat like debits or assets on a large balance sheet, on which we try to reckon and trace connections.

PART II

Systemic View

CHAPTER 6

Mass Contagions

So early as the year 1374, assemblages of men and women were
seen at Aix-la-Chapelle who had come out of Germany and who, united
by one common delusion, exhibited to the public both in the streets
and in the churches the following strange spectacle. They formed circles
hand in hand and, appearing to have lost all control over their senses,
continued dancing, regardless of the by-standers, for hours together in

wild delirium, until at length they fell to the ground in a state of exhaustion. While dancing they neither saw nor heard, being insensible to external impressions through the senses, but were haunted by visions, their fancies conjuring up spirits whose names they shrieked out; and some of them afterward asserted that they felt as if they had been immersed in a stream of blood, which obliged them to leap so high. Others, during the paroxysm, saw the heavens open and the Saviour enthroned with the Virgin Mary. . . . A few months after this dancing malady had made its appearance at Aix-la-Chapelle, it broke out at Cologne, where the number of those possessed amounted to more than five hundred; and about the same time at Metz, the streets of which place are said to have been filled with eleven hundred dancers. Peasants left their plows, mechanics their workshops, housewives their domestic duties, to join the wild revels, and this rich commercial city became the scene of the most ruinous disorder . . . too often found opportunities for wild enjoyment; and numerous beggars, stimulated by vice and misery, availed themselves of this new complaint to gain a temporary livelihood. Girls and boys quitted their parents, and servants their masters, to amuse themselves at the dances of those possessed, and greedily imbibed the poison of mental infection. Above a hundred unmarried women were seen raving about in consecrated and unconsecrated places, and the consequences were soon perceived. Gangs of idle vagabonds, who understood how to imitate to the life the gestures and convulsions of those really affected, roved from place to place seeking maintenance and adventures, and thus, wherever they went, spreading this disgusting spasmodic disease like a plague. . . . It was not, however, until after four months that the Rhenish cities were able to suppress these impostures, which had so alarmingly increased the original evil. In the meantime, when once called into existence, the plague crept on and found abundant food in the tone of thought which prevailed in the fourteenth and fifteenth centuries, and even, though in a minor degree, throughout the sixteenth and seventeenth. (Hecker, 1888:106–111.)

Talk to a disgruntled politician or weary preacher who has spent his life trying to stir audiences and one gets no picture of such extraordinary susceptibility to contagion as is given by the dancing manias of the Middle Ages. "Apathetic" public and bored congregations seem to be the rule. One gets a similar story from semanticists who talk about communication gaps and people unable to reach one another. Any teacher could confirm the same thing: Messages don't easily "contage."

But another group of phenomena give an entirely different picture: people going wild over some entertainer or favorite; extreme gullibility and credulity; messages spreading like wild fire in all channels, no "crowd" factor being necessary; almost everyone susceptible, traipsing off on crusades, rushes, and stampedes.

Such phenomena have no settled name. They are variously called hysterias, crazes, manias, booms, rushes, epidemics, stampedes, crusades, collective delusions. For convenience we shall call them mass contagions. Their chief characteristics seem to be: (1) extraordinary suggestibilfity and gullibility; (2) wide spread of messages or forms of behavior in the mass; (3) actions, energetic, extreme, or frenzied; and (4) some delusion or loss of normal sense of reality. All contagions have an excessive character that carries them beyond what is justified by common sense: Hysteria is not running to a bomb shelter during an air raid; scapegoating is not normal judicial process; riot and rebellion are not military operations. Because of their extraordinary character, we are forced to suppose that more or less urgent tensions or underlying conditions make people susceptible to them at some times more than at others.

We shall consider the following chief forms: (1) contagions of fear (hysterias); (2) hostile contagions, especially scapegoating and war fever; (3) contagious rebellion; (4) contagions of enthusiasm and hope; and (5) expressive outbursts. After reviewing some well-known examples from today and yesterday, we shall try to understand mass contagion in terms of tension theory and tasks of symbolic transaction.

Forms of Mass Contagion

Contagions of Anxiety

Hysteria refers to any outbreak of wild emotionalism; but, most commonly, it refers to epidemics of exaggerated fear and anxiety, "great scares" from disproportionate causes. That is, a massive bombing attack does not cause hysteria; but rumors, hoaxes, the imagination of "silly girls," and so on, might. It is generally recognized that mass anxiety is not neatly proportionate to causes of fear; just as "little things" can give rise to anxiety, disasters can occur without causing panics. For example, there was no serious panic in the sinking of the Lusitania; morale held up and the passengers helped one another (A. A. and M. Hoehling, 1956:99). Orson Welles' famous broadcast of a fictional "invasion from Mars," reached six million people and put one million into some kind of panic activity, such as heading for the hills, praying, or searching for a basement to hide in. It showed for the first time how much mass anxiety a radio drama presented as news could trigger, without help from rumor or the "crowd" factor. What it mainly showed was that most people are not very critical, and if one can convince them that something scary is really happening, they will be scared. Cantril, Gaudet, and Hertzog (1940) analyzed factors such as the prestige and apparent authenticity of the source, and tabulated characteristics of those who were disturbed, such as education, economic status, and personality. The main characteristic of those who resisted panic and interpreted the play correctly was "critical ability," as shown in checking up on the broadcast or analyzing its internal evidence and finding it to be untrue. Most of those who were panicked made no attempt to check.

Rumor, however, is a more common medium of anxious hysterias: a story arises—from nowhere that one can ascertain—spreads like wildfire, and carries fear with it. One interesting example is the Great Fear of France in 1789:

> The months of July and August may be called the months of the "great fear." Men were afraid, both in town and country of they knew not what. How this universal feeling of terror arose cannot be proved, but it was deemed necessary in some districts for a strict denial to be published to the report that the King had paid brigands to rob the people. This "great fear" was generally expressed in the words "The brigands are coming." Who the brigands were, whence they came, or whither they were going, nobody knew; but that the brigands were coming, nobody doubted. (Ross, 1908:73–74.)

Superstition often provides the basis of a contagion of anxiety by rumor. "Devil baby" panics are fairly common among the natives of West Africa. The essential story is that a woman gives birth to a child, who turns out to be a devil, and gets loose and terrifies the people. A witness of such a panic reported that:

> The story, as it reached us in town, was that a woman had been working alone in her husband's cassava patch not far from Ibadan. Her baby of a few months, according to custom, was tied by a piece of material to her back. . . . Suddenly the mother heard a voice from behind her saying, "Mother, why are you working like this in the fields? Take me home!" The woman stood upright in alarm and looked about her to see whence the words came. But as she turned about they were repeated . . . clearly and distinctly . . . there was no doubt that it came from her baby . . . "Let me down, Mother, let me down!" peremptorily demanded the child. The mother, seized by sudden panic, hastily rid herself of her baby and began running away wildly. She was . . . terrified to see that the child was running after her. It easily overtook her and disappeared into the thick forest bordering the fields. The poor woman . . . ran by a circuitous route to her village, where her tale spread considerable alarm. . . . Houses were shut and barred and the local jujuman did a roaring trade selling amulets and charms guaranteed to keep away that particular devil.
> The night passed quietly but the next afternoon brought fearsome news. A woman of another village, also at work in her husband's fields with her infant strapped to her back, heard her child suddenly and unaccountably address her. "Mother, why do you keep me tied to your

back? I want to get down. I can walk quite well. Put me down, I say!" This second woman behaved much as the first had done. She tore the child's harnessing cloth from her back and ran away, terrified. She also was overtaken by her infant, who sped into the forest. Like the first child, it was never seen again.

Word of these occurrences traveled round the countryside and men and women were much too frightened to work their fields. . . . In no time the fearsome news reached town and . . . we noticed . . . many shops closed and with their doors and windows marked with large crosses in chalk. When we got home we saw that the doors and windows of our servants' dwellings were similarly boldly marked. . . . In a few days the scare was over and we heard no more of the changelings' frolics.*

In this case legend provides a ready symbolic vehicle for the scare, of which rumors provide variations. But fantastic stories need by no means be based on superstitions. A mass hysteria involving a "phantom anesthetist" occurred in Mattoon, Illinois. A woman reported that someone had sprayed a sickish, sweet-smelling gas into her bedroom window, which partly paralyzed her legs and made her ill. Soon others reported similar symptoms: nausea, vomiting, and so on. Newspapers picked up the story: "Anesthetic Prowler on Loose." The community was put on the alert, citizens with shotguns on guard; police calls coming in kept squads busy. It died out after twelve days. Poorly educated people were mainly involved. (D. M. Johnson, 1945.)

A similar hysteria, involving a phantom slasher who was supposed to be attacking children with razor blades, occurred in Taipei, Taiwan, China, in 1956. Mysterious cuts and injuries of many kinds were interpreted as slashings; for example, a gash on a shin while a child was waiting to board a bus. Interpretations included the possibility that the slasher was a sadist, or was engaging in a blood ritual. Investigation by the chief of police showed that many cases were due to accident, innocent misrepresentation, or deliberate hoax. But even the police commissioner, while warning the people to avoid being unnecessarily frightened by rumors, was unable to avoid the conclusion that certain mysterious rascals might be behind all these stories, perhaps communist agents. The stories were spread mostly by rumor, but newspapers helped spread the affair from one area to another beyond the city of Taipei to other cities on the island, and finally to a Chinese community outside the island.

The action profile may be characterized by (a) a rapid and steady buildup in the number of reported incidents and a growing intensity in the uncritical and hyper-suggestive nature of the cases reported;

* "Fearsome Story of the Runaway Babies," from a correspondent, *Times*, London, Oct. 31, 1964.

(b) a period of stock-taking and sober analysis with a consequent decline in reported incidents; but then (c) a spectacular but short-lived
revival of interest; and (d) finally, a rapid cessation of the affair. . . .
The major participants predominantly were drawn from . . . the lower
income, lower educated stratum, and within that stratum, women and
children. (Jacobs, 1965.)

Prior to the action phase, which lasted about two weeks, there was
a rumor circulation phase of from one to three months.

A more realistic context for wild interpretation of physical evidence was provided by a 1954 "windshield pitting" epidemic (Medalia and Larsen, 1958) in Seattle in which there was mysterious
damage to automobile windshields—little pits, which got larger and
grew into bubbles. Public alarm spread; hundreds of calls came in
to police, over three thousand automobiles were damaged. People
covered their windshields with floor mats and newspapers; some
claimed they had found tiny metallic particles that caused the damage. The hysteria lasted a little over three weeks, reaching its peak
(as measured by news space) at the end of the second week. When
people were asked where they first heard about windshield pitting,
they credited channels of first contact as: newspapers, 51 percent;
interpersonal relations, 19 percent; radio, 18 percent; television, 6
percent; and direct experience, 6 percent.

Some hysterias involve symptoms of bodily illness, which spread
contagiously. Thus, the bite of a "June bug" caused an epidemic
among women workers in a textile mill (Kerckhoff and Back, 1968).
Women claimed that a small bug had bitten them and caused them
to feel nauseated, nervous, numb; some of them even fainted. The
epidemic lasted for eleven days with 200 of 965 workers stricken.
The spread was rapid, in geometric progression. Only one small bug
was ever found in the plant, and no physical explanation could
account for the symptoms. It was found that the hysteria spread
more among workers suffering strains (such as much overtime
work), first appeared among women with close relationships, and
later afflicted isolates.

A mouse hysteria occurred among girls in a cotton mill, in which
a mouse put into a girl's bosom produced fits and convulsions, which
spread to twenty-four and stopped work (Park and Burgess, 1924:
878). A belief arose that it was a disease introduced by a bag of
cotton.

Perhaps the most famous example of insect-bite hysteria is that
associated with the origin of the dance, the tarantella, in Italy
(Dawson and Gettys, 1948:612). A peculiar interaction of hysteria
and art occurred. Near the town of Taranto was a native spider that
had a narcotic bite. It became the practice to keep the victim active
for twenty-four hours, to combat the narcotic influence. Out of it

grew a dance. When a person thought he had been bitten, musicians were called in to play and keep him moving; as he became weary, the music got faster and faster. But all this also affected the people who had come to watch. Many joined in the dance and some believed that they, too, had been bitten by the spider; an orgy of dancing developed and kept on until dancers lost consciousness from exhaustion. Every summer saw a fresh attack of Tarantism. The musicians became known as tarantella players, and the dance still persists as part of a summer festival in the district. In this apparent ritualization of a hysteria into a dance and festival, we have an illustration of the creative function of collective behavior.

Closer to daily political realities are the "scares" that periodically circulate among Americans, some approaching hysterias in intensity, at least for a few. One example was the A-bomb fallout-shelter panic of 1962–1963. A sudden realization of the dangers of nuclear attack, triggered partly by official discussion of the need for a national fallout-shelter program, caused a rush of people to buy plans and to construct underground shelters in their backyards with a 3-foot sod roof, or convert swimming pools for the same. Although only 12 percent of householders over the nation took such precautions, and only a small fraction actually equipped themselves with a fallout shelter (Levine and Modell, 1965), there is no doubt that there was for a time, in places such as California, a spree that set people digging in their backyards for what later turned out to be rather expensive wine and mushroom-growing cellars. The nation looked at itself with surprise, not without dismay at the sentiments of some who said that in the event of crisis they would keep neighbors from entering their holes, if necessary by guns.

Similar to these "scares" are the recurrent rumbles of "doomsday talk" among Californians after predictions or tremors of earthquakes. For example, in 1969 there was a run on survival kits after astrologers and soothsayers had predicted the imminent end of California in a giant earthquake, in which San Francisco, Santa Barbara, Los Angeles, and San Diego were expected to disappear into the Pacific. Preachers led hundreds of their congregations out of the state, convinced that California was a den of iniquity about to be visited by divine retribution. A book called *The Last Days of the Late, Great State of California* became a best seller. The matter was not helped by rumors that the noted Caltech seismologist Charles Richter was leaving the state. Doomsday talk reached a fever pitch. *Time* seriously reported that thousands actually believed that the end of California was at hand (*Time*, April 11, 1969).

Drug scares were another area where popular feelings showed some earmarks of hysteria in 1969. There was a return to "prohibition" psychology: College students were given five-year and longer sentences for possession of drugs such as marijuana; "Operation Intercept" went into effect as a border operation and cost a $30 million business loss in the first three weeks, antagonized Mexicans, and raised the price and profits of marijuana to a point where the Mafia became more interested. Communists were blamed for trying to undermine the national character by drugs. Thus, the drug problem became linked in the minds of many with the "red scare," which had reached several hysterical peaks in United States history, especially the "big red scare" of 1919–1921, which caused hundreds of aliens to be deported and people like Charlie Chaplin and Will Rogers to be suspected of being mentioned in "Communist files" (Allen, 1931:61–93). Then in the 1940s and 1950s there was the Joseph McCarthy era, so well treated by Rovere's biography (1959). Lipset reviewed three decades of anticommunism, the Coughlinites, McCarthyites, and Birchers (Bell, 1964:373–446), which leads one to suspect that "red scares" are merely hysterical peaks of a structure that runs continuously through American thought. Such scares are distinguished by paranoid style, a suspicion of what underground enemies may be up to, which is not characteristic of the hysterias we have previously mentioned. Paranoid style, as described by Hofstadter (1966), may prove to be a permanent part of American politics, in which case we can always count on some events or persons to generate hysterias.

Contagions of Hostility

Let us now enter the "world of paranoia" a little farther, first observing that hysterical fear is often associated with some kind of scapegoating, or irrational hostility and punishment. Indeed, it seems that the other side of the coin displays such reaction, for when people fear, they also hate. *Scapegoating* may be defined as unloading blame and punishment on parties who are innocent, or only partly responsible, for an alleged evil. Psychologically, it is a "displacement reaction," but sociologically, as we shall see, it proves to be more than that.

The most celebrated example of a hysteria that involved both anxiety and scapegoating is, of course, the witch mania of New England in 1692. This gave rise to an ugly picture of Puritan authoritarianism, and made Cotton Mather a villain in United States history, who hunted down witches and preached moral sermons to people about to be hung. The epidemic began in Salem, Massachusetts, and took place all in one dreadful year. It began with some "silly girls" playing at Black Mass with fantasies about the devil. While doing so they developed an unusual malady in which they would scream, go into fits, and sometimes scramble about on hands and knees, making noises like the barking of a dog.

> No sooner had word gone around about this extraordinary affliction than it began to spread like a contagious disease. All over the community young girls were groveling on the ground in a panic of fear and excitement . . . while . . . townspeople . . . could only stand by in helpless horror as the girls suffered their torments, (K. Erikson, 1966: 141–153.)

The town's doctor did what he could, but soon decided that the illness was beyond his powers. Then the girls began to blame people; court hearings were held in which the girls were star witnesses in pointing out the "witches" who had afflicted them. Hearsay— almost any kind of fantastic evidence in accord with the spirit of the times—was accepted. The mania was loosed, and spread from Salem to Boston and other places. Soon no one was safe; twenty people were hung or pressed to death, including a minister; even two dogs were accused of witchcraft and executed. The flavor of this remarkable era is well given by Starkey (1949) and by Hansen (1969). It is important to remember, however, that the extremes of Salem took place against a background of tradition of belief in witchcraft; witch burnings and hangings had been going on for centuries in Scotland, England, and the European Continent. The contagion was simply an extreme reaction overlapping tradition. Questions still remain: Why so many witches in one particular place in one particular year? Why did hysteria reach such a pitch that people were mistaken for witches, while some accepted the accusation, pretended to be witches, and imagined themselves to be in league with the devil? And why, then, did the whole thing suddenly fade, people become shamefaced, magistrates become careful about standards of evidence, and a general pardon release hundreds from jail? Superstition seems insufficient to explain a hysteria that developed on top of superstition.

The "Reign of Terror" is perhaps history's most outstanding example of contagious scapegoating, aside from the witch hunts. It was a rage of vindictive fury emanating from the people, who, after storming the Bastille, beheading the king, queen, nobles, churchmen, and partisans, one after another (22 deputies of the Girond were beheaded in one day), finally devoured most of its leaders, including Danton and Robespierre. Vivid accounts are in Dickens' *Tale of Two Cities*; Alphonse de Lamartine, *History of the Girondins* (1847); and Thomas Carlyle's *The French Revolution* (1837). The acute phase of the terror lasted over a year, and finally Napoleon acted as a strong man to put an end to it with a "whiff of grapeshot."

But we see that scapegoating is not just an outburst of popular fury—it is a very ancient ritual practice. The Old Testament tells of the Hebrews casting out evil by loading a goat ritually with the sins of the tribe. Abraham offered to sacrifice his son, and Jonah was thrown to the whale because he was believed to be bringing bad luck to the ship. Thus, we see that traditional scapegoating has the character of ritual expulsion, whose symbolic meaning is purification. Doubtless the Puritans felt this way about the witches they put to death—that they were getting rid of an evil which threatened them and their whole way of life. We may suppose some strain of moral tension is at the basis of such actions; as K. Erikson (1966) suggested, the moral "boundaries" of Puritanism were being threatened by forces such as secularism, heresy, and strangers. This ritual symbolism of scapegoating means that we cannot treat it as just a senseless outburst. It must be considered as a moral transaction, aimed at some kind of balancing of the scales.

Thus, it is impossible to entirely condemn even the Reign of Terror as totally evil, or, on the other hand, to be sure that what we call justice is free from scapegoating as the ritual expulsion of evil. Indeed, Americans seem to love casting blame as outbursts of popular, righteous indignation. Hofstadter said:

> Americans do not abide very quietly the evils of life. . . . There is a wide and pervasive tendency to believe . . . that there is some great but essentially very simple struggle going on, at the heart of which there lies some single conspiratorial force, whether it be . . . the "gold bugs," the Catholic Church, big business, corrupt politicians, the liquor interests and the saloons, or the Communist Party, and that this evil is something that must be not merely limited, checked, and controlled but rather extirpated root and branch at the earliest possible moment. . . . So we go off on periodical psychic sprees that purport to be moral crusades: liberate the people once and for all . . . restore absolute popular democracy or completely honest competition in business, wipe out the saloon and liquor forever from the nation's life, destroy the political machines and put an end to corruption, or achieve absolute, total, and final security against war, espionage, and the affairs of the external world. (Hofstadter, 1955:16–17.)

Hence it is that some such tendency must always be expected—at least in the fact-finding and blaming processes of disaster—when there is a great tension of grief and "injustice," and when there is enthusiastic popular support for any process of justice. We may call to mind some famous trials—causes célèbre—which acquired a scapegoating flavor because, on the one hand, the legal process seemed to have behind it an outburst of moral righteousness, as in the case of the trial of Oscar Wilde in England. On the other hand are the cases where sympathetic audiences felt that the accused was being singled out and punished as a representative of some larger cause for which he was not responsible—that he was only a martyr—as in the Dreyfus case in France, which stirred up liberals the world over (Halasz, 1955); or the trial of Sacco and Vanzetti in the United States, 1921–1927, which seemed less a trial for murder than an expression of class prejudice against Italians, the radical labor movement, and foreigners and the poor generally. The "dago Christs" were executed while crowds kept vigil outside the death house. This case underwent an interesting transformation, from the "red scare" atmosphere of the trial of 1921 (with judge and courtroom obviously prejudiced against the defendants and the prosecutor urging the jury to "stand together like true soldiers") to the pathos of "martyrdom" of 1927, when witch-hunt feelings had mostly subsided and liberal fervor to "save Sacco and Vanzetti" reached its peak. This change in symbolism and mood put Massachusetts justice and Judge Thayer in the role of a "Cotton Mather," the stress of which his suicide gives some hint (Klapp, 1964a:155–163).

Disasters, of course, are often an occasion for scapegoating when the tension of grief and sense of being wronged leads to the feeling that *someone* must be to blame. An example is the 1942 Cocoanut Grove fire in Boston (Veltfort and Lee, 1943), in which 488 nightclub patrons burned. Popular blame casting, by rumor and news stories, shifted from one scapegoat to another—the bus boy (who had struck a match), a "prankster," (who had removed the light bulb that the bus boy was trying to replace), the fire department that had approved the club a week before, other city officials, and the owners of the club. Such violent accusations, against whole groups, were attributed not only to the grief of the moment but "latent hostility" (for example, against Jews, and against federal officials, which had been smoldering for months).

However, there is no simple relationship between the physical magnitude of trouble and the demand for a scapegoat. Bucher (1957), studied aircraft disasters, found that the public was *not* looking for a scapegoat, "did not become angry first and look for an object later." Anger developed only as perception developed, of failure to act to prevent future disasters, or agents "standing in opposition to basic values" so that people became convinced they had "no intention of doing anything about the situation. Then the blaming process is underway."

The extraordinary animosity toward long hair, beards and sideburns, and toward hippies in the late 1960s had earmarks of scapegoating. Such people were suspected of being communists, homosexuals, drug pushers, and so on. The film "Easy Rider" (1969) showed two long-haired, "hippie" type motorcyclists, slain by savage local animosity while riding through the South. Such animosity is all the more extraordinary when we remember that Jesus and Abraham Lincoln, our two greatest heroes, were men with long hair. The impossibility of explaining antagonism to long hair by any tangible disaster resulting from it justifies supposing that it was a scapegoating response connected with collective identity, expressing a deep moral unease of the times that was harder to rationalize than that of the people of Salem.

War fever is another dimension of hostile contagion, a fever of militance against an outgroup. There is little doubt that societies can be swept into turmoil by such feelings. In our own history, the inflammatory and religious agitation of abolitionists, such as the Garrisonians and Harriet Stowe in *Uncle Tom's Cabin*, helped to stir up separatism and plunge the country into the Civil War. William Randolph Hearst gets no small credit for fanning the war with Spain, with his slogan "Remember the *Maine!*" In World War I, Congress not only voted for, but was also stampeded into, declaration of war by a "feeling" which caused many to vote against their better judgments. Congressman Fred Britten, Republican, Illinois, stated in the House, April 5, 1917—

> The truth of the matter is that ninety per cent of your people and mine do not want this declaration of war and are distinctly opposed to our going into that bloody mire on the other side. There is something in the air, gentlemen, and I do not know what it is, whether it be the hand of destiny or some superhuman movement, something stronger than you or I can realize or resist, that seems to be picking us up bodily and literally forcing us to vote for this declaration of war when way down deep in our hearts we are just as opposed to it as our people back home. (Millis, 1935:454.)

World War I was probably the last major conflict that America entered with a "flag waving" spirit; German-Americans were persecuted, the "Hun" became a mythical symbol for atrocity stories, and at the armistice celebration in New York City the Kaiser was burned in effigy. However, a wave of hysteria following the Pearl Harbor attack led to the imprisonment of over 110,000 West Coast Japanese, most of them native-born U.S. citizens, without due process, and dispossessed (and never fairly reimbursed) from their property. All later agreed that this was a violation of Constitutional rights, perhaps worst in United States history. There was at the time no effective voice of protest (Congress passed a bill supporting the move, with only one senator, Robert Taft, opposing); General De Witt appeared before a Senate committee stating that "a Jap's a Jap. It makes no difference whether he is an American citizen or not. I don't want any of them here"; a superpatriot chopped down four Japanese cherry trees along the Tidal Basin in Washington; the

Tennessee State Department of Purchasing declared "open season on Japs, no licenses required." (*Time*, Aug. 11, 1961.)

Contagions of Rebellion

Rebellion is different from mere conflict in that it is an attack on the authority symbols of one's own group; hence, it necessarily generates more inner tension as guilt. It becomes contagious when it spreads, sets off others into mutinies and defiance of law, and has the purpose or effect of stirring people—not just to disturb the peace but to try to upset constituted authority. Thus, the Boston Tea Party was a contagious act that stirred the colonies into defiance of King George, whereas Thoreau's refusal to pay a tax to his government was defiant but had little immediate contagious effect.

A prime example of contagious rebellion is the ghetto riots of 1967, which were not definitely political but "involved Negroes acting against local symbols of white American society, authority and property in Negro neighborhoods—rather than against white persons." Disorder usually began with rock and bottle throwing and window breaking. Once store windows were broken, looting usually followed. But there was something more than looting (just as there was something more than tea dumping in Boston in 1773). A "spirit of carefree nihilism" was observed to be taking hold; "to riot and destroy appeared more and more to become ends in themselves"; young people were seen "dancing amidst the flames." No deliberate insurrection, however, was occurring as in the case of the Boston Tea Party. "The urban disorders of the summer of 1967 were not caused by, nor were they the consequence of, any organized plan or 'conspiracy.' " Nevertheless:

> Militant organizations, local and national, and individual agitators, who repeatedly forecast and called for violence, were active in the spring and summer of 1967. We believe that they sought to encourage violence, and that they helped to create an atmosphere that contributed to the outbreak of disorder. We recognize that the continuation of disorders and the polarization of the races would provide fertile ground for organized exploitation in the future. (Kerner Commission, 1968:9.)

Thus the riots, though spontaneous, had some of the spirit of rebellion against White institutions, and even more of its effect. The basic conclusion of the Report of the National Advisory Commission on Civil Disorders (1968) was that: "Our nation is moving toward two societies, one black, one white—separate and unequal. . . . To pursue our present course will involve the continuing polarization of the American community and, ultimately, the destruction of basic democratic values." The typical rioter was a militant, not just a looter but—

a teenager or young adult, a lifelong resident of the city in which he rioted, a high school dropout; he was, nevertheless, somewhat better educated than his nonrioting Negro neighbor, and was usually under-employed or employed in a menial job. He was proud of his race, extremely hostile to both whites and middle class Negroes and, although informed about politics, highly distrustful of the political system. (Kerner Commission, 1968:7.)

The contagious quality of the rebellion was seen in the way it spread. The eruption in Watts in 1965 was a precursor, an omen. In 1964 there had been riots in eight cities, relatively unnoticed. In 1966 there were eighteen. In 1967 there was an eruption that spread over thirty-nine cities; for example: Nashville in April; Jackson and Houston in May; Boston and five more in June; Detriot, Newark, and sixteen more in July; Chicago, Milwaukee, and two more major cities in August. Undoubtedly some of the tension was spread by news itself to other cities; but behind it was the background of accumulated tension in all Black communities.

Disorder did not erupt as a result of a single "triggering" or "pre-cipitating" incident. Instead, it was generated out of an increasingly disturbed social atmosphere, in which typically a series of tension-heightening incidents over a period of weeks or months became linked in the minds of many in the Negro community with a reservoir of underlying grievances. At some point in the mounting tension, a further incident—in itself often routine or trivial—became the breaking point and the tension spilled over into violence. "Prior" incidents, which increased tensions and ultimately led to violence, were police actions in almost half the cases. . . . (Kerner Commission, 1968:6.)

The Berkeley revolt of 1964–1965, involving a very different class of people, also had the rebel spirit, and surprised everybody by starting a chain reaction on university campuses in the United States and elsewhere. It fused with some of the waning civil rights fervor to help make the "New Left" spirit, which crystallized about this time in statements such as those of *Ramparts* magazine. The spirit of this rebellion is expressed by one of the leaders, Mario Savio, as follows:

Last summer I went to Mississippi to join the struggle there for civil rights. This fall I am engaged in another phase of the same struggle, this time in Berkeley. The two battlefields may seem quite different to some observers, but this is not the case. The same rights are at stake in both places—the right to participate as citizens in democratic society and the right to due process of law. Further, it is a struggle against the same enemy. In Mississippi an autocratic and powerful minority rules, through organized violence, to suppress the vast, virtually powerless majority. In California, the privileged minority manipulates the university bureaucracy to suppress the students' political

expression. That "respectable" bureaucracy masks the financial pluto-
crats; that impersonal bureaucracy is the efficient enemy in a "Brave
New World."

In our free fight at the University of California, we have come up
against what may emerge as the greatest problem of our nation—
depersonalized, unresponsive bureaucracy. We have encountered the
organized status quo in Mississippi, but it is the same in Berkeley.
(Lipset and Wolin, 1965:216.)

This rebellion was distinctly different from the theme of Black power
and separatism expressed by leaders like Stokely Carmichael and
Eldridge Cleaver, but it was akin to that of Daniel Cohn-Bendit and
Gabriel (1969) who expressed the spirit of European students. The
spread of the New Left rebellion through the universities in 1968
and 1969 is too well known to need description, as are the crusade
to legalize "pot" and the "Yippie" demonstration at the Democratic
Convention in Chicago, 1968.

Thus, there emerged in this contagion a romantic image of
overthrowing the "Establishment" to bring in a new order, vaguely
defined in terms of Marxism, anarchism, humanism, and "participatory democracy." This movement formed uneasy coalitions with
Black power for specific demonstrations. But it remained largely
unorganized, threatened continually by splits into factions, and relying upon contagion and spontaneous *esprit de corps* for its effectiveness. It caught on widely among university and high school students
("never trust anyone over thirty"), though hardly more than 2 percent
could be classed as activists. Nevertheless, higher percentages of
youth participated symbolically in rebellious behavior. A nationwide
Gallup survey of university campuses in 1969 showed that, of males,
28 percent were sporting long sideburns and 6 percent beards; of
both sexes, 13 percent were displaying sloppy clothes and slovenly
appearance, 22 percent had tried marijuana, 4 percent had tried
LSD, and 66 percent thought premarital sex was all right. Thus, it is
evident that the definition of rebellion cannot be confined to physical
acts against the established order, but extends to symbolic actions,
such as dirty words or calling cops "pigs," when they express a
similar spirit. Actually, a new era of romantic style rebellion had
been triggered by the Berkeley "filthy speech" outburst and in no
small measure by the success of the Beatles, whose long hair and
satirical lyrics symbolized so much antagonism to the very Establishment that Savio was "uptight" about. Added to this was the
alarming voice of Timothy Leary, the "prophet of pot," who was
calling on dissidents to "turn on, tune in, and drop out" rather than
join the political ranks of the New Left.

Thus, we see that rebellion, whether by political acts or by gestures and style, is a symbolic process involving conversion of the

meaning of an authority symbol into an image that one can defy with a good conscience. One way to do this is to convert the authority into a "bad guy" (such as an authoritarian or tyrant who represses liberty, or a "fat cat" or exploiter), or a fool whose views are out of date and whose bungling and ineptitude have aggravated social problems (the very image of the "square" or "straight"). When authority is translated in such terms, there is no disloyalty in criticizing it nor is there treason in attacking it. Guilt is allayed and rebellion is legitimized as a way to values that existing authorities no longer serve but defeat. Merton said—

> When the institutional system is regarded as the barrier to the satisfaction of legitimized goals, the stage is set for rebellion. To pass into organized political action, allegiance must . . . be withdrawn from the prevailing social structure . . . [and] transferred to new groups possessed of a new myth. (Merton, 1968:210.)

Defining themselves as good guys fighting for a noble cause, sometimes as martyrs suffering from the injustices of authority, the rebels build the morale of a resistance movement—no less a "Yippie" than a patriot of '76.

Nevertheless, from the agitations, crime, and civil disorder (Gurr, 1969) of the late 1960s, we are likely to exaggerate the rebelliousness of Americans. For all their talk ("a little rebellion now and then is a good thing," Thomas Jefferson said), Americans are not a very rebellious people, and are conservative economically compared to Europeans. Disorderly yes, but rebellious no. The urban riots of 1965–1967 came as a surprise to the White establishment, and actually showed the great patience of the Blacks, who had waited a hundred years for an emancipation that had not come and who would, by Latin American or Middle Eastern or European standards, probably have expressed their feelings a lot sooner. Most American political uprisings stop short of full revolt at protest: Coxey's Army march on Washington, 1894, "a petition with boots on"; the "bonus" march of veterans in 1932, a protest that ended in violence but produced the Bonus Bill of 1936; the Poor People's Campaign, climaxed by Solidarity Day in Washington, D.C., 1968, which was committed to dramatizing hunger for the sake of nonviolent democratic change; the New Mobilization to End War in Viet Nam, 1969, which brought 250,000, the largest crowd ever in Washington, D.C., to "March Against Death," and which was on the whole peaceful and "inspirational" in spirit, disappointing militants.

Such instances of restraint with serious grievances somewhat offset the impression of general rebellion created by the ghetto riots and New Left demonstrations by university students. Although the campus trend was strongly to the left in 1969, as shown by

Gallup reports ("conservative" was almost a "dirty name"; 53 percent were liberal versus 21 percent self-described as conservative), the national picture showed a solid majority (three-fifths) of "middle Americans" who expressed the following sentiments: local police do a good job, 78 percent; police should have more power, 63 percent; Black militants have been treated too leniently, 85 percent; college demonstrators have been treated too leniently, 84 percent. The "middle American" stood firm, supporting President Nixon by large majorities, reasserting traditional values, and festooning his automobile windows with American flags. Eric Hoffer commented: "The common man is standing up and someday he's going to elect a policeman President of the United States" (*Newsweek*, Oct. 6, 1969: 29, 35).

We turn from the dark to the bright side by looking briefly at two kinds of popular contagions that express optimism, enthusiasm, and expressive satisfaction instead of anxiety, aggression, and rebellion.

Enthusiastic Contagions

Rushes, booms, bubbles, and crazes may be called, for want of a better term, enthusiastic contagions. Common to them is an extraordinary enthusiasm and optimism, a dream of magical wish-fulfillment, religious or secular, which draws in the common man and sustains his hope with a "pot of gold" image. Typically, such contagions burst like a bubble after a time. During the time of their growth, word gets around, usually by rumor, of extraordinary opportunities that are accepted with gullibility. An example is the Great Tulip Mania in Holland, England, and France, 1634–1636. The collecting of bulbs became a gentleman's hobby, which became a rage and finally a frenzy. The prices for rare tulips increased so much that marts for their sale were established in the stock exchanges of Amsterdam, Rotterdam, and other towns. People were known to invest half their fortune in a single root. The middle classes, merchants and shopkeepers, and even those of moderate means were drawn into the speculation. A sailor happened to see what he thought was an onion on the counter of a merchant and picked it up, thinking to have it with his lunch as a relish. He went to the dock to eat and had hardly finished his meal before the place was in an uproar of search for the missing tulip. He was caught and put in prison for some months on a charge of felony.

> Many individuals grew suddenly rich. A golden bait hung temptingly out before the people, and one after the other, they rushed to the tulip-marts, like flies around a honey pot. . . . Nobles, citizens, farmers,

mechanics, seamen, footmen, maid-servants, even chimney sweeps and old clothes women, dabbled in tulips. People . . . converted their property into cash, and invested it in flowers. . . . At last, however, the more prudent began to see that this folly could not last forever. Rich people no longer bought the flowers to keep them in their gardens, but to sell them again at . . . profit. It was seen that somebody must lose fearfully in the end. As this conviction spread, prices fell, and never rose again, confidence was destroyed, and a universal panic seized upon the dealers. . . . Those who were unlucky enough to have had stores of tulips on hand at the time of the sudden reaction were left to bear their ruin as philosophically as they could . . . but the commerce of the country (Holland) suffered a severe shock, from which it was many years ere it recovered. (MacKay, 1932:89–97.)

Another example was the South Sea Bubble, a frenzy of speculation in South Sea enterprises, which occurred in England in 1717 (MacKay, 1932:46–88). The craze began in the House of Lords, spread to the stock exchange, and finally to the people generally, who hurried to put as much or as little money as they had into any kind of South Sea venture, with "visions of ingots dancing before their eyes." It seemed "as if the whole nation had turned stock-jobbers." Innumerable companies started up for all kinds of wild enterprises. The most extraordinary was one that asked for investment to carry on "an undertaking of great advantage, but nobody to know what it is." The day this stock was put on sale, the entrepreneur sold a thousand shares and took off the same evening for the Continent, never to be heard of again. This bubble collapsed and ended in a parliamentary inquiry to find the rascals who were responsible for it, but there could be found nobody to blame for the general foolishness.

Such events match the American gold rushes of 1849 in California, excited by the discovery at Sutter's Mill near Sacramento; and in Alaska, 1898, the "Klondike fever," which drew over 30,000 people, most of whom had never mined for gold before and still less had ever lived in a climate like that of Alaska. Two major speculative frenzies occurred in America during the 1920s, one of which was the Florida land boom of 1925. This brought on a trek of population, searching for prodigious profits like those realized by a poor woman who bought a piece of land near Miami for $25 and sold it for $150,000. People bought indiscriminately, with only one idea—to resell, even land that was entirely under water. The optimism grew, helped by bubbles and dancing girls of promotion, until a hurricane suddenly put an end to it (Allen, 1931:301–321).

Even bigger was the stock-market boom of 1929, in which stories of fortunes made overnight were on everybody's lips, and brokers' offices were jammed with crowds of men and women watching the

message of the ticker tape; the little people crowded in, eager for
a part of the pot of gold, along with the big operators. Rampant
rumors of profits told of a valet who made a quarter of a million
dollars; a trained nurse who made $30,000 by following tips given
her by patients; a cattleman who bought and sold thousands of
shares a day by telephone from his ranch; an ex-actress in her Park
Avenue apartment, surrounded by charts and financial reports, playing the market on a lavish scale; "grocers, motormen, plumbers,
seamstresses, and speakeasy waiters were in the market. . . . The
Big Bull Market had become a national mania." When the crash
came, the panic was equally severe; people fought to sell, rumors
spread wildly that eleven speculators had committed suicide in one
day; troops guarded the New York Stock Exchange against an angry
mob (Allen, 1931:322–377).

Such secular, profit-motivated crazes invite reflections like those
of Tawney (1920) about the overemphasis of an "acquisitive" society. It may seem a long jump from secular frenzy to religious
fervor like that of the "people's crusade" of 1096, and the "children's
crusade" of A.D. 1212. Yet, the general characteristic—the common
man drawn into a dream of magical wish fulfillment—was there;
nor was the material pot-of-gold promise a small element, since
historians have chronicled the looting of the crusaders as they
passed through Europe and the Middle East. It seems to be a matter
of what people are interested in. In other respects the patterns of
contagion are similar. For example, a report is given of a crowd of
between 100,000 and 150,000 people who jammed into a place in
Puerto Rico to see the expected miraculous appearance of a dead
saint. People came from all over Puerto Rico, as well as from Haiti,
the Dominican Republic, Cuba, Miami, and New York, blocking the
road, pouring by thousands off the train, and overwhelming the few
hundred police and guards who had been recruited to maintain order.
As the crucial hour of eleven approached—

the tension in the crowd grew to great proportions. . . . In those last
fifteen minutes . . . various people reported seeing different miracles:
the rain fell in many colors off the garments of the children; the
Virgin appeared silhouetted in the clouds; wondrous rings of color
appeared around the sun; people who had felt sick for years suddenly
felt well. Finally, just after eleven, a cry went up that the Virgin,
dressed in black, was walking down the west hillside toward the well.
It took considerable time for the crowd to be persuaded that in fact this
was not the Virgin, but only an old woman dressed in black. Shortly
thereafter another cry spread through the crowd that the Virgin, dressed
in white, was walking up the east hillside; but again, this turned out to
be nothing more than an old man in a white shirt. For hours thereafter,
people kept watching the skies and the hills and the trees and thousands

continued edging their way slowly toward the well . . . until, at about 5 P.M., the crowd . . . began to desert in droves. From that date until March 1 of the following year, a steady stream of people, roughly two hundred on every weekday and three thousand on Sundays, have come to Sabana Grande. . . . (Tumin and Feldman, 1955.)

In 1966, flying saucers (UFO's) were sighted by fifty people in Ann Arbor, Michigan. At least twelve policemen and forty other persons said they watched a weird flying object, guarded by four sister ships, land in a swamp. Descriptions of the UFO's tallied closely. The two persons who were reportedly closest, a man and his son, said they ran to within 500 yards of the object. It was shaped like a football and was about the length of a car with a "grayish yellow" hue and a pitted surface "like coral rock." It had a blue light on one end and a white light on the other. It took off with a sound like the echo of a ricocheting bullet when his son broke the silence by saying, "Look at that horrible thing!" A policeman said four other UFO's hovered in a quarter-circle over the one in the swamp, and when it took off they vanished with it. Six police cars chased the formation. The Air Force remained noncommital, while the Flying Saucer Society claimed another vindication. The extraordinary agreement of some flying-saucer enthusiasts seems explainable only by the truth of their observations or by a social contagion among people made extremely suggestible by hope, since panic in many cases was negligible. In fact, optimism was more prevalent, as in the case of one man who brought his fiddle to the scene and began playing, hoping the phantom pilots would hear and come to earth; another man sat in his car blinking his headlights in code, hoping to communicate with the visitors. Table 6.1 lists the varying numbers of sightings reported by the U.S. Air Force UFO Study Committee. Do peaks show the work of contagion?

Expressive Contagions

Expressive contagions draw people into outbursts for sheer joy, the "hell" of it, or into indulgence in sentiment and pathos—for example, a "good cry." Unlike enthusiastic contagions, expressive contagions have no clear goal other than emotional release. Therefore, release of tension is a chief characteristic, though this does not rule out other functions, as we shall see. Many kinds of tension (relief, "high spirits," frustration, sexuality, guilt) contribute to expressive contagions and outbursts. In the case of religious revivalism, the prime motive seems to be guilt. The Great Western Revival, which was sparked by a six-day camp meeting in Cane Ridge,

Year	Number	Year	Number
1947	79	1959	364
1948	143	1960	514
1949	186	1961	488
1950	169	1962	474
1951	121	1963	399
1952	1,501	1964	526
1953	452	1965	887
1954	429	1966	1,060
1955	404	1967	937
1956	778	1968	392
1957	1,178	1969	(146)
1958	590		(Study terminated early in year)

SOURCE: *Christian Science Monitor*, April 22, 1970. Report by Dr. J. Allen Hynek, Director, Lindheimer Astronomical Research Laboratory, Northwestern University, of sightings reported by the U.S. Air Force UFO Study Committee, up to the time when the project was terminated in 1969.

Kentucky, 1801, swept the country in a wave of preaching, penitence, and prayer, and lasted for several years in both cities and backwoods areas. "Circuit riders," with Bible, gun, and saddle blanket for bed, carried the message to outlying hamlets and farms, knocking on the door of every cabin, to preach against immorality and "Demon Rum" (which was, indeed, rather a problem, since whiskey sold for twenty-five cents a gallon, full supplies were kept in every cabin, and almost everyone, including women and children as young as twelve years old, took part in the amenities). Calling these rough and sincere people to penitence was fairly easy. One circuit rider converted everyone on a Mississippi River steamboat—captain, crew, passengers, gamblers, even the piano player. He claimed to have converted 10,000 people, baptized 12,000, preached 14,600 sermons, and orated 500 funeral eulogies. The general effect was an orgy of repentance, with people "groveling among the fresh-cut stumps" (Wallace, 1955). A later offspring of this spiritual upheaval was the temperance movement (Gusfield, 1963). A similar revival occurred among the students of Wheaton College, Wheaton, Illinois, 1950, in which statements by a few students in the auditorium started an orgy of confession that involved most of the academic community and lasted a week. To some extent, the evangelism of Billy Graham has been an effort to create this kind of contagion, but we cannot always credit him with such success among the huge crowds he draws wherever he goes (K. and G. Lang, 1960).

The secular equivalent of religious revivalism in the nineteenth century is probably the worship of entertainers, popular music, faddism, and fun of the twentieth century. One of the early signs of displacement of the ethos from religion and morality to secular matters was the idolization of movie stars; the funeral of Rudolph Valentino, for example, drew between sixty and eighty thousand mourners the first day, produced riots, and required four policemen on guard while crowds milled about the street all night long. The end of the "great lover" produced an orgy of grief that no one had anticipated and which lasted for years (J. P. Chaplin, 1959:74–88).

On the entertainment side we began to see what might be called an era of musical evangelism with the development of "rock" music, which involved much of the youth of America, indeed of the world, in a mass expressive contagion, even penetrating the Iron Curtain. It grew up as a kind of rebellion against jazz, which never (except for the "swing" era of Benny Goodman) had acquired the popularity of a mass contagion. It was started by the pioneers of "rock and roll" like Elvis Presley, and Chubby Checker who started the dance craze, the "twist." However, the Beatles and Rolling Stones were the main triggers of the international craze that swept from Britain to America and European countries as a wild and devastatingly new kind of music, which broke with the traditions of classical, popular, and jazz composition and sound. Its deafening impact appalled elders, but youthful fans stormed the concerts and even picked up as souvenirs the chewing-gum wrappers thrown away by their idols. The main part of the message of "rock" was an invitation to let oneself go in mind-bending experiences, abandoning one's senses in wild, strident, and even ugly sounds, many produced by primitive "unmusical" techniques, helped by unheard of (but not unheard!) electronic amplification and distortion. Beyond the theme of self-expression was also a rebel spirit that could not be mistaken (Klapp, 1969:84–95). A connection of "rock" with traditional music was finally established when Leonard Bernstein listened to a Beatles' recording (the "Sergeant Pepper" album) and acknowledged it as music. By 1969, rock had adopted an evangelistic posture, dedicated to renewal of the world by electrical, mind-bending experiences, bringing in new awareness by wild celebration of the senses (aided electronically and chemically). If we ask about the "trigger" of rock (what made it contagious?), we must take some note of the fact that the "hypnosis" of evangelism was in its vehemence of preaching, arousing guilt, whereas with rock it seemed to be a gigantic "beat" that shook and numbed the nervous system, reverberated buildings, and sometimes damaged hearing (Eisen, 1969; Belz, 1969).

We have looked at several kinds of extraordinary mass contagions that sweep people out of normal life—constructing images that approach collective delusions—into actions that are frenzied, various, and prolonged. Thus, they go beyond the ordinary character of crowd phenomena in that they have wider mass participation, even spreading over the world; person-to-person transmission is unnecessary, nor is circular interaction (the "crowd factor"), and they last longer, enduring for weeks or even years. Such things imply considerable buildup as symbolic processes with many inputs (in this sense, Orson Welles' "invasion from Mars" was not typical). Hysterias and such contagions are much more complex than a mere outburst such as a riot, mob, or panic. Whereas a crowd, for all its diversity, does pretty much one thing (such as flee or attack), a hysteria is a variety of collective and individual actions over a period of time, all in the grip of a predominant mood and conception that is collective and which develops (as well as spreads) during this time by processes such as rumor, achieving in a short time something very much like what legend building accomplishes in centuries. On the quantitative side, ignoring change in image, we see a developmental curve like that of the Mattoon and similar epidemics —namely, a slow beginning, increasingly rapid rise to a peak, and a rapid falling off. But the span of such epidemics may range from weeks to years.

The inputs of a contagion seem to be multiple, usually not one channel but a combination of firsthand experience (perception), person-to-person chains ($A—B—C—D$ . . .), mass communication, and crowd interaction.

From a psychological viewpoint, contagions seem to be periods of extraordinary suggestibility, leading to actions that disturb the normal tenor of life. Suggestibility rises to a level of gullibility, where people are willing to accept anything relevant; rumors that would ordinarily die, now spread and grow like weeds, or, if you prefer, like wildfire; and there is a rapid spread of patterns of behavior, which go off like firecrackers. Such excessive response is not organized or calculated, but is a spontaneous letting-go, which is described by words like panic, mania, and frenzy. All this means that during the time of a contagion, triggers become more potent: "silly girls" who are usually ignored are now listened to; suspicion magnifies what can be considered suspicious; anger, anxiety, and hope make people look more eagerly for signs, perhaps for scapegoats. At some point in contagion, trigger "strength" becomes zero (or almost meaningless), since people need no triggers to develop responses such as those of the Sabana Grande miracle, or the flying-saucer enthusiasm, or the Salem hysteria.

At the point where triggers are least necessary, the contagion seems to become most delusional, that is, able to manufacture its own signs and out of touch with reality as science defines it. Superstition is obviously at the root of some of this (as with devil babies). But bubbles are not so easily accounted for, nor does "rock" as an expressive contagion need any particular established vision to sustain it. We must suppose that contagions develop images that are transitory and part of the mood of the moment, but the longer the moment lasts, the greater the chance that rumors will fixate in a manner similar to legends. However, we note that loss of reality does not come only from delusional content of belief, but occurs in anyone whose feelings become so high or whose actions so frenzied that he pays little attention to the cues of his environment—as the saying goes, he knocks things about like a bull in a china shop.

We turn next to a consideration of tension, which is generally considered to have an important part in mass contagions.

Tension Theory

We have seen five types of mass contagion: anxious, hostile, rebellious, enthusiastic, and expressive. The standard picture is of unrest, which begins with some individuals, spreads to others, partly by witting or unwitting agitation, and finally becomes visible in forms like outbursts, protest, and social movements (Blumer, 1939). But the questions are: Why does unrest develop and spread more at some times than at others? Why to some persons more than others? What makes unrest "contage"? At this point, tension—both as an individual and systemic variable—seems a necessary part of the picture.

Various theories have been put forward as to the psychological mechanisms involved in contagion. At times, it seems mechanical and senseless, like the transmission of a germ, which led Tarde (1903) to attribute it to a mechanical imitative tendency (which he called "interpsychical photography") and which he held was a tendency in all human beings to duplicate the idea or action presented to them by others. Other writers said it was an instinctive herd tendency (Trotter, 1917; McDougall, 1920). Neither of these theories was very satisfactory because variations of contagion were the big problem. Most sociologists who discussed the matter relied upon the concepts of suggestion, and considered suggestibility as a tendency to respond uncritically, varying with individuals. Miller and Dollard (1941) treated imitation as a response developed in people by various conditioning. Freud (1922) introduced the concept of identification as a means of relating ourselves to others by finding in a leader something we have within ourselves. Turner (1964) reviewed various theories and asked whether what we call contagion is not an emergent norm that puts pressure on us. It seems plain that there is little consensus yet as to just what goes on in contagion. Even instinctivists still have their day. About all that everyone is agreed on is that Tarde (1903) was wrong.

Perhaps, then, we can be excused from trying to settle all these questions. Indeed, we might confine ourselves to two minimal propositions that seem consistent with what is known (not necessarily sufficient): (1) If tension (unspecified) is high, people are more likely to engage in any kind of activity of which they are capable. (2) If a certain meaning of a situation is communicated, people will respond in a manner that seems to them appropriate, considering the other information and meanings which they already know. This may seem a long way from understanding what goes on in contagion, but it does focus on two things, which undoubtedly have an important part: tension and what is commonly called suggestion, for which one conventional definition is "a form of symbolic communication—by words, pictures, or some similar device—aimed at inducing acceptance" (K. Young, 1956:52). Suggestion depends on beliefs, attitudes, and energies within the subject, which make him able and potentially willing to do what acceptance implies; it has no magical power to create capacities not already there. Even the feats of hypnotism prove no more; hypnotism merely allows us to see the full scope of potentialities that are ordinarily restrained and unused.

Tension, then, becomes our term for tendencies in the organism that are pressing for release by a suitable trigger (stimulus or symbol). Everyone is familiar with tension as a kind of surplus energy expressed in displacement activities, such as scratching one's head, biting nails, licking lips, lighting a cigarette, and polishing glasses. Such signs of tension occur among all the primates (Morris, 1967b:127, 139). In 1969 an American firm put on the market an "executive sandbox" as a "creative piece of furniture" for the homes of tense businessmen. "It's surprising how often I sit there and play in the sand," one delighted customer is reported to have said. "And when friends come over, they all look for the best place to sit on the ledge so they can play." Ordinarily, tension is hidden below the surface, held in—bottled if you please—by external or self-restraints. But "nervous" and insecure people often become more talkative (both suggestive to and suggestible from others). Also, as we often see in everyday life, tense people are easily overmastered by their own feelings or others' suggestions, if given the right trigger, so that they let go with force, like a door against which someone is pushing that is suddenly unlocked. Such may be the case of the rigid-but-tense person who is not easy to unbend but may be grateful for release (as in T-group therapy), or who swings from one rigid extreme to another in the manner of the Thurber fable, "The Bear Who Let It Alone" (the moral of which is "you might as well fall on your face as lean over too far backward").

For our purposes, the main point is that it is generally recognized that rising tension increases the likelihood of both individual and collective behavior when triggers are appropriate. Or one may put it as: Whatever the "strength" of a trigger may consist of (threat, authority, persuasiveness, etc.), tension reduces the strength needed, that is, lowers the threshold of response. In this sense, tension increases the readiness to let go. It is necessary to assume that tension can in some way build up, be stored, and spill over if the level gets too high; or it may burst forth if the right trigger opens the door. This is, of course, only an analogy and does not imply that there are no important differences between human and physical systems such as reservoirs and batteries, which store energy—these are not literal assertions but merely models, useful within limits.

For a whole society, the readiness to let go is well expressed by Boulding's (1965) term "supersaturation," which implies that protest acts as a kind of trigger for precipitation:

> Protest is most likely to be successful where it represents a view which is in fact widespread in the society, but which has somehow not been called to people's attention. . . . Societies, like solutions, get supersaturated or supercooled; that is, they reach a situation in which their present state is intrinsically unstable, but does not change because of the absence of some kind of nucleus around which change can grow. Under these circumstances, protest is like the seed crystal or the silver iodide in the cloud. It precipitates the whole system toward a position which it really ought to be in anyway. We see this exemplified in the relative success of the protest movements in civil rights. . . . Wherever there is hypocrisy, there is strong hope of change, for the hypocrite is terribly vulnerable to protest. On the other hand, in the absence of protest, the supersaturated society may go on for a long time without change, simply because of what physicists call the nucleation problem.
>
> When the society is not supersaturated, a protest movement has a much rougher time. It then has to move the society toward the new position, from which change can then crystallize out, and this is a much more difficult task than crystallizing change in a society that is ready for it. . . . That is, the techniques for creating the pre-conditions of change may be very different from the techniques required for crystallizing it. (Boulding, 1965:vi–viii.)

We may say that when President Nixon used the American gesture for "fed up to here" (hand below chin, palm down) with civil disorder, shortly after his election, he was expressing a state of tension among the "silent American" majority that would be equivalent to what Boulding meant by supersaturation, namely, a systemic leaning that could easily be helped by a push.

But everyone does not lean the same way, nor equally far; we need a simple model that takes account of both tension and suggestibility, and find it in the metaphor of tilted dominoes on a board which is also subject to tilt. We all know how dominoes fall when they are lined up, standing on end close together. This expresses how contagion would flow if there were a strong suggestion, everyone were susceptible, and conditions of communication were good. But we know that everyone is not equally vulnerable to contagion, even under good conditions of communication. This may be represented by supposing that each domino has its own "tilt," consisting of lack of squareness of the end on which it stands.

"Tilt" comes from two main variables, tension and suggestibility. A person who is tense wants to let go, and a person who is suggestible is ready to accept messages that urge him in certain directions. The most "tilted" (tense and/or suggestible) individuals will fall first, and carry along with them other members in a chain sequence that are sufficiently tilted in the right way. We must suppose that some of the dominoes are standing sideways to others and are sufficiently square on the bottom to be stable even when another falls against them. This would describe the situation of the person who stands firm in the midst of an almost universal contagion. But it also implies that a "tilted" domino *can* tip a straight one if general tension and suggestibility rise; that is, if there comes a time when "silly girls" can sway sensible judges and paranoids can make normal people suspicious. At some point, presumably, all the dominoes would fall over.

We can express this possibility of all dominoes falling by supposing that a general rise in tension is like a tilt of the board on which the dominoes stand. This is a systemic state of tension. When it approaches the tipping point for the "normal" domino, it enters that range which Boulding calls supersaturation. Yet, there seems to be no way of making the analogies match here except by supposing that a little glue of some kind holds the dominoes upright on the board for a time after they would ordinarily have fallen. Both metaphors have some, though limited, value for representing the availability of people for response to contagion.

Pursuing the domino analogy, we may say that suggestibility is represented by the direction in which dominoes face and the direc-

tion of their leaning. It is the factor that makes people more discriminative and which specifies the direction of contagion. It helps
answer the question of *which* people are most influenceable and to
what are they influenceable. A person is suggestible according to his
beliefs, attitudes, and values. It is also recognized by psychologists
that general persuasibility is a personality trait, which varies with
individuals regardless of topic. Women are generally more persuasible than men. Among men, the more persuasible are those with
rich imagery and strong empathy, low self-esteem, and who are
other-directed (Janis et al., 1959). It is generally recognized that
anxiety and insecurity increase suggestibility; for example, Sherif
and Harvey (1952) found that when subjects were asked to make
judgments of the autokinetic phenomenon in situations made uncertain by darkness, lack of spatial orientation, and so on, there was
greater convergence with the judgments of others.

Psychologists distinguish at least three types of suggestibility:
(1) primary (or psychomotor), in which people carry out a motor
movement upon repeated suggestion; (2) secondary suggestibility,
in which people will perceive or remember the thing suggested; and
(3) prestige suggestion, in which people change their opinion after
learning that a prestige person holds a different one. People who are
religiously conservative rate high on prestige suggestibility; likewise for authoritarians. More interesting, perhaps, for our purposes
is the finding that religious conservatives are higher in psychomotor
suggestibility, which seems to be especially strong among members
of revivalist churches, where responses like twitching, jerking, and
sudden conversion are common (Argyle, 1958). In general, such
findings help us tell which people in a mass will be most susceptible
to contagion and to what kind of pushes (suggestions) they will
topple.

The process of contagion, by this theory, would be expected to
have four main stages: (1) the fall of the first—most tense and
suggestible—"dominoes," which might or might not affect the majority, depending upon the general tension level; (2) the spread of
contagion to the middle of the group, the fall of a substantial number
of the respectable rank and file; (3) the "bandwagon effect,"
in which it seems that practically everyone is participating and that
failure to do so seems deviant; (4) the exhaustion of tension and
return of almost everyone to normal unresponsiveness and restraint
(standing dominoes). The boom, bubble, hysteria, or mania is over.

We may presume that the bulk of tensions that dispose many
people to such extraordinary collective actions are *systemic* in
origin, that is, come from *strains* generated by typical relationships
and chronic situations within the system. Structural strains are defined by Smelser (1962) as an "impairment of the relations among

and consequently inadequate functioning of the components. . . . 'Pressure' and 'malintegration' would suffice. . . ." According to Smelser, some form of structural strain "must be present if an episode of collective behavior is to occur. The more severe the strain, moreover, the more likely is such an episode." (Smelser, 1962:47–49.) This does not go so far as to say that every collective outburst or contagion must be preceded by a *structural* strain; but it does, on the other hand, tighten the connection of strain with collective behavior by defining it as a tension-producing factor. Systemic strain is nothing more than a continual source of excessive tension "built into" a system of relationships. For example, the prolonged presence of a mother-in-law in a wife's home is commonly recognized as a strain-producing tension in individuals, whereas an altercation over an automobile accident would not be systemic strain unless there were a high level of tension as part of a high rate of accidents produced by a traffic system or a culture of driving. Then you would have a systemic strain. In this way, strain as a major underlying source of widespread tension is the "tilt of the board" that favors mass contagion. Figure 6.1 illustrates this systemic relationship.

Much of the "tilt of the board" for Americans comes from the high cultural value placed on work and the drive for achievement, which leads to the famous pace of living ("drive, drive, drive") and the stress of adjusting to rapid change. Not the sluggish pace of bureaucracy (which has its own irritations) but the forefront of competition and innovation ("where the action is") is regarded as ideal. An expert on rocket construction, Dr. Kurt Debus, described the built-in stress of space work:

> There is so much tension, so much anxiety in putting man into space. And we've lived with it so long now. Yes, we've lost men because of family problems. When a man is so dedicated that the NASA program becomes his personal life, it takes much time away from wife and children. We need a great many understanding wives here and we devote a great deal of time in trying to make them so. We take them on tours and we entertain them—but in the end we usually have to tell them their husbands will be working even harder next year. Such exposure to stress is rare elsewhere. We live with it constantly. In fact, it is so much with us that we are studying it—how is it affecting our hearts, our nerves, our functions, our aging process? We don't know yet. (J. Rogers, 1969.)

The fact that the United States ranks twenty-sixth among modern nations in life expectancy suggests that systemic strain is widespread and has little or no relation to sheer hardship and low standard of living. Indeed, the high standard of living increases the strain of mobility and stress from such things as overeating and

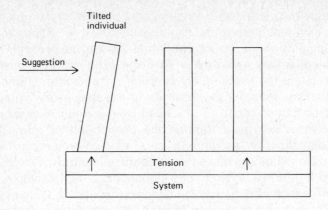

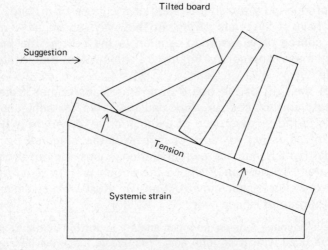

FIGURE 6.1.   Systemic strain as the "tilt of the board."

noise, which is coming to be recognized as a serious source of
tension caused by the increasing number and audibility of gadgets.
Urban congestion is an important strain; so are information and
education when they cause an underprivileged class to perceive
more clearly what they are not getting, leading to a tension of
blockage favoring deviant behavior (Merton, 1968:211). But even
prolonged television commercials are a systemic strain that makes
many people uptight. Defining strain as chronic tension production
in a system does not require that we show it to be inadequate
functioning. This is perhaps a better way to view the problems of
abundant societies, which often seem to be functioning quite ade-

quately in the distribution of material goods, yet which have dispro-
portionately high tension.

A direct connection between systemic strain and social contagion is seen in the matter of inadequate communication. When
channels on which people rely for news and reassurance are dis-
rupted, outbursts become much more likely. Failure of the "grapevine" of gossip or of the supply of public news, or loss of confidence
in the credibility of news (for example known or suspected censorship) increases the flow of rumors. Shibutani said—

> Unsatisfied demand for news—the *discrepancy* between information
> needed to come to terms with the changing environment and what is
> provided by formal news channels—constitutes the crucial condition
> of rumor construction. . . . When activity is interrupted for want of
> adequate information, frustrated men must piece together some kind
> of definition, and rumor is the collective transaction through which
> they try to fill this gap. (Shibutani, 1966:62.)

Likewise, "wildcat" strikes are seen to be a product of systemic
strains consisting of inadequate communication flow between labor
and management; for example, poor grievance procedures and disruption of the plant "grapevine," which cause a rise of tension that
cannot be eased through institutionalized channels (J. F. Scott and
Homans, 1947; Gouldner, 1954). However, although disorganization
of communication usually means strain, we cannot conclude that
organization of communication necessarily means less tension.
Organized groups may have more tension precisely because they
communicate better. For example, an experimental comparison of
organized and unorganized groups (French, 1941) in situations of
frustration (insoluble problems or motor-skill tasks), and also under
conditions of fear, showed that the organized groups—which had
higher "we" feeling, motivation, interdependence, and participation
—also had more frustration (because better motivated) and more
interpersonal aggression in the form of blaming, joking, and scapegoating, though these tensions were not severe enough to disrupt
the groups. In short, because they were better motivated, the groups
were more frustrated, and because they communicated better, tension spread more easily. Another point to bear in mind is that improved communication, in terms of sheer amount of information
available, can become a systemic strain in terms of "information
overload," to be discussed in Chapter 9. In such cases it becomes a
question of whether "poor" or "good" communication produces a
higher level of tension.

Another relationship we need to take into better account is that
between systemic strains and popular moods. It seems plain that

contagions which involve whole nations, millions of people, and which may last for years (red scares, war fevers, stock-market booms, crusades, gold fevers, revivalism, witch hysteria, persecution of Christians in Rome, Reign of Terror, ghetto rioting, style rebellion in America and Europe) are sustained by more than the momentary tensions that seem to be discharged within days or weeks (invasion from Mars, Mattoon gasser, windshield-pitting epidemic, and so on). Of course, such brief epidemics may be only a "storm squall" of a larger one. Historians characterize such periods as epochs; for example, a "season of heroes"; the mood of austerity in England after World War II; American guilt following the Civil War bloodbath (which historians recognize as having influenced the symbolism of the Lincoln assassination; Basler, 1935); a "gilded age"; and "age of reform" (Hofstadter, 1955)—in all these examples, a certain outlook and temper seem to prevail and give a style to the era. We may think of this as a collective mood, moving in like a storm front and, during the time it lingers, making "showers" and "squalls" likely, that is, impelling people toward certain kinds of activities. Such a mood presumably consists of a common way of looking at things because certain kinds of perceptions, images, and sentiments are uppermost in people's minds in a milieu of tensions arising from the system. A meteorological analogy enables us to relate such emotional "weather" to systemic factors that are as observable to the sociologist as water evaporation, air circulation, and cloud formation are to the meteorologist. We presume, in other words, that careful observation of the formation of images, moods, and tensions will permit us to predict well in advance the kinds of contagions likely to occur. Prediction such as this depends on whether the changes are—

1. capable of being charted
2. continuous and gradual, or discontinuous and sudden
3. cyclical
4. fluctuating between extremes

Such moods are probably systemic by-products, and the time of their formation may be the "supersaturation" phenomenon of which Boulding speaks. To build up a mood may require a complex interaction of systemic tensions, millions of words and pictures in publications, and an undercurrent of rumors before the mood is mature enough to be crystallized by a slogan, an accusation, or dramatic deed of a symbolic leader.

To summarize, the preceding consideration of tension theory suggests the following propositions:

1. Without excessive tension, extraordinary contagion is impossible; the less the tension, the more trigger is needed. Trigger "strength" (authority, threat, persuasibility, and so on) declines with rise in tension.

At some point, threshold resistance becomes zero; that is, no trigger is needed.

2. It is possible for a system or an individual to hold excessive tension, in a manner suggested by Boulding's supercooling metaphor, past the point of first possible outburst (probably by homeostatic mechanisms), but the longer it is held, the less trigger needed.

3. The most tense and/or suggestible people are leaders of contagions.

4. Widespread contagions are likely to be the result of systemic strains; reduction of systemic strain reduces the number and severity of contagions.

4a. Scapegoating will increase with rise of aggressive tension or systemic strain.

5. The direction of contagion is not determined by the amount or source of tension, since usually there are many possible outlets and displacement occurs easily (the analogy is of a flowing and spilling stream).

6. The probable direction of contagion depends on what people are suggestible to, that is, pre-existing symbols and attitudes; but this does not preclude emergence of new symbols and attitudes, especially in crisis.

7. The number of people involved in extraordinary mass contagions will depend upon their availability (Kornhauser, 1959); that is, the extent to which group relationships favor or restrain their participation—for example, role obligations, absorption in work or community activities,

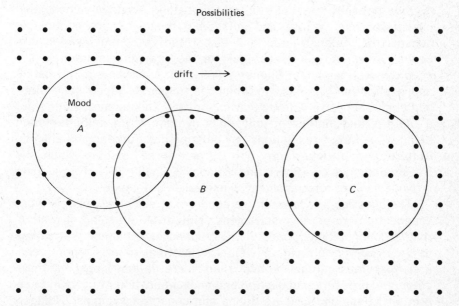

FIGURE 6.2. The changing "weather" of popular moods: moods as emotional learning or suggestibility; and mystiques as non-rational symbolic formations.

peer-group pressure, mobility, alienation, isolation. The sociometry of mass contagion is still much in need of study.

We turn now from physical metaphors to the theory of symbolic transactions.

Mass Contagions as Symbolic Negotiations

The "tilted domino" theory helped us to visualize in a simple way how tension and suggestibility favor mass contagion—why it spreads to *some* people at *some* times and not to others. But it is only a model and, like any model, has limits. One limit is that it does not explain emergence of symbols in transactions as collaborative, creative processes. According to tension theory, if a "toppling of dominoes" occurs, it does so only when the meaning of a "trigger" as a symbol has been adequately established and perceived (the right interpretation made). Until this time, tension waits "in storage" within individuals, unable to collectivize (contage). Tension makes people more ready to look for, and read meanings into, signs, but the question of how situations and signs become meaningful is ignored.

The basic premise of symbolic interaction theory is that men do not respond to mechanical triggers (stimuli), but to situations as defined, that is, meanings constructed and communicated. Neither do they transmit messages as impulses along a pathway unchanged except for energy loss and noise, but meanings are continually constructed, reconstructed, and elaborated as communication proceeds. To remind ourselves again of the symbolic interaction perspective, we may quote Blumer (1969a): Interaction is a "formative and explorative" process in which participants "judge each other and guide their own acts by that judgment." The human being is not a "neutral and indifferent unit" in a system, but a self-interacting being who "forges his actions" by defining his situation and objects. Culture and structure are only "frameworks" within which the transaction goes on (Sherif and Wilson, 1953:199–201). This judging is what negates the mechanical nature of any model.

The question arises when we equate that seemingly simple word "suggestion" to another statement: If a certain meaning of a situation is communicated, people will respond in a manner that seems to them appropriate, in the light of information and other meanings that they already know. Then there is no longer uniform, automatic pressure; suggestion becomes a question of how we interpret situations and how we define and construct symbols. "Triggering" becomes a function of what goes on as men construct interpretations that permit action to proceed on a new basis, and its progress determines how many stages of definition there are, each requiring time and collaboration. The best metaphor is not "transmission of an influence," but "men constructing a platform," each level of which rests upon preceding levels or stages of a negotiation through which parties must go together, and which will break down if they cannot construct common ground for the next step.

A mechanical transmission model fits cases where there is little elaboration of meaning, and output is close to input. For example the "invasion from Mars" panic took place within a few hours; there was no way to tell that the popular definition of the situation varied greatly from the program input. But in a hysteria that lasts weeks, months, years, it is quite another matter to say input equals output. The historical evidence is that the perspective of an era does change, and along with it the definitions of situations. Multiple inputs—by word of mouth (person to person), crowds, other kinds of groups, and various media—would lead us to expect development of new images, even if a mechanical model of transmission were retained; and all the more so if each person reconstructed the situation each time he received and passed on a message. Therefore, the presumption is that prolonged "contagion" involving many people in many kinds of interaction does not keep a character that matches the input, but develops according to laws of its own. Rumor, for example, follows several different courses of development, none so simple as the patterns supposed by Allport and Postman (Allport and Postman, 1947; Peterson and Gist, 1951; Buckner, 1965; Shibutani, 1966).

Even in "fast fuse" contagions—as we may call those that occur in a few minutes or hours—defining processes seem to be there at the very beginning. Beliefs and stereotypes are, of course, readymade symbols. But even when an established situation or stereotyped view of things is suddenly shattered, as in a disaster, defining processes seem to go right to work to provide interpretations by which people can act together. Interviews of about a thousand persons involved in disasters (conducted by the Disaster Team of the National Opinion Research Center of the University of Chicago) contradicted the prevailing view of panic as an animalistic stampede, and showed a considerable development of imagery, definitions of the situation, and "high order sign behavior, including complex and socialized emoting, perceiving and remembering." (Quarantelli, 1957; Schultz, 1964.) Sociologists who have arrived at the scene of a disaster shortly after its occurrence have been impressed with the amount of spontaneous cooperation and mutual understanding that developed very quickly. It is no surprise, of course, to find people helping themselves and their own families, but it is another thing to engage in rescue and service to strangers. Of a tornado that hit a community in Michigan, Form and Nosow (1958) reported that, contrary to some commonly held opinions, "people do not become completely incapacitated during a crisis." Rather, "most persons tend to do things that they have learned are appropriate for emergency situations, even though they may never have been involved in an actual crisis." Activities are "not random," but "there is a tendency for rescuers to assume functions that are most appropriate for them." Many of these are, of course, traditional patterns, such as helping neighbors. But more impressive was the ability of the rescuers to improvise common actions that might be expected to come from professionals, such as fire departments and Red Cross:

> Perhaps the most striking fact about the rescue activities was what the Beecherites did for themselves. There was unanimous agreement among both victims and rescuers that the Beecher people had gone a long way toward taking care of themselves before any other outside groups came into the area. How did they do this in the rainy darkness without electric power, without special equipment or outside aid? The same questions were asked when Londoners and Berliners were being bombarded nightly. And yet the people took care of themselves, not without casualties, but without the predicted panic and disorganization. . . . Their earliest activities were looking for and aiding specific family members, friends, and neighbors; in cases where family members, friends, and neighbors were unhurt, other types of activity emerged first. People tended to look around and appraise what had happened. They took stock of propetry damage, but usually did not stop there. They began looking for victims whether they knew them or not. They performed first aid, transported victims to aid stations, and did other things to facilitate rescue. The feverish, purposive activities, the lack of shock, and the constructive organized behavior of both victims and rescuers are difficult to conceive. Perhaps what was most remarkable at this time was that the activities were selflessly directed toward others. (Form and Nosow, 1958:61–62.)

Specific actions during the temporary allocation of functions in the emergency stage included: stock taking, testing telephone and radio, salvage of property, search for others, announcement of survival, first aid, summoning aid, providing shelter and clothing, care of children, calming, general search for victims, clearing roads and accesses, directing traffic, digging out victims and loading them in cars, evacuation of injured and corpses to collection points, obtaining and providing equipment, and providing drink and food. "Those exhibiting symptoms of panic or shock were not less active than others . . . as a matter of fact, as a group, they maintained a consistently higher activity rate." Nor did professionalism have much to do with it. Firemen reported that tasks performed by volunteers "were the same as their own" (Form and Nosow, 1958:23, 61–

63, 86, 166). Loomis (1960) noted the development of "an amazing consensus" within a few days after a disaster.

> The much stepped-up rate of interaction largely dealing with the disaster tends to standardize all the reports of what constituted reality. . . . Group solidarity usually begins to increase. . . . An aura of euphoria, of brotherly love, of altruistic endeavor. . . . Thus . . . mounting solidarity is observable in the afflicted area at the time the second phase becomes operative: the arrival of community agencies . . . . Sentiments coalesce a considerable time after the events that precipitate the sentiments. The listener hears weird, bizarre, and horrifying stories: the bus driver who was hampered in helping the passengers by his almost severed, dangling thumb which he tried to bite off; the automobile that shot up in the air and descended with a woman's body draped across it, landing without even blowing a tire. . . . When the . . . disastrous events are finally seen in retrospect by the participant, and as he interacts at a high rate with other participants on the constant theme of the disaster, the burden of sentiment assumes great proportions. . . . Anyone who has visited a disaster area within a few days after the disaster can testify to the onerous burden that is communicated to anyone who will listen. Later these doleful sentiments are sometimes communicated by improvised songs in cultures like the Mexican. . . . As the third stage of disaster comes into prominence, what has been called the "halo effect" of the very generally shared goal coupled with a satisfying internal interaction pattern, lingers so that the heightened community solidarity can be noted well into the rehabilitation stage. (Loomis, 1960:136–142.)

Nor does halo effect require a pre-established community. An earthquake in Los Angeles, in February 1971, which killed over sixty people and inflicted over a billion dollars in damages, brought out "a wave of neighborliness and good Samaritanism" among people who did not know one another:

> A wave of neighborliness and good Samaritanism is washing across the stricken area. "This is a time when we come to realize just how good people can be. . . . Friends found us and offered us use of their home . . . And neighbors came around and gave us food and water." . . . "As soon as we checked our own families, groups of neighbors went from house to house to see if everybody was all right." . . . "People responded abundantly. Families came and offered rooms in their homes. They brought clothes and supplies. The supermarkets, drive-ins, and other stores gave us more food than we could possibly use. Even the long-haired hippies dove right in and helped us." . . . A 14-year-old boy took it upon himself to direct traffic for 10 straight hours in a jammed intersection when no policemen were available. (Sitomer, 1971.)

Quarantelli (1970) calls such Samaritans *emergent accommodation groups*, in which internal activities are highly cooperative and external aims and actions are integrative. Such collectivities emerge in a *"consensus crisis* situation," in which there is general agreement about goals and what should be done; and looting, panic, and other antisocial behavior are rare. By contrast, *"dissensus" crises,* in which factions are in sharp disagreement about goals and values, give rise to the *conflict groups* that comprise so much of the traditional subject matter of collective behavior. (See also Barton's analysis of altruistic community response in disaster, 1969:203–279.)

So, panic and disaster—which we may call "short fuse" transactions—are not vacuums of meaning but are collaborative processes in which rich consensus and improvised cooperation are generated. There is apparently no raw perception at the beginning of new events or at the point where old structures break down. Symbols intervene at every juncture, but we cannot identify them because rarely does one sit around watching closely, hoping that with luck, insight, or technique, he can catch the unfolding of meaning.

In "slow fuse" contagions—as we may call those that last a considerable time and have many inputs—we are in a position to sit and watch, and can see that more is going on than the transmission model (toppling dominoes) can handle. As an example, consider the contagion of unrest that developed in America during the 1960s over deterioration of the environment. Americans began to perceive that their environment was contaminated. People had breathed bad air in big cities for decades (bad air has existed in Chicago for over twenty-five years) and had never given it a thought. Rather suddenly, pollution became publicly visible; one could see— in air, rivers, lakes, ocean, soil, foods—an environment steeped in poisons. Even color television was dangerous when viewed nearer than six feet. How did this happen? Was it due to any dramatic increase in pollution? On the contrary, the environment had actually *improved* greatly for most people (think, for example, of the life of a chimney sweep in London at the time of Oliver Twist). But the ability to *see* faults had increased much faster than any change— for better or worse—in the environment. It was a change in *vision* —our images, not physical conditions—that produced the tension about pollution in the 1960s. This was a symbolic task, a development that could be traced through various symbolic events. It really began, perhaps, with the publication of Rachel Carson's *Silent Spring* in 1962, which opened people's eyes about the effect of insecticides, especially DDT, on wildlife. The agitation of groups like the Sierra Club for the protection of the environment became more urgent. Dramatic news stories such as the Santa Barbara oil spill created a vivid image of destruction of environment and wildlife. The "smog" of Los Angeles spread to cities which had not seen it before. Industries responsible for pollution began to feel apologetic and published advertisements like the following:

> THE EFFLUENT SOCIETY: HOW CAN WE HELP CLEAN IT UP. Each day, 173,000,000,000 gallons of sewage and waste flow into the waters of America. As a result, many of our rivers and lakes are dying. Some are already dead. And year after year, the rate of pollution is steadily increasing as our population continues to grow. . . . But there is no reason why our useable water supply cannot be saved. . . . X Corporation is a major supplier of water pollution control equipment . . . .

A bustle of "environmental studies" programs in universities began in 1969. A boiling political issue was ready to burst into steam; politicians began to line up. By the end of the decade, spontaneous drives for laws against polluters of the environment were springing up all over—for example, the California "People's Lobby." The point is that in these years a *view* of things was taking shape. "Environment," "noise," "ugliness," "conservation," "ecological balance," got new meanings. Even man got new meaning as he began to see himself as destroyer, polluter of his own environment. This was a significant symbolic change. Only after such meanings of the environment had been built up, which made people "uptight," could agitation "contage"; people could get excited, indignant, and alarmed about something they could see and talk about. Contagion had to wait for a symbolic development.

This is seen just as clearly in the widespread rebellion against "repressive" culture and institutions, which became so prominent among university and high school students during the later 1960s. Everywhere the refrain among campus rebels was how insensitive and inhuman the educational system was; yet how desperately did teachers try to develop curricula that would be more student-centered and "relevant." But they could not keep pace with rising demands and expectations. Students vied with each other to find faults and infringements on their freedom. Dissatisfaction became contagious; asking students to air grievances led to discovery of others they had not thought of before. It was like opening a Pandora's box. The truth was that the educational system had never been so good and so unrepressive for so many people. But an unexpected by-product of modern living was that it was generating images of what one had a right to expect—an ability to see faults—much faster than its real improvements could keep up with.

The tensions of modern society were largely the result of proliferating *images* (from many inputs) that made it possible for more and more people to become discontented with conditions that were getting better and better. One began to see the spectacle of teachers experimenting desperately with programs—almost pleading with students to like what they were trying to do—while students took the attitude of sitting back with folded arms, saying to each other, "Just look at the tricks they are up to now!" This deterioration of images could not be explained by the worsening of the educational system or the gross failure of teachers trying to do a good job, for it was not in underprivileged slum schools that such reactions were happening but in some of the more advanced and favored programs.

This tension in the schools was only one sector of a larger front, a contagion of unrest fostered by the idea that there was something wrong with abundance and, by implication, progress, which stood in the way of full self-realization. This has been called the *new romanticism* (Klapp, 1969:87). A frustration of self-realization began to be blamed on the "plastic" values of the "establishment." The sources of this explosion of discontent are so numerous it is difficult to list them. Some came under the guise of "civil rights" agitation, though the new romantics could not fully harmonize and coordinate their demands with those of minorities. A signal event for the new rebels was the 1965 Berkeley uprising, including the "filthy speech" demonstration. A "new left" point of view took shape in publications like *Ramparts* magazine and the writings of Herbert Marcuse. Student leaders, such as Daniel Cohn-Bendit on the Continent, went from country to country spreading the new point of view. Demonstrations of students in many other countries showed the worldwide character of the discontent. The claims of the new romanticism became established in America by symbols such as "doing your thing," escaping from "hang-ups," "repressive culture," "plastic" values, "turn on, tune in, drop out," "make love not war," "groovy," and "mind bending."

But the new romanticism was not confined to one group; it became inextricably mixed with the discontent of all kinds of groups that began to find voices. Brown power and Red power joined Black power. In 1969 even the "silent majority" began to demand a voice. *Time* reported that even women were beginning to regard themselves as a minority (51 percent) and declare war on what they called "sexist" society, picketing the Miss America contest and dumping brassieres into trash cans because they were symbols of female "oppression" (*Time*, Nov. 21, 1969:53). Everybody seemed to be "getting into the act." Looking at somebody else's claims made people look back at their own. This was a trigger to invidious comparison and self-examination, which was sure, if it looked long enough, to find cause for complaint, especially since symbols were becoming so available and numerous. What the new romanticism did was add new dimensions to the "explosion of expectations" that had been so visible in developing countries.

Since the new romanticism was not grounded in material, economic, or political grievances, it helped a contagion of unrest to flow easily into affluent countries. The paradox, then, was that the wealthiest country in the world, with one of the most liberal constitutions in the world, could claim leadership in unrest, and could explode at many levels. All this made little sense if viewed in the light of how much worse off others were in underdeveloped countries. The fact that things had been getting materially better (constant rise of GNP, per capita income, welfare services, and proportion of population with educational opportunity) did not prevent this contagion. To trace the actual sources of tension is beyond the scope of our study here. The point is merely that the appearance of images and symbols of discontent made contagion easy in classes for which it would otherwise have been difficult; that is, these classes were inert until appropriate symbols (and the realities they made visible) had been constructed. The particular directions in which unrest could "contage" depended in part on what symbols lay ready and waiting.

What this all adds up to is that people can generate innumerable tensions by images alone (independent of material realities), and that the abundance of such tension-producing images is an unexpected by-product of the modern system. New troubles were becoming visible that no one had seen before and had never suspected would be possible in an abundant society. (Such a radical change of visibility of troubles had happened a century before with the discovery of disease germs. But the tensions these images produced were not worse than the superstitious terrors they replaced. We cannot be so sure about the images being produced by the modern world.)

Symbolic Thresholds and Tasks

The preceding examples are meant to illustrate that contagions do not diffuse in a mechanical way but depend on the development of appropriate symbols that enable people to see certain realities and communicate such images easily. They suggest that there are certain symbolic tasks and negotiations which must be completed before mass contagions can proceed, and that the resistance to communication without adequate symbols must be thought of as a threshold to be passed. Indeed, it is possible that such symbolic tasks might constitute a series of necessary stages for mass contagions if they are to run their full course. At this time they cannot be put into empirical sequence, but we can begin by postulating that contagions must pass certain thresholds, each of which is associated with a symbolic task; we can distinguish five such symbolic tasks and put them in what seems a logically plausible provisional order:

1. Formation of a preconditioning mood
2. Symbolic bargain transaction:
   (a) Formulation of tensions as grievances
   (b) Dramatization
   (c) Collective collaboration to make a symbol that belongs to all
3. Construction of goals and programs, including anticipatory consummations
4. "Bandwagon" as legitimation
5. Morale and "we" formation

For the sake of comparison with another theoretical scheme, all this occurs within stages 3 through 5 of what Smelser (1962) calls "value-added" process. Each stage is discussed below.

(1) It is *formation of a preconditioning mood* that causes people to lean unwittingly toward certain kinds of expression and involvement before they have adequate symbols that represent what they themselves feel. We have already encountered the "emotional weather" that comes in like a storm front, lingers, and creates an epoch with a characteristic outlook. The probable source of such moods, as suggested, is probably tensions resulting from systemic strains. At the beginning, systemic tensions, like those that are truly individual, are private; each person—if he recognizes them—imagines himself alone to be the deposit of these tensions, doesn't know how to verbalize them, and lacks confidence in them as legitimate grievances. He may discover through experiences such as those of T-groups that others have such feelings, but they must be publicly voiced and rationalized (consensual validation) before they can be shared.

(2) Even with a preconditioning mood, contagion is by no means inevitable. It depends upon *symbolic bargain transactions* by which people construct a situation that can be shared. (a) To begin a symbolic bargain, tensions must be *formulated*; otherwise, individuals are alone with their problem. Suppose something bothers you, such as a need for animal regulation because dogs are upsetting your trash cans. Your neighbor is "uptight," perhaps about a marital tension. The third neighbor down the line is having trouble with his work. What will bring all three together into a symbolic bargain so that you can agree upon the nature or source of trouble?

Perhaps no bargain is possible. A changing society is generating all kinds of tensions that cannot—and perhaps never will—be formulated as problems and grievances about which anything can be done.

However, perhaps a leader (often called a demagogue) will find a way to tie together a considerable amount of this pervasive tension into one symbol—gather it up, like lint, into a ball and throw it to people. There is no rigorous logical connection between sources of tension and objects of action (psychologists call this *displacement*, whereas logicians might call it *faulty abstraction*). But if an activity can occur, such as a public protest or demonstration (in which there is a satisfying catharsis of tension) or a hostile confrontation that drives people into opposite camps, there will not be much objection to the logical difficulty of the symbolic bargain that results. Once a symbolic bargain is reached, it serves as a vehicle for both arousing and working off more and more tension as people become more involved in activities.

Such a symbolic bargain, especially when it comes from widely different sources of tension, cannot be considered as a simple mirroring of each other's views, an imitative kind of consensus. There may remain considerable differences of feeling among those who share the same symbolic bargain. Scheff (1967) distinguished three kinds of consensus from "dissensus" in which people do not agree, and who understand that they do not agree: *monolithic consensus*, in which a majority agrees and understands that there is agreement; *pluralistic ignorance*, in which a majority agrees but thinks there is disagreement; and *false consensus*, in which the majority do not agree but think that they agree. For widespread mass action a gigantic compromise of various kinds of consensus must be achieved. But, once an acceptable symbol is formed, though people may still have different kinds of tension, they are no longer alone. They have a voice, at least, which they can share together.

(b) *Dramatization* is one of the most helpful vehicles for mass symbolic bargains. Drama has a universal appeal; that is, its basic forms can be appreciated by people from widely differing cultures because it is based on the human capacity for identification, the ability to put ourselves in the shoes of others in differing circumstances, even to feel sympathy with animals and natural forces. A dramatic event (such as Mrs. Rosa Park's refusal to give her seat to a White man, provoking the Montgomery bus strike) is often seen as the threshold over which a movement passes to a new level of consensus and action, drawing in people who were not previously interested. In such cases, it might seem that contagion could not proceed until a dramatic view supplemented the factual representation of the problem, since drama has more power to create meaning, to transfer tension to a new symbol, than does a logical or verbal connection. Meanings do not emerge from dry, mechanical transactions and logical arguments as often as they do from dramas; when feelings run high, people confront one another and reveal themselves with spontaneous expressions, and rich language and metaphor open realms of imagery. At such times, meanings "come alive," the image shines, the moment blooms. So, as we well know, public speakers and leaders strive constantly to dramatize and metaphorize, to get their point across, to make the meaning come alive.

The *audience* of drama is that kind of collectivity in which one is taken out of oneself (that is, diverted into self-forgetfulness) by a vicarious journey. In such experience there is privatized dreaming with minimal crowd interaction—indeed, the audience may be dispersed. The transaction of vicarious experience is through *role taking*, not discussion as with the public; that is to say, the salient objects are roles and plot patterns rather than verbal issues and problems. In general, drama tends to unify people at a nondiscursive level, whereas discussion tends to divide the public. (See Chapter 8.)

The abstraction (symbolic bargain) of drama occurs through the process of role casting, in which certain parties become representatives (as heroes, villains, fools, victims, martyrs, scapegoats, and so on) of things that concern people. The dramatic action is usually what assigns the roles and enables people to see more clearly the meaning of the issues as personal actions (symbolic gestures). Thus, dramas become vehicles for mass vicarious experience—bringing people together on the common ground of sympathy for a victim or in admiration of a hero or hatred of a villain—and the catharsis of dramatic climax. Drama is precisely the kind of transaction that allows an audience of diverse tensions to pour all their feeling into one encounter, issue, or role by virtue of the great, distinctively human, capacity for identification. Its dynamics and patterns as a principle of mass action have been explored in various studies (Duncan, 1962; K. and G. Lang, 1961; Klapp, 1962, 1964a,b).

Rebellion is a form of mass action in which drama has an especially important role in helping people to formulate a situation in which they can share. For rebellion to occur, it is not only necessary to arouse hostility toward some villain and allow people to share such feeling as a symbolic bargain. It is also necessary to help people recognize that some villain is the source of their frustration, to help them cast blame against "they who" cause the frustration, and to see authority (of law, leadership, government, the establishment) in a villain role. Thus, conspicuous stages in the development of almost any historical rebellion have been dramas in which people were seen as victims suffering injustice from authorities cast as villains; or scenes in which heroes had the courage to stand against authorities. Thus, the nobility of these rebellious roles proved both that the authorities were weak enough to dare to attack and bad enough to deserve attack. Hence, the task of dramatizing rebellion is to destroy legitimacy of authority (by converting erstwhile heroes into villains by roles showing "you can't be good and do that!"), and to legitimize rebel roles. Such legitimation rallies and mobilizes people to join protest and revolt (topples the dominoes) and helps build rebel morale. It is plausible to hypothesize that mass contagion of rebellion cannot proceed very far until such a drama has been completed.

(c) Once an initial symbolic bargain has been struck, perhaps by a drama that aroused great interest, multiple inputs such as rumor, biography, and news add to the image and allow quick formation of a symbol even more satisfactory to many people and which becomes a common focus for *collective collaboration.* The initial drama may have been a lucky "hit," only momentarily satisfactory, but rumor and popular interpretation weave a more satisfactory formulation. The more inputs, the better—for of all that is thought and said, the most dramatic and colorful will be singled out to find pragmatically a symbolic bargain most satisfying to most people. Of course this does not rule out factionalization of audiences who see the same figure in opposed terms (as villain and as hero). In any case, if a public figure can reach the stage where there is widespread popular collaboration in building his image, he is almost assured of success as a popular symbol, though not always on the terms he bargained for.

(3) It is fairly plain that *goals and programs* are symbolic constructions that often occur after contagions get under way. Obviously, if a contagion is to go anywhere as a movement, it must create pictures of what it wants that will last over time and of what it is going to do to get where it wants to go. Otherwise, it will be, at it were, stopped at the expressive stage of outbursts, which lead to nothing. One of the images it may need to create is that of a dramatic consummation, a symbolic payoff that is expected to occur at the end of the agitation or movement. The lack of these things is a handicap. For example, during the late 1960s, the New Left agitation, though it had rich images of discontent, was vague about goals and open to charges of being "anarchic" and of having destructive divisions within its own ranks. This happened because leaders were unable to formulate a clear picture of goals (beyond vague talk about "participatory democracy") and methods of achieving them, beyond sporadic outbursts and opportunistically riding on the coattails of other group demonstrations, especially those of "Black power." Stopping the war in Vietnam was, of course, a goal shared with various groups, including Senate "doves" and "Mothers for Peace," but left little that the New Left could claim as its own. Thus, the New Left, at the end of the 1960s, was unable to recruit

larger numbers, or even hold together its own ranks, unless it could achieve a dramatic, symbolic, anticipatory image of a distinctive payoff that would be realized sooner or later.

If vilification is viewed as a social process of spreading and organizing popular hostility against "enemies," it may be conceived as having certain symbolic tasks. One is creating moral alarm: We find the collective symbolic construction of the villain and his treatment to be a process having four stages: (1) development of unrest by a general feeling of moral alarm—that there is a moral crisis, not merely a disaster, produced by and calling for the image of the evil work of a villain; (2) growth of demand through communication for a specific villain to fit the moral alarm that has been aroused; (3) organizing and carrying out collective action against the villain— whether institutional processes or spontaneous collective action; and (4) creation through communication, such as drama and ritual, of a consummatory image of the fate or treatment of the villain, which will imply that society has been strengthened or saved (entropy reduced), and will leave a residue of satisfaction in group memory (Klapp, 1959).

On the other hand, mass contagions in the brighter end of the spectrum (booms, bubbles, expressive movements) have to focus on the symbolic task of building a rosier picture of consummation. Some of the films of 1969, which featured a hippie-style fulfillment ("Alice's Restaurant," "Easy Rider," "Midnight Cowboy"), seemed to be helping create a popular image of self-fulfillment through "kicks" of one kind or another, and unquestionably appealed to some American youth as attractive life styles. (See Chapter 11.)

(4) The *"bandwagon"* effect in mass contagion can be considered as a symbolic task. In this sense, the bandwagon effect is not merely the weight of large numbers swinging the remaining holdouts into coming along (as we saw in the baboon troop when stragglers followed the move of the center)—sometimes called the "mass principle"—nor is it simply the "prestige" of majorities. Rather, it is the point where enough of the right kinds of people *legitimize* an action as right, respectable, not merely popular. At such a point, people who have been "stuffy" about participating in an activity that seemed silly or somewhat disreputable, give up their objections and join the action. Moreover, such a legitimation provides not merely an example to imitate, but also normative pressure; that is, "you are wrong if you don't get on the bandwagon." Viewed in this light, the "rightness" of the bandwagon effect is a symbolic stage comparable to a graduation, professional certification, or a court conviction or exoneration. What the symbolic view of bandwagon effect does is take the emphasis off numbers and

put it on the symbolic value of the kinds of people who ride the bandwagon, and the meaning of the actions in which they are engaged. As with other symbolic stages, it negates the mechanical character of the concept of contagion.

Panic is usually viewed as a demoralization of a crowd or mass by fear, in which cooperation and concern for others are lost, consensus breaks down, and each looks out just for himself (K. and G. Lang, 1961:83; Quarantelli, 1970). Yet it, too, is conceivable as sometimes a symbolic bargain of legitimation rather than merely the mass effect of everyone running away. In such cases, panic would involve what might be called a reverse bandwagon effect of legitimizing flight by implying that the organization to which loyalty was owed is no longer in existence. The sight of others fleeing then signifies the all-rightness and respectability of running away.

(5) *Morale* must be built if there is to be any movement beyond temporary involvement in contagion. Morale is a kind of "we" feeling about goals, a sense of participation in collective purpose. Its beginning was observed in the "halo" effect of disasters. But the full development of morale is plainly a long-term process, belonging at the end of the series of symbolic tasks of contagion, because it grows on inputs from shared tasks and sacrifices and is based upon retrospective of what we mean to each other together. However, quick spurts of "we" feeling can occur as part of the development of contagions. For example, the "Six Day War," of Israel with Egypt was an electric wave of excitement, not only to Jews everywhere but also to non-Jews, for it reached outside its arena and stimulated all sympathizers with a kind of vicarious "we" feeling. No small number of immigrants to Israel (for example, Scandinavians) were captured by the romance of joining the cause.

To the extent that symbolic tasks we have reviewed here—formation of preconditioning mood, symbolic bargain transactions, construction of goals and programs, bandwagon as legitimation, and morale and "we" formation—are part of the process of mass contagion, the spread of such messages depends not only on the amount of tension people feel about a matter, but also on the symbolic tasks they can negotiate to share their mood with others. Seeing contagion as symbolic transactions shows the inadequacy of the "domino" theory to explain the long-fuse—and for that matter, the short-fuse—transaction. At every point, meanings must be constructed and shared by symbolic bargains that have to be worked at if not already made. However, this does not mean that sheer mechanical tension theory is not useful as a model for looking at popular contagions, especially when they occur rapidly and have few different channels of input.

Conclusion

In this chapter we surveyed five common types of mass contagion: anxiety, hostility, rebellion, enthusiasm and hope, and expressive outbursts.

Tension theory is applied to these by means of a "domino" metaphor, which envisages people succumbing to mass contagion, that is, responding to triggers, when sufficiently "tilted" by tension and suggestibility. General tension—the kind most likely to involve the most people—is related to systemic strains. The main proposition is that the greater the amount of tension generated by systemic strains, the greater the likelihood that mass contagion will occur. However, tension level gives little hint of what direction contagion might take, this being better answered by the question of what people are suggestible to or about.

Shortcomings of the tension model were pointed out, especially the assumption that the operation of a trigger and the transmission of contagion from person to person are mechanical processes rather than symbolic transactions in which people continually create new meanings and construct by symbols the situations to which they respond. This view is offered, not as the "right" one but simply as an alternative model, for trying to understand collective contagions, especially when they are longer lasting and have many inputs. In this view, a contagion is seen to proceed by passing thresholds that mark negotiation of symbolic tasks in which the tensions of people, coming from various sources, are pooled in one symbolic bargain.

Whatever view is taken of mass contagion, one cannot help seeing the great importance of tension management in modern society. This may open a new province of government, to which official attention and planning are given, with a scientific effort to keep track of levels of tension, of what people are "uptight" about, and how high tension has risen. Perhaps there will be not only an economic policy but a tension policy, aimed at damping undesirable contagions or stirring up appropriate enthusiasm for public policies. In keeping track of the level of tension and in evaluating the effects of policies, obviously public opinion polling is not enough; an array of psychological and sociological indicators is needed (R. Bauer, 1966). Presidential commissions on the causes of civil disorder and violence in the United States show the inadequacy of present indicators, and are more like "locking the barn after the horse is gone." Franklin D. Roosevelt started the "trial balloon" technique of using subordinate officials in his administration (or perhaps people independent of it) to test the public temper. Likewise, President Nixon used Vice-President Agnew during the late 1960s, whose florid phrases and epithets apparently had the double aim of appeasing the right wing and "silent majority" (in their tension for a crackdown), and testing the vigor of dissent and New Left resistance and regrouping ability. But, for all the skill of such maneuvers, it seemed that the President was better at economic management than he was at tension management, especially after the Cambodia riots of 1970.

Nor was this otherwise than to be expected, since the fact remained that there was no arm of government dealing specifically with popular tension *per se*. The United States Information Agency was prohibited by law from dealing with domestic tensions, and no one questioned the advisability of this. But it still seemed strange that, with mass contagions threatening the very fiber of American society, there was no public agency at the national level primarily assigned to study, maybe forecast, them.

CHAPTER 7

Systems and
Safety Valves

By the end of the decade of the 1960s the metropolis of
New York had 1,400 governments; it was a jigsaw puzzle of
sewer, water, school, highway maintenance and similar
special districts under municipal, county, and state jurisdic-
tions. It was somewhat the same for lesser cities. Everywhere in the country there was urban sprawl, with accom-

panying congestion and smog, deteriorating city centers, crowded minorities, widening gaps, and mounting tensions. An environmental crisis loomed as the imminent destruction of air, water, earth, and social conditions for the good life—even for the affluent classes. Crash programs were under way to provide low-cost housing and remedy the most serious environmental pollution. Yet the fact was that, by 1970, America had but three new towns (Reston, Virginia; Columbia, Maryland; Irvine, California). What brought dismay was a sense of widening gap due to an astonishing fourfold explosion in (1) population, (2) rising expectations, (3) leisure time, and (4) technological thrust (as we may call the impact of machines and their by-products such as noise). The nation had to contemplate a problem of increase in *population* times *expectations* times *leisure* times *technological thrust.*

To some Americans, this was only "business as usual," but to others (including some government commissions) the system seemed to be coming apart at the seams. Plainly, an end was approaching for the idea that things take care of themselves when "normal" forces are working. Decades before the government had quit laissez-faire as an economic market policy, but the implications of new solutions were still hard to accept. "Planning scares people," said an official of the Metropolitan Council of Minneapolis-St. Paul. In the midst of the urban and environmental crisis, aversion to planning remained a keynote of the American outlook. Yet the environmental crisis of the 1960s urgently signaled the fallacy of the idea that things work out best when no one is in charge. With economic disaster and environmental bankruptcy looming, what was the choice?

For those who saw no future in laissez-faire, it seemed that there was but one alternative to the reversion to moralistic ordering-and-forbidding legislation—piecemeal, mostly repressive—that had brought about things like Prohibition. This was to try to see the problem as a whole, in broadest terms over the longest span, using the best physical scientists, biologists, geographers, social scientists, architects, and other knowledgeable workers, and to plan. An era of general systems theory and management seemed to be at hand. A systems approach capable of making war and sending men to the moon could not fail when applied to the rest of society. With economic and technological planning comparatively well developed, sociologists were somewhat embarrassed to find that many of the gaps fell in their field.

This is not to say that sociologists had not long been talking about systems, from the philosophizing of Comte and Spencer to the structuralizing and functionalizing work by Merton, Parsons, and the anthropologists. But, as sociologists themselves admitted, structural-functional theory has a tendency to be static. The emphasis needed was a concept of communication flow, continual feedback among all parts of the system, as a dynamic process, the locus of function and change. This was crystallized in the formulation of cybernetics theory (Wiener, 1948).

> Society can only be understood through a study of the messages and the communication facilities which belong to it. . . . I do not mean that the sociologist is unaware of the existence and complex nature of communications in society, but until recently he has tended to over-look the extent to which they are the cement which binds its fabric together. (Wiener, 1950:27.)

This emphasis led to a rapid development of "general systems theory," which burgeoned in all directions, and brought the natural and social sciences closer together with an enlarged and sophisticated concept of information transmission (including such things as enzymes and genetic codes). General systems theory supported the small voice of "symbolic interactionism," which had been saying something like this since the time of Cooley (1909).

Nature of Systems Theory and Its Application to Sociology and Collective Behavior

The systemic view is that events seemingly isolated are inter-related and cannot be understood unless one considers how they work together as a system. An obvious illustration is that of economic "failure," which, before 1929, was usually considered as an individual fault (lack of thrift, prudence, foresight, character), but, in 1932, came to be seen as a system that was working so badly that an individual could not succeed however good he was. A *system* means some kind of interdependence among elements A, B, C, D . . . X so that a change in one means a possible change in all, and a change in all means a possible change in each. Some kind of accounting, therefore, is necessary for all important components: a balance sheet of gains and losses, inputs and outputs, debits and assets. Changes and redress of imbalances occur by inputs and outputs, actions and reactions, and between components, which in human systems include a large amount of symbolic communication. This notion of a balance sheet for everything is rather like the theological assumption that the sparrow never falls without God's noticing—that everything matters, at least we presume; jump on the earth, and you shake the moon ever so slightly; every collective outburst, however "senseless," means some happening in the system—perhaps yet to be discovered.

Systems extend beyond sight; humans usually act "blindly," and discover the implications for the system later. DDT was discovered in 1939 by Paul Muller. In 1948, he got the Nobel Prize. The increase in food productivity made possible by DDT was hailed all over the world; meanwhile a toxic residue was quietly building up in the environment. By 1962, Rachel Carson published *Silent Spring*, telling of birds killed and other damage by DDT. By 1969, the Food and Drug Administration had to seize 28,000 pounds of poisonous coho salmon from Lake Michigan; diving birds were dying from eating the fish in Clear Lake, California; Congress was creating a national commission on pesticides; and Arizona had outlawed DDT for one year, to find out just how harmful it was. Sweden was the first nation to ban the improper use of DDT, and this was rather ironical because it had also awarded its discoverer the Nobel Prize. Such a thirty-year sequence was required to reveal the systemic implications of a new chemical and generate appropriate responses to control it. Isn't it rather like this with almost every piece of legislation and every technological innovation? Ecological systems, being so large, involving whole species in balance, are perhaps among the hardest to see (a wit has even claimed a relationship between number of old maids and the linen crop of Ireland: Old maids keep cats, cats kill rats and mice, such vermin invade the hives of bees, bees fertilize flax from which linen is made; hence, the more old maids, the more linen). At the other extreme, physical systems, especially those we have made ourselves (machines), are among the simplest and easiest to see; for example, a bed spring. But, large or small, a system is defined as "a whole which functions as a whole by virtue of the interdependence of its parts" (Buckley, 1968:xvii). It extends to its boundaries, which are where interdependence stops and unrelatedness, strangeness, disorder, crisis, high entropy begin.

Static systems stay put until some external force changes them, and then remain as they are; but dynamic ones keep moving and changing, and some of the more complex systems have the capacity to return to their original condition, restore their own balance, by an activity called *homeostasis*. Homeostasis is usually defined as a self-adjusting process by which systems maintain a balance or "steady state" within a range of variation, by using a feedback mechanism. *Feedback* is the name for the continual flow of information about its own actions and the environment that enables a system to adjust so as to return to a steady state or reach limited goals. No one has described feedback better than Wiener (1950), who introduced this crucial concept into social theory:

> Man and the animal have a kinaesthetic sense, by which they keep a record of the position and tensions of their muscles. For any machine subject to a varied external environment to act effectively it is necessary that information concerning the results of its own action be furnished to it as part of the information on which it must continue to

act. . . . A gun-pointer takes information from his instruments of observation and conveys it to the gun, so that the latter will point in such a direction that the missile will pass through the moving target at a certain time. . . . It is necessary to put into the gun a control feedback element which reads the lag of the gun behind the position it should have according to the orders given it, and which uses this difference to give the gun an extra push. . . . Something very similar to this occurs in human action. If I pick up my cigar, I do not will to move any specific muscles. . . . I . . . turn into action a certain feedback mechanism; namely, a reflex in which the amount by which I have yet failed to pick up the cigar is turned into a new and increased order to the lagging muscles. . . . Similarly, when I drive a car, I do not follow out a series of commands dependent simply on a mental image of the road and the task. . . . If I find the car swerving too much to the right, that causes me to pull it to the left. This depends on the actual performance. . . . If . . . the information . . . is able to change the general method and pattern of performance, we have a process which may well be called learning. (Wiener, 1950:24–27, 61.)

Likewise, Deutsch (1966:88) defined feedback as "a communications network that produces action in response to an input of information, and *includes the results of its own action in the new information by which it modifies its subsequent behavior.*" Biology, of course, provides some of the most impressive examples of homeostasis, such as the means by which warm-bodied animals maintain their body temperatures, the balancing mechanism of the inner ear, or the disease-combating processes, mechanisms so beautiful and complex that they bafflle understanding.

Our concern, of course, is with social systems. Society, whatever else it may include, shows numerous examples of homeostatic mechanisms. The most familiar, perhaps, is the self-adjusting price mechanism of the economic market, which extends to a world division of labor and balances of trade. Another familiar example is a factory, which maintains product control and plans its output on the basis of continuing feedback. Many examples from daily life seem to show social homeostatic mechanisms. We might note, for example, how a friendly group keeps arguments from getting out of hand. If arguing members raise their voices too high, this becomes a signal of trouble. The group senses a threat to its solidarity, and begins to "shush" the parties arguing, tries to divert their attention and conciliate them. Should further signals of trouble indicate that tempers are rising, the group will make even greater efforts, even restrain people physically. Finally, after a variety of such responses, in no sense planned, feedback may indicate that "things are normal again," and the group returns to being just a friendly gathering with no further precautions necessary. Thus the "we" feeling is preserved without anyone giving particular thought to it, and we see that a group is a system of relationships capable of responding in ways that preserve itself.

A more complex homeostasis is seen in devices used (unwittingly) to keep a poker game going over a period of time. A poker game is a fragile system because players may come and go, and it may break up at any time; yet, in spite of high tensions and bad feelings of those who may be winning or losing, it shows an ability to maintain itself by homeostatic mechanisms. Sociologists report some of these: The dealer's role is to try to run a relaxed game with plenty of action, spotting friction, conciliating, and "serving as a sort of sponge to absorb the frustrations of the losers." Concepts of sportsmanship help keep the game going on an even keel. "An important distinction between good and poor losers, and good and poor winners, was whether their actions tended to provoke or reduce the amount of tension in the game." A "good winner" attributes his success to luck, so giving the loser a chance to blame his loss on bad luck. "Bad winners" attribute their success to skill and even needle the losers. On the other hand, it is all right to needle a winner.

> A certain amount of abuse is tolerated by winners. How much, as a general rule, is directly related to the offender's "action," that is, the amount of money he loses and how fast. Winning is its own compensation; from the loser a certain amount of bad feeling is acceptable, if only to keep the fellow in the game . . . to lose some more. (Martinez and La Franchi, 1969.)

The code calls for losses to be blamed on bad luck, and a heavy loser may be allowed to hurl insults at the dealer "because the heavy losers 'make' the game." Consistent winners were found to exhibit traits expected of the model "good" winner, and the interactions seemed to be adjusting homeostatically to manage tensions and preserve the game (Martinez and La Franchi, 1969:30–35). The most conspicuous homeostatic mechanism in any social system, of course, is control of deviance, as the more or less conscious effort to keep people acting in such a way that the system can go on as before. "Facework" is also an important area of homeostasis (Goffman, 1955).

If homeostatic mechanisms were all that were operating in human systems, we should expect them to be continually restoring a balance of forces and working toward consensus and control which would become static. Society would be rather like a football game in which two teams playing on the fifty-yard line were equally matched and agreed perfectly on the rules: Barring accident, they could play on into infinity and the game would never move. Even the most traditional societies are not so static as this. The importance of homeostasis should not lead us to overemphasize stability in human affairs, which are notoriously disorderly. Human systems have a free and open character, flowing on to new resting and balance points. The higher the system is, the more fragile it is, and the harder it is to maintain homeostasis. Karl Jaspers said—

> Man can endure as a sheer existent, but he ceases thereby to be a man, just as every living being can die, and dead matter have victorious duration. The lower in rank, the greater the durability of a being. The higher levels are the more mobile, more imperiled, more perishable. (Matson and Montagu, 1967:527.)

Moreover, large information input often works against homeostasis and requires more change. Humans have more receptors and larger inputs than any other animal; therefore their data-processing load is greatest. Thus, homeostasis is necessary for human life, but it is a *non sequitur* that *this* homeostasis is better than all others.

Homeodynamics does not require a conservative orientation. "Moving on" is handled by an *adaptive* or *open-system* model in which feedback serves change, not just stability, and the homeodynamics of society is like the constant regrouping of men on a battlefield, or the poise of a surfer on the wave. In other words, the presence of a homeodynamic tendency does not force us to see society as always returning to old positions. Theorists such as Cadwallader (1959), Deutsch (1966), and Buckley (1967) think of feedback as information helping to steer society toward new goals—not just back to old equilibria. The constant input of information leads society to change its self-conception and its goals and to seek modification of methods to reach goals. The feedbacks of society, said Buckley (1967:124), "constitute a complex adaptive system—not simply an equilibrium or homeostatic system—operating as an ongoing process or transaction which is continuously generating, maintaining, or altering meanings and patterns of behavior." On the other hand, the goal-seeking behavior of an open system should not cause us to lose sight of the fact that every goal is a new potential equilibrum; that is, to abandon equilibrium altogether would be to destroy all system at the human level. We must therefore think of an open system as moving toward new goals while maintaining a certain amount of balance by homeostatic mechanisms. Nor should enthusiasm for "progress" lead us to suppose that we can disregard homeostatic mechanisms in either the society or the person. A psychologist notes that some of the homeostatic mechanisms governing our lives are exceedingly delicate and that we ignore their signals at our own risk:

> Organisms have self-regulating, homeostatic mechanisms built into them such that when balance is disrupted, signals are emitted, and

these elicit reflex and behavioral compensatory responses that restore dynamic equilibrium. At the human level, many of these signs
of disruption (I call them "all is not well" signals) reach conscious
awareness. They are capable of being discriminated and are identifiable as pain, depression, boredom, frustration, anxiety, or just generalized malaise. . . . In our culture we are trained from an early age
not to pay too much attention to our inner selves, to our own feelings,
wishes and needs . . . .

Pressures to play our various roles in the "proper" way actually foster increased self-alienation. (Jourard, 1964:142–145.)

Medical studies such as those of Hans Selye on stress show how
much health is essentially a matter of maintaining homeostasis in
the midst of change and challenges. There is no reason to suppose
that the average person is like a cork unaffected by the waves of
life. Homeostatic mechanisms may get him through, but he pays a
price for too much of anything. Is it so different with society, when
warning signals like smog and tension, burst forth suddenly as
crisis? Once we assume that homeostatic mechanisms are necessary even for the most progressive society, we must make sure that
excessive inputs are not overwhelming to many of them. One of the
first requirements is to get rid of the notion (seemingly held with
regard to progress) that unlimited intake of anything—food, medicine, information, technology—is progress for individuals or societies. No values are simply good when separated from the system
in which they obtain. This is the ultimate of relativism. Everyone
of the absolutes, including "happiness" and "liberty" will be seen
to require a system and to be limited by that system and its homeostatic mechanisms. So the progress of an open system should be
seen as a moving composite of change and homeostasis, not a
movement in which such mechanisms are ignored.

Another difference between human social and biological systems, besides greater openness for change, is that the functional
relationship, working connection of parts, is by communication of
messages that have *meaning*. There is some ambiguity between
language in common usage and its application in cybernetics, where
the word "information" sometimes means control (as in genetic
codes) or negative entropy (increased average order, higher complexity of organization, as in development of an embryo or complet-
ing a jigsaw puzzle); see Shannon and Weaver, 1949:103–104. Also,
"feedback"—either positive or negative—is merely a factor that
increases or decreases something else. Sociologists minced no
words in rejecting mechanical "push-pull" concepts of interrelation-
ships among human components of a system, as earlier systems
theorists conceived them. Duncan (1968) said—

American sociologists think poorly about communication because of their "trained incapacity" in the use of non-mechanistic models. The reduction of all science in sociology to research models derived from the physical sciences makes it all but impossible for the sociologist to deal with meaning. Sociologists of the behavioral persuasion . . . must, if they are consistent, do away with consciousness, intention, and meaning, in their research models. In place of "harmony," "order," "integration," we hear of "process," "equilibrium," "homeostasis," and "gearing." Order and disorder in human relationships are caused not by individuals enacting roles, but by "processes" which "occur" in "patterns" or "systems." Even those in the United States who style themselves "symbolic interactionists" often seem happier when they talk about "interaction patterns" and "structured responses," and employ other kinds of mechanistic imagery. . . . It is impossible to talk about human relationships without saying *something* about meaning. And meaning, even when it is called "pattern maintenance," is usually studied through the interpretation of symbols, for it is only in symbols that meaning—as attention and intention—can be observed. (Duncan, 1968:5.)

People have to understand their feedback before functions can occur; people are connoisseurs, not robots. Functions above the biological level are meanings communicated (payoffs with meaning). The older functionalism saw institutions "functioning," but never felt obliged to trace messages and feedback. This is the modern sociological task: seeing communication as the vehicle of function, the exchange of messages making possible cooperation, and the meaning of payoffs and the payoffs in meaning.

Now social scientists are more and more studying systems in terms of symbolic communication flow and feedback loops. Deutsch (1953, 1966) and Easton (1965) treated entire nations in this way. Sellers (1965) analyzed the American two-party system as an equilibrium maintained by symbolic realignment of voters.

There seems to be at work a constant tendency toward equilibrium that is built into the very structure of the American two-party system. The persistent narrowness of the margin between the parties is one of the most striking characteristics of the system. . . . Americans do not form deep and irrevocable attachments to parties based on fundamental ideologies or social cleavages. . . . Realignment seems . . . to be caused mainly by . . . a strong shift to the advantaged party by younger people and other new voters still in the process of forming their identifications. . . . Since in the American electoral system only a bare majority is necessary to win all the power, there is a tendency not only for a minority party to readjust its image so as to detach groups from the majority coalition, but also for a party with an oversized majority to force out groups in the process of deciding which part of its coalition its policies will favor. . . . Hence we may observe in

American political history a steady pressure toward equilibrium. (Sellers, 1965.)

Sociologists operate on a more modest scale, preferring to observe institutions or small, simple societies as communication feedback systems. Homans' (1950) classic application of this showed the mutual dependence of sentiments on which systems are based on interaction that supplies appropriate feedback:

> . . . when the members of the Bank Wiring group are put in a room together for the first time, . . . we can . . . watch their social system begin to elaborate itself. . . . Beneficent or vicious circles . . . are characteristic of all organic phenomena. We can say that the feedback of the internal system may be either favorable or unfavorable to the group, making its action on the environment more or less effective. . . . From the point of view of the Hawthorne management, the feedback in the . . . group would have been judged unfavorable: it resulted in restriction of output. On the other hand, the members of the group itself . . . might have judged it . . . favorable. They certainly said . . . that if output increased continuously the piecework rates would be lowered, someone would be laid off. . . . The mutual good feeling that accompanies close interaction may make the necessary practical work of a group go more easily: the group creates its own morale. . . . The internal system includes the mutual relationships between interaction, sentiment, and activity as these relationships elaborate themselves upon those of the external . . . system and then react upon the external system. But in analyzing the . . . Tikopia family we encounter a difficulty that was not present in . . . our analysis of the Bank Wiring Observation Room. . . . In the . . . Observation Room we could follow the actual process of social buildup and feedback. . . . In analyzing the . . . Tikopia family we are in no such fortunate condition. The family has a long history behind it; the . . . buildup took place long ago. . . . But . . . perhaps we can use . . . the same method we used in analyzing the Bank Wiring group, though in Tikopia the process by which the internal system continually elaborates on the external and reacts upon it has reached a steady state and is not, so far as we can tell, leading to further social development. (Homans, 1950:153–154, 240.)

So, McCleery (1961) and Barton and Anderson (1961) analyzed the flow of communication in a prison as a feedback system. Charting this flow in terms of input and output of various components, they made some interesting findings. One was that the more successful the control by authoritarian measures, the greater was the order— but the less was the participation of prisoners in treatment activities —and the stronger became the power of an inmate elite in alliance with custodial officers, which engaged in a certain amount of illegal activity as part of its privileges. Thus, the price of authoritarian success was defeat in other ways:

In this system, the maintenance of a power elite among the prisoners is dependent on a steady input of arbitrary administrative behavior producing anxiety. The powers exercised by the inmate elite group give them something to offer the custodial staff in return for privileges, which in turn strengthen the inmate elite. The cooperation of the guards in the maintenance of their privileged position makes the inmate leadership "accommodative" rather than rebellious or reform-minded and willing to use some of their powers to hold down the rate of disorderly behavior among the prisoners. This set of conditions therefore favors a low rate of disorder. At the same time, since the arbitrariness of the administration creates a strong hostility toward the prison among the rank-and-file prisoners, their participation in treatment activities is minimized. Thus one goal of the prison is achieved, but the other is not. . . . Here is one of the key mechanisms by which the equilibrium of the authoritarian system was maintained—a set of relationships which permitted the maintenance of order at the expense of rendering impossible the other nominal goal of the prison, rehabilitation. (Barton and Anderson, 1961:408–409.)

Another interesting observation was that when liberal reforms were introduced into the prison, the immediate price was a great increase in disorder as the old coalitions were broken up, since "the new programs did not immediately create new primary group controls favorable to a more liberal prison. . . . Only gradually did a new informal control through prisoner group consensus arise to hold disorder in check." (Barton and Anderson, 1961:408–409, 415).

Thus, systems theory, when applied empirically to the study of feedback loops, allows us to see more clearly what might be called the balance sheet of the system, the total of balancing relationships; deficits leading to changes in other components; homeostatic mechanisms, what they are, how they occur, and how they fail; vicious circles of feedback; and consensus as a major homeostatic element and the feedback cycles needed for it.

There is no reason to suppose that collective behavior is not a part of such systematic balance and does not have a place in the feedback loops. Systems theory has been so applied to collective behavior by Buckley, the general idea being that the forms of collective behavior found in social unrest are institutional by-products that lead to revision of institutions by feedback loops. How does this circle occur? The general picture is that the system generates strains that lead to spontaneous behavior, individual and collective, some of which takes the form of collective redefinition and organization for action, such as protests and movements. These feed back through civil debate into institutional reorganization. Figure 7.1 shows the process as Buckley (1967) visualized it. This scheme is tentative, of course, and much research is needed to fill in the intricate flows and loops; but it enables us to see collective behavior

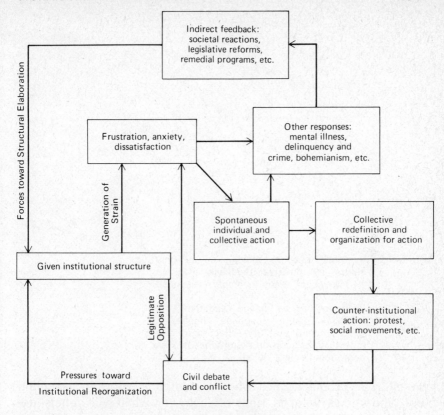

FIGURE 7.1. Systemic view of collective behavior.
(From Walter Buckley, *Sociology and Modern Systems Theory*, Englewood Cliffs, N.J.: Prentice-Hall, 1967.)

in systemic perspective, as a spillover from organization, a free-flow phase of action resulting from systemic strains, involving symbolic transactions, feeding back into institutional structure in various ways, whether for conservation or change. As pointed out before, the essential point is that collective behavior is part of a systemic balance sheet, the reckoning and redress of which is in terms of communication. Homeostasis is only part of the picture; the system can return to its original balance or move on to a new state, as diagramed in Figure 7.2.

So, from this point of view, there are no isolated outbursts, hysterias, rumors, fads, and so on. It is useless to talk about parts without concern for wholes, since the whole governs subvalues (as the ancient Greeks long ago said). All forms of collective behavior are part of a systemic balance sheet that we might be able to construct, if we knew the items and transactions. Piecemeal approaches are notoriously futile and mutually defeating as long as there is no accounting of the total balance sheet. We know neither what our

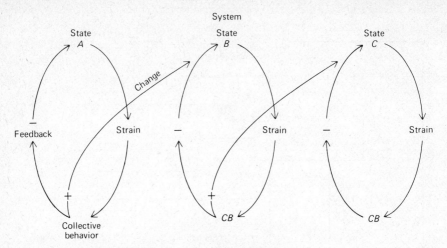

FIGURE 7.2. Systemic change: moving on to new
states by positive feedback. Positive
(+) feedback tends to amplify response
(input to system); hence, it is more
likely to lead to change. Negative (−)
feedback damps response; hence, it
tends toward stability—encourages the
individual to keep on doing what he has
been doing or not doing.

own effort is producing nor whether another's effort is canceling
ours. Who knows what is right ethically, or what will satisfy demands, or what goals to work for, without the systemic balance to
guide him? Injustice, viewed systemically, does not comprise the
bad deeds of villains but is a system working to distribute strains,
overloads, and short payments to some, and the easy life and oversized rewards to others. To cure such a strain, one does not attack
villains; he studies ways to change the system, what inputs will
have the desired total effects. One thing learned from studying systems is that simplistic solutions (most moralistic responses) often
do not correct but instead produce vicious circles. On the other
hand, one of the most encouraging things that systemic study
teaches is that small things can sometimes make big differences
(paralleled in medicine by the fact that a small pill can sometimes
take the place of major surgery).

To repeat, a systemic point of view, while emphasizing the importance of homeostasis, does not commit us to conceiving a closed
system, nor does it enshrine equilibrium (conserving the *status
quo*) as a *sine qua non* of social order. On the contrary, it posits
an open system in which homeostasis is important but in which collective behavior is part of the feedback process generating change.
Within an open system in which collective behavior is producing
change, we find the "conservative" mentality as a sign of those

wishing to emphasize homeostasis and preserve the *status quo*. But this does not imply that progressive change in the society is accomplished by abandoning all homeostatic mechanisms. It is impossible to find a tolerable state of human life where there are no forces working for order against disorder; in other words, some degree of homeostasis is necessary to preserve a living system from death, and a social system from anomie. Breakdown of homeostatic mechanisms, unless repaired, leads to ill health for even the most dynamic individuals and society. This applies as well to the most liberal, open systems (what is the English debating tradition but a homeostatic mechanism?). Indeed, one might argue that in an open society, the homeostatic mechanisms present, however few, are all the more vital because of the high level of disorder. In Chapter 9 on information overload, we shall go into the effects of an overwhelming input on the homeostatic mechanisms of an open society and the kinds of collective behavior that are likely.

Now, however, our attention centers on the homeostatic side, how certain arrangements help to keep tension from spilling over into collective behavior.

Safety Valves and Spillover

In Chapter 6 we treated mass contagions as symptoms of excessive tension, using the "falling domino" model to illustrate the spread of contagions to those who are most tense and/or suggestible. Then we tried to surpass some of the oversimplifications of this model by treating contagion not as a mechanical transmission but as passing over symbolic thresholds, tasks to be completed by symbolic transactions. Then we added the systemic view, emphasizing homeostasis through feedback, which makes a much broader treatment possible.

As already said, we are not in a position to draw up a precise balance sheet, but surely the major items to be entered in the ledger are how the system handles strains by homeostatic mechanisms, some account of the most serious strains (anxiety, aggression, frustration), where they come from, how much of a load they make, and when they approach crisis. We may also try to conceive crisis as a "spillover," loss of balance between tension-handling arrangements and excessive tension, too much negative feedback for the system to handle without drastic change or emergency response. (You will recall that we defined systemic strain as nothing but excessive tension in a large number of people, resulting from a systemic condition.) Excessive tension is more than the exuberance that is an essential and normal part of human life, an asset within limits. Even exuberance and enthusiasm can be debits on some occasions (a funeral, firing somebody), but certain unpleasant kinds of tension reckon largely as debits because, even in small amounts, they are damaging to relationships and to people and may require special buffers or safety valves. If positive feedback builds up these kinds of feelings, we are more likely to refer to them as vicious circles, whereas such a term is rarely used for buildup of hilarity, enthusiasm, love, or other pleasant feelings (though the rule "nothing in excess" seems to apply ultimately to every feeling). A "spillover" model, then, can be employed to conceive the point at which debits of destructive tension and vicious circles exceed the assets, and at which cutoff mechanisms are expressed in terms of safety valves and adaptive decisions.

In the rest of this chapter, then, an attempt will be made to draw up a number of items on this balance sheet: (1) how anxiety is generated and allayed by institutions of reassurance; (2) how aggression and frustration are partly handled by safety valves; (3) vicious circles and oscillations that lead to crisis; (4) a spillover model conceived as an imbalance between tension inputs and tension management; and (5) a larger view of the overall balance of a system in terms of five major components and ten vital relationships to be studied as communication problems.

Anxiety and Institutions of Reassurance

There is little doubt that at the beginning of the 1970s, the world suffered excessive fear and anxiety from many sources—some obvious, some not so obvious. Developing countries suffered the breakup of traditional cultures and authority systems as well as outright threats such as starvation. Modern countries suffered insecurities that were focused more on demands and expectations than the mere business of keeping alive. But international tensions and the threat of aggression hung over all. The paradox was that countries not threatened by obvious evils like war and starvation—indeed, many most favored economically and politically—also suffered high levels of anxiety.

Plainly, America was such a case. She had the highest level of prosperity and also (as far as one could tell) every sign of high anxiety. Some of this distress focused on fear of riot and violence. A Harris poll (*Life*, July 11, 1969) showed fear rising more sharply than the rise in crime, three-quarters of the people having changed their lives at least somewhat because of fear of crime, a booming sale of Doberman Pinschers and German Shepherd dogs, and a national chain of surplus stores selling 1,200 pocket tear-gas devices per month. Citizens were rushing to buy guns and install home-protective devices; in Atlanta, three thousand housewives took courses in self-defense in one year, the rich were taking refuge in condominiums surrounded by fences and patrolled by dogs. Such signs of fear were only part of the picture. There was a phenomenal sale of tranquilizers; a symposium at the School of Medicine, University of California, 1968, reported that one-fourth of the population were using sedatives. There was also a large sale of literary tranquilizers, if we might so designate books with titles like "Peace of Mind," and "How To Stop Worrying." A full-page photograph in *Life*, showing anxious, brooding faces of people on the street, asked "What are all these people so worried about?" It was, as many said and no one disputed, an "age of anxiety."

What is the difference between fear and anxiety? Fear is an appropriate emotion toward something rather specific that one has good reason to feel threatened by, such as war. Anxiety, on the other hand, is commonly defined as a vague worry, the source of which is not clearly understood, which has a tendency to be "free-floating" and seems excessive to an outside observer. For example, a rose cultivator in La Jolla, California, said, "I just lie awake at night listening to the wind whip my roses about." Because anxiety seems excessive, it may be necessary to have a belief that rationalizes it, that is often far from the real cause. It is, of course, the level of anxiety that is crucial: Normal anxiety, which occurs to most people some of the time, is called worry; acute anxiety is panic; and chronic high anxiety is characteristic of neurosis. So, in speaking of an age of anxiety in America, one means that the nation is suffering not just from fear but from symptoms that are rather like those of neurosis. To summarize by an oversimplified hyperbole—America's problem is anxiety. Israel's is fear. Again, people in some countries such as India, greatly threatened by starvation, show not so many signs of anxiety as do some Americans over health foods. (The fact is that the world is a dangerous place, but normal people don't worry much about it. The paradox is that if you worry as much as you should, you are anxious.) The case of America raises the question of whether favored nations make up in anxiety what they lose in fear. Is anxiety a price of progress?

Such a paradox is possible because concern in advanced societies is not focused on survival, nor merely on "existential" problems that humans must face everywhere, but on those presented by a complex and changing social system. Many anxieties are connected with the alienation and loneliness of life in a mass society, attested by a large literature (Stein, Vidich, and White, 1960). Status anxiety is a prominent characteristic of modern society. C. W. Mills (1951) called attention to the "status panic" of middle-class people because white-collar status symbols are found to be insecure, ambiguous, and unrewarding; a white-collar worker might, for example, find that he is making less than a blue-collar worker and that, despite all his better education, his clerical duties are as mechanical and monotonous as work on an assembly line; further, while the job market is being flooded by people as well educated as he is, he has no union or political party to protect his specific interests (C. W. Mills, 1951:240–247).

A survey of two thousand managers in the metals industry found that 42 percent expressed fears about their ability to keep up with advanced methods. Much strain was found in middle managers, harried by the competition of rising young men, many of whom were burning out in their mid-fifties. A best-selling book, *The Peter Principle*, claiming that every employee tends to rise to his "level of incompetence," showed how many were worrying about whether they were equal to their jobs. Riesman, Glazer, and Denney (1950) showed the anxieties of other-directed living. Such things might be called Horatio Alger in a bind.

No small amount of anxiety was generated by advertising, which told people that if they did not buy deodorants, dentifrices, anti-wrinkle creams, diets, reducing formulas, vitamins, pep pills, they would lose friends, status, or even health. At very least, they raised the question, "What's wrong with me?" Such institutional features justify the statement that anxiety does not just come from life but is manufactured by systems. Much of what has been written about the Protestant ethic suggests that this is indeed true; Fromm (1941) for example, arguing that Protestantism created a feeling of power-lessness, insignificance, and doubt about one's future after death, which led to a "frantic activity and a striving to do something," which we see dramatically depicted in Babbitt's hell as "failure" and in the price paid by Willy Loman. Likewise, in traditional societies, the evil eye is accepted as an almost universal superstition (Schoeck, 1955), and we see ghost fear and sorcery filling many societies with a dread that cannot be banished but which keeps them endlessly doing ritual to protect themselves from it (*Fortune*, 1932; Benedict, 1934; Miner, 1956).

The systemic view, however, takes notice not only of sources of anxiety but ways of handling it (once it has arisen) by *institutions of reassurance*. These have a primary (manifest) function to protect us from anxieties and fears coming either from life itself or the social system. We see a kind of battle between anxieties generated by the system and its own institutions of reassurance. Needless to say, police and courts have such functions, both at the practical and ritual level. A ritual element is strong in court drama, to *symbolize*, not just *do*, justice. Likewise, therapeutic institutions, such as hospitals and the Red Cross, symbolize more than they do, and vice versa. White magic—medicine men, good luck charms, horoscopes, occultism—promises that "things will come out all right." Folk tales and ritual drama are important in both traditional and modern societies for reassuring people that crime will be punished and things will come out all right; this is a primary (though latent) function of fairy stories with their happy ending, a pageant such as the Ramayana in South Asia (in which the hero Rama defeats the monsters and rescues his loyal wife Sita), morality plays, whose modern versions can be found in TV westerns and radio soap opera (Warner and Henry, 1948), or in a tragedy like "Macbeth," analyzed as a ritual catharsis. Ceremonies of recognition (rites of passage) like birthdays and testimonials to loyal employees are also institutions of reassurance: "We like you."

But the prime institution for reassurance in most societies is, of course, the church. It functions against primary anxiety induced by death, disease, and other causes by prayer and propitiation; its ultimate meaning is to symbolize as a "rock of ages" what eternal security is possible for man. The church also functions to relieve secondary anxiety—that which results from breach of rites and tradition (Homans, 1941) by ceremonies of purification and ways of expiating sin. There is no question, for example, of the great relief that Catholics feel after confession and forgiveness, or that Protestant converts feel from the experience of being "saved," or that all Christians get from the promise of Heaven, or the assurance that misfortunes necessarily endured in this life are "God's will." From a systemic point of view, such contributions of ritual and faith are homeostatic.

Even where there is no explicit promise of salvation, all the major religions quiet the restlessness of man in some way by a message of peace. This is not to say that the effects of religion in human life have not been quite opposite, as is well proved by religious wars. No institution always does what it tries to do. If we inquire how churches are working today in relation to anxiety, we see that they are not altogether successful as institutions of reassurance. The uncertainties of faith today are so great that no church is able to offer the rock of assurance by dogma—"this is it." Ministers find it safer to adhere to a middle-of-the-road humanism, with which no one can disagree, and cannot risk splitting their congregations by coming out strong on a dogmatic point. Modern churches have abandoned a literal concept of hell as the punishment for the wicked, and have become vague about the promise of Heaven. The church, as we know, should be a close fellowship of faith, a warm primary group; but all too often the congregation is a crowd of strangers who have little relationship with each other than what they might have in a department store. For such reasons, it is regrettably true that the churches, for all their best intentions, are hardly more reassuring than the rest of our society, and many religious problems and activities are full of the same anxiety as one might find in any other organizational activity (financial problems, unwelcome obligations, "do they like me?" "do I belong?").

So, especially in urban areas where, because of mass anxiety, spiritual ministration is needed most, we find churches falling down, through no fault of their own, as institutions of reassurance. The religious revivalism of the early 1970s reflected the insecure position of the church, anxiously searching for new techniques to reach lost audiences. *Time* noted hopefully the efforts of the "new ministry" to "bring God back to life" (Dec. 26, 1969). All this was in line with a curious finding by a sociologist that there was a *positive* correlation between formal religious affiliation and anxiety; namely, that believers complained more of tension, sleeplessness, and anxiety than did nonbelievers (Rokeach, 1965). This finding raised a question: Does contemporary religion bring peace of mind, or does it scare people, or perhaps attract scared people? In the midst of these perplexities, outside the church, movements such as encounter group therapy, hippie communalism, and anti-Communist crusades did what they could to provide reassurance.

So we seem to have a picture of society overburdened by anxiety, some of which it generates itself, and at the same time the traditional institutions for handling anxiety working less effectively. In such a situation, we would expect a spillover of excess anxiety into such things as hysterias, panics, and paranoid reactions and styles. We see such outbursts as symptoms of an imbalance between tension and one kind of homeostatic mechanism.

However, this is only one part of the picture. Let us look at the balancing of aggression and frustration.

Aggression, Frustration, and Safety Valves

On ceremonial occasions an elephant is . . . "dressed." He is made to lie down by his mahout, and then he is washed like a child, raising his head or leg at a word. . . . When the washing is over, he is dressed. First the forehead, trunk, and ears are painted in bold patterns. . . . Then the howdah is girt on with cotton ropes which do not chafe the skin. . . . The elephant goes through all this with great patience, but sometimes when all is ready he will suddenly fling a bunch of leaves and fodder over his back to give his mahout a little extra work before the parade begins. (Bond, 1969.)

Social systems, like individuals, seem to have "safety valves" for letting off excessive or undesirable tension harmlessly. The concept of "safety valve" is fairly well established in sociology (Par-

sons, 1951:304–308; Coser, 1956:151–156), but it is far from clear
yet how such institutions work and what their scope is. The essential
idea is that some arrangement channels undesirable tension such as
discontent and hostility away while preserving the relationship from
which the tension arose. William James, in his essay "The Moral
Equivalent of War" (published in 1910) was the first to enunciate it;
he argued that it was a waste of time to talk of universal peace and
disarmament because "the plain truth" was that "people want war."
But it would be possible to "invent new outlets for heroic energy"
that would be more useful, at least less harmful, such as conscript-
ing an army to fight poverty (which idea was finally launched by
Franklin D. Roosevelt in 1933 as the Civilian Conservation Corps).
Reformers such as John Dewey (1922) hailed this seminal idea for
the design of new institutions to handle impulses society doesn't
want. Dewey argued, on the basis of Freud's insights, that there are
three possibilities: unintelligent discharge; suppression (which is
"the cause of all kinds of . . . pathology . . . license . . . rebellion"),
or sublimation, constructive use of the energy for something that
society wants, such as a crusade for justice or a work of art (Dewey,
1922:156–157, 166).

What is essential to the idea of safety valve is that there is a
type or level of tension that is a debit to a system if uncontrolled,
but there is also an option for using tension in a more advantageous
way. The net advantage, then, that this sublimation gives is its function for the system. The definition of safety valve does not require
that the substitute activity be totally constructive; for example,
play is better than fighting within the group, even if people get hurt
in play. It might be argued, of course, that any activity is a substitute for something else that people might have been doing; but a
safety-valve institution is diversive, not only in that it keeps people
busy but also that it is in the long term an alternative in institutional
development. In the long or the short run, a safety valve must
"spend" something (energy, resources, time), the lessening of
which reduces the likelihood of activities the group does not want
(wants less than what it actually did).

Very often, asset expenditure is appeasement of particular motives, such as revenge, blame, honor, which otherwise might lead
to escalating hostilities (see Rosman and Rubel, 1971). In the sense
of appeasement, gift giving is an important safety valve in every
society; there is no way of knowing how many aggressions have
been "bought off" by gifts. The failure of such tactics to always work
does not argue against their general usefulness as safety valves.
Likewise, children often misbehave; but common sense tells us that
allowing them to have a good run in a play yard, or holding up a

vision of Santa Claus once a year, has something to do with causing them to act a little better than they might otherwise do at a particular time.

In short, if among two or more possible courses one is less destructive than the others and can become a standard arrangement that in one way or another reduces the likelihood or magnitude of the alternatives, then we may reasonably call it a safety valve.

Because the idea seems valuable, and because there is no evidence to justify throwing it away, let us proceed on the assumption that most systems, whatever their merits, generate destructive tensions such as hostility and frustration and that these effects can be partly managed by safety-valve mechanisms. Presumably, highly disciplinary systems (such as ancient Sparta and Japan, seventeenth-century Puritanism, or Crow Indian society) especially needed safety valves.

We can sort these matters out by classifying safety-valve institutions roughly into three types and distinguishing them from mere *buffers* or *accommodations*. A buffer mechanism is a social device for avoiding strain (such as rules requiring separation of the sexes in certain circumstances to reduce tension from sex or taboo violation, or a rule for a "cooling off" period in strike negotiation). Let us distinguish three types of safety valves: *diversive*, *cathartic*, and *aggressive*.

Perhaps the simplest safety valves are those that merely *divert* activity into less harmful channels than they might otherwise take; hence they function to "keep people busy." "Busy work" and games are a familiar device of teachers. Such tactics have been used by police, for example, to control a Hell's Angels gathering, as noted in Chapter 2 (Shellow and Roemer, 1969). It has been argued, and challenged, that the image of the Western frontier operated as a safety valve for a developing industrial society (H. N. Smith, 1957: 239). Let us call *diversive institutions* those that help keep people out of trouble by offering substitutes. Institutionalized gambling provides perhaps the best studied case (Devereaux, 1950; Tec, 1964). In countries like Ireland, Mexico, and much of Latin America, activities such as lotteries and horse-betting, heavily engaged in by the poor, seem to take people's minds off their troubles and reduce the likelihood that they will think of more revolutionary or criminal alternatives. Tec examined gambling in soccer pools in Sweden, and found that—contrary to suppositions that it would have dire moral and economic consequences such as ruining people—betting was confined within reasonable limits porprotionate to income, and did not interfere with normal involvement in friendships, associations, responsibilities, and offices. More to the point for our purposes, Tec found that bettors were "slightly more concerned about their work and more likely to take the initiative in improving their working conditions than non-bettors" (Tec, 1964:106). Further, betting was more frequent in the lower class (especially the upper part of the lower class) than in the middle and upper class. Tec then developed the theory that because "wagering keeps alive dreams," it functions as "an unrealistic and unconventional avenue of status advancement" for those blocked in other ways but not too discouraged to dream.

> By keeping alive hopes for social betterment, gambling alleviates some of the frustration derived from the obstacles which segments of the population encounter in seeking to fulfill their mobility aspirations. . . . The hopes provided by gambling, although almost never realized, tend to make a deprivational situation less acute and less urgent, thereby contributing to the well being of the bettors. This in turn has beneficial effects upon society. For, to the extent that socially-induced frustrations can be regarded as potential sources of deviant or revolutionary behavior in that they might find expression as outright attacks against the existing social order, relief of these frustrations is beneficial to the continuity of the social order. Thus, instead of turning against the original source of their deprivations and unfulfilled aspirations, bettors are relieved through gambling of some of the frustrations and, hence, are less likely to attack the existing class structure. Particularly significant . . . is the fact that the highest proportion of bettors comes from the "elite" of the lower class. For while the upper segment of the lower class . . . is more likely to aspire to unattainable social position and, hence, is more likely to experience frustration, its members, because of their "elite" position, are particularly effective in influencing the views and actions of the rest of the lower stratum. The fact, however, that the socially-induced frustrations of the lower class "elite" may be partly absorbed through gambling reduces the likelihood of potentially deviant acts on their part . . . also . . . of an attempt to incite the masses. Interpreted in such a fashion, gambling falls into the broad category of activities referred to as "safety-valve institutions." (Tec, 1964:108, 113–114.)

Tec also noted that gambling in Sweden provides revenue for the state while depriving criminals of a source of income. The whole sports picture needs to be looked at as diversive activity; as well as O. T. B. in New York City and State lotteries in New York, New Jersey, and New Hampshire. A less convincing case is provided by passive entertainment, such as television drama, as "action" for desk-bound bureaucrats and frustrated assembly-line workers. The best diversive safety valve presumably involves people in some kind of action, or at least a hope, which is more than they can get out of merely watching other people do things.

A second type of safety valve, *cathartic*, provides an occasion for a marked general release of tension or indulgence in feeling that is satisfying, recreational, self-fulfilling. Its main goal is a kind of euphoria from catharsis or peak experience.

> Those of us who have experienced the Nirvana of folk dancing, know that when we approach that state we experience some of the supreme moments of our lives. There is something electric, spiritual and communicative in the hoolyeh. . . . [It is] repetitious enough to be semi-hypnotic, the music is exotic and primitive, and the locked arms in a circle of brotherhood is symbolic of the best in folk dancing.
>
> Things happen to your body and mind. Your glands pour chemicals into your blood stream releasing pools of energy, your joints get flexible, your muscles get supple. You can perform *prisiadkis* with ease that you could not attempt while cold. Your heart and lungs work like mad, and you feel a surge of being alive and awake as you never feel otherwise. Your head reels with excitement and exhilaration, your wits sharpen, you laugh and yell and stamp your feet. Your inhibitions just slough off. It is a form of communal intoxication. And love, oh you just overflow with love, you're just in love with the whole wide world, you want to hug everyone. This spiritual side of the hoolyeh is one of the most satisfying parts, and leaves you glowing for days after. It is an emotional experience of the finest, richest, and healthiest sort. (Denov, 1954:10–11.)

Institutions such as carnivals, corroborees (Australian aboriginal dances), and school pep rallies also have this function of allowing an intense letting-go not possible in ordinary life. Let us call these institutions *expressive*. A number of holidays and festive occasions have some of this character, at least in theory, in American life: Christmas, Thanksgiving, Easter, New Year's Eve, Fourth of July, TGIF (Thank God It's Friday) and term-end parties, rock and jazz festivals also perform such functions for modern life. Religious revivalism rewards the poor and disfranchised for deprivations, as noted by Pope (1942). Finally, all kinds of confession, from church to the "bull session" in the dormitory or the role of the friendly bartender as "big brother" for "bar flies," or interaction in encounter groups and therapeutic sessions serve in these ways. When such safety valves are successful, typical feelings are an "aura of harmony" and of satisfying communication, which "wipes the slate clean." Such an institution, offering many kinds of fulfillment, satisfies many needs; but, whatever its manifest function, one of its by-products is reduction of frustrations that might otherwise lead to destructive conflicts.

A third category of safety valves includes institutions that pointedly *use aggression*, therefore presumably "spend" it in some way, so reducing the long or short term potentiality for conflict that the group does not want. We note, for example, that some of the "rock" music of the 1960s was more than generally cathartic; it was pointedly aggressive, and seemed to invite the audience to a vicarious orgy of hostile feeling, most of which led to no substantial damage and might reasonably be supposed to be serving as a "moral equivalent of war" for frustrated youth. The "Rolling Stones" were one of the most aggressive "rock" performing groups. Their collective performing personality was characterized by "raw, unadulterated insolence." Violent outbursts were frequent at their concerts, but seemed to be an involvement of the audience with the entertainers and to have few significant political consequences. A critic describes their performance:

> Violence? The Stones typify it; they don't imply it. A Stones concert is a raging assault, a fiery menace of music and freneticism choreographed by the devil's disciples. The Stones confront their audiences; they don't mess around. Jagger on vocals, and various rhythm instruments, dances like a dervish, moves like a matador, teases, threatens, and taunts his crowd into submission; half the show is in the fight they give him. Performers and audience are one in a desperate, cathartic drama, and everyone loves each moment of the fray. The energy is siphoned off, the crowd breathless, elated, spent. The group stalks dramatically off stage. (Sander, 1969b:68.)

Here we see an expressive institution with a clear function of aggressive catharsis, though it is impossible to settle the question of its ultimate contribution to political violence. Likewise, many sports, such as football, boxing, soccer, and hockey, seem to be pointedly aggressive and, in this sense, "moral equivalents of war." An American professional football player commented:

> Let's not kid each other. Pro football is legalized violence. If we did the things on a street that we do on a football field, we'd be locked up. But when you give a human being the chance to be very aggressive, I guess there's a satisfaction to hitting people, hurting people and getting away with it. . . . The most satisfying thing in football is the good stick. The thing you remember the most is when you hit somebody and they don't get up. (Meyers, 1969.)

Similarly, certain kinds of drama have a high, pointedly aggressive content, ranging from the violence of melodrama and tragedy to the joking, clowning, and knockabout of slapstick comedy and Punch and Judy. Such sports and entertainments seem to be institutions for sublimation of aggression, for rendering riot, feud, mayhem, and murder, into legitimized forms, the least advantage of which is diversive and the most of which is to provide the euphoria of emotional fulfillment and the happy ending—specific catharsis for aggressive motives. While the question of vicarious catharsis of aggression has not been settled, there is little doubt that some institutions with high aggressive content do substitute for forms of conflict that would be worse. Let us call these *aggressive safety valves*.

Such is the role of an ombudsman, who invites complaints and charges and takes the case (as did the champion of medieval times) to the appropriate parties for redress. Indeed, the whole process of justice, insofar as it uses adversary procedures, may be called an aggressive safety valve. The forms of punitive and restitutive justice grew up historically as substitutes for blood feud and internecine warfare. Such a function of violence mitigation by a substitutive procedure, which allows opponents some measure of fair satisfaction with less harm to the group than by fighting, can be seen in the drum duels of the Eskimo, where men who have quarreled face one another dancing and singing insulting songs while the people watch. A convincing case has also been made that sorcery in primitive societies serves as a safety valve for aggression, by keeping people busy with relatively harmless witchcraft against one another. This substitutes for overt aggression and results in other beneficial side effects such as group solidarity, administration of justice, therapy, and faith in the future by such things as divination and astrology (Kluckhohn, 1944; Hallowell, 1940; Fortune, 1932; Warner, 1937; Evans-Pritchard, 1937). Such examples show us some of the various institutional ways in which societies can make aggression less harmful within the group, by using it or at least diverting it.

These institutions, of course, are not infallible. Some do not work because of the very fervor with which they are pursued. For example, a sociologist noted that soccer was an "opium" in Latin America, "an all-consuming commitment bordering on fanaticism." But this absorption in a supposedly satisfying sport did not prevent riotlike, even warlike, outbursts from occurring; for example, El Salvador severed diplomatic relations with its neighbor Honduras:

> The first two of the three-game World Cup regional finals were enlivened by riots as the fans from both countries attacked each other on the field. As a result, the final game was played in the shadow of 1,700 riot-ready police who had been called in to guard the stadium. The feelings aroused by the game were intense; and it was a short leap from the soccer arena to the political arena and El Salvador's decision to shut down diplomatic channels with Honduras. (Lever, 1969:36.)

Such a "safety valve" seemed to be producing more trouble than it prevented.

One of the best examples against which to compare such excessive effects of safety valves and which allows well-controlled aggression is one that clearly seems to serve a status system and its authority. This example does not involve the force of law against offenders, but is concerned with status-reversal ceremonies in which the "low man" gets a chance to kick back at authority and relieve himself of aggression that has presumably accumulated while he was taking orders. Thus, in Japan, year's-end ceremonies include saki parties in which employees sit on equal terms with the boss. After prolonged imbibement and conversation, under the supposed influence of alcohol, etiquette relaxes and the employees begin to unburden themselves of criticisms and complaints that they would never think of voicing under normal circumstances. The boss hears and accepts these remarks without any loss of face, and is supposed not to hold a grudge afterwards. Such catharsis occurs within the context of the paternalism and corporate warmth of Japanese industrial life, and presumably contributes to it. Likewise, among the Ashanti of Ghana, the Apo ceremony, an eight-day feast, allows a license for anyone to speak out against whomever he pleases and thus cure the complainant's "sickness of soul." The result is "a discharge of all the ill-feeling that has accumulated in structural relationships during the year," a purification that restores community feeling (V. Turner, 1969:179). Such also must have been the function of the ancient Athenian comedies, during which a license was given to lampoon leaders such as Pericles, community institutions, and even the gods. Nor is it so different when university students, in annual skits, make fun of professors and deans; or when newsmen in the annual Gridiron banquet in Washington ridicule to their faces the president and other officials who have been invited, and who with good humor endure, with the understanding that no quotation or publication of the transaction will occur afterwards. Such safety-valve institutions function by, so to speak, reversing the flow of frustration in the authority system, which normally flows downward, and gives the underdog the satisfaction, for the moment, of giving back, of being "king for a day." And the effect is to stabilize, not upset, the status order.

A more common way for aggression to serve the social structure, however, is by displacement outside the group toward enemies. Durkheim (1895) was the first to fully state the theory that such displacement is more than merely group defense but is also a *rite* by which the "collective conscience" is affirmed, satisfied, and strengthened. So, Durkheim argued, society, not always having external enemies to arouse its sense of solidarity, needs crime—continual action against deviants—to remind itself of what it feels and thus to bolster its unity. Paradoxically, Durkheim argued that society needs the criminal as much as the criminal needs (for his profits) society. In this way, the enemy, by whatever name he is called, is only a symbol for a role that the group needs to institutionalize for its own solidarity: the eternal drama found in myths and morality plays, occasionally acted out in courts of justice. Thus, Durkheim was the first to explain with any satisfactoriness how society wars against the deviant, to maintain its own solidarity, not only by displacing aggression but by making a solidarity ritual—a communion —out of it.

Along this line, Dentler and Erikson (1959), based on a study of Quaker work groups and of prepsychotics in an army camp, put forward the intriguing thesis that groups not only unwillingly allow deviation but also tend to "induce" and "institutionalize" it because it has functions such as "boundary-maintenance." So groups, instead of casting deviants out, try to keep them around if they are not too dangerous. A familiar example is the fool. By having deviants around, a group is able to get a better sense of its own norms and boundaries and "reaffirm its essential cohesion." The deviant also serves to displace aggression away from leaders or the group itself. A fuller overview of this idea was provided by K. T. Erikson (1966) in a study of New England Puritans and how they treated heretics, Quakers, and witches. Were these successive persecutions an effort by the Puritans to restore their own weakening sense of community by defining more clearly what it was that they were combating, that is, undercurrents of grievances that were in fact eroding their way of life? And did the execution of heretics and witches now and then appease hostilities that might otherwise have erupted against the Puritan leaders or divided the community?

Aggressive safety valves take us to the vexed question of *scapegoating.* Are there times when sacrifice of a victim spares the group a more destructive conflict? The standard civilized position was stated long ago by Gordon Allport (1948): Scapegoating is cowardly and pathological; educated people, such as scientists, are relatively free from scapegoating tendencies; the battle for democracy, which means respect for the person, is a battle against scapegoating. In witnessing the uses of scapegoats by totalitarian governments (Leites and Bernaut, 1954), one can only reaffirm that an ethical society should remain vigilant to see that no group is allowed to use such safety valves for its own emotional satisfaction or political advantage (Lowenthal and Guterman, 1949). But, recognizing its injustice, and its role in pathological prejudice, should not prevent us from seeing displacement of aggression for the benefit of the group as a normal social mechanism. It was so when the ancient Jews ritually loaded a goat with the sins of the community. It was so when the Christian community relied heavily upon the image of a satanic adversary to maintain its own moral vigilance, and when it occasionally blamed individuals for being in league with the Prince of Darkness. It was so when the Tlingit Indians of the American Northwest settled their interclan feuds by a procedure such as the following: If an important warrior was killed, a man of equivalent rank from the offending clan was arbitrarily chosen to go forth in mock battle against a kinsman of the dead man and allow himself to be killed while the tribe watched. It was his duty to die, and it would have been impossible for him to defend himself without running the risk of adding a second death to the score his people had to pay. He was a scapegoat for the good of his clan.

Such an institutional arrangement plainly worked as a safety valve to reduce the total amount of aggression which the people as a whole would suffer. In the absence of rational courts, such as we understand them, they had no better device by which to save themselves. It might be argued that, with better education, a more effective safety valve could have been devised; but that institution, primitive though it was, made the Tlingits better off than other tribal peoples suffering under the burden of bloody feuding, such as New Guinea head hunters (Berndt, 1962).

There must, of course, be many unanswered questions about safety valves, especially aggressive ones. Are they truly satisfactory or frustrating? Do they arouse more aggression than they avoid? Are they fully functional? Are they in balance functionally, and how does one tell unless one has examined the balance sheet for the entire system? Are safety valves needed only if a system is rigid, not if it is an open adaptive one? Coser (1956) took the position that—

> Safety-valve institutions may serve to maintain both the social structure and the individual's security system, but they are incompletely functional for both of them. They prevent modification of relationships to meet changing conditions and hence the satisfaction they afford the individual can be only partially or momentarily adjustive. The hypothesis has been suggested that the need for safety-valve institutions increases with the rigidity of the social structure, i.e., with the degree to which it disallows direct expression of antagonistic claims. Safety-valve institutions lead to a displacement of goals in the actor: he need no longer aim at reaching a solution of the unsatisfactory situation, but merely at releasing the tension which arose from it. Where safety-valve institutions provide substitute objects for the displacement of hostility, the conflict itself is channeled away from the original unsatisfactory relationship onto one in which the actor's goal is no longer the attainment of specific results, but the release of tension. (Coser, 1956:156.)

Such questions as to whether an adaptive society can do entirely without safety valves must wait not only further research but also considerable improvement in present institutions, to see what a life with minimal frustration and good adjustment would be like. The questions about aggressive outlets as safety valves are perhaps the hardest to answer. It is very much in doubt whether any aggressive outlet (whether a "moral equivalent of war" such as sports, or a drama of violence, or a small war that manages to avoid a larger one) does, in fact, reduce the short or long-run tendency to aggression and violence? Rather, do they not teach and build up such habits? For example, can it be plausibly argued that punching a bag makes a man less likely to fight? An especially important question is to what extent a *vicarious* experience of aggression can substitute for a real one. Does it teach, increase tension, even trigger such responses? Experiments have shown, for example, that children, after watching aggressive events, are more likely to knock dolls about (Bandura, 1963). Some psychologists argue that there is no such thing as free-floating aggressive energy that can be released or drained off by watching violence.

> Nobody has ever maintained that sexual desires can readily be satisfied through watching a couple make love. If aggressive urges are drained through seeing aggression, why aren't sexual urges lessened by watching sexual activity? As far as sex is concerned, just the opposite probably occurs . . . I think the analogy should hold . . . people may become somewhat aggressively excited through watching aggression for a period of time. . . . Our experimental research has demonstrated that the observer's attitude toward the scene he witnesses is an important consideration . . . if the observer thinks the filmed violence he sees is bad, morally improper, relatively strong restraints against aggression are often aroused. He may then lean over backwards to avoid acting aggressively. But, should the observer believe that the filmed aggression is good or proper, there is a somewhat greater likelihood that he, himself, will act aggressively, for a few minutes at least, after seeing the film. (Berkowitz, 1966:273–293.)

An expert, after surveying the laboratory and clinical evidence, concluded that "exposure to media violence does *not* drain off aggressive tendencies. But the pursuit of evidence goes beyond psychological issues and proceeds in places beyond the laboratory" (Larsen, 1968:117).

A laboratory study lending some support to the safety-valve theory showed that boys watching *mild* television programs (such as the Ed Sullivan show) were *more aggressive* than the group watching aggressive programs (such as "The Untouchables"), in the following ways: more than twice as many fistfights, angry and loud arguments, and criticizing or insulting others; about three times as much manifestation of jealousy. *No* group became *more* aggressive as a result of watching aggressive TV programs; some subgroups actually became *less* aggressive. Boys watching nonaggressive programs became more aggressive (Feshbach and Singer, 1970). Such findings suggest the possibility that violent programs might be used to reduce or control aggressive behavior.

To sum up these unsettled questions, we do not yet know whether vicarious experience of aggression drains off or increases aggression or whether a less harmful aggressive activity (such as boxing) can substitute for aggression. Does it teach, or does it reduce the total amount of aggression in the systemic balance sheet by fulfilling the total functions of safety-valve institutions?

Moreover, a question remains with regard to scapegoating. Though there is doubt that scapegoating reduces aggressive activity, and though it is generally conceded that such activity is a sign of inadequacy—an inferior solution to problems not well understood—nevertheless an emotional satisfaction (catharsis) in it must be considered among the safety-valve functions, especially when one recalls the position of Durkheim (1915) and Fauconnet (1920) that punishment is a moral affirmation of the collective conscience, which should occur in drama if not in life.

This leads us to the position that, regardless of physical inadequacies, *ritual* scapegoating is of great use to society. Things may be going wrongly in actual life, but they come out right in "horse opera"; for instance, the bad guy gets his deserts. Is this of no value to the public? The contribution of morality plays in mass communication has been well established (Warner and Henry, 1948). And once the ritual scapegoat is seen to include such symbolic figures as the Devil, the religious sacrificial victim (Warner, 1959; Duncan, 1962), the martyr (Riddle, 1931), and the fool (Klapp, 1949a), one can only conclude that there are enormous positive contributions of the ritual scapegoat to the morale of societies.

What, then, can be inferred from the present situation? As we have said, no conclusion is final yet concerning whether safety valves work or which one is best. For example, does the appalling level of aggression in the present situation mean that safety valves are failing or that they are being overwhelmed by too many sources of frustration and aggression? If we assume that they *do* work, then the search for better ones (diversive, cathartic, or aggressive sublimations) is justified.

Once one assumes that safety valves work the argument that they are necessary is confirmed, whether one takes the position that aggression is biologically inevitable (Lorenz, 1966) or that aggression is a product of the form of society (Dewey, 1922). If Lorenz is right, then safety valves for aggression will always be needed because displaced aggression is the price paid for formation of the social bond. If Dewey is right—that institutions produce warlikeness, that authoritarianism and conflict produce frustration—then safety valves provide, by sublimation, a way-stage to a better social order, easing the frustrations and allowing society to have as low an aggression level as possible in the less than Utopian circumstances. Even if it is granted that a society without internal frustration and aggression is possible, it would be Utopian unreality to expect this to be true of most societies, especially rapidly changing ones; perhaps it would be possible only in small, isolated communal groups. Moreover, do not systems where aggression is now low achieve it *by* applying safety valves? For example, a prominent part of the Hopi Indian cachina ceremonies is the role played by ritual clowns called "mudheads." These individuals, bedaubed with clay and paint into weird and comic appearances, are allowed to freely insult and accuse anyone in the community, and few escape their verbal raking. It might well be asked, how long would the famed Hopi peaceableness and cooperation last without such a safety valve?

We conclude, then, that safety valves for aggression and frustration (assuming they work) are needed by most societies, and will be for some time. A realistic present position would be that modern society is generating aggression too high to handle without such "crutches," that an aggressive society cannot afford to pass up safety valves. The argument hinges on the increase of aggression in the United States. The National Commission on the Causes and Prevention of Violence reported in 1969:

> Violence in the United States has risen to alarmingly high levels. Whether one considers assassination, group violence or individual acts of violence, the decade of the 1960's was considerably more violent than the several decades preceding it and ranks among the most violent in our history.

Crime rates (normalized) reported by the FBI have been rising continually. The mass media tirelessly repeat the same themes, leaving open the question whether vicarious public anticipation is increasing or decreasing actual violence. Leading psychiatrists, such as Karl Menninger (1968a), have conjectured that people really like violence; that's why we have so much of it.

> The inescapable conclusion is that society secretly *wants* crime, *needs* crime, and gains definite satisfactions from the present mishandling of it! We condemn crime; we punish offenders for it; but we need it. The crime and punishment ritual is a part of our lives. We need crimes to wonder at, to enjoy vicariously, to discuss and speculate about, and to publicly deplore. We need criminals to identify ourselves with, to envy secretly, and to punish stoutly. They do for us the forbidden, illegal things we *wish* to do and, like scapegoats of old, they bear the burdens of our displaced guilt and punishment—"the iniquities of us all." We have to confess that there is something fascinating for us all about violence. (Menninger, 1968a:22.)

A comparative study of civil strife ranked the United States first in magnitude of strife and turmoil among democratic nations of Western Europe and the British Commonwealth (Gurr, 1969:552).

All this aggression was associated with (and presumably to

some extent caused by) numerous frustrations prevalent in spite of affluence, and was by no means all attributable to inequities of material distribution (Klapp, 1969:47–70). The truth is that there are many causes of frustration, systemic in character, that cannot be reduced to poverty or ethnic discrimination; for instance, to mention a few of them: crowding, environmental deterioration, urban sprawl, noise and poor communication, irritation of conservatives at rebellious styles (long hair, hippies, etc.), frustration of the public at criminals getting away without punishment. A general explosion of expectations has led to frustrations and identity problems at all age and social class levels. Many of these frustrations can be associated with the explosion of expectations and psychic mobility accompanying social change, especially liberation from traditional patterns (Lerner, 1959).

Social scientists attribute increasing political instability to a rising frustration ratio, a disparity between level of expectations and means of achieving satisfaction, in changing countries (Davies, 1969; Feierabend, Nesvold, and Feierabend, 1969). Once the frustration ratio (depending upon high level of expectations) is kept in mind, it is plain that abundant societies in rapid change are likely to have very high levels of frustration, since it is easy for the wants and vexations made visible by communication to outrace the means of satisfying them. Indeed, as sociologists have shown, the anomie of rapid change and urban mass living is a poor condition for human fulfillment.

Such things (increasing aggression and frustration) argue either that safety valves are useless or more needed than ever; but there was no way at the end of the 1960s to be sure which was true. Was the need for safety valves decreasing with progress? On the contrary, one might as easily make the argument that various tensions connected with progress were threatening to overwhelm the remaining homeostatic mechanisms while offering few satisfactory new ones. Outbursts of all kinds were happening in spite of progress or because of it.

Vicious Circles and Oscillations

We turn now to another systemic communication problem: how faulty responses of components lead to worse rather than better adjustment—widening gaps and rise of tension levels—within a system. This problem, commonly called *polarization*, is due mainly to what in communications parlance are called lags and vicious circles. *Lags* are failures of a system to respond promptly enough to new information, so that what is being done is too late to be of much use or may even be directed toward a situation that no longer exists. A common statement of lag in a social system is found in the expression, "things have to get a lot worse before they can get better." Very often lags of a democratic society are caused by the difficulty of arousing public concern to the point where it prods officials to act. Thus, Senator Edmund Muskie in 1969 analyzed the reasons for the slow organization of the fight against environmental pollution.

> Until the Congress or the people feel strongly enough to insist that these programs have priority over some others, we are not going to get the money, and we are not going to clear up the pollution. You keep hounding it. I can cry alarm about this. I have for eight or ten years. And it is like the old story of crying wolf. You do it so often that pretty soon people get used to it and don't pay any attention to it until a disaster happens, such as Santa Barbara. . . . I suspect that dirty water and air and littered environment, dirty homes, streets, add to the depression and the frustrations and the restlessness of the peoples in the cities. So it is an interaction. You have to do the whole job. (*Christian Science Monitor*, March 1, 1969.)

This politician saw himself as a kind of gadfly stinging the great leviathan of the public and its official agencies into action, overcoming lags at various levels, beginning with the failure to connect societal tensions with their causes and to respond to the cry of "wolf."

A common sign of lags in response of a system (aside from sheer failure to respond) is *oscillations* of policy, that is, going too far one way before adapting to new information. This may be likened to a bicycle rider who zigzags because he is too slow in correcting his course. If he were to read the signals farther ahead, or if his muscles were better trained to respond, or if his cycle did not have a loose handlebar, his course would consist only of straight lines and smooth curves. As it is, he may run into a curb or a passerby before straightening out.

But a more serious matter is failing to recognize a *vicious circle* in time and continuing to do something that makes a problem worse. A vicious circle of positive amplifying feedback occurs when something that is done to solve a problem progressively makes it worse, as is the case when one continues to give medicine to a patient who is already dying of an overdose. This happens because the signals that ought to tell us to stop the dose are being read as a sign that the patient needs even more—*positive feedback*. Call this a lag in understanding, or a mistake in interpretation, as you please. Sociologists speak of *deviance amplification* (Maruyama, 1968) when progressively severe control measures lead to increasing alienation and defiance of rules, and therefore to less order in society (Lindesmith and Strauss, 1968:400; T. M. Mills, 1959; Wilkins, 1965). For example, it is well known that prisons aggravate the criminal outlook. Deutsch (1966) sees panics and other outbreaks of undesirable collective behavior as products of amplifying feedback.

> In cases of amplifying feedback, information about the response of the systems serves to reinforce that response in the same direction, and information about this reinforced response may produce further reinforcement of this behavior. Panics in crowds, market panics, cases of runaway inflation, armament races, or the growth of bitterness in an extremely divided community are examples of amplifying feedback systems in social or political life. . . . Amplifying feedback situations may . . . get out of control, and may damage or wreck the system. . . . Perhaps the decisive quantitative consideration . . . is the increasing or decreasing character of the series of increments in response to the mutual stimuli at each cycle of operation. If the sequence of reinforcements of behavior, due to the feedback phenomenon, forms a uniform or even an increasing series, then the total response must grow until it exceeds the limits of the system and ends in some form of breakdown. If, on the contrary, this sequence of reinforcements forms a decreasing series, so that, on the whole, each new reinforcement tends to be smaller than the ones that went before, then the total reinforcement will tend to approach an upper limit that need not be beyond the capacities of the system. (Deutsch, 1966:192–193.)

In human terms, a vicious circle is nothing but an interaction that escalates beyond the range of payoff to loss, by reinforcing responses. Anyone who has seen a friendly argument grow into a fight, or a flirtation become a tragic affair, or social drinking lead to an alcoholic binge, knows what a vicious circle is. Almost any relationship can develop vicious circles; for example: parents with disturbed children (Bettelheim, 1950; Redl and Wineman, 1951), paranoid interpretations (N. Cameron, 1943), violent strikes, escalating wars.

Emotions of a vicious circle need not be unpleasant at all stages. Joking is fun until it goes "too far." Conceivably, even love, good will, and generosity could have vicious circles if they went beyond the point where behavior was appropriate and beneficial and people lost freedom to draw out of interaction. What is vicious, in other words, is not the sheer content of the feeling but how it works: the fact that parties are "locked in" and are carried beyond the range of payoff (optimum or minimum) to serious loss. If, foreseeing such outcomes, parties could refuse to respond to challenges, flirtations, etc., or could hold down response so that interaction remained within the range of payoff (in ethics, commonly called "moderation"), no vicious circle would occur. The fatal thing, then, is inability to foresee the outcome and break the chain of reciprocal amplifying responses. In cybernetic terms, this means the conversion of positive to negative feedback.

So, ominous examples were noted in the tendency to "overreact" to civil disorder in the late 1960s, as in the police riot at the Democratic Convention, Chicago, 1968. The President's Commission on Violence (1969) reported urban melting pots getting hotter and hotter, and growing polarization of relations between Blacks and Whites, and misunderstanding by the Blacks of Whites' efforts to help them (fearing a Trojan horse by the "White power structure"). Response to protest by university students ranged from lenience to severe repression. In California in 1969 some sixty-five bills were introduced, cracking down on campus violence. Former Governor Edmund G. Brown accused Governor Reagan of "throwing gas on the fire" of campus revolts. "Merely prosecuting, merely calling out bayonets, merely calling for martial law, calling for a confrontation—these are things that are throwing gas on the fire." Yet Governor Brown admitted that he and the Democratic-controlled legislature in 1961 made the same mistake when they drastically stiffened narcotics penalties to end trafficking in drugs. Since that time, narcotics use had increased sharply. The "People's Park" issue at Berkeley, 1969, was settled by refusing use of this university-owned property by "street people," driving them off by force, and in the ensuing riot one man was killed and 130 injured. Two months later, nearly a thousand students and "street people" assaulted the fence that had been built around the area, cutting holes with wire clippers, under the rallying cry of "Bastille Day." And, though further attacks on the "People's Park" did not flare up, could one be sure that the despair and alienation into which some students lapsed—to say nothing of the increased bitterness of conservatives—was not also part of a vicious circle? Only further study of the course and consequences of vicious circles, it seems, could settle the question.

One thing that systems theory seems to make plain is that simplistic solutions do not always work. That is, if common sense says throw water on a fire, there are at least a few kinds of fire in which such a procedure acts like gasoline. Thus, biologists quickly found that obvious things like controlling disease did not by themselves improve the human condition but led to overpopulation, which made things worse than ever; the Pasteurian must be followed by a Sangerian revolution to restore equilibrium (Hardin, 1963). And, if relatively sophisticated efforts to change social systems led to such unexpected effects, was it not even more likely when moralistic responses were used to try to control a pluralistic society? A familiar cycle seemed to be endlessly repeated in efforts to suppress "dirty" books and plays, and to forbid drugs and alcohol: (1) suppression; (2) increased public interest; (3) stimulation of "under the counter" sales, with price and profits rising, and banned books becoming best sellers; (4) growth of a racket organization to supply the illicit demand; and (5) side effects, such as police corruption, public hypocrisy and cynicism, and growth of criminal enterprises. On the other hand, the unexpected method, diametrically opposed to conventional logic,* seemed sometimes to work. For example, Denmark tried legalizing pornography for adults and found that sales, prices, and profits of dirty films and magazines declined; sex became boring when prurient interest was not excited by curiosity; there was no increase in sexual crimes; pornography was "no longer an issue" in Denmark (*Time*, June 6, 1969).

Toward the end of 1969, yet another unexpected consequence of simplistic measures for controlling social systems was intimated: the "silent Americans" were becoming much more resentful, community workers reported that "everybody wants a gun," people were calling for even stronger measures to achieve law and order.

While the causes of vicious circles of rebellion and hostility are far from clear, in the absence of systemic research, sociologists are agreed that the popular tendency to overuse police and repression fails on several counts: (1) It does not deal with the underlying causes of tension; (2) it closes off avenues of legitimate protest, thus creating a structure conducive to violence (Smelser, 1962); (3) it does not take account of systemic consequences beyond the immediate situation; and (4) it inflames feelings of resentment and injustice, and therefore is likely to start a vicious circle of retaliation.

Such a vicious circle can often be seen as a *semantic sign change*, as a person who makes a claim to authority in the effort to create order actually puts others in a position where they are more likely to deny his authority and see him as an enemy. A few examples may explain this. The essential fact seems to be that the one who is claiming authority does something to destroy his bond of common ground with those whom he is trying to control. For example, why did the phrase "cool it" work so well in damping the urban riots of 1968 and 1969? The answer seems to be that it was felt as a call of "soul brother" to soul brother, to imply that "our" interest is not served by rioting and "we" have got to stick together. Now, contrast this "soul brother" way of claiming authority by gaining consensus with the opposite approach, which casts blame on dissenters and tries to put them down by calling their action "treason." This rallies a certain number of conservatives to use force against dissenters, but relentlessly pushes dissenters into the role of rebels who repudiate the authority of the blame caster because they see *him* as a villain—one who has wronged them by denying common ground and access to legitimacy, and who refuses to listen to their grievances.

* Jay Forrester argues that intuitive or commonsense thinking is "wrong most of the time" in solving systemic problems (1969:110).

They strike out at the same time against whatever force and insult were used for control. In other words, the authority has burned the bridge he might have used to communicate with the dissenters. The sign of his authority changes from positive (hero, author*ity*) to negative (villain, authorit*arian*). All he has left is his trump card, naked force. Thus, a staff report by Joseph R. Sahid for the National Commission on the Causes and Prevention of Violence (1969) compared two protest demonstrations that were organized and attended by many of the same people, but whose results were markedly different. The anti-inaugural march in Washington, January 1969, was quiet and orderly in response to restraint, indeed a friendly liaison between police and the younger generation. But the antiwar demonstration in Chicago at the Democratic Convention, August 1968, a terrifying explosion of repressive violence, "proved self-defeating; when officials decided to 'get tough,' chaos rather than order resulted."

A somewhat similar effect of polarization is seen when a group uses patriotic "flag waving" to rally support for what are presumed to be American principles and to imply that those who do not accept these are un-American. Flag decals, red-white-and-blue arm bands, and slogans like "love it or leave it," make patriots visible, and have the advantage of gaining cohesiveness among them; but the price in a pluralistic society of rallying people by symbols, which imply that others who do not rally are traitors, is to put people on the other side of a line and to turn the line into a gap. Moreover, since the real consensus that holds Americans together is faith in a game in which one bargains with others to reach compromises (called prices and laws), when an excited patriot yells "un-American," he places others outside the game and they see each other no longer as bargainers but as enemies. The moral of this is that with rallying, as with authority, you cannot destroy consensus or spend more credit than you have without incurring the danger of a vicious circle of alienation, in which each comes to regard the other as outside the game of bargaining.

A sociologist (Janowitz, 1968) analyzed the development of *escalated riots* in American cities, from communal expressive outbursts to more or less planned guerilla warfare. "The stark reality of the new type commodity riot is in the use of weaponry. It is truly an escalated riot." In the old-fashioned communal riot, the fighters used mostly brickbats; now there is dispersal of firearms and stockpiling. Sniper tactics are used by paramilitary groups. In the new violence there is more "defiance politics."

> The new type of rioting is likely to be set off by an incident involving the police in the ghetto, which is defined as police brutality, where some actual violation of accepted police practice has taken place.

The very first phase is generally nasty and brutish, while the police are being stoned, crowds collect and tension mounts. The second stage is reached with the breaking of glass windows. Local social control breaks down and the population recognizes that a temporary opportunity for looting is available. . . . The third stage of the riot is the transformation wrought by sniper fire, widespread destruction and the countermeasures created by police and uniformed soldiers. There can be no doubt that the countermeasures employed deeply influence the course of rioting—even in prolonging the period of reestablishing law and order. (Janowitz, 1968:13.)

Janowitz notes the curious role of the bayonet, a traditional part of American riot control:

The bayonet is completely useless as an instrument of riot control and the management of civil disorder. As a device for separating hostile groups or controlling mobs, it has some of the impact of a police dog, in that it produces countereffects that are not desired. (Janowitz, 1968:25.)

Modern riot control requires a minimal use of force; and for whatever is necessary, nonlethal means are more effective: helmets, water hose equipment, batons, wicker shields, and the like, rather than "display of the ceremonial bayonet." Another point noted in this study is that television coverage of rioting tends to aggravate the vicious circle of aggression by selecting provocative scenes, by portrayal of "symbols of identification" used by rioters (such as African headdress and costumes) which awaken group consciousness, sympathy, and factionalism in the audience (Janowitz, 1968). Thus, we see some elements in the standard American handling of riots which contribute to vicious circles leading to breakdown of authority, especially: police brutality, the symbolic role of the bayonet, and mass media treatment.

A cross-national study of seventy-three countries scrutinized for over twenty years of their recent history shows that political coerciveness sometimes increases, and sometimes decreases, frustration and violence, but that an important predictive factor is the *consistency* of political coercion:

Political regimes employing consistent levels of coerciveness, either high or low, reinforce social expectations of similar levels to follow. Hence previously permissive regimes which suddenly turn coercive will sharply disappoint social expectations of permissiveness. Furthermore . . . this fluctuation in level and deterioration of political liberties may be felt as illegitimate and tyrannical by the citizens. . . . Fluctuation in coerciveness levels breeds violence. . . . Undue and repeated flux in any social, political and economic performance or environmental condition is postulated as an important source of systemic frustration and anomie. (Feierabend et al., in press.)

Sociologists found that when there has been "sensitizing experience or predisposing ideology" (say, a publicized injustice against a minority or a community belief that certain groups are unfairly treated), the public is more likely to see a disturbance as legitimate protest, whereas it is more likely to see unwarranted violence if identification of grievances and the "call for help" are "too soft to be heard, or when the threat to the hearer is so loud that it drowns out the appeal" (Jeffries, Turner, and Morris, 1971).

Such things show us some of the difficulties in preventing vicious circles of feedback in the American social system. There are no easy answers; much more study of vicious circles is needed. About all that is known now is that the conventional wisdom of simplistic measures, moralism, and repressive force are not the whole answer. To keep "law and order" in a social system requires considerable restraint, sensitivity, and knowledge of the working of social systems which goes far beyond what is available to legislatures and law enforcement agencies today. From the systemic point of view, the vicious circles represent the failure not only of communication and control, but also of the various homeostatic mechanisms in our society, of which we know so little as yet.

Spillover Model

We are now in a position to visualize better some of the major elements of systemic balance that probably have much to do with outbursts of collective behavior. Figure 7.3, showing a kind of balance between tension level (the result of strains, lags, vicious circles), on the one hand, and homeostatic factors (institutions of reassurance, safety valves, tension management), on the other, summarizes the picture we are trying to reach.

Keeping such a balance in mind, we see that politics is unavoidably concerned with tension management, the main job of which is to view in one picture the systemic relationships and the level of tension. The objective is to manipulate these factors so that undesirable outcomes—such as hostile outbursts, damaging rumors, hysterical contagions, rebellion, deviance, and quitting the system as dropouts—will be less likely. By attacking the systemic strains, much can be done to improve the quality and happiness of life. But in the case of lags and vicious circles, it is equally—perhaps more— important to remedy the communication and decision problems that have so much to do with failing to use the resources we already have.

As it is, government is in a position of managing a system in spite of tensions resulting from failure of institutions and response to feedback, which is like trying to ride a horse with a burr under his

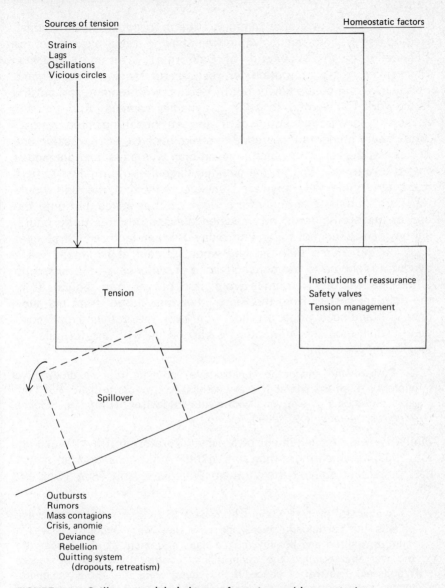

FIGURE 7.3. Spillover model; balance of tension and homeostasis.

saddle. A better way than expert rodeo riding would be to find the burr and remove it. So, we see politics today as trying to manage a restive horse while commissions of one kind or another hunt for the burr. President Lyndon B. Johnson was a master of "consensus politics, " but the Vietnam War overthrew him in midstream. President Richard Nixon showed a skillful pragmatism in avoiding extremes and courting the "silent majority"; but riots continued among minorities and students. On university campuses after such ex-

periences, one saw a new administrative preoccupation, to channelize and use student tension rather than having it boil over. Thus, the
Chancellor of the University of California (Riverside), Dr. Ivan
Hinderaker, got a reputation for resourceful tension management,
not by invoking police power but by dealing with tension and putting
it to work: "I wanted to build a dynamic campus. And for this
reason, I encouraged activism in the strongest possible terms."
When angry students threatened to strike because of repressive use
of force at Berkeley, in which a young man was slain, and demanded
that the American flag on the campus flagpole be run down to half-
mast, Dr. Hinderaker answered unexpectedly that the flag would
remain at half-mast not only for a week, as they asked, but until the
end of the spring term; he canceled classes, not for three hours,
as they had asked, but for an entire day. He then lectured the student
body on the theme that the flag would remain at half-mast "as a
symbol to face up to the consequences of violence. . . . It makes no
difference whether it comes from students or from police, from
the political Left or from the Right." For this, he got from his audience a standing ovation. He had won over the activists and completely disarmed the militants. He carried on with his formula for
tension management:

> Reward and encourage constructive activism; repress destructive
> violence. I am the friend of every activist who wants to build. But I am
> also the enemy of everyone who wants to destroy. (*Christian Science
> Monitor*, November 9, 1969.)

Similarly, wise management of M-Day (Moratorium Day), Washington, 1969, in which more than one million Americans took an active
part in protest against the Vietnam War, was, said *Time* (Oct. 24,
1969)—

> A peaceful protest without precedent in American history because
> of who the participants were and how they went about it. It was a
> calm, measured and heavily middle-class statement of weariness with
> the war that brought the generations together in a kind of sedate
> Woodstock Festival of peace. If the young were the M-Day vanguard,
> many in the ranks wore the housewife's apron and the businessman's
> necktie, and many who clambered to enlist were political leaders. . . .
> Hundreds of thousands of Americans found, face to face, that they
> had a common cause. . . . Probably the majority of the country were
> touched in some way by the outpouring. . . . What M-Day did raise
> was an unmistakable sign to Richard Nixon that he must do more to
> end the war and do it faster. (*Time*, Oct. 24, 1969:17.)

Thus, the successful management of M-Day apparently drained off
potentially explosive tension and helped build up new decision and
awareness of position of others—a contribution to the national will.

Presumably, an unwise handling of this demonstration could have had very much the reverse effect.

The job of tension management is to watch how the "general fund" of tension (anxiety, hostility, frustration, territorial crowding, hunger, sex, seasonal peaks, sheer restlessness, etc.) builds up, and seek the most sensible way to channelize it or, if possible, use it, taking account of existing safety valves or inventing new ones. Very much needed is an improved array of social indicators of such things as frustration ratio, alienation, exploding expectations, feedback deficits, and all other similar influences on systemic tension (Bauer, 1966). Of course, systemic tension management aims not to eliminate tension but to direct it to optimal level and uses.

> We must view tension as a normal, ever-present dynamic agent which, far from being "reduced" by automatic system processes, must —like the level of variety—be kept at an optimal level if the system is to remain viable. "Tension-reduction" theories must not lose sight of the positive contributions of tension-production in complex systems. . . . Communication networks and information flows can be seen as vehicles whereby tensions, intentions, and expectations are communicated as social pressures or interpersonal influences, and whereby selective responses are made whose sum total at any period contributes to the "institutional" order (or disorder) at that time. This transactional process of exchange, negotiation, or bargaining is thus inherently a morphogenic process out of which emerge relatively stable social and cultural structures; that is, definitions, expectations, motives, and purposes developing within (and outside) a given institutional framework act to reconstitute, elaborate, and change it by a complex of various levels of feedbacks. (Buckley, 1967:160.)

Expressive Movements and Systemic Balance

Let us, then, stand back somewhat and try to get a broader view of systemic balance as the relationship among five major components in which a deficit in any component changes the balance sheet for the system; hence, all components are affected. In this sense, tension management is a kind of payment on account, whereas social movements are an effort to make a large new deposit of principal. In our scheme we shall sketch ten vital relationships of exchange, or communication. From this it will be apparent that systemic debts cannot usually be localized in a single debtor-creditor relationship; that is, one cannot rob (or pay) Peter without paying (or robbing) Paul, John, James, and Mary.

Sociologists have various ways of classifying institutions; perhaps the most common categories are economic, political, religious, educational, welfare, recreational, and the familial. For our purpose of understanding the role of collective behavior in balancing or disturbing a social system, we need another kind of grouping in terms of function for tension management. In this regard, it is not so important to distinguish all different kinds of institutions as it is to see how institutions might work together, or in opposition, in relation to systemic tension and balance. Accordingly, we try to distinguish our five *"accounts"* (general categories of inputs and outputs) among which to keep a reckoning for the systemic balance sheet.

It might be supposed that two accounts would be sufficient for this purpose: the services by which the system meets the needs of people, and the protests that register the people's awareness that the system in some way has failed to meet their needs. But this is plainly inadequate, since so many expressive outbursts and other forms of turbulent collective behavior defy neat rationalization as protest. Against what are they a protest? What demand do they make? In many cases, people do not or cannot say. Take the following expressive demonstration on a university campus:

About fifteen students move in a procession into a grass quadrangle between classrooms, yelling and beating on wastebaskets. Their spirit is apparently cheerful and gay. They settle in a circle on the grass and begin rhythmic drumming. A student grabs a waste disposal can and improvises a "bass drum," which adds magnificently to the noise. The rhythm settles in, becomes catchy; you find yourself tapping your feet. Other students look on, some yell, but few come to join. New sounds are added to the orchestra as, for example, a bottle makes a syncopated bell clink. "What is it all for?," people begin to ask. Now, after twenty minutes of constant drumming, a screaming yell goes up, and the drumming reaches peaks of frenzy with screams. The crowd has, after twenty-five minutes, gotten larger; now one hundred are watching passively. No one has said anything; everything that has happened is nonverbal. Now chanting begins, and a few dance. The crowd has grown to three hundred. New pitches of frenzy with screams are reached after thirty-five minutes; now the noise is truly thunderous. By fifty-five minutes the last peak is over, drumming dies to clapping, and the demonstration stops at sixty minutes. Only a few outsiders have joined the demonstration; most of the crowd remained intrigued spectators. What did it all mean? At no point was any word uttered to explain. Something had happened that was apparently significant, and clearly deliberate, but no one could or would say what. There was no obvious issue of protest. If something was wrong with the school, why did they not say what it was? Even "rock" songs are more explicit. But, if no protest was pinpointed, perhaps it was because the source was too broad and could not be easily verbalized as a fault in a particular institution; perhaps a whole range—an entire series of transactions—was involved; perhaps there were communication failures in the system at the nondiscursive level, which could cause strains but leave people speechless about them.

Let us take the students at their "word," that is, that it was not a specific verbal protest issue, but that their demonstration had expressed a general feeling of something needed in life that was not simply traceable to one institution, that perhaps an entire complex of institutions and transactions was involved.

Without trying to specify all of these, let us posit five components of the systemic balance sheet. Let us call the first *expressive outbursts.* This includes spontaneous drumming, dancing, yelling, improvisations in "rock" music, rioting, and so on, when done for their own sake—the joy of participating and letting go—as distinguished from protest, which is not *inherently* much fun but aims at telling what is wrong and finding means to remedy a problem—the expressive satisfaction of protest is only incidental to its practical purpose; in expressive outbursts, "letting go," is the main thing. An analogy from medicine would be that play is fun, and play therapy can be fun because expressive; but, in general, the symptoms, diagnosis, and medical regimen (corresponding to social protest) are not fun. However, when expressive outbursts increase beyond a point (as when a person becomes too playful), we may suppose that something is wrong, that some deficiencies in the rest of the system are reflected in the outbursts. Deficiencies in what? Perhaps, if protest is difficult to verbalize, the deficiencies are in not meeting nonverbal emotional needs—an emotional deficit in some of the latent functions of institutions, which people do not understand clearly enough to complain about. This is where collective behavior may come into the picture most significantly, that is, to express kinds of tension not usually recognized as matters of political concern.

It is possible that expressive outbursts are in part a reaction against the general experience of too much control. Let us define as *control* those features of society which restrain action without *in themselves* providing material or personal rewards. For example, a policeman orders you to move your parked car (formal control), or a father's frown tells his son to shut up and eat his dinner (informal control). Such experiences are inherently frustrating because they do not in themselves provide rewards, but instead require a person to imagine and believe in future satisfactions that will come from obedience to the control. On the other hand, with rewards enough to become ends-in-themselves, control arrangements would be safety valves of the diversive type, as they have been described before (for example, a convict enjoys playing football within the penitentiary so much that he regrets being paroled). Obviously, control, because of its lack of rewards, is very likely to be complained about in political protest; and, when causing vicious circles, it can give rise to intolerable levels of tension and disorder.

A third part of our picture is *protest*, defined as verbalized expressions of grievances, more or less rational, usually in terms of "injustice." Explicit collective protest states in discursive symbols some failure of institutional services (manifest functions) and demands their remedy. Protest focuses on obvious, practical points; rarely is a failure of expressive life regarded as injustice (indeed, a Puritanical culture may even frown upon it). Protest, expressed in collective behavior, becomes a pressure of public opinion upon the system and its officials, or becomes the early stage of a social movement if a remedy lags.

The fourth element in the balance sheet, then, is *institutional services*, which keep society going by manifest functions (Merton, 1968:105) and are experienced by members as more or less measurable personal payoffs; for example, education can be measured in literacy, occupational achievement, and status symbols. Manifest functions may be so important that they are required by law; to receive them is a right, and to be denied them is injustice or grievance. Protest obviously focuses on such deficits.

But now, from our discussion in this chapter, we add a fifth component, *safety-valve institutions*, which presumably drain off tension from protest and provide various outlets, reliefs, and compensations: *expressive* (diversive, cathartic, aggressive) and *reassuring*. For example, expressive institutions such as Halloween and Fourth of July presumably have some effect in holding down aggressive outbursts at other times. Of course, institutions of play, religion, ritual, drama, and festivity have an important part in meeting emotional and identity needs (Klapp, 1969). Cox (1969a) analyzed the decline of festive institutions in modern society and the resulting tensions implied.

An important part is also played by images of a highly satisfying future (chiliastic visions, pie-in-the-sky, Sorel's myth of violence). Such things help make control and service experienced within the system feel more satisfactory. Hence, they are homeostatic. Changing systems, suffering the pangs of institutional birth, presumably need such buffers to offset or mask the thrust of the catalysts. Looking at all the safety valves, particularly at expressive institutions, we might hypothesize that loss or poverty of expressive culture could create an emotional deficit that would be repaid by an increase in expressive outbursts.

With these five basic components fairly accounted for, we are in a better position to begin talking about systemic balance. Surely, fewer terms would not be adequate. As has been said, protest usually focuses on two kinds of deficit: failure of services and overcontrol where no compensatory reward is visible. But it seems plausible also that a deficit in safety-valve (particularly expressive) institutions as emotional outlets could pay into protest without people knowing it and add vehemence to nonverbal outbursts. Conversely, if expressive institutions work well and give bonuses of personal payoff, they should take some of the steam out of protest, however real the grievances. Indeed, none of the five elements can be really satisfactorily discussed without reference to the other four. They must be considered working and changing together, simultaneously.

For simplicity, we can discuss them one at a time as they interact with the relationships indicated in Figure 7.4. These ten relationships need to be studied in terms of communication-flow problems existing among interpersonal relationships, mass contagions, meaningful transactions, feedback loops, vicious circles, and personal payoffs.

For example (referring to Fig. 7.4), expressive movements would be a trend along the line *EI-EO*, toward more *EO* because of a felt deficit in *EI*. For example, the great upsurgence of "rock" music, the new romanticism, and "revolution for the hell of it" (S. and I. Hoffman, 1968; Simmons and Winograd, 1968) in the latter 1960s might be attributed less to political and economic causes than to some deterioration of expressive culture that had made it necessary for younger people to seek new emotional outlets. How otherwise was one to interpret the movement of encounter groups, focusing on emotional experience and promising feedback and intense joyful experience; the Women's Liberation Movement, seeking a new feminine identity; entertainers and actors taking off their clothing; the Scientology technique for exploring your mind; phonograph recordings like "Signs of the Zodiac"; Witchcraft Coven (an authentic Black Mass, recommended only for those who have thoroughly studied Black Magic and are aware of the risks involved); and mind-bending experiences through the use of drugs. Such trends, when they become very widespread and are not merely a matter of more or less deviant minorities, seem to indicate that people are seeking new kinds of expression because old ones are felt to be lacking; taken together they indicate a systemic emotional deficit. Such things lead us to ask: What ails modern society? Is expressive culture inadequate; are festive institutions declining; do the arts lack spontaneity and opportunity for participation (in museums and concert halls); are people not having much fun—not even good conversation—at parties; is the role playing of a mobile society too shallow; are there not enough ceremonies of recognition where the focus is on *you*; is calculation displacing meditative thinking and "openness" to mystery, causing a loss of meaning (Heidegger, 1966)? Such deficits lead us to see meaning-seeking movements as

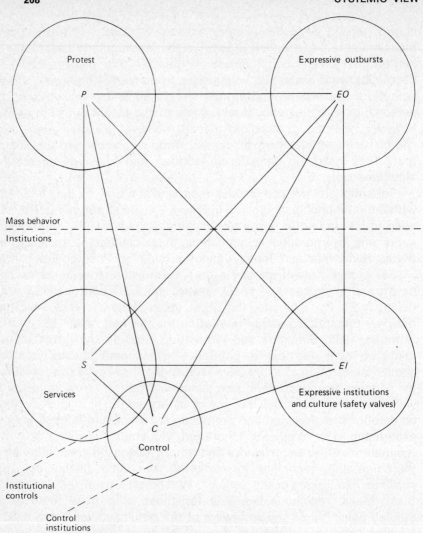

FIGURE 7.4. Systemic balance sheet: ten vital rela-
tionships of communicative feedback.
Problems of positive or negative feed-
back discussed in text: (1) C———S;
(2)   C———P;   (3)   C———EI;   (4)
C———EO; (5) S———P; (6) S———
EO; (7) S———EI; (8) EI———EO; (9)
EI———P; (10) P———EO.

an effort to compensate systemic deficiencies, one important transaction of the systemic balance sheet.

Another application of the chart would be to a Puritanical system
(as we saw in the case of the witch hunts of New England). Presumably, heavy discipline and the repressive effect of control would
have to be compensated by vivid images of future satisfaction. We

would expect safety valves to have a major function in relieving tensions: the more activities were banned by Puritanism (such as dancing), the more important the remaining expressive institutions would become. The Spartans and the Japanese Samurai had sports such as wrestling, swordsmanship, and archery as "moral equivalents of war." The Puritans had 3-hour fire and brimstone sermons as part of a rich ritual life, blame casting in an orgy of righteousness (Hester Prynne), and finally witches and heretics if nothing else would do. We would expect, in other words, an inverse relationship between control and the use of expressive institutions in a sector outside the range of activities repressed.

We can visualize several ways in which a system might fail to make its "payments" and hence favor outbursts of collective behavior: simple failure of control, leaving people free to do as they please (and others "uptight" because of their freedom); overcontrol, which increases frustration with vicious circles; failure of institutional service, with grounds for grievance; loss of meaning and satisfaction in expressive institutions, such as ritual, leading to emotional frustration; failure of safety valves; failure of communication that increases tension, such as protest not listened to and gaps of understanding; and overload of irrelevant information (a problem to be dealt with in Chapter 9).

The argument here is that there is a kind of push-pull relationship among these components (P, C, S, EI, EO). This is not a mechanical relationship, however, but a flow of communication of messages and symbolic transactions that encourage or discourage, increase or decrease, the working of other components (positive and negative feedback). Such relationships are, in fact, hard to trace and require much research. Many of the consequences are unexpected; for example, why did removing control of obscene literature in Denmark cause the problem of obscenity to vanish and its purveyors to go broke? Plainly, direct, simplistic suppositions do not always fit the facts. Nevertheless, we may state plausible hypotheses about the ten relationships among the five variables, all needing investigation in social systems. (Refer to Fig. 7.4.)

1. *Control—Services (C–S)*
   a. Overcontrol (additional restraint without actual or visualized rewards) favors—
      1) frustration.
      2) vicious circles of hostility and rebellion (loss of authority).
   b. The more services (manifest and latent functions), the more control tolerated, but the less control needed to preserve order, and vice versa.
   c. (A three-way relationship.) The more control without services, the greater the need for expressive institutions (safety valves).

2. *Control—Protest (C–P)*
   a. The more control without increase in services, the more protest.
   b. The more protest, the more political instability (defined in part as loss of control).
   c. The more protest, the greater the likelihood of overcontrol as a simplistic response, leading to a vicious circle.
      1) Overcontrol is more likely if protest is not perceived by the public as such, but felt to be illegitimate threat. Public interpretation of protest varies (R. H. Turner, 1969; Jeffries, Turner, and Morris, 1971); therefore, response varies, either as constructive remedies or overcontrol and more disorder.
3. *Control—Expressive Institutions (C–EI)*
   a. The more control, the more expressive institutions (safety valves) are needed.
   b. Even if control is constant, safety valves are needed as a cushion in the event of failure of services.
   c. The more expressive institutions, the less control is needed because tension is lower.
4. *Control—Expressive Outbursts (C–EO)*
   a. The more control (other things constant), the more expressive outbursts.
   b. The more expressive outbursts, the greater the likelihood of overcontrol and resulting vicious circles.
5. *Services—Protest (S–P)*
   a. The more services (manifest functions), the less protest, and vice versa.
   b. The more protest recognized as legitimate, the more quickly services are increased and improved. [see also 2b.]
6. *Services—Expressive Outbursts (S–EO)*
   a. The less services (manifest and latent functions), the more expressive outbursts and movements, and vice versa.
   b. Latent functions are more closely related to expressive outbursts than are manifest functions.
7. *Services—Expressive Institutions (S–EI)*
   a. Expressive institutions as safety valves help stabilize (reduce disorder and outbursts) in systems short on services.
   b. The less services (manifest and latent functions), the more expressive institutions are needed to compensate.
      1) The price of inadequate expressive institutions (especially when other institutions are lacking in services) is frustration, including identity problems (Klapp, 1969).
      2) Certain modern mass communications perform an emotional compensatory function for loss of functions in other institutions; for example, the family.
8. *Expressive Institutions—Expressive Outbursts (EI–EO)*
   a. The more (and better) the expressive institutions, the less expressive outbursts, and vice versa.
9. *Expressive Institutions—Protest (EI–P)*

    a. The more (and better) the expressive institutions, the less protest, and vice versa.

    b. There is less relationship between protest and expressive institutions than between protest and services, since protest focuses on manifest—easily verbalizable—functions and hence is not so responsive to deficits of expressive institutions.

10. *Protest—Expressive Outbursts (P–EO)*

    a. The more protest, the less purely expressive (cathartic) outburst, since such activities "drain off" each other.

or

    b. The more protest, the more expressive outburst, because they reinforce each other (open a "Pandora's box" of unrest).

    c. The more protest concentrates on specific service deficits (manifest functions), the less expressiveness there will be as a part (side effect) of protest.

    d. The more frustrating the response to protest (failure of communication, overcontrol, etc.), the more expressive outbursts there will be.

Such hypotheses suggest significant questions that students can ask about modern society, its conflicts and movements—what kinds of symbolic transactions will occur to redress imbalances. They give us a perspective, for example, on the strains of modern technology (too much control without expressive institutions?). At the research level, they point to a need for systems research on multiple relationships among these and other variables. To repeat, the argument does not assert a mechanical push-pull relationship, but rather the flows of symbolic transactions that need to be empirically traced. Experimental programs are needed on small and large systems, tracing message flow (formal channels, rumors, interpersonal relationships, mass media input, emotional contagions, ceremony and drama), and trying out policies with social scientific appraisal. There should be no more "Operation Intercepts" unless one knows, and is willing to pay, the costs in terms of consensus as well as economics. There should be no more use of tactics like those of Chicago police at the Democratic Convention of 1968, unless one is willing to pay the price in vicious circles. Adequate research will make it possible to find some kind of accounting of deficits and shifts in a system, and tell us what kinds of "payments" should be made and where. We need no longer regard "irrational" outbursts of collective behavior as sporadic events that just happen because of high tension.

It may be asked how, without such relationships being understood, can legislation, management, and planning be made possible? Once these relationships have been studied, we may hope to see more clearly what to do—besides the obvious need to repair service institutions—to reduce protest and political instability: abandon simplistic ordering and forbidding; avoid mistakes of overcontrol; learn how to improve feedback cycles; and repair and revitalize expressive life, perhaps by building new safety-valve institutions (an investment in leisure and religious institutions?). Once the systemic balance sheet is understood, the options should be clear and society can move in the direction it wants. "Progress" will mean something more than the thrust of technology into human affairs.

CHAPTER 8

Gossip, Rumor, and Talk

The feeling of "powerlessness" and lack of "participatory democracy" so widespread today is very much related to the fact that people feel they *can't talk* to those who actually control their lives. Normal political channels for talking to representatives (or to directing boards of corporations through stockholders' meetings, or to councilmen at city government meetings, or writing letters to Congressmen) are viewed with doubt, if not disdain, by many as mere tokens—not real ways to influence—and often thwarted by pressure groups working behind the scenes. Especially in cities, it seems futile to talk to a mayor or councilman if, as is sometimes the case, power is wielded by cliques of businessmen who do pretty much what they want to (Hunter, 1953, 1959; Rose, 1967:8, 492). When the formal leader does come forth to talk to his constituents—perhaps by receiving a delegation—many believe that this is only a public relations tactic, not true dialogue, and that his real talk is with different groups. It would be misleading, however, to suppose that loss of confidence in the effectiveness of communication is merely a political trend; it would be even more simplistic to attribute it primarily to chicanery. The broad trend of our society is, in balance, against talk that relates persons one to another and in favor of impersonal and monological communication through mass media. Eddies of dialogue (whether by telephone conversations with television viewers or by panels of experts discussing public affairs for the benefit of mass audiences) do not reverse the tide. The old-style New England town meeting, where it survives, is only a vestige of earlier days.

Faith in the power of talk is strong only when you feel you have some claim—either of responsibility or familiarity—on the person talked to. Buttonholing a politician as he pushes his way through a crowd is a poor substitute for this. But other reasons for lack of faith in talk exist, not all coming from modern society. In Puritan days, for example, talk had to be pretty much to the point—businesslike or religious—or it would be regarded as idle and vicious. The fact that the Puritans talked themselves into witch hunts does not gainsay this low opinion of idle talk. But modern reasons for the low repute of talk come from our media-oriented society. It is recognized that the printed word has more prestige than the spoken, except in special, close relationships. Even then, if the person who speaks to us says, "I got it from a book," he gains in credibility. The mass media are regarded as a reliable source of "news," whereas gossip and rumor are thought of as "wild," unreliable, harmful, without which we would probably be better off. All oral processes are somewhat at a disadvantage. Story telling gave way to story reading, and reading in turn to television. People seem so "plugged into" public media today that they pass up opportunities to talk, even to relatives.

All this has been summed up as the *monological trend* of a media-oriented society. Matson and Montagu (1967) said—

. . . The field of communication is today more than ever a battle-ground contested by two opposing conceptual forces—those of *mono-*

logue and *dialogue*. The "monological" approach, which defines communication as essentially the transmission and reception of symbolic stimuli (messages or commands), finds its classical formulation in the art and science of rhetoric and its characteristic modern expressions in cybernetics, combative game theory, and the repertoires of mass persuasion. The "dialogical" approach, which regards communication as the path to communion and the ground of self-discovery, found its original champion in Socrates and has its spokesmen today in such diverse currents of thought as religious existentialism, post-Freudian psychotherapy, and sociological interactionism. . . . These writers have made us aware that human communication, wherever it is genuine, is always a person-to-person call—never a transcribed message from an anonymous answering service to whomever it may concern. The symbolic paradigm of this interpersonal encounter, formulated by both Marcel and Buber, is the relation of *I* and *Thou*. . . . The end of human communication is not to *command* but to *commune*. . . . It was John Dewey who observed that "there is more than a verbal tie between the words common, community, and communication." Just so there is more than an alliterative connection between the terms *democracy* and *dialogue*. (Matson and Montagu, 1967:viii, 3, 5, 6, 10.)

Early in the 1950s it had become fashionable to view with alarm the "totalitarian" implications of this trend toward monological communication. Aldous Huxley's *Brave New World Revisited* seemed to confirm the dismal picture painted of 1984 by George Orwell. Huxley (1958) wrote—

. . . If the great impersonal forces now menacing freedom continue to gather momentum . . . the best of constitutions and preventive laws will be powerless. . . . Under the relentless thrust of accelerating over-population and over-organization, and by means of ever more effective methods of mind-manipulation, the democracies will change their nature; the quaint old forms—elections, parliaments, Supreme Courts and all the rest—will remain. . . . The ruling oligarchy and its highly trained elite of soldiers, policemen, and mind-manipulators will quietly run the show as they see fit. . . . In my fable of *Brave New World*, the dictators had added science to the list and thus were able to enforce their authority by manipulating the bodies of embryos, the reflexes of infants and the minds of children and adults. . . . Under a scientific dictator education will really work—with the result that most men and women will grow up to love their servitude and will never dream of revolution. There seems to be no good reason why a thoroughly scientific dictatorship should ever be overthrown. (Huxley, 1958:110–111, 118.)

But scientific students of mass communication, summarizing available research, were reaching a rather different picture: The media are not omnipotent; their power to influence people directly is greatly exaggerated (for example, to convert voters or to cause crime); they work mainly to reinforce and to channelize existing attitudes rather than to create new ones (Schramm, 1954, 1960; Klapper, 1960). The power of mass media to change attitudes and behavior is mediated by the personal influence of a more articulate segment of the audience, called *opinion leaders* (Lazarsfeld, Berelson, and Gaudet, 1944). Opinion leadership is stronger than mass communication and has the power to buffer it. Whatever the effects of mass communication, they are "two-step"; that is, certain messages from the media are usually picked up by opinion leaders, who in turn pass them along to their followers. The effect of the media is brought about when opinion leaders exert personal influence on a following or circle of acquaintances. For example, certain gregarious, middle-class women have quite a voice, whether as models or by their opinions, in what fashions other women adopt (Katz and Lazarsfeld, 1955). In general, their mediation consists of: (1) being exposed to more messages than their followers, (2) filtering messages, (3) embodying them in their own choices, and (4) exerting personal influence by modeling, talking, or even deliberately acting as "change agents" (Rogers, 1962).

Was it, then, a surprise to find that in spite of the "power" of the media, which seem to be binding society together, a malaise called "alienation" is very common, an "anomie" that is the opposite of morale, cohesiveness, and "we" feeling. Far from the nightmare of 1984, the reality, especially in urban centers, is a poorly knit society, with many people "apathetic," wanting "escape," and "dropping out" (Klapp, 1969). And even totalitarian societies like Soviet Russia, for all their monopoly of communication, have substantial portions of dissenters—for example, liberal artists and writers, who have somehow managed to withstand the omnipotence of mass communication and the omnipresence of Lenin.

How is this possible? We can put it in perspective by concentrating in this chapter on talk as a collective process, especially gossip, rumor, and public opinion formation. In general, the argument is that the low opinion of oral communication—regarding either its power or reliability—is not justified, and that the "unreliable" processes of gossip and rumor in a media-oriented society more than earn their keep.

Talk in the Small Community

Talk is the lifeblood of the small community, whose basic transactions are oral and interpersonal, though it may receive input from mass media. The small community is a little world whose internal affairs seem more important than what goes on outside. The main medium of internal news is gossip.

One of the best pictures of the social role of gossip is provided by Blumenthal (1932), whose study of "Mineville," a Western town of 1,800 population, shows some of the advantages and disadvantages of living in a small town. "Mineville" was a hotbed of gossip; the main hobby was talk about somebody else. Since everyone knew everyone else, there was plenty to talk about. Most of the people took part in this talk, though if asked about it, they would outwardly condemn gossiping. They tended to minimize the significance of their own gossiping, yet became upset when they were the focus of talk. Whether or not one was a "bad" gossip depended on one's relationship with the teller. The chief gossipers were "social historians" who could remember everything about everybody. In 2 hours a story would completely circulate the community, though most would know it in a half-hour.

Over half the residents had telephones, and the women were able to gossip on the phone while the men were at work, then summarize for their husbands at night, who in turn had their share to contribute. Intimate tidbits of personal information were usually fed into gossip through betrayed confidences. Blumenthal analyzed the reasons for the inability to keep a secret. Because all the townspeople were so closely related by kinship and friendship, there was no one in whom one could confide who did not have some other relationship equally confidential. So the spread of information was due not so much to irresponsible information purveyors ("bad" gossips) as to normal disclosures of intimacy. Moreover, if the relationship was broken, as in a quarrel, the situation was ripe for a wholesale breaking of confidence. Moreover, many disclosures came from accidental slips, which might happen in the effort to tell an interesting story, to win a point in an argument, or to seem important in other people's eyes. Finally, many confidences were broken because people simply forgot they had received the information in trust. Not only did people tell what there was to know, but they also knew each other so well that they could deduce the channels through which the news traveled and thereby evaluate its reliability.

The chief gossip centers were the school (children were important agents of gossip) and "Sid's Tailor Shop," which was for Mineville's men what the modern beauty shop is for today's women. It was a center for discussion of everything by way of news and the best place to sense shifts in public opinion. The tailor was like a newspaper editor in that he would hear both sides of a story quicker than most others, and try to arrive at a true statement of the situation. He took pride in his informal status. Thus, if one wanted to find out quickly what was going on, one went to Sid's Tailor Shop to talk to those who liked to "hang around and talk."

Thus we have a picture of a community both fascinated by gossip and afraid of it. It was a community ruled by Dame Grundy (as we epitomize that sharp-eyed little old lady who looks out from behind the lace curtains). Gossip was like a weed in its irrepressibility as part of the general love of story telling. But, unlike a weed, "gossip is the lifeblood of the town which makes every person's tongue a whip to discipline his neighbor and, at the same time, put every neighbor at his mercy" (Blumenthal, 1932).

This means that, sociologically, gossip is the main means of informal social control, not only in pressure to conformity but also in expression of criticism leading to change. It is an oral, public, opinion-forming agency. Its power to work as a sanction lies in the fact that, along with what parties know about each other, moral judgment is passed along the chain from A to B to C, which takes shape as social opinion (consensus) and leads to various activities of control (whereas a stranger's values would be of no significance). It is the ability of gossip to formulate moral judgment that makes it so important to the community. Moreover, we must not conceive it as simply cruel (as it might be to strangers) but protective and even forgiving. For example, in Mineville, police found certain difficulties in law enforcement: They could not easily arrest their own neighbors and buddies; an offender was not merely an individual but a member of the Jones family, whose reputation helped him. There was a general concern of people for each other and a sense of responsibility to those they had known all their lives. There was a unique credit system, in which, knowing everyone, merchants extended credit to everyone. The community took care of its own, and outside agencies such as the Red Cross were not called upon. Thus, we see that gossip is part of the texture of a living community.

Because of its functions, we find gossip institutionalized in various ways in social systems. For example, among the Azande, an African tribe, it serves as a mechanism of law enforcement and crime detection. Witch doctors are called upon to divine, by examining a chicken's entrails, who has committed an offense against tribal law. But they know well enough the guilty party, for the witch doctor is also a gossip expert and hears everything that people are saying. It is no surprise that law enforcement often coincides with tribal consensus (Evans-Pritchard, 1937).

Another use of gossip is found in the classic study by Willard Waller (1937) of rating and dating on college campuses. The pattern of association—therefore, ultimately the social class system—depended upon what students said about others as dates in dormitory and fraternity and sorority "bull sessions." Thus, gossip made its contribution to stratification.

Yet another function of gossip is found in what is sometimes called the "cosmic ooze" system in promotion of college professors and others whose performance has to be rated, in part, by what people say about it, especially when it is difficult to apply technical criteria. In short, gossip is highly functional for social systems. But it becomes dysfunctional when so wildly inaccurate and harmful that it disturbs a system more than it helps it, perhaps because it lacks intimacy of relationships or the sharp eyes of Dame Grundy to help it tell the truth.

Under favorable conditions, the gossip-monger is not the irresponsible slanderer, the agitator arousing discontent and breaking down confidence in institutions, but an agent of *homeostasis.* Where gossip loses credibility, perhaps because stories come from strangers who do not know or care much about each other, and distortions become wild, then we are in the realm of rumor, about which more needs to be said. But, even where rumor is rife and irresponsible, perhaps because mass media lack credibility, the journalistic gossiper can have a function, as illustrated by the column of Drew Pearson, "The Washington Merry-Go-Round," which became a Washington institution. As the *Christian Science Monitor* commented, "Every corner-cutting politician quaked lest some disgruntled secretary, some irate constituent, some blackmailing enemy telephoned his tale to Pearson."

But reporting to the newspapers and adding to the amount of news carried by the mass media is not the proper function of gossipers, whose duty is to the oral system of the small community. Gossip carries opinion about the common life of people who know one another. A community buzzing with gossip gives proportionately less attention to the outside world; it is ethnocentric, introverted; in an isolated primitive tribe or rural village, gossip and rumor may be all there is. Its affairs are local: the size of the fish catch, a coming festival, a child that died. According to the ideal model of Redfield (1947), a folk society has no information input other than its own affairs. While such insulation is rare in reality, it is true that news of the outside world typically comes to a primitive society as rumor input to the gossip network. For example, the Tikopia, according to Firth (1956), have no word which distinguishes news as we understand it (verified, known source) from hearsay or what people are saying, though they do take an interest in whether accounts are true or false and suspend judgment when in doubt. They have a great interest in news, both from the outside world (such as the arrival of a ship) and local (the fishing, an illness or death, what the chief in the next village is doing), and get it by word of mouth daily.

Folk are continually traveling up and down the beach and along the inland paths, and exchange of news is part of regular social intercourse, as it tends to be in any rural area. Between districts there is less contact. Formal visiting is not very frequent . . . when it occurs, as for a dance festival or some other large-scale ceremony, or when a vessel arrives from overseas, the visitors are apt to remain separate from the local residents, to hang about together under the trees or to sit together in a house. But even then there is plenty of exchange of information between the parties. . . . An arrival from one side of the island at a ceremony on the other is usually asked first for news. (Firth, 1956:122–132.)

News is also passed from one island to another by ceremonial whooping and firing of guns. Likewise, drum signals are used to extend the oral system.

Among the Arapesh of New Guinea, Mead said—

When . . . some event of importance occurs, a birth or a death, a quarrel of proportions, the visit of a government patrol, or a recruiting European, or the passage through the village of a traveling party of strangers . . . there are shouts and drum beats from hilltop to hilltop. But all that the signals convey is that something has happened about which the listeners had better become excited. A furious drumming on one hilltop starts off a series of shouted queries in a relay system from hilltops nearer to each other, or a child or a woman is dispatched to find out what has happened. The listeners immediately set about guessing what all the excitement can be about, speculating rapidly as to who may be dead, or traveling, whose wife may have been abducted, or whose wife sorcerized. A dozen explanations may be introduced and, according as they appear plausible, the movements of all the listeners will be altered or not. If no one can think of a plausible reason for the commotion, most of the listeners are likely to set off in the direction of the sounds. There is some slight attempt to differentiate drum beats, but . . . the distinctions are always getting blurred. The point of communications is to excite interest and bring together human beings who will then respond, on the spot, with emotion, to whatever event has occurred. . . . Interestingly also, when people tell stories about past events, they tend to impute to the moment when the drum beat was heard from a distant hilltop, a full knowledge of what they learned only after they had responded to the drum beat. (M. Mead, 1964:9–26.)

Another South Pacific people, the Manus, are more specific in their drum signals. A certain pattern of beats means, for example, "I am about to announce the date at which I will give a feast." The drummer beats out the number of days before his feast carefully, and the listeners take note. Each houseowner has a special pattern of beats, which is his signature. Another extension of the oral system is found among the Balinese; the town crier goes through the streets announcing a coming feast, according to a precise calendar, and specifying what each household is to contribute, and which groups in the population are to appear at the temple at what time and for what services (M. Mead, 1964). Festivals that bring tribes together are also occasions for extending the oral network. During the summer gatherings of Eskimos, drum duels between hunters who have quarreled allow each to challenge and insult his opponent, and incidentally to bruit a lot of gossip. A similar news spreading is found in the improvisation in calypso songs in the West Indies, in which one puts to rhyme some foible or secret that is as yet unknown or gilds a known fault more brightly.

Oral communication networks by such primitive means may be very extensive; indeed they sometimes seem to work almost as well as mass media in spreading news over wide areas. Rural villages of India, for example (Dube, 1967), show an amazing ability to know by word of mouth what is happening far away. In 1962, when Communist China attacked a remote part of the Himalayan border, a national survey of 198 villages randomly chosen from different states, some far away from the event, showed that 83 percent of the villagers had heard of the attack shortly after it occurred. Only a small proportion of the communication could be attributed directly to radio and newspapers; by far, the majority had gotten their information from face-to-face oral communication through traditional channels. "The proverbial isolation of the Indian villages is a myth. The economic, social, and religious networks that join together a number of villages are accompanied by their own channels of communication" (Dube, 1967:139–146.)

Thus, it seems useful to make a distinction between *gossip* and *rumor* as types of oral communication, depending upon where they come from and what they tell about. Both are hearsay and unverified by modern standards of news. Gossip is internal news and the small community or primary group is its locus, whereas rumor comes from the larger society, the world outside. Gossip is intimate and personal in focus, whereas rumor is more impersonal and tells of the doings of strangers. Gossip is chatty and conversational; there is a sense of relationship between the teller and hearer which help make the news interesting; whereas the interest of rumor arises from external urgency, the possible importance of remote events. In gossip there is high consensus among the participants because they belong to the same community and know and have a lot in common, whereas there is lower consensus, greater heterogeneity of opinion, and greater ignorance of actual events shared by the participants of rumor.

Finally, gossip clearly creates consensus and serves community action, whereas this cannot be so often said of the larger area integrated by rumor; conflict and divisive (wedge driving) effects are more likely. Gossip has an insuperable advantage over rumor: the thousand eyes and ears of those who live in the same community and can speak dialogically with one another. Within the smaller system, gossip often follows sociometric lines, such as visiting patterns, which can easily be charted (Loomis and McKinney, 1956), but this is not so easy, if not downright impossible, for rumor.

Traditional societies rely heavily, if not altogether, on oral systems to preserve the culture, socialize the young, and share information. In our own society, oral systems are a vital underpinning of mass communication and public opinion formation, and to appreciate their effects we must understand their features. Often we can see these most clearly where speech is the predominant medium, not competing with mass communication.

To keep its affairs going, an oral system depends primarily on word-of-mouth communication between persons present and known to one another. There is little reference to writing, print, or other mass media; and what there is is interpreted, filtered, and made effective through the oral system.

Such a system, partly because of its need to preserve an unwritten tradition, puts a premium on ability to tell and remember. The story teller is not just an old grandmother serving as babysitter in disadvantageous competition with television, but a person with a respected function for the whole group, listened to as seriously by adults as children. There is stress on oral performance; status goes to those who are wise, that is, who remember and speak well. The social historian is not just a gossip (as in Mineville), but has the duty to remember protocol and tales of importance to the group, whether legend or history. Firth (1956) said of the Tikopia:

> The Tikopia are great narrators. They delight not only in hearing news as items of information; they also delight in giving and hearing a presentation of news in elaborate aesthetic form, with dramatic emphasis. They dwell on incidents, the narrator taking time to explain in particular his own emotions and thoughts as an event takes place. Such narratives are normally presented as a record of actual events. In this the reproduction of remembered items may be often extremely accurate. In 1952 I heard a Tikopia describe to others many details of my movements in 1928–29. A stone on which I had sat under a tree in a pause in a walk 23 years before was pointed out. A funeral gathering was told by one man of a song which I had not finished writing down at his dictation then (the remaining stanza was dictated to me on the spot) and so on. And in 1928 I was given details of the visit of H.M.S. "Mohawk" thirty years before, including loss of one of her anchors off Tikopia—a story which on checking recently (in 1955) I found to be quite correct. (Firth, 1956:122–132.)

Such memory and narrative feats remind one of the ability of Swazi herdsman to remember each of hundreds of cattle, reported by Bartlett (1932). It depends on what one is interested in and how important it is. The most important stories may be preserved in ritual by dramas, dances, and other performances; and the performers have a correspondingly important status.

Regardless of who has the responsibility of keeping traditional stories alive, it may be said that status governs all communication in oral systems; that is, people want to know *who* said it and what right he had to speak; the source is just as important as the content of the information. A person speaks at appropriate times, and in different ways, depending on the status of the other; to some he speaks not at all (as in brother-sister avoidance). Not knowing the proper style in which to communicate may nullify the message. For example, the Japanese are very sensitive to status and have different modes of address for males to males, males to females, youth to age, and so on. One American Nisei, who studied Japanese before returning to the country of his fathers, was embarrassed by puzzling reactions to what he knew to be excellent pronunciation, until he discovered that he had been taught a *feminine* style of speaking. In oral systems, age usually has the advantage in speaking because with long memory goes a reputation for wisdom and perhaps the *mana* of the warrior or medicine man. Where status governs in communication, there is a high ratio of prescription (for example; advice, moral judgment, command) to merely descriptive information because people who speak the most also have the right to say how things should be done. Since they are used to this, people living in oral systems prize wisdom, proverbs, omens, moral tales, and so on, and do not prefer the "objectivity" of factual information.

In an oral system, where status governs who speaks when and to whom, there is not likely to be a democratic equality in expression of opinion. Nevertheless, lack of voting and the right of everyone to talk equally does not rule out *vox populi*, because the status of he who speaks may include the obligation to speak for those who are silent. Thus F. and M. Keesing (1956) described opinion expression among Samoans. An opinion poller would have "thin pickings" among these people because a "wall of inhibition" surrounds individual judgment; few are ready to express personal opinions outside the proper communication channel on any issue of concern to the group. Even leaders are not willing to give opinions or "spot" decisions in fields of their responsibility. The reason is that elite decisions involve group responsibility; and, to be effective, they must have marshaled behind them support from adherents, peers, and superior groups concerned. To know what a decision means, you

must know all the "voices" involved. The leader does not know
what his opinion stands for until he has been through an oral
communication process:

> A titleholder is essentially a responsible group representative. His
> "voice" is correspondingly a group voice. He must therefore correctly
> consult back to his adherent supporters as well as deal with his peers
> or superiors . . . which might provide "voices" in a traditional deliber-
> ation process: the household, close kin, and community assemblies
> and the supra-village elite or *matai* assemblies of extended family, re-
> gional, and "all Samoa" character. Which deliberating group would be
> appropriate to handling a given problem is defined by tradition and
> custom. . . . Whether or not . . . all adherents of a given titleholder
> are actually consulted the weight of their support is nevertheless
> ideally always there as a generalized "voice," back of his personal
> "voice." . . . It must never be forgotten that each elite member, in
> speaking publicly, has by implication his group back of him. . . . If
> he fails to carry these with dignity, honor, and satisfaction in his
> supporters' eyes he can be rendered powerless, replaced, and even
> banished or otherwise punished. (F. and M. Keesing, 1956:91–129.)

On the other hand, having group support, a leader may seem authoritarian and overbearing. His sensitivity to the group he represents
determines how far he can go. With these nuances of meaning and
implied powers, the Samoan assemblies take the form of a verbal
game in which there seems to be delight for its own sake and little
explicit formulation of decisions.

> Samoan leaders delight in talking . . . what is enjoyed and sought
> is not the decision but the prolonged drama of the *fono* proceedings.
> A speaker is applauded not for what he says but for his control of the
> nuances of the speaking art.

One who plays this subtle game must know the rules, the bounds
beyond which he may not go; but he is allowed all kinds of individual
plays that display his virtuosity, the exciting gambit, the trick, the
daring maneuver, the disguised stroke, in the way of a player performing to please his audience rather than merely win points. This
game goes on, seemingly endlessly, "until by suasion, compromise,
or downright weariness, at least an outward appearance of unanimity
is forthcoming"; the Samoans avoid any conclusion that aligns a
majority against a minority (F. and M. Keesing, 1956). Thus, though
there are status differences in Samoa and no "individual" opinion,
equal or otherwise, everyone—even the women who sit outside the
men's circle—shares in the leader's "voice" in some appropriate
way, not only when he rarely takes a definite position but when he
performs orally for the glory and fun of it in the assembly. No one
feels left out of the political process.

An oral system not only allows a person expression through the status of others who "speak for" him, but the high rate of personal feedback in day-to-day transactions means much expression as well as support to the ego. A balanced oral system allows maximum interplay of person on person throughout a day, week, or season—continuous dialogical exchange at many levels, a time for joking, love, solemn ceremony, convivial eating, physical contest, body contact, debate, drama, rhythm—even orgy—all the modes of interaction which together can make a full person. (Which is not to say that oral systems cannot make people dour, stilted, Puritanical, paranoid, and so on, as anthropologists can well attest.) But the potential range of interaction makes great self-expression possible. Nonverbal cues and interactions by tone, manner, gestures, etiquette, kinesics (Hall, 1959; La Barre, 1967; Birdwhistell, 1970), together with the whole range of ritual (Klapp, 1969), are important parts of the oral system—it is never a matter of words only. Even where the rule "silence is golden" is applied, there is a great deal of personal expression and recognition; just because a person is noticed, people are responsive to him, he matters in the status system.

This returns us to a point already made: Where gossip is of high value, everything a person does matters, a thousand eyes and ears take account of his performance in a festival, his presence or absence from a gathering, his success in enterprises, his attitude and demeanor from day to day. He may complain about intrusions into his privacy (as if he were a city person), but not about lack of concern.

In an oral system, information disseminated by the media is filtered by *gatekeepers*, usually people one knows (or people known to people one knows) who occupy central statuses and key positions in interpersonal communication networks. In a traditional system, the right to speak and convey information, and the duty to listen, may be established by status; and the centrality of a status in a communication network (for example, a telephone operator, or a person in an information booth in a railway station) can make almost anyone who occupies that status in some sense a gatekeeper (Leavitt, 1951). A classic picture of the traditional gatekeeper is provided by Lerner's (1958) description of a Turkish village leader:

> At the time of Tosun's visit, there was only one radio in Balgat, owned by no less a personage than the Chief. In the absence of any explicit orthodox prohibition on radio, the Chief, former soldier and great admirer of Atatürk, had followed his lead. Prosperous by village standards, being the large landowner of Balgat, he had bought a radio to please and instruct his sons. He had also devised an appropriate ceremonial for its use. Each evening a select group of Balgati foregathered in the Chief's guest room as he turned on the newscast from

Ankara. They heard the newscast through in silence, and at its conclusion, the Chief turned the radio off and made his commentary. "We all listen very carefully," he told Tosun, "and I talk about it afterwards." Tosun, suspecting in this procedure a variant of the Chief's containment tactics, wanted to know whether there was any disagreement over his explanations. "No, no arguments," replied the Chief, "as I tell you I only talk and our opinions are the same more or less." Here was a new twist in the ancient role of knowledge as power. Sensing the potential challenge from radio, the Chief restricted the dangers of innovation by partial incorporation, thus retaining and strengthening his role as Balgat's official opinion leader. (Lerner, 1958:26–27.)

It is obvious that Balgat's Chief was both a gatekeeper by virtue of his control of radio messages and, at the same time, an opinion leader who, by interpreting the received messages, influenced the ideas and attitudes of his clique. However, there was a less orthodox opinion leader in the town, the Grocer, who had views at variance with those of the Chief. He had been to the city and had had opportunities to listen in the coffeehouses of Ankara. "It is nice to know what is happening in the other capitals of the world," said the Grocer. "We are stuck in this hole, we have to know what is going on outside our village." Nevertheless, he did not openly challenge the Chief's views, but only expressed his opinions obliquely (Lerner, 1958:27).

In such a traditional oral system, where people are enmeshed in group relationships, they are hard to reach except through their gatekeepers; there is little or no direct exposure to mass media. And if exposed to mass media, they do not respond readily but prefer to have messages transmitted personally to them by their leaders. This is illustrated by some 250 families of immigrants to Israel, who came from Yemen, Yugoslavia, North Africa, and central and eastern Europe (Eisenstadt, 1952). The problem was to assimilate them into the modern State of Israel. A program of oral and written instruction was provided in three spheres: economic, to instruct them as to working opportunities, and housing and relief facilities; cultural and educational, to induce them to send their children to schools, study the Hebrew language, participate in lectures, folk dances, festivals, and so on; and political, to instruct them about civic rights and duties. However, it was found that the way in which information was transmitted had a great deal to do with whether it was accepted. Three types of transmission were tried: (1) direct, impersonal appeals to the whole group in meetings, or through newspapers, proclamations, and the like; (2) personal appeal to a specific individual or small group by an official; (3) transmission of messages to them through their communal leaders. As might be expected, the formal, impersonal contacts were least effective; the best way of reaching them was through their opinion leaders, and they fully accepted nothing unless it came to them in this way. Data showed that, after six months of communication effort, only 10 percent had been affected by formal, impersonal methods of instruction and 25 percent by direct personal appeals from an official; whereas 65 percent had changed their behavior when information came to them through their leaders. As the immigrants said: "In all these things we know that we have to rely on our teachers and rabbis as they understand these things much better than we do; and if they would have thought it right, they would have told us themselves"; or "We have joined in these social activities mainly because" leaders we trust "have talked about it with us and have persuaded us that it is good and worthwhile. In all these matters we rely very much on them and we would heed them much more than any stranger." Moreover, even the leader's messages had to come to them in a certain way: If formal and impersonal, it was likely to fail; communication was effective only when it was direct and personal, in which authority was intermingled with primary relations and identifications. As one immigrant put it, "We do not want only to hear orders from far-away people, even if they are very wise and know everything. Our rabbis know that the best way is to gather all of us in the synagogue and to tell us about it and to explain it to us. Otherwise, we do not listen." However, over a period of time, such exclusive reliance on opinion leaders was lost; the immigrants began to receive more information directly from the absorbing social system, to go to the movies, and to participate more in the mass media. Among the reasons given for turning away from traditional opinion leaders were disillusionment with the elites' ability to interpret the new social system and its values, even the feeling that clinging to the old elites blocked achievement of full status within the new society. As one said, "Lately I began to feel that whenever I meet the old leader, whenever they try to explain things to us, to organize us, I live in our imaginary world, a world of yesterday. I feel they really do not belong here. They are trying to keep us in our old life. But I feel that we really belong to the new life here, and that they are real obstructions on our way here." (Eisenstadt, 1952.)

Both examples, the Turkish gatekeeper and the immigrants coming to Israel, illustrate that in an oral system an individual is not alone; he is enmeshed in a network of primary oral communication and must be reached through such a network. The gatekeeper interprets and largely controls messages coming from outside the system, and the opinion leader interprets, authenticates, and validates these messages. If outsiders (such as Peace Corps or public health officials) try to work with such communities, they must do so by appealing to the opinion leaders, not by going around them to try to achieve direct contact with the man on the street or the woman in the home (Schramm, 1964:192–194). Long after newspapers and radio broadcasts are available in a developing society, said Schramm, traditional media, such as the bazaar, coffeehouse, puppet show, village meeting, continue to be influential, and interpersonal channels may have to carry most of the job. To reach people as a change agent, you do not circumvent the oral system but use it and build upon it in some way.

Here is an example of piping a message from mass media, as it were, into an oral system, a parade in a small village of central Tanzania.

> First came the children's fife and drum corps. Now, you have never heard a fife and drum corps until you have heard the African version, with the drums wandering off into after-beats and syncopation. Behind them came the Tanu Young Pioneers, in their green and red uniform shirts, picking up the rhythm and shouting Tanu songs. Tanu . . . is the Tanganyika African National Union. It is not often called a party. . . . But it is their version of the single party, which so many of the new African states are evolving. After the Young Pioneers came the Tanu Chairman and council, and the local government officers, the dancers, and the people of the village. They were going to help lay the cornerstone for a new community center, which they were building with their own hands and largely with their own materials.
>
> It was Tanu that I had come to see in action, and I must say that it performed very impressively. Not merely in drumming up the parade, which is easy in Africa, but in all the field activities of national development. To put it simply, Tanu's function is to mobilize the people. Tanu and government come together in the district commissioner who made the speech. . . . Tanu gets out the people . . . to build the community center . . . volunteers to teach literacy classes . . . to attend . . . the classes; smooths resettlement of families from inadequate land to a new village . . . .
>
> The mass media seemed to have very little to do with the process. I saw one or two broadsheets, a technical pamphlet, a few radios in individual houses but no community sets. . . . Most . . . communication came through Tanu. . . . The plans were widely discussed . . . sometimes changed . . . occasionally a complaint went up through the commissioner. . . . the people seemed to consider it . . . their own effort. (Schramm, 1967:11–12.)

The preceding examples illustrate the main features of talk in the small community, where tradition and primary group interaction are more important than mass media input, where opinion leaders filter the information that does come from outside, where gossip rules not only as a source of news but as a means of social control, and where the individual is not alone either in his opinions or his access to information or even his private life. But this is not the situation of most people in the modern world, in which mass media of communication and urban living have superseded the gossipy focus of village life, and oral systems play a much more limited role. We turn now to a brief consideration of how, in terms of communication, social scientists conceive this transition.

Transition from Oral to Media System

The "great transition," which in Europe was called industrialization and in underdeveloped parts of the world is now called modernization, can usefully be described as a shift from an oral to a media system. Into the primitive village comes the oxcart bearing a transistor radio. Modern roads link villages with one another and with the city. New goods and ideas come in; people go to the city for trade and for work, and come back with new ideas. The aspirations of young men are awakened, people become aware of modern ideas, and the authority of the gatekeeper (epitomized by the Turkish Chief) is undermined. An irreversible trend toward greater media exposure and political and economic participation commences.

In other words, modernization may be conceived as not merely use of technology or certain kinds of political and economic organization but ways in which information is put into and used by the system. For a picture in terms of communication of what happens in modernization, we are indebted to Lerner's ground-breaking work. The shift from an oral to a media system is schematized ideally by Table 8.1.

TABLE 8.1
Systems of Public Communication

	Oral Systems	Media Systems
Channel	Personal (face to face)	Broadcast (mediated)
Audience	Primary (group)	Heterogeneous (mass)
Content of communication	Prescriptive (rules)	Descriptive (news)
Source	Hierarchical (status)	Professional (skill)

SOURCE: Lerner, 1958:55.

An oral system spreads messages by mouth-to-ear communication within and between "natural" primary groups of kinship, worship, work, or play. A media system spreads (broadcasts) its messages through impersonal channels, such as print, film, and radio, to large mass audiences. The mass is a far more heterogeneous collectivity than is the primary group, because its members come from all walks of life, even from different races and cultures. In the oral system, the one who speaks does so by virtue of status, or hierarchical position, as we have seen in previous illustrations, whereas in the media system the source of information is usually someone who has no status other than a professional communication skill—for example, a newscaster or television actor.

Because the professional communicator lacks the authority that goes with status, his messages are more likely to be descriptive and factual, rather than prescriptive, that is, having the character of moral injunction or command. As Lerner (1958) pointed out, these are idealized models, to which few societies perfectly fit. But the distinction has profound implications, for it is not only correlated with but also is a major cause of other important features of society, including urbanization, literacy, and political representation and participation, democratic or otherwise, including the growth of nationalism. Lerner contends that urbanization has a crucial role in the early phase of modernizing a social system, and it does this by bringing people into contact with the information and values of the media system. And literacy is both an index and agent of widespread modernization, since literacy provides the basic skill required for operation of a media system. High literacy and media participation make possible a "take-off" toward widespread participation both in economic development and in representative government by devices such as voting.

Lerner's theory of modernization might be summarized by the following sequence: (1) urbanization draws people into cities, accompanied by population growth and increased economic investment; (2) increasing media participation, especially need and opportunity for literacy as a skill for operating a media system; (3) increasing psychic mobility, an awakening of wants and ability to imagine oneself in a different style and status of life than that to which one is accustomed, including a willingness to by-pass traditional gatekeepers; and (4) increasing participation, in the market, industrial process, and representative government. Lerner distinguished three stages of development, using the crucial criteria of urbanization, literacy, and media development, as listed in Table 8.2.

Politicization, then, is a consequence of shift from an oral to a media system. National feelings can develop under the urging of leaders using the mass media. A self-conscious public opinion can emerge, which not only knows what it wants but also has the expectation that opinions matter and leaders will respond to them. Moreover, a media system is well on the way to becoming a mass society in which large numbers of people are unattached to status systems and group ties, and therefore available to new kinds of

T A B L E 8.2
Types of Social System

	Traditional	Transitional	Modern
Urbanization	Under 10%	10–25%	Over 25%
Literacy	Under 20%	21–60%	Over 60%
Communication system	Oral	Media-oral	Media

SOURCE: Lerner, 1957: 266–275.

political appeal, including totalitarian movements (Kornhauser, 1959).

Modernism is seen as a set of attitudes that can be measured on a Likert type of scale* and which comes from a life in which there is high media participation, stress on individual achievement, and low integration with relatives and other status groups. The marks of a "modern" man, perhaps anywhere in the world, are (Kahl, 1968): (1) activism rather than fatalism, including planning the future and using technology to shape the world; (2) role stratification of life chances, that is, seeing a system open in which status can be achieved; (3) low community stratification; (4) occupational primacy, or determination and driving ambition to succeed; (5) low integration with relatives; (6) individualism, that is, independence of close ties and pushing one's own career; (7) low distrust of outsiders (contrasted with ingroup mistrust of strangers); (8) high participation in mass media (versus gossip and the oral system); (9) preference for urban life; (10) accepting work with big companies and bureaucracies (versus the primary group). Thus we see something of the state of mind and style of life of the psychically mobile participant in the media system.

The transition to a modern communication system does not mean wiping out the oral system, as the above schematization might seem to imply. The gatekeeper and informal opinion leader is not driven away by the professional communicators of the mass media. Rather, the media system is laid over the oral system, which has become looser in the process. The analogy might be used of water (representing mass-media messages) flowing so rapidly through a lawn that it loosens the roots of the grass and separates clumps from one another. Such a view of how a media system coexists on top of an oral system of informal opinion leaders is given by Pye (1963:24–29), who said that mass media do not always weaken the

---

* Likert scale is an attitude-test that provides a five point response-scale for each item as follows: agree strongly—agree moderately—neither agree nor disagree—disagree moderately—disagree strongly.

oral system but may, paradoxically, increase reliance upon direct word-of-mouth communication from those whom one knows. One reason for this is that increased ease of travel makes it possible for people to get about and consult with one another more; for example, in professional associations. Another reason is that professions, more specialized and better organized today, may make it possible for experts to find out who their counterparts are and exchange information, either personally or by letter or bulletin or phone call. So the interplay of modern mass media with oral systems is usually characterized as the previously mentioned "two-step flow"; that is, messages arising from the professional communicators of the mass media (for example, advertising) reach people who are, for the most part, not alone but enmeshed in networks of associations that strongly influence whether or not they accept the media messages; indeed, the consensus of experts is that:

> (1) the influence of other people on specific decisions tends to be more frequent, and certainly more effective, than the influence of the media; (2) influentials are close associates of the people whom they influence and, hence, tend to share the same social status characteristics. . . . (3) intimate associates tend to hold opinions and attitudes in common and are reluctant to depart unilaterally from the group consensus even when a mass media appeal seems attractive; (4) there is specialization in opinion leadership—a woman who is influential in marketing is unlikely to be influential in, say, fashion. . . . Opinion leaders tend to be more exposed to the mass media, particularly to the media most relevant to their spheres of influence. (Katz, Levin, and Hamilton, 1963:82.)

Thus, the mass media impinge upon people who are subject to even stronger group pressure. Doctors are more likely to try a new drug if they have high contact with colleagues who have used or recommended it personally; farmers who adopt new kinds of seed do so usually after personal interaction with trusted professionals, neighbors, or friends.

The critical feature of a modern communication system, said Pye (1963), is not—to repeat—elimination of the oral system but "orderly relationships" between the two levels in which there is "sensitive interaction between professional communicators and those with influential positions in the networks of personal and face-to-face communications" in which "feedback" mechanisms adjust the flow of media output; that is, the professionals running the media are "constantly on the alert to discover" how their messages are being "consumed" by opinion leaders, who are especially sensitive to what is going on in the media and which is helping them to interpret the trend of public opinion.

In short, a modern communications system consists of a fusion of high technology and special, professionalized processes of communications with informal, society-based, and non-specialized processes of person-to-person communications . . . the real test of modernization is the extent to which there is effective "feedback" between the mass-media systems and the informal, face-to-face systems. Modernization thus hinges upon the integration of the formal institutions of communications and the social processes of communications to the point that each must respond with sensitivity to the other. (Pye, 1963.)

By contrast, said Pye, the *transitional* system (as an example of which we may take a country like Greece or Turkey) is characterized by a "bifurcated and fragmented" relationship between the media and oral levels, an urban-centered media system that penetrates only erratically into a separate village-based system, which is autonomous in the sense that it does not interact with the urban system. Further, the villages are actually isolated subsystems, which have less communication with each other than they separately have with the urban centers; this linking might be likened to "the spokes of a wheel all connecting to a hub but without any outer rim." The adjustment problem of a transitional society therefore, is, to bring the informal rural systems into relationship with each other and to the mass-media system rather than to pour investment into the modern sector, which might create even greater imbalance.

Finally Pye noted a difference in function between the opinion leaders of the traditional oral system—who are mainly concerned with interpreting a limited body of information—with those of modern society concerned with screening and keeping up with an enormous input.

The sheer volume of communications . . . in a mass-media system means that much of the function of the informal, person-to-person level . . . centers on screening out specialized information from the mass flow for the consumption of particular audiences. The role of opinion leaders is thus one of investing time and energy in "keeping up" with particular matters and insuring those who are dependent upon them that they are "fully informed" and "up-to-date" on the special subject. . . . In a traditional system the prime problem . . . was generally the inadequate volume of information to provide a complete picture. People turned to opinion leaders to learn what could be made out of the limited scraps of information received in the community. The skill of opinion leaders was not one of sorting out specialized information but of piecing together clues and elaborating, if not embroidering, upon the scant information shared possibly by all present. Thus the traditional system depended upon the role of the wise man and the imaginative story teller who needed few words in order to sense truth and who could expand upon the limited flow of messages. (Pye, 1963: 24–29.)

In contrasting gatekeepers of traditional and modern systems, it may be added that, whereas the traditional gatekeeper is a wise person we know and trust, selecting for us certain information, the modern gatekeeper is likely to be a stranger unrelated to us by status or primary group trust, who is screening the information which comes to us in terms of his interest, not ours. He may be an advertiser buying television time, a news editor (White, 1964), a committee chairman, or a political censor—perhaps only a policeman—who can claim no wisdom greater than our own. The nature of information flow is therefore a matter of the gatekeepers who are chosen in personal relationships versus innumerable, unknown gatekeepers who are not so chosen. In the modern system, whereas an opinion leader may be a colleague or friend, the gatekeeper is more likely a stranger.

The transition from an oral to a media system has two more consequences important to our study of collective behavior. One is that rapid urbanization, helped by mass media, often makes populations masslike, with some of the frustrations of anomie. The other is that expectations (fostered by "psychic mobility," the capacity to dream and empathize) grow faster than the means (that is, usually the institutions) by which to satisfy them. The "want-get" ratio becomes dangerously unbalanced. Ten years after his first, rather optimistic, formulation of the effect of mass media on developing countries, Lerner commented with some foreboding:

> The naive idea that it is good for a nation with a very high standard of living to communicate its own image to a nation with a very low standard of living . . . is a very dangerous assumption. I think on the contrary, that we are doing such psychological harm in the underdeveloped world that our children's children will pay some of the price for this. We have conveyed a picture of a better life, of the availability to all of the good things in life, and thereby helped to accelerate the desires (and demands) of peoples for these things. We have done this with the best will in the world.
>
> I think that no nation has ever been more well-meaning than the American nation. But what we have done is to create a set of wants which cannot be satisfied within the lifetime of the people now living. We have helped to unbalance the ratio between the wants and the means to satisfy those wants by our insistence on operating directly and psychologically on individuals elsewhere in the world. This disruption of the want-get ratio—for people are taught by the mass media primarily to want—has gone so far that I don't think it is an exaggeration to say our psychological operations in recent years have been preparing a "revolution of rising frustrations." When people learn, as they must, that they cannot hope to get what they have been taught to want, there will follow a global acceleration of frustration with its attendant reaction-formations of aggression and regression, neither

of which is a state conducive to the modernization which American aid was intended to promote in the first instance. (Lerner in A. Hoffman, 1968:134–135.)

This gloomy conclusion was supported by research on political instability by Feierabend, Nesvold, and Feierabend (1969), which threw more light on the scope of the effects of the gap between aspirations and social achievement. In a survey of eighty-four countries, a substantial correlation was found between political instability (measured by an index taking an account of such things as protests, riots, assassinations, and coups) and a gap between aspirations and social achievement, which is assumed to be greatest in transitional countries that have been exposed to the ideas of modernity but which have not made much progress along the path. Of countries classed as traditional, thirteen of twenty-three were rated unstable; whereas of transitional countries, twenty-five of thirty-seven, or roughly two to one, were unstable; and, by contrast, of modern countries that had made progress in closing the gap, only four of twenty-four were unstable (Feierabend et al., 1969). Clearly, much more is needed to be known about the effects of information input on developing societies where, for example, studies of frustration ratios, the rate of institutional development, their homeostatic needs and optima and limits of change, and side effects of innovation, have neglected to account for the feedback loops discussed in Chapter 6. Some of the assumptions about the revolutionary tendency of the urban poor in developing countries were examined by Nelson (1970) and found to be overdrawn.

However, in summarizing the differences between the oral and media systems, we should not lose sight of what is perhaps the overriding fact: Media systems are monological. They have great power to spread information rapidly and widely *one way*. Monological communication, while it can stimulate talk (and other collective reactions) is more likely to damp it. We all know the effect of television on conversation in the average home. Nor have videophones to any extent made mechanical communication two-way, nor have "telethons" and other audience-participation devices been able to approach the feedback of the oral system. (And even if they did become two-way, there would be considerable reservations about their ability to transmit the nonverbal cues that are so important in human interaction.)

Still less do status rewards to celebrities have any power to confer recognition on the average person comparable with what he can get from any oral system. The main theme we wish to emphasize is that the *oral system is superior in personal feedback*, however inferior in technical information, to the media system. This is an inherent advantage of oral communication for dialogical exchange. The trend toward media in modern systems, however offset by "opinion leadership," cannot make up for this shortcoming by more monological information—"hot," "cool," or otherwise. The member of an oral system gets lots of feedback in day-to-day inter-action in every matter that concerns him. Everything he does mat-ters; many eyes and ears take account of him, his personal life, how he dances, the results of his hunt or fishing, his crop success. He is subject to the flattery of being gossiped about (which may re-call Oscar Wilde's remark that worse than being talked about is not to be talked about at all).

By contrast, the member of the media system usually does not get sufficient opportunity to air his opinions and test them by others; he watches others perform on mass media; *they* are ex-pressed, he is a spectator—to some degree frustrated. He feels himself of little account, lost in a crowd; nobody pays attention to him. Gossip is lacking or discounted as trivial, but "human interest" news about celebrities and people selected at random by the media fills the void. Our member of the media system finds that the main source of his information is in people he doesn't really know, that is, no personal chain of trust connects him with them. His gate-keepers are unknown, resented as censors and authoritarians, or suspected as manipulators.

On the other hand, the man whose main source is an oral system knows the people from whom he gets information and is in a position to evaluate it, perhaps make a claim if it fails; he trusts his gate-keepers. Though he may not be a leader, he has no feeling of powerlessness; he has a "voice" expressed through his leaders. The member of the media system, for all the information that comes to him, often feels he has no voice; *vox populi* may be an empty phrase or a mere poll finding; he feels unable to reach the public on one hand or the leaders who insufficiently represent his opinion. The man in the oral system uses and accepts a high ratio of norma-tive judgment (prescription) in the information he exchanges, for he knows which opinions are shared and that there is a group sup-port and sanction for what is said.

On the other hand, the man in the media system speaks usually without group support, often in conflict with the opinions of others, with varying degrees of reference-group salience. For this reason there must be a high ratio of "objective" factual information, and a low ratio of judgment (prescription), which is usually discounted as "preaching," or "bias." Such differences are summed up in the statement that oral systems are dialogical, and that media systems tend to be monological.

Another way of saying this is that there is a tendency to *com-*

munication imbalance in media systems; that is, a person may not be well served by a system that becomes too monological, whereas an oral system, even without media input, has all the potentialities for balanced personal life. A media system, however much information it puts in, tends to deprive people of feedback and forces audiences into a spectator position. Unless the media system is offset—and its messages mediated—by thriving oral systems, it tends to move toward the negative features of a mass society.

So one sees a loss of oral culture—as one might call it, a "rocking-chair" culture—in modern society. People less often linger to chat on front porches, around pot-bellied stoves, on wharves, in stations; or all day in coffeehouses, taverns, or open-air cafes. The skills of conversation and storytelling decline. Few talkers are used to being listened to. Such a lack of oral activity is reflected by the urban setting: streets, eating places, plazas, even parks are inhospitable. There is no place to "be"—only some place to "go." "Street people" are a problem. In such environments, there seems to be nothing to do but seek commercial entertainment or go home and watch television.

So, as "rocking-chair" culture declines, one often sees people who rely rather too heavily on electronic and print input. "Talk shows" displace live talk; in the friendly bar, television or the jukebox drowns out what talk there might be. Multimedia inputs are common and easy. For example, a man might talk on an intercom, watch a video or radar screen, while listening to a radio. In a restaurant an observer saw a man eating while reading a newspaper, listening to a ball game on his transistor radio, against a background of piped music (Musak). It is commonplace for today's art to hit you with several things at once. Thus, it is possible today to live almost entirely on the communication feast provided by the media, talking into machines and enjoying transmitted messages and entertainments; some—especially old people and those confined to institutions—have to do this. When it is by choice, we might call such a person a media man, that is, one plugged into some kind of mass communication almost all his waking time, who is rarely alone with his own thoughts or engaged in dialogical relations.

A vicious circle is possible when plugging into a media system takes the place of dialogical relations one might be having were it not for absorption with media input, as can be illustrated by the effect of television on conversation in the home. As interaction declines—perhaps resented as an intrusion because it is not so interesting and entertaining as the media—we approach the dependence of the media man, who is a caricature of a normal human being. He may congratulate himself on extension of his senses, especially after reading McLuhan (1964a,b), who claims that electronic media are restoring the sensory balance lost in a print culture. But our consideration of oral systems suggests that one would not be really "retribalized" (as McLuhan claims) by plunging into media systems but would be more than ever deprived of dialogical encounter such as that recommended by Martin Buber. Indeed, such a person would probably have a severe identity problem (Klapp, 1969). Media-filled hours—what will this mean for man? Opinions now range from a joyous extension of the senses to universal inanition and boredom. Of one thing, however, we may be sure: Extension of media *at the expense of* the oral system means trouble because it is on dialogical communication that human health, wisdom, happiness, and freedom depend.

With this perspective, we consider the contribution of talk-forming opinion and rumor as a response to media-input called news.

Talk Processes in Media Systems

The triumph of monologue is never complete, not even in the most relentlessly efficient media systems. Eddies of talk rise up and counter the inflow of news and technical information, to embroider and interpret, to supplement, even to oppose and refute on occasion.

The American President's public relations problem illustrates this constant battle of media with talk. A *Life* writer (Sidney, 1970) noted the effort of President Nixon to build up a screen of what in business would be called good public relations. Unlike Lyndon Johnson, his predecessor who had managed, by explosive relations and idiosyncrasies such as exposing operation scars and pulling beagles' ears, to make himself a thoroughly unlikeable person to many citizens, Nixon's role was controlled and poised, a model of deportment that might have been taken from "a textbook on executive thoughtfulness." When irritated, he became "excessively polite." He was assiduous with personal touches, dropping in unexpectedly to talk, personally delivering boxes of candy to White House employees. There was "not a single provable story" of his blowing up at a reporter, staff member, or cabinet officer. Nor were disgruntled employees spilling secrets of the household and office family (as happened with Mrs. Kennedy).

But such a commendable effort to maintain a good image is enormously difficult for one who has a public role, and is even more difficult for a highly placed celebrity. There is not only the relentless eye of television exposing quirks that might have otherwise remained hidden (except to intimates) in an age of print, but also a gossip network, including those writers who are eager to speculate and feed the public hunger for news about the "real man" and his private life. In such a situation, "little things" count more than they should and tidbits are irrepressible. The paradox, too, is that in image making, a colorful item, however trivial, has more power than the most important issue or sententious utterance that is not colorful (Klapp, 1964a).

The point of this for our purposes here is that talk always has its day and say, and rises against news and even the best planned public relations to add its own interpretation. In doing so, it gives meaning to what otherwise might be a raw input of information, embroidering, adjusting for credibility gaps. It forms public opinion dialogically within what is usually called the "two-step" process. And, not least in conditions of mass life, it helps to compensate for anonymity and impersonality by gossipy speculation about the lives of celebrities who are "famous yet unknown," the media bending to feed this process by assuming the function of Dame Grundy.

This can be considered in two aspects: the public opinion-forming function of talk, and the new functions of rumor and gossip in the media system.

1. Public Opinion Formation by Talk

"The public is, what the crowd is not, a discussion group." (Park and Burgess, 1924:799.)

According to what might be called the classic theory of public opinion in sociology, public opinion forms as a result of talk processes that are stimulated by the constant input of news. That is, news starts, but discussion creates, public opinion. Without talk, in which people express differing viewpoints about the meaning of news, there would be no public opinion in the true sense, although there might be a community decision on the basis of custom and mores, or a crowdlike unanimity. Thus, if we imagine a sleepy Mexican fishing village, cut off from telephones, newspapers, and radios (as an example of a traditional oral system), there would be local events to talk about, mostly in the realm of gossip, but no input sufficiently novel, disturbing, and continuous to require constant discussion to decide what such things meant.

In these matters it is perhaps best to let Park speak for himself. Ordinarily,

news has no influence upon political action or morale. Its tendency is to disperse and distract attention . . . the ordinary function of news is to keep individuals and societies oriented and in touch with their world and with reality by minor adjustments. (Park, 1955:140.)

However, dramatic front-page news and continued stories focus public attention and create a need for interpretation that leads to talk and the public-opinion process. The ultimate function of this process is to

> bring into existence a collective will and a political power which, as it mobilizes the community to act, tends to terminate discussion. . . . It may seem a far cry from public opinion to the "rights of man." . . . However, both are products of the same political process . . . public opinion is the form which the collective will takes when it is in process of formation. Rights are public opinion in one of its ultimate forms, after it has been incorporated into the mores. (Park, 1955:116.)

But, said Park, news input does not lead immediately to collective decision; indeed, it is more or less at odds with morale and mores. This is because

> it intensifies differences. Public opinion is on the surface of things and does not reflect the attitudes and points of view on which the community is united. The very existence of public opinion is itself evidence that we are not at the moment as one in regard to what as a nation or a people we should do. However, as things get discussed and drop out of discussion, the direction which public opinion takes in the course of time indicates the direction in which collective will, in the process of formation, is taking. (Park, 1955:141.)

In other words, there is a kind of circular, generative relationship between collective will and news as input that challenges opinion, creates problems that cannot be readily solved by mores and custom. Such problems must be settled by interpretation and discussion, making decisions ultimately feeding into the deeper consensus of mores and culture, which are largely unconscious unless challenged (Park, 1955:116, 140–141, 290). This book distinguishes between the two levels of what Park calls *public opinion* and *mores* by the terms *rational* and *nonrational consensus*. In this sense, "rational" does not mean logical agreement but merely an awareness of something sufficient to make one think about it and discuss it.

In systemic terms, this might be called an eruptive theory of public opinion; namely, that the constant intrusion of news causes talk to erupt out of its normal channels of gossip into discussion that leads to public opinion. Typically, therefore, there is no public opinion in isolated traditional oral systems nor, for that matter, is there in very closed media systems. Behind it all is the assumption, voiced by John Dewey (1922), that there is no thinking without problems and challenges, and that things taken for granted will drop out of thought. Further, in an isolated or very traditional system, because the input of news and problems is not large enough to generate an attitude of public concern with events of the day that one must know and make decisions about, there is no habit of public opinion and therefore no institutionalization of it as a political process and, finally, no habit of political participation, by means such as voting, to express opinion. The implications of news input for a system are therefore very great indeed; and politicization usually requires stepping out of the oral system to the greater input of a media system.

But it is important that the media system, for all its monological input, provide opportunities for the talk process to thrive. If talk processes are suppressed, not only may public opinion be stunted but strains also may lead to contagions and systemic readjustments of kinds discussed in Chapters 6 and 7.

Another point about Park's theory, besides the importance it attaches to news input as a source of the public-opinion process, is that public opinion is a collective, not merely an individual, thing; as Cooley put it, "an organic process, and not merely . . . a state of agreement about some question of the day" (Cooley, 1918; Blumer, 1948). That is to say that there must be some group relationship and transaction among the individuals forming public opinion, and it is this process on which our interest focuses.

Likewise, the *public*, in sociological conception, consists not of people in general nor even of people having opinions, but comprises those sufficiently interested in a topic to talk about it and form opinions over a period of time—whether or not they agree. The public, in short, is a collectivity focused on a topic, loosely integrated and sporadically interacting.

Within the public are smaller groups where the real business of public-opinion formation occurs: primary groups, forums and discussions, work groups, associations like the League of Women Voters and American Medical Association, women gossiping in a beauty shop, or merely four old codgers on a park bench. By being formed in such groups, public opinion becomes a collective process rather than people independently interpreting events and making up their minds.

Because of such interactive processes, public opinion is shaped socially in various ways.

1. It expresses group norms, whether or not people are conscious of it (Sherif, 1936).
2. It rapidly crystallizes into stereotypes and verbal nuggets, such as slogans, cliches, epithets, and "pro" and "con" positions, which emerge as "coins of thought" (Sumner's, 1906, phrase) in communicative exchange, a selective and leveling process similar to what goes on in rumor.
3. In forming opinions, people seek others with their own view and avoid cross pressures from those with different opinions; audiences are

self-selecting and self-reinforcing (Lazarsfeld, Berelson, and Gaudet, 1944; Kriesberg, 1949).

4. Gregarious opinion leaders with high exposure to the media have more influence upon opinion than do other individuals or the media directly— the two-step theory (Katz and Lazarsfeld, 1955). The moral of this is that, if you want to influence people's opinions, influence their opinion leaders.

5. The opinion a person expresses is not a matter of simply how he feels but what reference groups are salient and what definition of the situation is favored by these groups (M. and C. Sherif, 1964; Campbell et al., 1964:161–183). That is, when a person expresses his thoughts to others, or with others in mind, he shapes his thoughts in accordance with their viewpoint—not necessarily agreement but taking them into account, and this is more than tact or courtesy.

For example, an experiment showed how the group definition of the situation influences the opinion expressed. Americans were asked to say in the presence of others what they thought about Soviet Russia. The subjects showed acute consciousness of pressure coming from others who listened to what they said. The opinions given in such circumstances were found to shift in the direction of what the subjects thought (usually accurately) the audience opinion was. "In general, the individuals tended to conform to their conception of the group norms when giving their public opinion. The typical pattern was for the individual to compromise between his private opinion and his conception of the group opinion when expressing his public opinion" (Gorden, 1952). Again, if a reference group is made salient, it will pull people's opinions in the direction of the norms of this group; for example, if people are reminded that they are Catholics, Jews, and so on, they will take a more definite stand and talk more in accordance with the views of these groups. Awareness of their reference group made Catholics less likely to accept, and more resistant to, arguments aimed at changing their opinion away from Catholic norms (Kelley, 1955). Yet another illustration of group influence upon opinion is seen in the research finding (Janis and King, 1954) that if you are called upon by a group to take an active role by verbalizing your opinion, you will talk yourself into the opinion more than if you merely listen to such messages, as was shown by an experiment in which active participants who played a role in which they gave a talk to a group changed their opinions more than those who merely read and listened to the same message.

Such findings show us that public opinion is far from an individual process and is highly subject to group processes and pressures. Even marked difference of opinion from others is subject to polarization by collective transactions, as discussed in Chapter 2 (see also M. and C. Sherif, 1953).

The longer-term process of public-opinion formation can be visualized by conceptual models that show stages of collective decision. One of these is a scheme developed by Foote and Hart (1953) of the process of opinion formation as it leads to group action in a democratic society. Five phases are distinguished:

1. *Problem* formulation—a number of people recognize a problem, which is vague at first; a public forms to discuss its concerns; public and the problem emerge together.
2. In the *proposal* stage there is a conviction "something ought to be done," but no clear idea of what to do has developed; discussion of proposals becomes the central issue of public opinions.
3. The *policy* stage is reached when out of the clash of proposals comes a group decision that can be adopted as a policy—something "we" can do (equivalent to collective will in Park's terms); "only at this stage can the public begin to be described properly as constituting a group."
4. In the *program* phase, the decision-making body of the opinion-forming group (let us say, a labor union) "empowers its agents to act"; they become "a self-conscious organization of functionally differentiated persons cooperatively pursuing common objectives"; for example, a pressure group systematically influencing legislation.
5. The *appraisal* phase completes the public-opinion process, if it goes that far and does not "abort" at one of the earlier stages. In this stage, opinion formation centers on whether the program was successful; "people may find that what was sought is not what was wanted after all," which could spark the beginning of another cycle prefaced by unrest and collective behavior appropriate to the problem phase. (Foote and Hart, 1953.)

These five phases state a number of symbolic tasks through which public opinion must pass, in more or less logical sequence, if it is to accomplish anything by working in a democratic way from the "grassroots" beginning. There is no implication that public opinion must go through these stages; indeed, by far, the majority of opinions probably never get beyond the discussion of proposals; for example, "there ought to be a law" or "why doesn't somebody do something about this?" An unknown amount of public opinion never gets out of the alienation stage, in which people barely recognize what is wrong but do a lot of grumbling and hence contribute to unrest. One trouble with this model is that it assumes the public to be rather like a big committee; there is little account of the less rational reference-group and opinion-leadership processes.

Another long-term model of public-opinion formation is that developed by students who investigated *how innovations are accepted*; for example, the use of a new drug by doctors, or the way farmers make up their minds to adopt new agricultural methods. Such studies find that in the early stages of opinion formation, only the venturesome—perhaps only the deviant—will try out the new idea at all; such *innovators* have little influence on either the opinions or practices of others who remain enmeshed in interpersonal networks. Sooner or later, however, some *opinion leaders (early adopters)* will begin to take up the idea. But they have to try it and succeed before they can convince *their friends.* With some success, and personal testimonial, influence begins to flow through the opinion network and the adoption curve begins to rise markedly as the timid *majority* begins to accept the opinions of trusted professionals, colleagues, and friends, who legitimatize their decisions. At a yet later stage, the *holdouts*—the older, more conservative, and more isolated members of that particular public—fall into step. Such theory points out that the public may be aware of something, even interested, long before it is ready to act on its opinion by trial or adoption into their own lives. The early innovators are less group-influenced. The *majority need reinforcement* by peers and opinion leaders before they will adopt. The testing (corresponding to "appraisal" in the Foote and Hart scheme) must occur early as an opinion-leader function before the majority will adopt (Beal, Rogers, and Bohlen, 1957; Lionberger, 1960; Rogers, 1962; Katz, Levin, and Hamilton, 1963). (See Table 8.3 and Fig. 8.1.)

Doubtless, different kinds of publics—urban, rural, professional, laymen, modern, transitional, democratic, totalitarian—need their own models of public opinion development. The common factor, however, is the importance of group processes—and high among these talk processes—in the formation of opinion. Conversely, direct media impact is less important; the stronger these group processes are, the less the content of media is able to help us predict what opinion actually will be.

Rationality of Public Opinion

Because of their role in public-opinion formation, talk processes are a mainstay of a democratic society. The classic theories of liberal democracy (Locke, Jefferson, Mill, Bagehot, Tocqueville) assume that free talk is necessary to rational decision by electorates, assemblies, and courts, and that from this free talk come improvements in public policy, discovery of new knowledge—in short, the progress of mankind. In this conception, discussion is an open market of ideas in which debate clarifies and tests the alternatives and the individual independently makes up his mind, naturally,

Diffusion Process: Types of Adopters

Adopter Category	Salient Values	Personal Characteristics	Communication Behavior	Social Relationships
Innovators	"Venturesome"; willing to accept risks	Youngest age; highest social status; largest and most specialized operations; wealthy	Closest contact with scientific information sources; interaction with other innovators; relatively greatest use of impersonal sources	Some opinion leadership; very cosmopolite
Early adopters	"Respect"; regarded by many others in the social system as a role-model	High social status; large and specialized operations	Greatest contact with local change agents	Greatest opinion leadership of any category in most social systems; very localite
Early majority	"Deliberate"; willing to consider innovations only after peers have adopted	Above-average social status; average-sized operation	Considerable contact with change agents and early adopters	Some opinion leadership
Late majority	"Skeptical"; overwhelming pressure from peers needed before adoption occurs	Below-average social status; small operation; little specialization; small income	Secure ideas from peers who are mainly late majority or early majority; less use of mass media	Little opinion leadership
Laggards	"Tradition"; oriented to the past	Little specialization; lowest social status; smallest operation; lowest income; oldest	Neighbors, friends, and relatives with similar values are main information source	Very little opinion leadership; semi-isolates

SOURCE: Everett Rogers, *The Diffusion of Innovations* (New York: The Free Press, The Macmillan Company, 1962), p. 185.

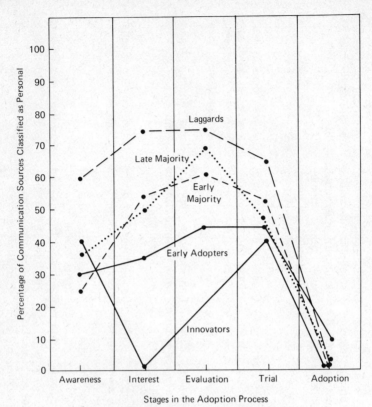

FIGURE 8.1. Personal communication in opinion formation and adoption process. (From Beal
and Rogers, 1960: 19; reprinted in Everett Rogers, *The Diffusion of Innovations*,
New York: The Free Press [The Macmillan Company], 1962, p. 180.)

if he is rational, choosing the best idea just as he would choose the
best detergent if he knew results of consumer tests. The ideal
situation for such a free market of public opinion is well-informed
and carefully moderated debate and deliberation, as is found in
scientific assemblies, parliaments, jury trials, or the famed New
England town meeting.

Actually, we seem far from such a rational democracy in most
of our public-opinion formation, considering such things as the
monological input from media, heavily biased by owners and spon-
sors; failures of rationality when public debate becomes vitupera-
tive, shouting-down and forceful confrontation; or subtle official
suppression of dissent, as was common in America during the early
1970s. For example, antiwar protesters were jailed and fined for
acts nominally permitted under the First Amendment: seventy-three
people, including clergymen, were arrested for holding a worship

service for war dead across the street from the White House; the actress Jane Fonda was arrested for handing to servicemen petitions calling for an end of the war; two men were arrested for holding a hunger fast in Lafayette Park, which faces the White House, because they displayed a sign explaining what their fast meant, police preventing them by the technicality that displaying a sign meant they were "participating in a public gathering without a permit." Though such policies would fill Thomas Jefferson with gloom, hardly better than suppressed opinion are apathetic publics, manipulated by the media, who avoid all responsible decision (C. W. Mills, 1956). Worse yet are "available" mass publics captured by a totalitarian elite (Kornhauser, 1959).

Other trends discouraging to the ideal of liberal democracy included the development in America during the 1960s of "image politics," the packaging of candidates in terms of media appeal as "personalities," and the avoidance of any issues more thought-provoking than being in favor of peace, good government, and lower taxes. This meant that the public, deprived of real issues in its choice of candidates, had to decide on mere liking of personalities or a kind of hopeful psychoanalysis to tell them in whom they could best put their trust. Another trend, described by Boorstin (1962), and heavily attacked by Marcuse (1964), was the growing power of the media to create "pseudo-events," indeed, a pseudo-environment of more or less pleasing fabricated images.

In the light of such things and the group processes that form opinion, can we say that public opinion is rational? Obviously it is not, if what we mean by "rational" is conformance to the liberal democratic model of responsible, temperate discussion in a free market of ideas. Such a model is only an ideal, not necessarily a description of what is happening. Social psychological findings about the strength of conforming tendency (Sherif, 1936; Asch, 1952; Milgram, 1963) show that opinion cannot reach the independence assumed by Locke and Mill; that is, the possibility of an individual free from conscious and unconscious group constraints in making decisions. Yet, for all these difficulties, it is possible to characterize the public, by virtue of its discussion, as more rational on the whole than a group bound by mores, which Sumner (1906) showed to be nonrational, and also more rational than the crowd whose unanimous and coercive decisions were analyzed in Chapter 2. This is, perhaps, all we can hope to expect from a public, but it is enough to be worth the effort of studying the aspects of public rationality.

This hope, however, centers on creating higher levels of free public discussion, not merely increasing the numbers of people involved. Many have tried to improve democratic participation in America by "getting out the vote" with the slogan, "Vote as you please—but vote!" We feel somewhat ashamed that voting turnout should fall to less than 50 percent, that even election of a president hardly calls out 65 percent; yet, studies of nonvoters, according to Rienow, show—

> nonvoters to be civic wallflowers. They are inclined not to be members of any groups that might put them in touch with civic life; they appear to live on a different wavelength from people interested in politics; they are consequently shockingly short on information. When questioned about their attitude on public issues, many more of the nonvoters are in the category "I don't know" or "Undetermined" category. . . . The typical citizen who doesn't bother to cast a ballot . . . tends to demonstrate strong egocentricity; he is almost oblivious to anything but the most self-centered activities. The voter, on the other hand, usually displays a broad outlook that encompasses the world. Indeed, a foreign issue may often interest him more than a bread-and-butter question. The characteristic nonvoter will brighten considerably when the issue is brought down to a level with his pocketbook. On any higher plane, he presents a vacuous stare. This, then, is the character we campaign so ardently to bring to the polls. (Rienow, 1960:9.)

If the nonvoter is such a civic incompetent as Rienow paints him, it is hardly to be expected that bringing him to the voting booth will raise the general level of public decision. We had better, perhaps, be content with the smaller proportion who freely and interestedly enter the debate of public affairs.

Let us return now to rumor and gossip, their functions and possible contribution to the rationality of media systems.

Functions of Rumor and Gossip in Media Systems

Again we take up gossip and rumor and kindred activities such as joking, which are usually not dignified as rational public opinion. No matter how copious, indeed overwhelming, the input of news from the media, these forms of participation never stop. They belong in the larger realm of *anonymous interpersonal communication* (or, if you prefer, statusless communication) among strangers in the mass, by way of contagion (dealt with in Chapters 2 and 3), imitation in fad (see Chapter 10), and rumor (as distinguished from gossip), to be considered here. None of these forms of communication basically follows lines of either sociometry (structural lines of established relationship such as friendship and work association) or mass communication channels. What they seem to do is add to, modify, and embroider communication that occurs by established channels.

Therefore, we begin with the hypothesis that rumor and gossip are not displaced by media input (however copious and reliable),

but get new functions in a media system: mainly, to add meaning*
to information by interpreting and embroidering it (if need be, supplementing and correcting credibility gaps), and to compensate for
the monologicality of media and anonymity of mass life—that is, to
give the man on the street a chance to talk back and be heard.

The interpreting role of rumor has long been recognized. Its
"basic law," according to Allport and Postman (1947), is that the
amount of rumor in circulation varies with the importance of the
subject multiplied by its ambiguity or cognitive unclarity. To be
highly concerned about an event, yet deprived of clear knowledge
of it, is the prime condition for rumor. Take as an example the in-
quest into the tragic death of Mary Jo Kopechne in an accident in
which Senator Ted Kennedy was involved. There was an exasperat-
ing ambiguity in the news of what happened. Kennedy maintained
silence and spoke only through his lawyers. He did so, presumably,
to discourage rumors and bias before official findings were reached.
Yet, it is doubtful if he did in fact discourage rumor by his deliberate
ambiguity: A *Time*-Harris poll showed that his silence had cost him
heavily in public sympathy and that disagreeable opinions had been
formed in a two-month interval: that he had not told the truth,
agreement shifted from 44 to 51 percent; that he dove into the
water to save the girl from drowning, agreement declined from 63
to 50 percent; that nothing immoral had taken place during the incident, agreement declined from 51 to 32 percent; that Kennedy was
not driving under the influence of alcohol, agreement declined from
38 to 23 percent; that he had suffered enough, agreement declined
from 68 to 57 percent; and that he had displayed qualities that
disqualify him for high public trust, agreement increased from 40
to 47 percent. This shows the kind of price that a public figure can
pay when a shortage of hard facts—far from damping—encourages
rumor and speculation. The work of rumor is to fill gaps, especially
some point of logic, evidence, or meaning that is missing from the
picture.

The work of rumor seems dysfunctional because it inflicts such
harm to reputation and because it is so often associated with riots,
unrest, and mass contagions. During times of stress, said Leighton
(1946:159, 268–269), a community becomes "a prey to vicious
rumors and vivid fears." Stress causes misinterpretation of ordinary
events; for example: a train whistle becomes a scream, stories of
deaths and cruelties become common—"the similarity of rumors in
all reports on situations of human stress is very striking." Many
rumors unquestionably have a wedge-driving function, setting groups

* "Information must not be confused with meaning." (Shannon and Weaver,
1949:99.)

against one another at the expense of the larger community; one sample of 1,089 rumors showed that 66 percent were wedge-driving (Knapp, 1942). When trouble starts, said Lee and Humphrey (1943: 109–112), "rumor mills" of demagogic groups take advantage of it and start stories. The rumors of a "fever-heightened verbal milling process" furnish the riot-participant with a justification, an "anesthetic for his conscience." Yet, even such effects are seen to be functional for some groups; it is a matter of level.

How distortive is rumor? Is it as wild and unreliable as some think? Allport and Postman (1947) found, by transmission of stories through chains of subjects, that rumors are subject to leveling (simplification by loss of information), sharpening (heightening certain details selectively), and assimilation (changing the rumor to better fit local prejudices, culture, and concerns)—a process close to what psychologists call stereotyping. Higham (1951), replicating this study, found similar effects (for example, by the third reproduction, 74.5 percent of the details had been leveled out), but that ego involvement increased the accuracy with which a person repeated a story: "material affecting a person's interests is less likely to suffer distortion than material in which they are not ego-involved." A later study threw light on the loss of accuracy in rumor transmission: A review of conflicting findings—those who saw it as leveling, those who saw it as snowballing into a more elaborate version (Peterson and Gist, 1951), and those who saw it becoming more accurate and valid (Caplow, 1947 ; Bauer and Gleicher, 1953)—found that it was a matter of the conditions and attitude with which the story was transmitted. This study distinguished three kinds of orientation or "set": (1) critical, in which a person is knowledgeable and able to check the story by some kind of reference to what he knows; the effect on the rumor in this case is to eliminate false and irrelevant details, or, if accurate, to keep it intact; (2) uncritical set, in which there is a need to believe or no opportunity to check (for example, we may presume Flying Saucerians fit this category), the effect of which is that rumor picks up new details and meanings, becomes a "better story"; and (3) transmission set, in which the only interest in telling the story is passing it on (as in a laboratory experiment), whether or not it is true, in which case the main loss is due to forgetting or noise, though there is some elimination to help a story make better sense, and assimilation to linguistic habits (Buckner, 1965).

By this theory, we expect markedly different kinds of leveling or elaboration, depending upon the audience, its set, and the amount of collaboration in transmission (which is greater in a "net" of interaction with feedback than a "chain"). A common objection to the studies of serial ("chain") transmission in a laboratory is their artificiality and lack of the urgency and multiple inputs of real life; further, the laboratory chains are short (usually from eight to twelve), whereas real rumors doubtless go through hundreds of transmissions. Clearly, distortion, whether by leveling or elaboration, is by no means inevitable in rumors. The real-life situation is yet another story. A survey of studies of rumors planted in real-life situations, together with an experiment in which a rumor was planted in a girls' school, found no distortion and that cognitive unclarity helps the spread:

> Rumors will spread when there is (a) a state of cognitive unclarity about (b) an important issue which is (c) common to all or most members of a group . . . under conditions of widespread cognitive unclarity there is far more transmission of a planted rumor and far more speculation involving new rumors when the issue is important than when it is relatively unimportant. In distinct contrast to expectations created by studies using the technique of serial reproduction, there is absolutely no indication of distortion of the planted rumor. (Schachter and Burdick, 1955.)

So, to say the least, there is little reason to conclude that rumor is necessarily wild and distortive. Rather, we may presume that this depends very much on the attitudes of people participating in rumor and the situation and social system in which it occurs. In the small community, as previously noted, rumor has the sharp eyes and historical memory of Dame Grundy. In such a community, the storyteller is likely to be ego-involved, well informed, and able to check his interpretation by excellent feedback.

Another principle that helps us to understand whatever changes occur in rumor is called by Festinger and associates (1948) "integrative explanation"; that is, "there will be a tendency to reorganize and to distort items so as to be consistent with the central theme" of the rumor once it has been established. For example, once the people living in a housing project had been convinced that there were Communists working in their community, it was easy for them to organize new incidents into "an integrated explanation" of what had been taking place (Festinger et al., 1948). According to this principle, we see not only the possibility of a rumor becoming more consistent, but also a whole complex of rumors fitting together into a sort of legendary view—distortive, perhaps, but also capable of fitting together with scientific, or paranoid, logic.

Shibutani's (1966) comprehensive study of rumor helps us to better see what this form of "improvised news" does within a social system. Shibutani treats such things as tension, and cognitive unclarity and dissonance, as aspects of crisis. Rumor is one of the collective responses to a crisis of information. When something

unusual happens and disrupts established relationships, people become uncertain and feel they must consult one another, to be sure
that their respective definitions are sufficiently alike to enable them
to continue cooperating. They become—

> highly sensitized to one another. They ask questions; they compare
> experiences, they make suggestions. . . . Transactions proceed in a
> halting, tentative manner. . . . Thus, men in crises continually reinforce
> one another as they build up together a working orientation toward
> their changed environment. (Shibutani, 1966:174.)

But the most important part of Shibutani's theory is his view of the
development of new definitions through a process of *natural selection*:

> Out of the welter of reports, comments, and speculations that
> surround any unusual event certain items are tentatively accepted
> while others are rejected. Rumor construction at least in the beginning
> is a trial-and-error process, a form of collective experimentation. . . .
> *Selection* occurs as ideas are picked out and tested in use. . . . Of the
> mass of verbalizations . . . a few items stand out as being sufficiently
> deserving of serious consideration. Thus, a rumor is not something
> imposed from the outside, as in experiments on serial transmission,
> but what is selected spontaneously from the mass of communicative
> acts that constitute the hub of group life. Choice is usually uncon-
> scious, and when the developmental cycle runs its course, a stand-
> ard version gains general acceptance. Since rumor is a collaborative
> process, selection is necessarily *collective* . . . what is of interest to
> only a few is rejected . . . and soon forgotten. . . . The common defi-
> nition . . . takes shape through . . . the gradual integration of those
> items that have *survived*. (Shibutani, 1966:176–178.)

How reliable is a rumor? Here Shibutani makes an important
distinction: As long as collective excitement is moderate, informal
controls are maintained, and men retain their critical ability, selection takes place on the basis of *plausibility*. In such a situation, men
use auxiliary channels to build a view with the "best available
evidence." Though plausibility is no guarantee of accuracy ("reports
that are implausible are rejected, or viewed with suspicion, even
if they happen to be accurate"), rumors do not run wild, and
they change "in the direction of greater harmony with shared assumptions." However, when tension and collective excitement run
high, rumors act more like mass contagions, and "prevailing mood
replaces plausibility as the basis for selection."

> As men become more and more excited, their outlook becomes
> constricted . . . standards of judgment are . . . temporarily transformed.
> When conventional norms are no longer operating, it becomes possible
> to consider seriously proposals that are alien to established beliefs.
> (Shibutani, 1966:178–180.)

Further, during collective excitement, suggestibility leads to relaxation of self-control; they are less concerned with their self-images (for example, less concerned about seeming absurd); therefore they are no longer protected against impulsive behavior and foolish interpretations. This is the condition, then, for wild rumors: "if rumors occasionally prove inaccurate and implausible, this is more likely to be the result of a temporary suspension of critical ability than of defects of oral transmission," (Shibutani, 1966:180–181).

The thrust of Shibutani's view is that rumor is not an irresponsible, idiosyncratic process but part of the building of knowledge by society; and, on the whole, it is subject to the same standards as public policy, institutions, and the rest of culture. It is a functional view of rumor, in which natural selection winnows out what is least useful and keeps what the group regards as the best.

Indeed, the long view of symbolic transactions requires us to see rumors, jokes, songs, fads, stories, popular opinions, stereotypes, legends, heroes, and villains as part of the societal process of growth of collective ideas—the social construction of reality (see Chapter 5). It does not at all follow, then, that rumor ought to be stopped as an altogether irresponsible and dysfunctional process, that is, by better official reporting and such things as "rumor control clinics" (which, nevertheless, have their place in situations of tension). To wipe rumor and gossip out, as if they were harmful weeds, is something we could hardly wish to do. And the first to agree with this, probably, would be reporters and inside dopesters, whose success depends upon keeping one's ear to the ground and using the "grapevine" a little better than others do.

Thus, to supplement the official media is an important and irreplaceable function of talk. It serves to interpret the input and to supply a socially acceptable meaning to information, present or lacking. Media commentators serve the public alongside countless anonymous commentators, wits, and wiseguys. Where there is a credibility gap, the news-supplementing function becomes particularly important. It is recognized by people who work in the news and public relations field that material which can be labeled as "inside information" has greater credibility than ordinary news. Why is this so? It is unquestionably because people have found that inside dope can be more right than the official version, and that public fronts hide secrets of one kind or another, hence public statements are suspect, and information that seems to have leaked out has greater credibility. Margaret Mead (1964) commented on the mistrust of mass media, which is so common in our society.

> The local American emphasis has . . . been on resisting high powered communication pressures. . . . In our American system of

communciations, any interest, wishing to "sell" its products or message to the public, is able to use the full battery of available communication techniques, radio and film, press and poster. It is characteristic of this system that the symbols used to arouse emotion . . . have come into the hands of those who feel no responsibility toward them. In a society like Bali there is simply no possibility that such a symbol as "The Village," also spoken of as "Mister Village" and as "God Village," could be used by a casual vendor or rabble rouser. The symbols which evoke responses are used by those whose various positions in the society commit them to a responsible use. But in the United States, most of the value symbols of American tradition are ready to the hand of the manufacturer of the most trivial debased product, or the public relations counsel of the most wildcat and subversive organizations. (M. Mead, 1964:20–23.)

Because Americans experience such fragmented and contradictory symbols, they develop a "heightened threshold to any sort of appeal," and a cool attitude that gives them a "sence of immunity," which make them overlook the messages they are continually absorbing. Suppose a dishonest correspondence course uses the name of Florence Nightingale to gain nursing students. Will experience with this phony course cause the name of Florence Nightingale, and finally those of other venerated American symbols, to be surrounded with an aura of phoniness? And is there any escape from this communication gap as long as the insincere and irresponsible use of symbols continues?

One possible response to the confused state of our symbolic system and the dulling of our responsiveness is an artificial simplification, a demand for the return of control to central authorities who will see to it that there is no more of the haphazard and contradictory use of important symbols. (M. Mead, 1964:20–23.)

We may venture the hypothesis that the lower the credibility of media, the higher the relative credibility of rumor.

This may be clearer if we consider the role of rumor in a closed totalitarian society where the media give even better reason for mistrust. The Soviet Union controls almost all of its own media input, yet has not been able to avoid a substantial credibility gap. All information is interpreted ideologically, the movement of people in and out is restricted. Yet, somehow, the Russian people find out that that isn't all there is to the news. People are bored with constant propaganda. A ferment of free opinion is kept alive by talk and rumor; forbidden books and manuscripts circulate from hand to hand among the intelligentsia; a distinguished author, Grigorenko, confined in a lunatic asylum, was able to circulate his notes and observations not only to Russians but also to the world. It is clear, therefore, that a *covert public opinion* exists in Russia with ideas

different from those of the official Soviet view of the world. There
is grumbling about lack of consumer goods. But this covert opinion has not been able to develop an alternative ideology. A *Christian
Science Monitor* correspondent reported—

> The great mass of Soviet people, contrary to any misconceptions in
> the West, do not think of themselves as languishing under an authori-
> tarian, oppressive regime while waiting patiently for its overthrow.
> For the vast majority of Soviets an alternative to the Communist sys-
> tem . . . is inconceivable. . . . Said one youthful, intelligent office
> worker: "I can't even imagine that there is something else besides
> Marxism-Leninism." Since there is no tradition of political dissent . . .
> Russians do not miss it and are in fact apathetic to it. . . . Open dis-
> senters are only the tiniest fringe of Soviet society. (Saikowski, 1970.)

We get some idea of the Russion public-opinion process by
looking at Rose's (1954) description of it. He holds that the Soviet
state, like any totalitarian society, is really "one large audience"
and lacks an active public opinion with real voice in affairs.

> The distinction between the audience and the public is a most im-
> portant one for . . . contemporary society . . . while both may exist in
> a democratic society, the audience, when it is the dominant form of
> group . . . is actually conducive to totalitarianism. . . . While the
> totalitarian state provides something for the people to belong to, it
> still keeps people apart and out of communication with one another.
> No dictatorship can survive if the common people form publics and
> freely discuss their situation. . . . Fascism, therefore, sets up the
> strongest barriers to certain kinds of communication among citizens
> . . . yet tries to create the illusion that they are fully integrated mem-
> bers of an understanding and protective state. . . . The communist
> leaders know that a sense of participation . . . and a *feeling* of being
> free to discuss . . . are important . . . . They therefore outline a set
> of discussion topics . . . which can be discussed without endangering
> the leadership in the exercise of power. To make sure the discussion
> does not take a "dangerous" turn, they specify . . . the "right solu-
> tions" at which the discussion should eventually arrive. Every adult and
> adolescent . . . is . . . pressured into . . . attending . . . a small dis-
> cussion group . . . who work or live in the same place. . . . topics are
> handed over to a trusted group leader who is a member of the Com-
> munist Party, and . . . people are encouraged . . . to arrive at the
> predetermined solutions. . . . discussion . . . gives the appearance
> of being free, since any kind of argument can be raised if . . . properly
> refuted. . . . Through his . . . participation . . . the . . . citizen is given
> the impression that he is one of the controllers . . . . He, of course, is
> given only a choice of . . . the "right" candidate . . . and . . . activities
> . . . or not participating at all. . . . Actually . . . the Soviet state is
> . . . one large audience because there is no connection between . . .
> communication . . . participation at the lower level and the ultimate
> control . . . . (Rose, 1954:43–45.)

The development of true public opinion, by this analysis, is the key to the difference between a totalitarian system with a captive audience and a democracy with a participating public.

The kind of talk that *does* go on in the Soviet Union is, therefore, of great interest. And here rumor comes into its role of being almost, one might say, a hero and savior of public opinion. Apparently its role is to supplement, correct, and offset the official media and their propaganda. Inkeles and Bauer (1966) reported a thriving "rumor factory" in the Soviet Union, especially important among the peasants, who rely for news on conversations with people coming to the *Kolkhoz*, such as truck drivers and fellow farmers who had been to city markets. Technicians in the country also were eager for rumors: "We were always trying to get information from people who had come from Moscow." Three-quarters of collective farmers reported "frequent" exposure to *none* of three official mass media; therefore their main source was rumor. And, even though the intelligentsia used the official media, they also most frequently used rumor and had most confidence in it (Inkeles and Bauer, 1966). The rumor network in the Soviet Union is so powerful that it circumvents some of the regime's control and they would suppress it if they could. As it is, the regime taps it to sound out public opinion. Rumor is found not only to supply information but also to have tension-cathartic and "myth-busting" effects. The control of the regime over information media and propaganda makes rumor all the more important: "It is the Regime itself that is responsible for the elevation of what is ordinarily an incidental information source to the status of a parallel system of communication outside of official control" (Bauer and Gleicher, 1953). Thus, we see that as long as rumor thrives, the Soviet public is not quite the captive audience that Rose supposed it to be.

These observations should convince us of the great importance of rumor as a source of fairly reliable information and part of the talk processes on which democracy rests. Where there is a credibility gap, as there is in our society as well as in the Soviet Union, it helps people to penetrate the shield of privacy and secrecy and get the inside dope. Thereby they come into fuller contact with reality than they would if they simply accepted the "front" presented by a public image or the official view offered by the selected information and ideology of the media.

But, beyond this, another function of rumor in modern life is curiously like that of gossip in the oral system. As we noted, gossip in the small community provides everyone with continual scrutiny that is also a kind of recognition and status, making it impossible for anyone to be lost in the faceless mass. Gossip keeps people interested in one another and provides continual feedback in terms of personal information, not only what others are doing but also how they are responding to what one has done. Rumor cannot do all this for the mass society, but it can to some extent compensate for the monologicality of media and the anonymity of mass life. Gossipy speculation about the lives of celebrities goes on irrepressibly. This gives the *feeling*, if not the reality, that people know about each other and care about each other. Celebrities get the feeling of a relationship, a kind of loyalty, to "my public"; they have to watch their step to avoid disappointing their fans, if they happen to be entertainers, or their constituents, if they happen to be needing votes. So, the existence of gossip, making "little things" important, is a force that acts as some constraint on public people. As we saw in the example of President Nixon's effort to control his image, this constraint is considerable.

But, aside from the feeling of relationship with celebrities and the constraint upon them exerted by gossip, another function can be found in the fact that gossip about celebrities helps to feed their function as a compensatory symbol for the identity problems of facelessness, which is also called the "Mitty syndrome" (Klapp, 1969). That is, the price of being pushed into the role of a passive audience by monological media is a considerable amount of frustration, in spite of the vicarious entertainment received. The recognition given to the celebrity rewards the faceless viewer; watching others succeed is a substitute for his own success. Thus, all the gossip about celebrities helps feed this need for visualizing vividly what the hero's life is like, what the satisfactions are that are being enjoyed vicariously. Seeing the celebrity in his swimming pool; on his yacht; gossiping about girlfriends, boyfriends, cosmetics, love affairs, and business deals; listening to chatty interviews in which celebrities pass small talk to television audiences, all help the public to feel close to its favorites, and thus compensate for the anonymity, impersonality, and monologicality of mass life. The illusion of an oral network, as well as some real disclosures by rumor, seem to have some value in a media system.

So, we have examined the forms and functions of rumor and found it to have some important functions in a media system:

1. Perhaps the most important—whether in a closed or an open society— is that it is an important part of the talk process that keeps public opinion and democracy alive.
2. Rumor (like other forms of mass contagion) defies channels and thereby threatens secrecy; and secrecy, we know—whatever its value in war —is the enemy of a democratic society, which must keep most of its vital information public.
3. Another advantage of rumor is more subtle: Unlike conventional public discussion, rumor allows people to speak contrary to conforming

pressures and perhaps to their own announced positions—to say what is unpopular, unpleasant, dangerous, libelous, below one's dignity—irresponsibly. If stuffiness and gobbledegook are the official language, then, like wit and satire, rumor is a fresh voice. Thus, rumor frees us from what we would say to please reference groups and audiences.

4. Nor is rumor as wild as some think. It is sometimes surprisingly accurate and sticks closer to truth than one would have a right to expect, considering the number of liars and imaginative storytellers in the rumor chain—hence, its role as a form of news even when the media are well developed.

5. Rumor acts as a sanction on public officials and policies. It keeps them more on their toes and good behavior than they would be were media only supplying information about what they are doing.

6. Rumor gives the public an alternative source of information for reality checking. In an age of credibility gaps, especially where there is totalitarian control of communication, this function is priceless.

7. Rumor, by stimulating small-town gossip and feeding the appetite of the public for tidbits about celebrities, compensates for the anonymity and monologicality of a media system.

Conclusion

In this chapter we have looked at talk processes in both traditional societies and modern media systems, open and closed. In these societies we have seen that public discussion, including gossip and rumor, and mere talk, idle or subversive, are important and functional. In a traditional oral system, they are the very fabric and texture of togetherness. In a media system, they have the vital role to give meaning to a vast amount of information input, and to offset and supplement the monologicality of the media system (especially the closed system).

One of the important conclusions that emerges is that the function of talk processes—especially gossip and rumor—is *homeostatic.* That is, as a response against the input of new and disturbing information, these processes serve to interpret the world, to bring people together in common understandings, and sometimes to punish people for deviating too far from the norms of the system. To repeat, the function of talk processes is not so much to give people new information (the media do this to distraction), but to help people put facts together in meaningful and socially useful ways. Therefore, the main function is individual and social integration.

All this is therefore part of consensus making as the maintenance and creation of a social order; or, as we put it in Chapter 3, the construction of social reality by symbolic transactions. Symbolic transactions not only rebuild the old order by interpreting information in traditional ways, but also grope toward new definitions (as implied by Shibutani's treatment of rumor). Considering the flood of information, disturbing and undigested, which the media bring in, we must credit the oral processes with more function for bringing things together into meaningful wholes than do the media, for all the wealth of their technical information and for interpreting what they transmit. Especially in the developing societies, where the traditional gatekeeper is giving way to the modernization process, we see the media breaking down homeostasis by increasing psychic mobility leading to an explosion of expectations, often without supplying either a new conception of the world that hangs together or the technical means and institutions to satisfy the wants of the unbalanced want-get ratio.

We can see better the implications of this struggle between monologue and dialogue, media and talk, by considering the effect of the vast flood of information on modern open systems, the subject of Chapter 9.

CHAPTER 9

Information Overload
and Meaning Gap

As they rattled off down the road in the cold, clear morning, the boys, round-eyed with excitement, studied every house and barn with such prolonged interest that their heads revolved on their necks like those of young owls. . . . Rock River had only one street of stores, blacksmith shops and taverns, but it was an imposing place to Lincoln. . . . When Lincoln spoke he whispered, as if in church, pointing with stubby finger, "See there!" each time some new wonder broke on his sight. . . . The buying of boots was the crowning of joy of the day. . . . Then there were books to be bought, also, a geography, a "Ray's Arithmetic," and a slate. . . . At last, with all their treasures under the seat, where they could look at them or feel of them, with their slates clutched in their hands, the boys jolted toward home in silence . . . Lincoln was pensive and silent all the evening, for he was busily digesting the mass of sights, sounds, and sensations which the day's outing had thrust upon him. —Hamlin Garland, *Boy Life on the Prairie*, 1899.

This glimpse of boys' life on the prairie during the 1870s is meant to illustrate how it was in America before our transition to a media system, how thrilling were the simple sights and sounds of a small town to a boy who had no notion of movies, television, or, for that matter, newspapers. His world was quite as interesting to him, it seems, as ours is to us, though not so loaded with sensations. In Chapter 8 we saw how modernization can be conceived in terms of information theory as a change from oral to media systems, displacing dialogical communication and gatekeepers by monological communication from people one does not know, increasing psychic mobility and politicization; and sometimes changing the want-get ratio when things happen too fast, that is, too great an input of information destroys old culture, poses new problems, or arouses new expectations while failing to develop institutions that can deliver. We noted also that transition to a modern media system was associated with development of a mass society in which there was a loss of cohesion and morale and an increase in alienation, presumably connected with poor communication.

The question posed here is: How does increasing information act on social systems? We have seen the traditional gatekeeper (embodied in the Turkish leader) trying to protect his society from the overwhelming impact of new information, which he sees to be his duty. We pity his constituents and resent him as an old fogy, an authoritarian trying to place on progress the "dead hand" of the past. This seems justified when we see the eagerness with which transitional peoples grasp the input from transistor radios, cinema, and news. Pye (1963) said—

In most of the new states the atmosphere is not saturated with communications; the mass media are novel and can still provoke curiosity. In many Asian and African countries there is only one local radio station or at best two stations that compete for attention; and the volume of newspapers and magazines is so limited that competent readers are usually constantly hungry for more reading matter. Under these conditions of relative sparsity of media it appears that people do not develop the same attitudes of selectivity, and therefore in transitional societies the media can in fact play a far more potent role in political education than in the saturated societies. (Pye, 1963: 126.)

We take due note, however, of warnings by anthropologists that a flood of information can destroy simpler cultures. For example, the Brazilian government tried to protect the Xingu Indians from ethnocide by setting up a model reservation program, a kind of zoo for people, in which they received medical care but in which no other influence from civilized life penetrated; nevertheless, it was estimated that oblivion would be the fate of such tribal cultures by 1980. Modern peoples, we presume, do not need such protection; they can take in their stride the inputs that would swamp less advanced societies, because they have institutions for change, efficient communication and data processing, and selectivity toward information. Pye said—

> In the West the individual finds himself in an environment which is nearly saturated by the mass media, and he must develop mechanisms for warding off the massive and omnipresent pressures of all the different competing forms of communications. Clearly it is impossible in such societies for a person to expose himself to the overpowering bulk of the communications being disseminated, and therefore, as a means of self-defense, he must develop the capacity to ignore much and to become selective in his responses. (Pye, 1963:126.)

America has long been a world leader in modernization, though other societies, such as Japan and Turkey, have made startling leaps. Whatever the qualifications, America still stands first as an open system, with maximum mobility and media input, and rapid change in institutions and loss of traditions. She prides herself on being ahead in progress and absorbing everything and all comers.

Does she, by virtue of this history and philosophy, also have the honor of being the first to discover the negative effects of extremely high information input?

We are beginning to see, at any rate, that the modern era has undergone a crisis in the concept of progress, and that this has occurred, ironically, in the midst of more information than we can use. At the first level, the crisis is felt as the sheer multiplicity of problems as unexpected side effects of technology. At a deeper level, the effect is difficulty in combining new information into a meaningful picture of existence. The sense of absurdity grows; Samuel Beckett wrote—

> this old body to which nothing ever happened, or so little, which never met with anything, loved anything, wished for anything, in its tarnished universe except for the mirrors to shatter . . . and to vanish in the havoc of its images. (Beckett, 1967:30.)

Time seems out of joint; it is grotesque to have so many problems in the midst of abundance of both goods and information. Something is wrong. What?

Social scientists have not been slow in suspecting that some of the trouble might be found in the increase in communication itself, that we might get too much of a good thing. Deutsch (1961) noted "communication overload" as a "disease of cities," in which the possible freedom of choice is jammed by "coincidences of choice" resulting from the very efficiency of communication and transport. Because of the multiplicity of things needing attention, people find no time to attend to anything or anyone. He noted also the price in human meaning that has to be paid for this: loss of responsiveness to other people. A psychiatrist (Meerloo, 1967) commented—

> The technical means of communication via telephone, radio and television have become ensnarled in a gigantic traffic jam . . . indeed, there exists a positive communication explosion, a prelude to an avalanche. I have already observed in some patients the breakdown of their communication systems as a result of this overloading. We are in danger of being crushed under a mountain of information debris unless we find new condensations and simplifications to pull us out. (Meerloo, 1967.)

In this chapter we take the input called "information" and try to show that it contributes the most good only under optimal conditions; and at a certain point it ceases to be functional and becomes a source of strain. At the same time that information creates this strain, meaning (which is a product of total system functioning —not a mere item of information) can break down. Neglected inputs that are not usually thought of as information are part of the reason for the collapse of meaning when they suffer deficits. The thesis here is that modern society is subject to a malaise of communication coming *in part* from information overload. Actually there is a combination of three elements: (1) loss of cohesiveness and increasing alienation, due to poor communication of social feeling; (2) too much monological input at the price of dialogue and the oral system; and (3) too many facts without prescription, which people cannot put together in a meaningful way because there is no gatekeeper or interpreter they can trust and they are flooded with cross pressures. The small defiant peer groups and subcultures of our society are actually a defense against these conditions.

Information Overload

Our information output today is staggering and growing. It is estimated that in science alone approximately 2,000 pages of books, newspapers, and reports are published every *minute* in the world; the amount of scientific information is doubling every six years

(Stanford, 1971). The libraries are submerged by this "paper flood"; "keeping up" is a farce and professionals feel guilt, though they read all the time; it is a myth that facts somehow find their way to the people who need them. Hopes center on improvements in the technology of information retrieval (Gross, 1964). The Authors Guild reported that in 1970 there were 30,000 new books published in the United States alone.

The flood of new technical ideas was equally impressive. The U.S. Patent Office reported that in 1970 there were 230,000 patent applications pending and that such a backlog had existed since World War II (the normal waiting time to process a patent is three years).

To handle this flood of technical information, over 30,000 computers were operating, and the amount of computing power available in the United States was doubling each year (Armer, 1966). So, we get the picture of a kind of battle between print technologies and machines to process data into more usable form. Washington officials rely on capsule digests prepared by underlings. It was estimated that the official cable traffic into the State Department is as much as 10,000 incoming and outgoing messages a day (Manning, 1968:162–163).

But the main input of information was by no means into the minds of experts and officials. The common man was being inundated too, though he might not read a word. It was estimated that the average person had almost 3 hours of television viewing a day (Roper, 1969); Federal Communications Commissioner Nicholas Johnson reported in 1970 that by the time a child entered kindergarten, he would have received more hours of instruction from TV than he would later get in college for obtaining a bachelor's degree; an average man of 65 would have spent nine full years of his life watching TV. Actually, an interaction among the media multiplied the amount of apparent information from the original facts. An expert (Manning, 1968) said—

> The newspapers thrive more than ever because radio and TV titillate with small bits of news and make us thirsty for more detail. The news magazines thrive, often by dressing up what the newspapers have already said with spicy verbs and aromatic adjectives, because the daily and Sunday press are found inadequate. Yet while the news weeklies reach for more and more millions of subscribers, the fortnightlies and monthlies go up in circulation too, because all that precedes them is assumed—correctly—to be not sufficient to slake the thirst. In addition, more than 1,500 newsletters . . . are prospering because hundreds of thousands believe they are not getting enough of the pertinent facts from the other publications they read. Add to this the explosion of "book journalism" . . . . (Manning, 1968:158–159.)

Boorstin (1962) commented on this fine line between real and pseudo-information; to the receiver it may not make much difference. Advertising makes its contribution to the information flood; it was estimated that the public is exposed to 1,600 selling messages per day from all media.

While there was little question about the amount, opinions of the *value* of the information transmitted by the mass media varied greatly, from those who saw in it the opportunity to spread culture more equally and extend the sensory horizon of man, to those who would agree with Aranguren's (1967:155) view: "Most of the information transmitted by mass media of communication is worthless." A sociologist (Wilensky, 1964), analyzing media exposure of 1,354 American men, ranging from highly educated professionals to the working class, found them, on the whole, happy with the content of their communications; but he also found that the distinction between "class" and "mass" audiences was being lost; intellectuals were becoming "permeated" by the mass media. "What *is* new, unique to our time, is a thorough interpenetration of cultural levels; the good, the mediocre, and the trashy are becoming fused in one massive middle mush" (Wilensky, 1964).

Yet, marring this picture of contentment was the fact that the news media, television especially, were bringing certain new kinds of unpleasant facts directly into the home that had formerly had some kind of editing. Families watched political assassinations, riots, and Vietnam body counts with their TV dinners. Margaret Mead (1969b) commented, "This is the first age that has not had the chance to *edit*. Things are thrown on the screen just as they happen."

Intrusiveness of communication is a growing problem: Technology increases the thrust of information into the lives of people whether they want it or not. What was called the "jukebox problem" in the 1930s has grown into a pervasive feature of life in the 1970s: Everyone has portable equipment, whether at home or on the beaches and in the public parks, to thrust his tastes upon others; the volume of sound, stimulated by competition, has risen. This imposes a strain on the ideal of a free society: A stimulating difference of opinion becomes intolerable when technology gives the power to thrust upon others—"my taste is your garbage." Advertisers use every device to intrude selling messages into what has become a communication bedlam. Pornography is a related issue, since it becomes more difficult to protect oneself from shock, sudden damage to the superego, from stimuli thrust through one's defenses. Technology, even without amplification, increases mobility, and hence speeds up the impact of persons upon persons and scenes in ways that are not always mutually agreeable.

Fashion changes impose a further gratuitous burden upon people, of keeping up with information which they know is trivial and will lose its validity. In the early 1970s, the difference between a miniskirt and a midiskirt was of no permanent usefulness, but its significance at that time was earthshaking. Language proliferation is another source of burden: the endless changing catchwords, "in" phrases, jargons, neologisms, many of which are not technically needed but are simply a result of illiteracy (as defenders of the English language complain).

New marketing names, creating pseudodistinctions among products, add to the confusion:

What do you suppose Magic Moment, King Vitamin, Elephant, and Born Free have in common? They could be a soap opera, a super-sized vitamin tablet, a zoo, and a rallying cry for a militant movement—in that order. In the packaged goods business, however, they are all new products. Magic Moment happens to be a woman's hair coloring . . . King Vitamin is . . . [a] new children's cereal . . . Elephant is a malt liquor . . . and Born Free is . . . [a] new shampoo . . . .

Marketing managers have stretched their minds to crank out these product names. . . . The name game . . . is driving an increasing number of firms to the U.S. Patent Office in Washington, applying and registering brand names in record numbers. An all-time high of 32,631 applications for names were processed last year, compared with 28,294 in 1968.

In the U.S. Patent Office today, there are already more than 400,000 brand names registered, a total swelling annually by 20,000 plus. (*Saturday Review*, June 13, 1970:60.)

From such things we see that a modern media system has an enormous capacity for pouring information into people, much of which is beyond what they at the moment need and want. The part they do not want becomes a psychic burden—and in systemic terms, a strain. "Irrelevance" becomes a salient problem of the system because the sheer amount of information makes the likelihood small that any particular bit will apply to the individual. Yet, the knowledge that most information is irrelevant does not reduce the strain upon the individual, who in his own interest must sort his way through the information, much of which is "garbage," and in any case cannot protect himself from intrusion. In the broadest sense, the problem of information irrelevance merges with environmental pollution. It depends on how far one wishes to carry the concept of information—for example, whether a particular smell is just a smell or a clue to a problem that must be dealt with.

We may now try to define *information overload.* In normative terms, it might be said to be any input past the ideal rate for digesting new information and making it part of one's philosophy. Students will appreciate this because it is a description of their education. Imagine living on an island where a boat arrives each day and brings one piece of information of significance to *you*, leaving the rest of the day to think and talk about it. Such might be the optimal rate of input for a thoughtful response to life. Likewise, for society, overload would begin where news stopped being pleasantly stimulating and became a source of strain on decision processes, the authority of leaders, validity of cultural beliefs, socialization of children, and so on.

Information theorists try to define *overload* in terms of a measurable relationship between input and output of a system. The limit of a system, beyond which overload occurs, is usually called its *channel capacity*; all units through which communication flows, whether living things or machines, are regarded as *channels.* For example, a message may come from a human brain through a telephone wire to another brain, which in turn puts the idea into discussion of a committee, whose recommendation goes to an executive, whose decision solves a problem. All these intermediaries are channels, each with its own capacity for handling information. At the simplest level, it is a matter merely of transmission, that is, measuring the output (message received) against the signal originally sent. The message from a channel is always less discriminable than the input signal because of a certain amount of inherent *noise* (any stimulus that interferes with the reception of a message). For our purposes, we must remember that noise includes not only meaningless stimuli (which carry no signal) but also perfectly good information that doesn't happen to be what we want, or which is excessively *redundant* (repeating what we already know and therefore interfering with new information that we need and might have gotten).

Perhaps the most important thing to remember in trying to define information overload is that whatever the efficiency of some media (computers, cable lines, multimedia art, and so on), overload always occurs at the weakest link, which is often the human brain (Fig. 9.1). The human brain has great powers of abstraction, but is severely limited in channel capacity. Experiments by G. A. Miller (1967) showed that humans have difficulty making discriminative judgments of sound, color, taste, and so on, when alternatives go beyond the "magic number seven." "There seems to be some limitation built into us either by learning or by the design of our nervous systems" which limits what we can perceive immediately without help from some device such as counting.

"It can print information at the rate of 5,600 words per minute. Run a help wanted ad for someone who can read 5,600 words per minute."

FIGURE 9.1. The weakest link. (From *Saturday Review*, Jan. 31, 1970, p. 19.)

We are able to perceive up to about six dots (marbles, beans, dice marks, musical tones) accurately without counting; beyond this errors become frequent. . . . This ceiling is always very low. Indeed, it is an act of charity to call a man a channel at all. Compared to a telephone or television channels, a man is better characterized as a bottleneck. (Miller, 1967:8, 18–25, 48.)

It is not, of course, just a matter of the channel capacity of the human brain. Different modes of communication have different rates of transmission; for example, Quastler and Wulff (1955) found that the maximum transduction rate of impromptu speaking was about 26 bits per second, with a mean rate of about 18, whereas oral reading reached about 35 bits.

Groups, also, have different channel capacities; for example, a "wheel" or mesh has a better capacity than a "chain" because several lines can carry a distributed load (for example, a committee dividing up an assignment); but studies also show that strain increases on the central position in a "wheel" when information increases, as measured by increased time to perform tasks, reaching a "saturation" point that exceeds the ability of the individual to process information (Gilchrist, 1955). So, a wheel-like organization gains in efficiency by sending all its messages to one executive, but at some point it loses efficiency when the executive suffers overload.

James G. Miller (1960, 1971) studied information overload experimentally in terms of relation between input and output or performance. Overload is the point at which additional information causes a leveling or falling off of individual or group performance. In one situation, four people were required to cooperate in coordinating information that appeared on a screen. Individual A called out the slot in which an arrow appeared. B called out a letter representing that position. C, whose back was turned to the screen, pushed a button that registered the information he got from A and B. D watched some red light signals, which told whether C's push was correct. If the push was incorrect, D told him and C pushed another button until he finally got the right one. The performance of such a group can be charted as a relationship between varying rates of information input and output, in bits* per second. That is, how much information was handled in how long a time. The performance of two teams (A and B) is shown in Figure 9.2. The leveling off at about 3 bits of input per second shows the point at which overload occurred. The channel capacity is found to be between 2 and 2.5 bits of output per second. Two other findings (J. G. Miller, 1960) are of interest here: One is that the channel capacity of groups with this pattern is lower than that of individuals, though performance curves have the same shape. The second is that when overload occurs, certain kinds of behaviors (whether called mechanisms of adjustment or symptoms of failure) become frequent: (1) omitting information from the process; (2) processing erroneous information; (3) queuing—holding off some responses during rush periods with the hope that it may be possible to catch up during a lull; (4) filtering—selecting some kinds of information and leaving others; (5) cutting categories—discriminating with less precision (for example, instead of saying "I see yellow," saying, "I see a light color" or "I see a color"); (6) using multiple channels—spreading information through two or more channels, as in decentralization; and (7) escape from the task. See Figure 9.3.

* A bit is a binary unit of information; for example, whether "heads" or "tails." Technically, a bit is the logarithm of two (choices) to the base 2 (Rapoport, 1953). Hence, if a signal tells you which of four suits a card belongs to, it contains 2 bits of information.

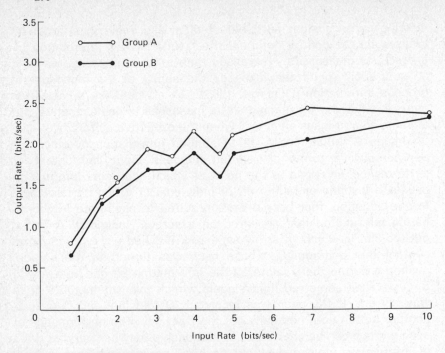

FIGURE 9.2.   Performance curves for groups A and B.
(From J. G. Miller, "Information Input
and Psychopathology," *American Journal
of Psychiatry*, vol. 116 [February 1960],
pp. 695–704.)

Fogel (1963) described the danger of information overload for
the executive in modern life:

> So great an amount of information may be furnished to the decision-
> maker that he no longer can maintain immediate availability of the
> relevant data. He may have to spend a large portion of his time filter-
> ing incoming data or searching the available store. . . . Further, there
> is the danger that such a vast quantity of information may divert him
> from his original task. He may lose sight of his goal or have this
> goal modified even without his being aware of the change. Too much
> information can degrade the decision. Obviously the "cocktail party"
> environment is unsuited to decision making. (Fogel, 1963:360.)

Students of management (Raymond, 1962) report that the typical
executive can receive and absorb only 1/100 to 1/1,000 of the
available information relevant to his decisions. Better data collection and processing often seem only to flood him; software cannot
keep up with the hardware. Again we return to the statement that
the channel capacity of the human brain is often the weakest link.
Such scientific studies, treating information overload in terms
of output and channel capacity, however valuable, fall somewhat

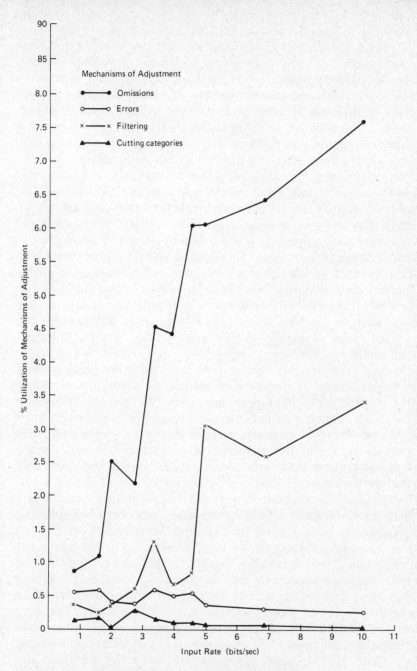

FIGURE 9.3. Mean utilization of mechanisms of adjustment by both groups at various input rates. (From J. G. Miller, "Information Input and Psychopathology," *American Journal of Psychiatry*, vol. 116 [February 1960], pp. 695–704.)

short of the full scope of the problem, as we have already seen. For one thing, outside the rather artificial laboratory setting, information comes to us not only in carefully controlled quantities but also in complex patterns of input, relationships, and symbols. Moreover, it is used in total living and not only in executive decisions. Therefore, we need some account of the whole psychic balance sheet, not merely the amount of information that enters into particular decisions. Actually, we suspect that information overload is not just too much information in a given time but an imbalance in communications caused, for example, by information that is monological, to which one can't talk back; coming so fast and so itemized, diverse, inconsistent, confusing, and irrelevant that one cannot fit it into a comprehensive picture (cognitive map); information received while unsupported by groups who could act as gatekeepers, guides, or generalized others (G. H. Mead, 1934); information coming from sources we do not trust; information that is poor in social feeling or which disturbs "we" feeling, perhaps because it is too impersonal, lacks concern, or breaks down faith in tradition or our fellows. Such an overload is not always a question of too much but one of too much in relation to too little of other kinds of information, all needed at the same time.

We may presume that information overload often occurs when there is not enough redundancy (repetition or contextual encoding of the signal). Most languages are about 50 percent redundant (Colby, 1958), which may indicate a homeostatic need not to have too rich a mixture of new information in any communication. For redundancy is one of the elements of communication balance we need to know more about—the kinds needed versus the kinds that are merely boring.

The thought of a homeostatic need for redundancy challenges us to try to understand a little better what happens when information floods the human mind. It has long been known there is a kind of screening (Freud called it a "censorship") that sorts out raw experience into categories which "make sense," leaving out the rest. Some psychologists call this "gestalt perception": seeing a pattern and ignoring the ground. Symbolic interactionists are likely to say that it comes from linguistic categorizing itself: The very process of forming cultural concepts and teaching a child a language acts like a grid imposed on his experience (Lindesmith and Strauss, 1968; Whorf, 1967). Aldous Huxley (1954) used the words of the English philosopher C. D. Broad to try to explain how psychedelic drugs flood the mind with unusual sensations.

> Each person is at each moment capable of remembering all that has ever happened to him . . . the function of the brain and nervous system is to protect us from being overwhelmed and confused by this mass

of largely useless and irrelevant knowledge, by shutting out most of what we should otherwise perceive or remember at any moment, leaving only that very small and special selection which is likely to be practically useful. . . . To formulate and express the contents of this reduced awareness, man has invented and endlessly elaborated those symbol-systems and implicit philosophies which we call languages. Every individual is at once the beneficiary and victim of the linguistic system with which he has been born . . . it confirms him in the belief that reduced awareness is the only awareness . . . so that he is all too apt to take his concepts for data, his words for actual things. Most people, most of the time, know only what comes through the reducing valve and is consecrated as genuinely real by the local languages. (Huxley, 1954:21–24.)

Huxley quoted William Blake, who said that if the "doors of perception" were opened, "everything would appear to man as it is, infinite." This leads us to ask whether there is any way besides psychedelic drugs to open the doors of perception. We see, if we do not attempt to conceptualize input, it is not all that difficult. Indeed, the mind is in some ways an almost nakedly open receptor. The following advertisement from a radio equipment manufacturing company will illustrate this:

A LITTLE-KNOWN FACT ABOUT THE HUMAN BRAIN CAN SAVE YOU A REMARKABLE AMOUNT OF MONEY. A brand new marketing research study . . . has unearthed an astonishing fact. An average of 73% of the people who have been repeatedly exposed to a television commercial will mentally replay the video upon hearing the sound track. Read that last sentence again. It could be worth millions of dollars to your company. Because the question naturally arises: Why pay for the picture all of the time? Take the sound track, and run it on the radio. . . . Radio and television, working together, can maximize impact.

Such a finding suggests to us that in some ways the mind is like an open tape recorder into which tracks can be inserted without our knowing it. Imagine yourself going about in public for 24 hours with an expensive machine switched on, taking everything that comes in, traffic noises, babbling conversations, and imagine how it would sound in playback, in what state the tape message would be. In some ways our nervous system is like this: on the one hand, the censoring conceptual screen; on the other hand, the open input. This is what makes an overload dangerous, not merely overwhelming the conceptual screen but constantly dripping in extraneous stimuli that have psychic costs difficult to estimate. So, the individual is in the dilemma of the unguarded input: antennae stretched out to hear what he needs, constantly intruded by what he does not want; for example, he must listen to all the traffic noise for the screech of wheels that can make him jump, because if he doesn't, he will not hear the message that saves his life. The unguarded input can build up all kinds of tensions and tendencies over which the individual has little conscious control.

So we see people engaged in a kind of strategy to keep their feelers out, yet avoid sensory flooding. Bats have an amazing ability to guide themselves in the dark by listening to echoes of tiny noises which they make themselves, even when loudspeakers are blasting sounds hundreds of times louder in an effort to "jam" their signals (Moore, 1967:85). Fortunately, humans have some of this ability to thread their way through the myriad stimuli of a confusing urban environment. One example is the cocktail party technique of "listening with three ears," tuning conversations in and out in various parts of the room. Another is flitting and hopping from one input to another, a strategy that might be called multiple-input management. Presidential adviser Henry Kissinger has been depicted working in a "steady babble of ringing telephones, sharp voices and electric typewriters." While talking to a visitor, his "hand reaches surreptitiously toward magazines on the table. On the phone he reads while the other person talks, his mind handling both at once, and puts aside the reading only when he responds" (Nevin, 1969). Such tactics enable people to manage complex conscious inputs, though we know little about the subliminal flooding.

Our American "open society" philosophy makes us especially vulnerable. We are taught to avoid snobbish tastes and to welcome everything that comes in, even advertising, even the devil's advocate. By contrast, we can see how Buddhism for many Eastern peoples acts as a sensory shield, rejecting much of the input of the senses as unreal and lowering expectations to a point where frustration is almost impossible ("he who sleeps on the floor will never fall out of bed"). Thus, we see that cultures can encourage or discourage information overload; it is not just a matter of how the mind works.

The immediate impact of conscious and unconscious information overload on a person's viewpoint has been described in various ways by students of communication. Barzun (1964), for example, notes that the inflow of jargon from social change has almost destroyed English as a "mother tongue." From the scores of technical vocabularies, abbreviations, trade names, and other neologisms added to the language—nearly half a million in the latest Webster—

> it would be difficult to choose a central group of words and phrases whose uses and connotations form a public idiom. . . . The user pays for it in the choppiness of his stream of thought and the crudity of the fragments of feeling it carries . . . becoming a foolish and discontinuous mind. (Barzun, 1964:201–202.)

McLuhan (1968) is not so discouraged by the discontinuity.

> It is worth much meditation that the news stories of the telegraph press are unified by a dateline rather than by a storyline. The discontinuity among the news items themselves creates a mosaic rather than a pictorial effect. The mosaic brings about deep involvement on the part of the reader who is obliged to create his own connections. (McLuhan, 1968:vii.)

Deutsch (1966) sees a threat of eclecticism to not only system integrity but also the human spirit.

> To accept the impact of outside information in a sequence of decisions may lead to decisions incompatible with one another. . . . the effect of indiscriminate receptivity may be the destruction of autonomy or even the destruction of the system. . . . We may conceive of spirit as the set of second-order values that might describe a pattern of decisions by which first-order values are chosen. Spirit . . . could represent a consistent strategy of values, as distinct from the "tactical" values that govern particular classes of decisions . . . the opposite of eclecticism. . . . Dignity is nondisruptive learning. . . . When we defend a man's dignity, we defend his ability to use his personality: we defend him against the imposition of an intolerably high speed of . . . changing his behavior . . . incompatible with the continuous functioning of his self-determination, his autonomous learning. (Deutsch, 1966:240–241, 131–132.)

Thus, for Deutsch, information overload threatens at the same time loss of integrity in both the individual and the social system. Social and individual projects are like a pile of blocks continually being knocked down; there is an endless flitting and frittering of viewpoints. A person may feel that his life is like a jigsaw puzzle that won't come together, either because pieces are missing or new ones added do not fit. If we search for a psychological term that best describes this state of affairs, we may find it in *cognitive dissonance.* In a society with information overload, the chances are good that a member will be in a chronic state of cognitive dissonance. He finds it difficult to pull himself together, close wounds, repair the fragmentation of his thoughts, tastes, and symbols. Dissonance, said Festinger (1957:3, 13), "being psychologically uncomfortable, will motivate the person to try to *reduce dissonance* and achieve consonance"; in addition, he will "actively *avoid* situations and information which would likely increase the dissonance." He will seek evidence to confirm decisions already made and avoid that which contradicts what he believes. If he belongs to a cult whose prophecies have failed, he will talk all the harder and more optimistically to persuade people to join (Festinger, Riecken, and Schachter, 1956). If he is doing something rather unpleasant, such as a dirty job that he got into without being forced, he will compensate by talking enthusiatically about it to himself or others, or by finding something interesting in the experience, as a strategy to make himself feel better about what he has already done. Some of the curious behavioral results of cognitive dissonance are reviewed in an excellent summary by Zajonc (1960). What concerns us here is merely to note that cognitive dissonance is a kind of distress from too much conflicting information, to which people respond in various ways that are quite familiar in our society.

The most logical response, it would seem, to an awareness of dissonance—say, the smell of the wrong kind of smoke in a kitchen, would be *constructive behavior*, such as thoroughly investigating the problem, arguing with others if necessary about what to do about it, and then doing it. This, of course, is the theory of our democracy. However, when dissonance is continual and problems are chronic or hydra-headed, or vested interests are entrenched, rational problem solving is not always the favored response.

More likely is *selective exposure.* For decades, public-opinion researchers have found that voters act in ways that are in contrast to the classic picture of the participating citizen. They listen to views mainly of those on their own side, they avoid propaganda and media that might change their opinion, they make up their minds before campaign argument begins; only a minority welcome new information from *cross pressures* (Lazarsfeld, 1944; Kriesberg, 1949). Campbell and his associates (1964) said—

> Identification with a party raises a perceptual screen through which the individual tends to see what is favorable to his partisan orientation. The stronger the party bond, the more exaggerated the process of selection and distortion will be. (Campbell et al., 1964:76.)

Behavioral scientists find that *audiences* are *self-selecting*, "people tend to see and hear communications that are favorable or congenial to their dispositions," and expose themselves more to chosen opinion leaders than to the mass media (Berelson and Steiner, 1964: 101–104, 529–533, 551). A basic response, when faced with people with whom one does not agree, is to draw together with one's own kind. In work and play, church membership, and especially in friendship formation, there is a tendency to select associates with similar value orientations and prefer to communicate with those who reinforce one's own values. For example, a liberal will seek other liberals and tend to avoid conservatives (Lazarsfeld and Merton, 1954). Intertwined with selective association is selective perception —that is, even if one looks at adverse information, one tends to see only that with which one agrees, or one tends to distort it in a way that is more consistent with one's own view. The classic

example is the study of the "Mr. Biggott" cartoon: "When prejudiced people saw a cartoon which made fun of their views, they
failed to see the humor and thought it was really a serious support
for their side" (Cooper and Jahoda, 1947). Most of this, of course,
is quite consistent with the idea that people dislike cognitive dissonance and avoid it when they can. The honest intellectual, bravely
facing all problems, seems to be far from the typical picture.

Another reaction to dissonance, especially when it comes in the
form of authority with which one may not openly disagree, is *compliance*: surface conformity, with pragmatic role playing and some
loss of inwardness. This often happens in education. For example,
Friedenberg (1963) argued that the American public high school
encourages in its students a bland submission to the conformist
values demanded by American mass society; consequently, it stifles
the adolescent's innate capacities for growth in uniqueness and
autonomy. Such students were hostile to individual privacy and inwardness, and rejected their most vivid and original peers in favor of
"good students" who accepted the school's authority. They identified with "the more powerful and frustrating forces" and closed
"their minds against the anxiety of perceiving alternatives." "Cram
and regurgitate" is known to all students. In broader terms, such
conformity is the other-directed response to varying group norms
(Riesman, Glaser, and Denney, 1950). External consonance achieved
by compliance, of course, is at the price of inner stress, which is
unmeasured and may take years coming to a head.

A fourth common response to information overload is to *attack
the sources* of bad news. An input of information into the system is
identified as a villain, and energy is devoted to fighting or sup-
pressing it. The most obvious form is censorship. Moralists may
view much of the input of the mass media as pollutants, as in this
letter to a newspaper about "the poison pool":

> What would be our reaction if a dose of poison were dropped into
> our water every day? We would either become immune to it or we
> would suffer through it. But first of all we would energetically protest
> against this infiltration of something disastrous to health and happiness.
>
> And what are we doing about accounts of crime, narcotics, etc., in
> the movies or television? We are blindly tolerating them, letting our
> young people get acquainted with the coarsest, brutal, and dangerous
> modes of life; giving them every detail of how to accomplish a burglary
> or murder. Isn't that poison? And isn't our responsibility greater than
> just to shrug our shoulders and reply "the public demands it"? In a
> civilized world of culture, high ideals, and motives we can hardly
> tolerate such a position, or stand by while the minds of our young
> people (and adults) are filled with ideas that we would certainly not
> like to experience.

When are we going to wake up to the fact that we have got to unite in an effort to forbid and suppress such broadcasting?

But it goes much farther. By 1970 it was fashionable to blame the schools, especially universities, for stirring up youth to dissent and rebel; a "backlash" of popular resentment deprived many schools of needed funds. The news media themselves also discovered that they were becoming villains; somehow they were to blame for so much "bad news," whether because of highlighting the sensational or too much criticism of public policies. A survey of fifty-three editors and public officials by the Associated Press in 1969 agreed that the following statement explained a substantial cause of public distrust of newspapers: "The press is always criticized and attacked during periods when the public is frustrated by the enormity of unsolved problems and this is one of those times." Some blamed the inpouring of bad news, smut, and sedition on the insidious work of Communists.

We may here try to interpret public "paranoia" as a response to the strain of information overload. The first persons to get "uptight" in a world of high information input are likely to be those with authoritarian personalities or social structures. This happens because the more rigid a system is, the smaller is the amount of information that can seem threatening. The authoritarian system has limited machinery for adjustive change and is easily overloaded. Clinical studies (Adorno, 1950; Sanford, 1950) showed that authoritarians tend to repress unacceptable impulses within themselves and project such motives to others when seen as hostile and threatening; they react extrapunitively (punishing others) to frustration unless the frustrating person is powerful, in which case they react intropunitively (punishing themselves). So, the simplistic response of attacking an enemy or scapegoat rather than the total problem input is a natural tendency of the authoritarian system to reduce its information overload.

A vicious circle of failure of response, increasing strain, and misinterpreting feedback could increase the "paranoia." The thing to remember about the paranoid response is that it fits all threatening facts into a consistent picture and provides a meaningful course of action. Here we have a theoretical connection between information overload and the collective hostile outbursts and escalations treated in previous chapters.

Yet another response to information overload may be called *insulation.* A person may try to create for himself an island of taste or moral consensus. This is seen in the esthete or connoisseur who makes discrimination his life style, surrounding himself only with esthetic things and sifting the environmental "garbage" adroitly or avoiding it altogether (Fig. 9.4). Another kind of insulation takes the form of "positive thinking," Coueism, or "psychocybernetics" (Maltz, 1960), which simply refuses to think about bad news and reinforces good thoughts. A sterner response is that of the monastic, who shuns the "world" altogether. Thomas Merton, after joining a Trappist monastery, advised—

> Do everything you can to avoid the amusements and noise and the business of men. Keep as far away as you can from the places where they gather to cheat and insult one another, to exploit one another, or to mock one another with their false gestures of friendship. Do not read their newspapers if you can help it. Be glad if you can keep beyond reach of their radios . . . keep your eyes clean and your ears quiet and your mind serene. (Merton, 1949)

"Every now and then Roger likes to cut himself off from all media."

FIGURE 9.4. Insulation from information overload.
(From *Saturday Review*, May 16, 1970,
p. 22.)

Others, sympathizing with the monastic point of view, try to carry on in the world, following the formula of Dwight L. Moody, the evangelist:

> Christians should live in the world, but not be filled with it. A ship lives in the water; but if the water gets into the ship, she goes to the bottom. So Christians may live in the world, but if the world gets into them, they sink.

Some sectarians, like the Mennonites and hippies, form colonies to cut themselves off from the information overload of modern society. And on a much larger scale, this seems to be the strategy of the closed political systems such as the People's Republic of China and the Soviet Union.

It is also possible to insulate oneself by work. *Specialization* provides for some a partial shield against information overload, by restricting their input to a narrow sphere of expertise or legal responsibility. But this game is, as we know, usually at a price of understanding the larger whole in which their work fits; the world becomes even more unrelated.

Such tactics throw light indirectly on the predicament of those who live discontentedly within an information-overloaded system without being insulated or engaged in overt fighting. Bad news pours in from their TV sets and newspapers. Noise penetrates their quiet. Issues come to them for decision about which they know little or nothing. (About other things which they know, no one asks their advice.) Books with titles like *The Population Bomb* (Ehrlich, 1968) warned that the world is approaching a crisis far too big to be blamed on scapegoats. It is plain that such a plethora of information can increase the sense of powerlessness, whether through ignorance of matters with which only experts can deal or helplessness in controlling changing world situations. Such an information overload is *alienating*: The world is thrust at the individual with intrusive noises, alarms, and appeals, about which he feels he can do nothing, even if he cares. The natural tendency to do something is smothered by input about the Los Angeles smog, Lake Erie pollution, the My Lai massacre, multiplying demands of protest groups, the nuclear menace. Apathy like that which followed the atomic shelter panic of the 1960s, or which usually accompanies political corruption, seems a natural response of people who say, "It's too much to think about, to heck with it!" Writers take note of "psychic numbing," closing off of public feeling from horrors in the mass media. In this sense, apathy is a homeostatic response to overwhelming cognitive dissonance.

It would be a mistake, however, to attribute all psychic numbing to alienation from bad news. A certain amount of boredom and jading seem to be characteristic of an overloaded communication system, even when the news is good. Nor is it attributable to the dullness of work routines, as some assume. Long ago, sociologist Simmel (1950) pointed out that jading came paradoxically from the very eagerness for sensations that the mobile urban world provided so abundantly; a city man, tasting so many pleasures and meeting so many strangers, finds his head sophisticated but his palate jaded; he develops a kind of psychic callus:

> He reacts with his head instead of his heart. . . . An incapacity . . . emerges to react to new sensations with the appropriate energy. This constitutes (the) blasé attitude . . . . (Simmel, 1950:410, 414.)

Thus, the blasé attitude works like a cliché of speech, whose redundancy makes the new seem like the old and takes the place of fresh insight. Art and entertainment fight a constant battle with jading, but seem only to increase the intensity of the sensory bombardment.

Finally, there is what we may call (in view of such difficulties) the heroic response to information overload, to try by every means available and those yet to be devised to master the flood: better educational methods, new Ph.D. programs, ever larger and more intelligent computers with the hope that their "brains" will stand between us and the growing complexity of problems, speed reading a thousand words a minute or scanning six books at a time. In 1970, *Life* magazine featured a computerized family, who had bought an $8,000 gadget and were enthusiastically applying it to all of their problems, grocery bills, income tax, even the children's homework. But it is plain that whatever victories have been achieved by improved data processing, the areas covered comprise only a small sector of the battlefront.

We have here reviewed some of the common responses to information overload. To summarize, they are: (1) constructive problem solving, (2) selective exposure and evasion, (3) external compliance, (4) attacking sources of bad news, (5) insulation, (6) specialization, (7) alienation and psychic numbing, (8) improved data processing.

But such closeups of information overload do not quite give us the systemic picture, the implications for the whole society.

Systemic Implications of Information Overload

On the systemic scale, individual problems like cognitive dissonance and alienation shrink into details of the larger question of how a society handles the information it receives or generates. The systemic trend may have a longer term than a life career—grandchildren may inherit problems; posterity enters the balance; the individual is only a link or channel. Questions of consensus, progress, symbolization enter. We assume that human society is an open, or adaptive, system that frames new goals, moves on to new equilibria, and is not merely homeostatic (Buckley, 1967; Deutsch, 1966; Cadwallader, 1959). Such a system reaches equilibria as way stations on a path of change. Its homeostasis is therefore a spiral rather than a cycle of return. (See Fig. 7.2.) For example, a friendly argument is likely to shift ground, move from issue to issue, and leave the opponents with points of view different from those they started with. An adaptive system uses new information to set up new goals; it adapts, if you please, not only to a present environment but to a state of things that does not yet exist: its own image of the future. But to frame and reach new goals, it may have to form consensus; for example, create a political party that will support policies that no current party accepts. There is some symbolic task in every societal movement to new equilibrium.

The most hopeful view of how a society handles a large input of information is that cross-fertilization will lead to new syntheses, such as the way Japan has reconciled modern industrial methods with familism, to produce corporations that are in some ways like great families. At best, we can hope for a cultural renaissance, a creative burst of ideas such as occurred in the Golden Age of Greece. Obviously, this is not the usual outcome of large information input into social systems.

1. Decision Lags

The most visible sign of strain from information overload is a lag in deciding what to do and getting people to agree with us. Lags come not only from failing to reach a solution, but also from taking too long a time to arrive with even the right solution, for the situation has changed and something else is now needed. In spite of being the world's most abundant nation, America has long been aware of widening gaps between problems and solutions, expectations and satisfactions—crime increasing nine times as fast as population, ranking twenty-third in world infant mortality rates, 10 percent of the population expected to occupy mental hospital beds, all of which led Gunnar Myrdal to refer to the country as being "backward" in social welfare. Such lags in meeting obvious problems indicate not merely a lack of technical information but of consensus; of time needed to communicate, persuade, and educate; perhaps rigidities in institutions and culture, which make it difficult for people to respond in new ways. Plainly, the societal response is failing to keep up with the information input.

Decision lags are especially important at three levels: (1) *Science and scholarship* fail to keep up, by theory building and research, with the flood of data from the environment. Causes of lag include lack of funding for research, overspecialization, retrieval loss of information already collected, and inability to develop a unified theory that puts bits of information together. Science and scholarship feed their lagging output into a second level of decision making, (2) *government and administration*, which has its own reasons for failing to use theoretical information effectively. Government and administration are flooded by crises difficult to handle by existing laws and bureaucratic rules. Operating largely without the benefit of scientific theory, they too slowly develop policies and measures, or by piecemeal and repressive methods actually make problems worse, which feeds back into the mounting crises. Below these two decision levels, is (3) the *public*, being flooded by "bad news," exerting some voting pressure on the inefficiency of government and administration, and living in a state of dissonance in which optimism and hope are offset to some degree by alienation, as evidenced not only by protests but by apathy and silent "gaps" in attitudes that prevent democratic discussion and encourage violence. Each of these lag cycles interacts with the others in complex ways.

Such decision lags raise the question of whether a democratic society is especially vulnerable to information overload because of features such as prolonged debate, lobbying by vested interests, and veto group action (paralysis of policy from fear of vocal minorities who lack the power to get what they want but have enough leverage to block a majority decision). Such factors mean that a democratic society, while open to information, is often unable to respond to it decisively and efficiently; for all its faith in the "free market" of ideas, it cannot process information fast enough when obstructed by the push and pull of special interests. A case in point is, perhaps, the fate of water fluoridation measures in American community politics. When fluoridation was put into effect quietly, there was no trouble; but when put to a referendum, angry opposition, and even paranoid elements often defeated the proposals (Crain, Katz, and Rosenthal, 1969). Here we seem to have a lag in needed measures resulting from democratic processes.

But information overload has a greater threat to democracy than merely failure to reach decisions quickly enough. A systems theorist (Vickers, 1968) tried to explain a vicious circle that occurs especially in developing societies undergoing rapid industrialization, which seem to be "hoist by their own petard"; that is, they cannot achieve by democratic process the rising expectations of the want-get ratio (Chapter 8):

> All societies where rapid industrialization is taking place are in danger of being unable to adapt themselves to the rate of change which their own activity produces. . . . Most disturbing, perhaps . . . are changes in the expectations, individual and collective, by which they are governed. . . . The regulative mechanisms become fully occupied with the short-term at the expense of the long-term, with the urgent at the expense of the important. This . . . may set going a vicious circle, which will . . . finally overwhelm the system. . . . There is here a *peculiar danger to Western democracy*. . . . Thus an increase in the rate of change places an increasing strain on the machinery of democracy. This, I believe, is why democracy has broken down—or has not been attempted—in many countres where rapid industrialization is taking place and why it is at risk everywhere. . . . The ultimate result of overload is certain . . . the system will fall back to a lower level of organization, discarding or modifying such of its governing expectations as cannot be realized. (Vickers, 1968:469–470.)

The fact seems to be that even the most open society has a high component of homeostasis, which can be disregarded only at its own peril. If it suffers too high an information input or frustration ratio, it may lose its stability and inner forces may push it over into some other kind of system. Deutsch (1962:162) said: "Communication overload or decision overload may be a major factor in the breakdown of states and governments."

Such a view of system homeostasis overcome by the wrong kind or amount of new information gives an updated view of what used to be called the "cultural lag" problem (Ogburn, 1922). It puts into terms of information theory what happens when a society undergoes a maladjustment in its ability to develop social institutions and culture that keep pace with input of technical information. Cultural lag theory puts the matter in terms of a disparity of rates of change in material and nonmaterial culture. It points to the fact that culture can change greatly, but that human nature is relatively fixed; particularly, it imposes biological limits on the rate at which individuals can learn and hence at which societies can change. Today we accept the fact that there may indeed be a saturation point beyond which societies cannot accept new information—set by the communication system, its channel capacities, and decision mechanisms—thus reducing the ability to form consensus and common symbols. In such terms it seems possible to treat the stresses of both modernizing societies and of modern ones; when governments are staggering with problems, adults have a feeling they can't keep up, and the generation gap widens ominously.

2. Failure to Integrate Information into
New Common Meanings

New information does more than create a crisis in decision making. It often works to reduce the amount of consensus about what must be taken for granted in order for decisions to be made. For example, we can imagine a group of engineers discussing how to build a bridge; but if they began to discuss whether to build a bridge at all, or even whether to be engineers, we would refer to this as not a decision difficulty but a lack of common meaning of what they were doing and how it fitted into the scheme of things. Meanings are usually the background, not the content of practical decisions. Yet much of the information coming into modern life questions exactly this. For example, how does a certain style of behavior—say, that of a hippie—fit in with the cultural norm of work or the moral rules by which one lives? Even a small fact can introduce dissent in scientific or political matters, but value differences can introduce prolonged and soul-searching discussions and confrontations that can shake the consensus of an entire system. In other words, dissensus goes much farther than dissent.

Thus, we see that every system has the task not only of responding to information by conscious decisions but also of building on a much broader scale in terms of styles, tastes, moral codes, ideologies, languages, and so on—the consensus by which people can make decisions together because they assume the same things. But systems may be unable to make sense out of new facts; they suffer a pile-up of bewildering and alarming symptoms, even show an allergy to certain kinds of information. This can be summed up by saying that social systems have limits to the amount and kinds of information they can integrate into common meanings; when they pass this limit, meaningless facts just pile up or, worse, put the system into a crisis that might be likened to indigestion.

To illustrate, our society abounds in trends of which people are unaware or unable to rationalize in terms of our present ideology; there is no place in their scheme to fit the new information. For example, ideas of the economy of scarcity persist in the midst of abundance, cybernation, loss of employment, and the looming age of leisure. People seem simply unable to grasp that idleness, as exemplified by hippies or people permanently on welfare, might make sense, especially to labor unions anxious to preserve what jobs they have. Again, the increase of pollution, effluence, and trash—flowing in part from overpopulation—fails to come through to people as a crisis affecting the very idea of progress, which they identify with material growth. They cannot fit the new facts into their meaning system. The old picture of national growth and prosperity resulting from increasing population, technology, and hard work simply do not fit the direction in which things are moving. Actually, the system is undergoing unparalleled stress from four huge factors, working in many ways opposite to these assumptions. These factors are exerting what might be called a "crunch"—a peak of systemic strain (see Fig. 9.5)—on an already weakening traditional structure: (1) information overload is leading to cognitive dissonance and exploding expectations; (2) the thrust of technology, including media, is increasing, with many adverse and unmeasured effects, such as unemployment and pollution; (3) population growth is increasing the crowding and resulting tendencies toward territorial aggression; (4) increasing mobility is multiplying the impact of people upon one another (hence aggravating the effects of crowding) and also contributing to status loss from rootlessness and poor personal feedback (as explained in discussion of the oral system, Chapter 8). Such confusing facts violate our assumptions that it is good to have more people and large families (*but that means more population pressure on environment and facilities*); that labor-saving technology frees people for leisure (*but increases population pressure and perhaps crime and misbehavior*); that technological power helps man (*but the thrust of technology destroys environment and perhaps liberty*); that movement is good because it gains a richer life

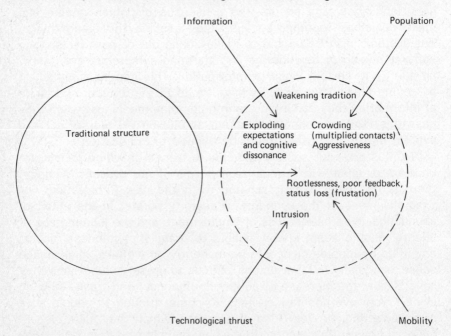

FIGURE 9.5.   A "crunch" (systemic strain peak).

and more opportunities (*but mobility destroys status and roots*);
that increasing GNP means abundance and the good life (*but it also
means mounting pollution and trash*); that information always helps
solve problems (*but not if it overloads decision and breaks down
meanings*).

Consequently, many people are unable to evoke the optimistic
picture of the world implied by the progress ideology, because too
many of its assets have been converted into debits, because it is a
leaky bucket with holes to be patched before doubts can be quieted.
By the end of 1969, a world Gallup poll showed that Americans were
by no means the world's leaders in optimism about progress. In
answer to the question, "Do you think, for people like yourself, that
the world in ten years' time will be a better place to live in than it
is now?" The more developed countries, including America, ranked
below less developed countries in agreement. Greece, Spain, Fin-
land, and Colombia were the most optimistic; even India outranked
the United States. Japanese and Canadians were the least optimistic, as indicated in Table 9.1.

TABLE 9.1
World in Ten Years?

	Better, %	Not So Good, %	Same, %	Don't Know, %
Greece	71	7	9	13
Spain	60	6	17	17
Finland	54	19	24	3
Colombia	53	30	13	4
India	49	15	19	17
W. Germany	43	9	32	16
United States	39	27	29	5
Canada	35	33	26	6
Japan	30	31	23	16

SOURCE: Data taken from a Gallup poll, Dec. 4, 1969.

Of course, if one's present position was bad enough, the poll
helped to make almost any future look better. But that hardly accounts for the lack of optimism in the most progressive countries.

Among the new facts that people were unable to relate to old
meanings were what we may call *symbolic violations*: the use of
symbols in ways that confused, flouted, or degraded their established meanings. The abuses of advertising have already been
mentioned. It is well known that those in the vanguard of the arts
and social movements often have difficulty conveying what they

have to say. If they use totally new signs, no one will understand; but if they use old symbols in new ways, it is almost as bad. People could not make out, for example, what the "pop" artist Andy Warhol was doing in painting a Campbell's bean can with perfect fidelity when he could get a real one (filled, too). Likewise, hippie styles displayed American Indian, pioneer, and other familiar costumes in puzzling ways. Some people used the American flag in ways (material for jackets, flying upside down) that brought on court proceedings. There were anomalies in the university graduation ceremonies of 1970. For example, of 1,336 Harvard seniors, many modified the traditional cap and gown by red-stripe arm bands, no academic robes (donating the rental fee to aid Cambodian refugees), or Viet Cong flags pinned to their back or hung from an aisle seat. In California, a graduated senior started hitchhiking in full academic regalia in hopes that it would help his progress somewhat.

Such symbolic usages were puzzling to the public; they seemed like language mistakes that make an English teacher or a native speaker wince. Let us call symbolic violations those misuses of symbols, whether from ignorance or with intent, that baffle, dismay, and sometimes outrage users of a language. Sometimes the intent is merely to attack established symbols, but more often the violator has a meaning of his own but has no way in the current communication channels to translate or to integrate it into the common meaning system.

3. Inability To Construct Meanings
(Consensus) Fast Enough

So, behind the information-decision problem, there may be a much larger one, a lack of common meaning to relate bits of information to, or by which to convey additional bits of information into, the public store. Decision lags can sometimes be speeded up merely by using computers or quicker data-collecting methods; but it is quite another thing to correct meaning lags that depend on more complex, slower, natural processes. The growth rates of languages and of mores indicate something of the scope of this symbolic task. While symbolic constructions can occur quickly, as in crowds (Chapter 3), on the whole the process is slower and difficult to control; it is not simply a matter of manufacturing an image as one would a motor.

As we indicated in Chapter 5, the special quality of human communication, unlike machines that handle programmed and monological input, is that it confers meanings to stimuli that create situations. In W. I. Thomas' well-known terms, the situation is not simply there but defined by the respondent. Marcel Proust constructed a whole novel of the past out of a cookie crumb. This is more than data processing—it is meaning-creating. So, along a communication channel are the ever-changing meanings of situations, things, persons, roles, information, culture, actions, tasks, games, self, frame of reference, world, as people interpret the signal that comes to them. This does not rule out reliability in human communication, but all the more emphasizes the need for common rules of meaning by which humans can make the same constructions when they wish.

A member of a simple culture lives in a world, most of whose symbols and information he is prepared to deal with; like an animal, he reads the tracks and signs of nature, and also reads a culture as familiar to him as his mother tongue. If disaster occurs, ritual and belief systems usually explain it. These simplistic solutions cannot be applied in modern societies, which are subject to the information overloads and growing new stresses such as we have described. Though the information flood becomes greater and greater, and sensory input reaches even orgiastic intensity, meanings do not grow with the same speed. One of the chief casualties is various forms of consensus ("we" feeling, morale, tradition, ideology), which do not hinge upon single information decisions but on a complex process of interactive support, largely through nondiscursive communication. For example, suppose that a company board making businesslike decisions has something happen that disturbs members' confidence in one another, perhaps subtle evidence of collusion revealed by some of the members. This will not be registered in the minutes of the meeting, which may record nothing but agreement. But the committee will have lost some of its meaning, and in the long run its output will suffer.

Thus, we designate as *meaning gap* a hiatus, a vacuum, or a fragmentation of meaning, which separates people in the same society even when they share the same factual information. Though they construct meanings (it is hard to keep a human from doing that), they cannot construct sufficient common meaning to reach one another with messages that go beyond mere transmission of technical facts, especially messages that generate "we" feeling, common values, and a sense of togetherness. Any such gap is a strain in a social system, but when it begins to paralyze the total response to major problems, such as crime control or keeping a school system going, it becomes social crisis.

Hence, we use the concept of *symbolic balance* to designate not merely a balance between information input and decision but also between that much larger proportion of new information and common symbols, and between meaning formation and consensus loss.

A heap of facts does not automatically add up to a world outlook, so the symbolic task is to construct common meanings that will give members of a system the same world (universe of discourse) to operate in as they solve particular problems. Symbolic balance is doubtless a complex function of ratios such as communication redundancy versus novelty, tradition versus innovation, dialogical versus monological communication, intimate versus impersonal encounter, homeostasis versus growth and challenge.

Symbolic balance, then, is a complex equilibrium of symbol formation to information input that goes with a societal equilibrium. When there are many symptoms of overload, such as decision lags or "paranoid" style, we have reason to believe that a system has lost equilibrium because it has passed its range of tolerance for new information. In other words, it is unable to construct common meanings fast enough to match the input. Such a concept of symbolic balance by no means implies a static culture, but one that is able to manufacture common meaning by which to move to a new equilibrium.

Meaning Gap and Search

Thus, meaning gap, as described here, is the other side of the coin of information overload. Together they make a symbolic imbalance of too much information and too slow meaning construction of a kind that can bring people together into a common world.

At this point we go a little more deeply into how meaning gap is felt in modern American society, and show its relation to forms of collective behavior that reflect a search for new meaning.

Deterioration of Success Goals

The managing editor of the "Harvard Crimson," a Radcliffe junior, aged 20, said—

> I am not certain that I believe in the good life at all any more, just as I am no longer sure that I believe in "education" or "social justice." It's common knowledge that the world is over. . . . And it doesn't really matter, of course, that I am losing my mind. I am not the only one. We are all tired of trying, too tired to blunder on through the garbage that keeps piling up. We can, if we like, wallpaper our minds with the Village Voice instead of the Wall Street Journal, but we won't be any happier. And it seems that somewhere in a discussion of the good life there should be some brief mention of happiness.
>
> On why the world is over: We are tearing ourselves apart. With systems and countersystems, labels and logic, the right and the left and fear. I'm not talking about the bomb here. If we do blow it all up,

then none of this matters. I'm talking about the end of the world as we know it, competition and nine-to-five idealism, and about why the brightest people I know don't want to do anything any more but sit around, and talk, and smoke dope. . . . The revolution begins with the recognition of total absurdity. The real revolution does not lie with those who think they can destroy the system. . . . It is not those who attempt to break the system on its own terms that are the threat (our hope) but those who slide from under. The point is to get out of it all. To break away from all systems, accept and embrace the world as insane. To have the courage to do nothing but what we really believe in, and to be nothing but loved. (Sternhell, 1970:36.)

Such a description of the entire social system as absurd is perhaps an extreme statement, but it is an interpretation by a person who is obviously sane and well educated. It mentions information overload ("garbage") and loss of faith in the "good life" that is associated with "competition and nine-to-five idealism"—the standard American economic success goal.

But meaning gap is not just a matter of loss of economic motivation. It extends through the educational system (as there is no need to demonstrate to students). It is found in church. It is found in the home; for example, the traditional role of the housewife is challenged. An article on "The New Feminism" asked whether housewives' drudgery is any worse than the "meaningless jobs most people have today?" It answered that "housewives are not paid for their work, and money is the mark of value in this society"; therefore, by implication, men get more value from their work (Komissar, 1970). But, unfortunately, there are numerous complaints about the identity problems of men, such as being emasculated by aggressive women or blended into a "third sex." The more one listens, the more one hears of those who have meaning problems, in terms of boredom, being unable to "relate" to work or people, feeling cheated, empty, or lonely. Such problems of meaning go beyond the mere question of monotony of work or emptiness of material success values.

Some indication of how widespread is the meaning gap has been given by language used by some of the younger generation to express their inadequate relationship to the system: plastic (values or persons that are phony), tell it like it is, can't relate, turns me off, do your thing, freak out (escape), "turn on, tune in, drop out," bad vibrations, "culture of death." (See Chapter 11.)

A list of names, such as those following can usually be sorted by college students into people who are (or were) "straight" or "square" and those who are "hip" to values that the Establishment does not understand.

Shirley Temple	Timothy Leary
Joan Baez	Burl Ives
John Wayne	Bob Dylan
Peter Fonda	Bob Hope
J. Edgar Hoover	Jerry Rubin

Sorting such names into two columns shows a meaning gap, not necessarily along generational lines. Bob Dylan sang, "something is happening, and you don't know what it is, do you, Mr. Jones?" Mr. Jones was Dylan's symbol in the song for the "square" who cannot perceive the new values of the "counterculture" (Roszak, 1969).

In the 1960s, a battle of the graffiti was waged on parked cars labeled with "square" signs such as "Love it or leave it," which were altered by counterculturists to read "Change it or lose it."

The term "square" showed not just a gap in communication but a kind of blockage, a closing of doors, in two senses: one was the unwillingness of youth to enter certain activities. For example, if Sunday school or Boy Scouts was "square," this meant that the youth would not enter this kind of activity; that door of opportunity (if opportunity it was) was closed. Such issues as beards and haircuts sometimes resulted in closing off career opportunities. The other kind of blockage was that these same doors were closed to groups who lacked the status to enter them, such as ethnic minorities.

In one sense, the complaint of the Radcliffe junior reflected the familiar literary theme ranging from Fitzgerald's *The Great Gatsby* to Herbert Gold's *The Great American Jackpot*—that success was a "rat race." But never before had so many who were favored by class and education to win—future leaders of the country—displayed so much boredom, not only with the rules (Parkinson's law, the Peter principle, and all that), but also with the very rewards of the game. One can see what would happen to baseball, if people stopped caring what was on the scoreboard—whether pitchers achieved "shutouts" or batters hit home runs—and left the stands before the game was over. So, it seemed that many upper-middle-class educated youth were dropping out of the great American game of earning as much as one can, to consume as much as one can, and display the status symbols registering the score. Hippies and political radicals were the more visible of such dropouts, but countless others merely ran the race more slowly and wandered off the course at the turns.

Poor Feedback and Loss of Social Feeling

It would be a mistake to expect an explanation of deterioration of success goals merely by pinpointing the faults of a material sys-

tem, even in information overload, without considering more pervasive sources of alienation in the poverty of feedback and shallowness
of social feeling. For example, Fuchs (1967) noted that Peace Corps
experience in the Philippines sometimes led to an identity crisis as
workers contrasted Filipino personalism and cohesiveness with the
"aloneness" of American life. Fuchs speculated that the "cult of
self-sufficiency" was "a cause of or at least . . . related to a widespread sense of loneliness, meaninglessness, and worthlessness in
American life," coming from absence of the "warmth, closeness,
lovingness, and dependability" often found in traditional, familistic
societies.

> Surely Americans are far behind others in their capacity to appre-
> ciate and understand mystery, or in expressing their bodies freely and
> rhythmically, or in absorbing and merging confidently and harmoniously
> with nature, or in feeling the joys of mutuality in relationships. (Fuchs,
> 1967:208–213.)

A similar report of the shallowness of American friendliness was
made by foreign students at U.C.L.A. (R. T. Morris, 1960:120, 125).
Difficulty in building up good social feeling is a kind of communication problem different from the flood of factual information
we have been considering, though both involve poor feedback. In
one sense, we Americans are communicating too "well," by a
monological input of irrelevant facts, bad news, and noise, all of
which are strains to sift and integrate. Hence, we have cognitive
dissonance, lagging government responses, and inability to construct
meanings fast enough. The "better" we communicate in terms of
pouring unrelated facts into the system, the worse such problems
become. But, in another sense, we are communicating not nearly
enough of the feedback that supports the individual—his social feelings, beliefs, and identity—because of interactional deficiencies that
are indicated by labels like "aloneness" and "shallowness."
In other words, for adequate meaning, there are two essential
cycles of feedback at two levels, both of which must be balanced.
One is the input of discursive information, which is the basis of
decisions, adaptive responses, and integrated theory when properly
balanced. The other is the cycle of nondiscursive feedback, the
circle of input from others, which supports our sentiments: how we
feel about ourselves and our lives. Trust in others, "we" feeling, and
morale depend upon this input. Discursive information concerns
what we do intellectually and technically; nondiscursive is at the
level of sentiments (consensus, "we"), how we act socially. The
two levels are indicated in Figure 9.6.
The roles we play toward others depend upon feelings such as
sympathy, friendliness, trust, sincerity, tact, feeling of common

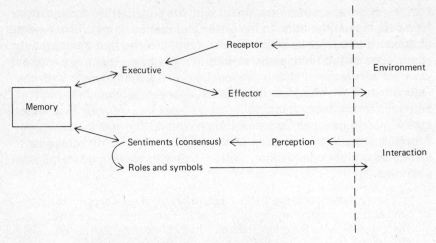

FIGURE 9.6. Two levels of feedback cycles: Discursive information (upper half of diagram)
concerns what we do intellectually and
technically; nondiscursive information
(lower half of diagram) is at the level
of sentiments (consensus, "we"), how
we act socially.

task, which we can sum up as a consensus of social sentiments and
which must be continually nourished by sincere display of corresponding sentiments by others. When anything interferes with this
cycle of feedback, social sentiments weaken, perhaps break down.
A breakdown of the consensus by which roles are played not only
interferes with relationships, but ultimately also confuses the identities of people, who must define themselves by the responses of
others and their own success in role playing. The basis of this is
explained by the theory known in social psychology as *symbolic
interactionism* (G. H. Mead, 1934; Blumer, 1969a).

It is commonly recognized that we live in a *mass society*. What
does this mean with regard to the second level of feedback, of
nondiscursive information needed for social sentiments? A mass
society is one that is increasingly crowded with people who are
poorly related to one another, in terms such as primary group instability, status insecurity and ambiguity, and lack of concern. For
example, a person does something that is important to him, and
nobody pays any attention; he gets in trouble or suffers a crime,
and nobody responds. Essentially the fault of a mass society is lack
of feedback to one's own behavior from a sensitive and responsive
network of relationships (versus monological communication). In a
mass society one's act is like "bread cast upon the water," but
which does not return; social reciprocity is weak. A familiar ex-

ample of strong social reciprocity is a village. If A does a favor for B, it may come back to him later as a service from X to Y—who happened to be A's and B's cousins, respectively. In a mass society, such a sensitive texture of reciprocity is lacking, even where there is wide involvement with many people who are nominally "friends," but most of whom are actually only acquaintances. Heavy involvement in shallow contacts with many such acquaintances does not supply adequate reinforcement to identity and social sentiments, but actually places a kind of overload on people (noted by Simmel, 1950) who must deal with so many strangers, sorting out responses, interpreting their signs and styles, playing games (Berne, 1964) divining the motives behind fronts, "facework" (Goffman, 1955), and so on. In playing such games, some people develop manners and defenses such as universal friendliness or wearing dark glasses, which further defeat genuine feedback and self-disclosure (Jourard, 1964).

What this means in terms of information input is that people, deficient in feedback that helps their social sentiments and identities, are deprived of a means of making significant what information they receive; that is, they do not know what attitude to take toward facts. For example, persons who have had their confidence in their own opinion shaken by contrary information will talk to others who agree in order to restore their level of confidence (Brodbeck, 1956); but if they do not have someone to turn to or have no confidence in the group to which they turn for support, how can it help them to strengthen their opinions? In such ways, we may say that mass society deprives an individual of emotional homeostasis from group feedback at the same time that it overloads him with information.

Six factors disturbing identity all over the world help us to understand why modern mass societies so often "cheat" people in meaning: (1) destruction of environment, places that constitute "home"; (2) loss of contact with the past and tradition—hence, collective identity; (3) lack of identifying social ceremony that recognizes the importance of the person; (4) excessive social mobility, destroying roots and weakening personal feedback and concern; (5) shallowness of feeling, whether from technical relationships, overinvolvement in media, or other causes; and (6) variety of role models, from media or peer groups, which is bewildering and frustrating because they are unsupported by guidance or assurance that they will pay off in careers. Such conditions could be expected more or less in any society with advanced technology and media, high urbanism, and rapid change; but they would be present hardly at all where oral feedback networks were intact and rich, as in a village in Crete or a kibbutz in Israel. The evidence to support these conditions as sources of identity and meaning problems were examined by Klapp (1969).

So, it is no surprise to see a growth of psychotherapeutic programs devoted to breaking through emotional walls—ironically trying to return to the rapport that might be found among half a dozen Arabs sitting together on the floor drinking coffee.

When such factors as we have been describing increase beyond a critical point, any social system will suffer meaning and identity failure. The basic reason is that a certain amount of *redundancy* (of the right kinds: culture, tradition, grammar, manners, premises, "we" symbols, trust, and so on) is needed for the transmission of any message, especially of the kinds needed by humans for personal reassurance. Beyond a point, novelty without sufficient context of redundancy becomes delusive, a frenetic gibberish. But long before this happens, humans lose interest in messages because of insufficient payoff. In other words, redundancy is needed just as much as information to keep communication going; all systems depend on redundancy as a framework of identity, memory, and purpose on which to hang information.

In such ways, it seems, the whole feedback network of emotion in modern life has become unplugged, the batteries of sentiment are not charged often enough, people feel a sense of emotional shallowness and emptiness.

If nondiscursive feedback to social feeling could be improved, then the deterioration of social interplay might be reversed: *People might play roles with more satisfaction, feel better about themselves and one another, like their work more, value the status symbols (now the expression of genuine concern); success goals would gain in meaning, and the "great American jackpot" would become, once again, the American dream.*

But the question remains whether modern society can find the leverage to change enough of these trends that destroy meaning, such as mobility and information overload, and restore *symbolic balance* at both levels at the same time. How could this be done? Two solutions might be sought: (1) reduce the information overload (by increasing redundancy or improving adaptive response) so that more people could put together a meaningful picture of the world; and (2) improve the payoff of nondiscursive feedback in day-to-day relations—perhaps by new institutions—so that people could feel richer sentiments, self-esteem, and mystiques embodying life's ultimate meaning.

Should symbolic balance not be restored and should crisis in the system take place, then people would be launched like Ulysses into the sea of change, not knowing where they would arrive, awaiting dubious rescues from collective behavior.

*Relation of Meaning Gap to Collective
Behavior*

Unable to restore meaning through old circuits, a society may be expected to release the tensions of the twofold stress described above by outbursts and movements that decrease information overload and dissonance, and which increase emotional payoffs in new kinds of activity together.

On the one hand, information overload means increase of tension to the point where a new bit of information can trigger a panic or a hostile response that attempts to destroy the source of bad news or imposes an intolerant demand for consensus to suppress further sources of information. This might lead to rapid acceptance of an ideology, a plunge into a cult that provides an answer to "everything," or a crusade against radical or heretical ideas. In general, the response of a society to severe stress of information overload might be expected to be expressed by efforts to simplify the problem by confining it to one source of trouble that can be fought, as in scapegoating; or it might be solved by reducing the variety and amount of information input by some kind of restriction on communication.

On the other hand, imbalance experienced as lack of meaning in present institutions should be expected to take the form of movements that have the character of meaning search; that is, not merely using the old methods to accomplish old goals, but groping toward new forms of interaction that foster more intense sensory experiences, new intuitions, values, and life styles.

For this reason, much of conventional politics and economics— for that matter, religion and education, too—is irrelevant to meaning search. While effort may be made to put "new wine into old bottles," there will be a strong tendency to move into unconventional modes of expression for which the old order lacks adequate accomodation or even language. Some of these movements will seem a rebellion against the very rationality of the system. Thus, some of the currently new movements take the form of a "mind-blowing" search for new sensations, which seem to have no place in any ordered way of life. But the social forms that might contain them are still emerging, though they have yet to prove their viability. For example, could a group survive in the world of tomorrow (assuming guaranteed incomes and vast leisure) if it was incapacitated for work much of the time by psychedelic drugs? Again, will technological arrangements be found in the city of tomorrow so that individuals can each enjoy new sensations in music at ninety decibels without disturbing one another? Most meaning-seeking activities, however, would have to be judged by subjective and romantic rather than practical criteria, because they aim at inner payoff, not practical results—what Eric Sevareid has called the "euphoria of action." Many would be in the realm of the occult, as the more respectable ways of knowing were found to be lacking. So, by 1970, innumerable articles and books showed that America was in the midst of an occult boom of astrology, Scientology, spiritualism, clairvoyance, ESP, Tarot card reading, ghost chasing, palmistry, graphology, phrenology, numerology, alchemy, witchcraft, Satanism, and Hare Krishna chanting.

Likewise, shattering encounters, though seeming to destroy the very basis for stability, can be experienced on second thought as therapy. A participant in a "marathon" encounter group reported:

> After 48 hours we were shook-up and angry at the encounter group's tastelessness and its unnecessarily headlong rush into defiance of personal and social norms. But these reactions were less important to us than our astonished realization that we had been doing the most intensely concentrated learning of our lives. I felt then, and I feel now, that we had been exposed to an almost-revolutionary format for educational and institutional change. Both Godsend and menace, Encounter is still a messy and imperfect tool. (R. L. Schwartz, 1970:16.)

Who is to have the final say? To prejudge a groping movement is like trying to describe the pattern of a stream before it has found its course.

Conclusion

This chapter describes an imbalance of communication leading to a social malaise that is expressed in certain kinds of collective behavior. The communication imbalance consists of an overload of information, largely from mass media, about matters that seem irrelevant (remote events, strangers, confusing problems, demands, propagandas, noise, intrusive appeals) at the same time as there exists a shortage of nondiscursive feedback for building good social feelings (sympathy, fellowship, "we" feeling, concern, trust, morale, self-confidence, identity) into a community network. Very often such an imbalance can be seen in a disproportion of media to oral input, though it is rarely so simple as that, since much of the feedback for good social feelings is nonverbal interaction that is not registered in what people say. Nevertheless, talk is a fair indicator; and a system may be said to be imbalanced when media input is so high and the community network so weak that people know the personal lives of celebrities better than those of their neighbors and friends.

System imbalance reaches *crisis* when the ratio of information input to nondiscursive feedback becomes so large that the world seems threatened and invaded by strangers; people feel their backs are to the wall and they must either fight or leave. They cannot restore good feeling by the ordinary means of communication, appealing to friends for support or umpire for rules; the game has broken down because others do not share the same meaning. The resulting collective behavior, then, expresses the tension of people who fight panic caused by information overload and try to overcome it by responses such as suppression and crusades against enemies who embody the strange input, or by searches for meaning and new styles of life through rebellions, cults, fads and so on. Figure 9.7 outlines this relationship.

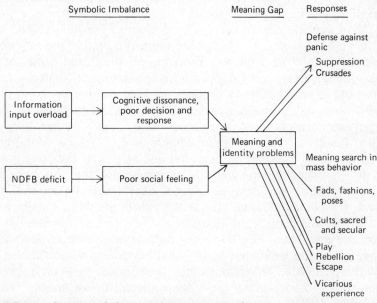

FIGURE 9.7. System imbalance and meaning search.

These considerations lead to some more far-reaching conclusions about society and its values. One is that greater attention should be paid to social needs for homeostasis and redundancy at two levels. Social balance needs redundancy (a certain proportion of familiar and old to new and strange information) both in factual input entering decisions, technical processes, and intellectual education, and in input from the responses of people to one another, which build social feeling. The movement of an open society is from one balance point to another, by changed communication processes at both levels; for example, political decisions and technical innovations are accompanied by talk processes, cathartic encounters, new cults, and so on, which enable the nondiscursive meaning

to be generated. Homeodynamics is not so much a return to a previous resting point as a new balance of discursive and nondiscursive
communication.

This focuses a certain amount of blame on technology as a prime
source of input, via the media, and new conditions and side effects
disturbing the meaning of our way of life. The very efficiency of
technology in the mechanical sense becomes a thrust of noise, intrusion, coercion, and boring sameness (banality), which threatens
the meaning of the communication system and hence of society itself. One suspects that technology has ruined more human games
than it has ever improved; at least a critical look at the noise-to-
signal ratio of all technological innovation, within the equation of
symbolic balance, is called for.

These considerations are a severe blow to the modernistic bias
that change is always good, and the more the better. The modernist
thinks of himself as a pioneer throwing off the "dead hand" of the
past; but he rarely considers the homeostatic mechanisms he is
disturbing or whether he is putting any kind of balance in its place
(see Toffler, 1970, on "future shock"). New things must be scrutinized and subjected to questions other than whether they are
larger, faster, or cheaper than what one had before. Mobility—a
prime cause of information overload and stress in relations among
people—is especially suspect in the assumption that the more people move about, see strange places, hear from one another, and
reduce the communicative size of the world, the more tensions will
be lowered and change go more smoothly. Also, a severe blow has
come to those ideas that there are natural mechanisms (Darwinian
competition, the "invisible hand" of the market) automatically balancing systems when changes are introduced. In a time of eco-
crisis, this old confidence has been replaced by an uneasy feeling
of uncontrolled forces loose in the world, forces over which automatic laws do not and cannot work in our favor. The growing faddism and style rebellion of modern times are other sources of disappointment to those who adhere to the belief that everything new
must be good.

It is strongly suggested that change, mobility, and modernization are good only within limits set by the system's ability to balance itself at new levels. When enthusiasts talk about the advantages of progress, they are actually talking about a middle (optimal)
range in which there is a stimulating input of information that people are able to use in a meaningful and creative way to reach the
goals of their own culture. But to speak of progress from information
input in a society exploding from identity and meaning problems
seems the height of fatuity. Modernism in such a setting is a pep
pill for a Mad Hatter's tea party.

Finally, all these considerations lead to some revision of the classic liberal theory about knowledge and society. The good old liberals (Voltaire, Locke, J. S. Mill, Bertrand Russell; Popper, 1952) assumed that the ideal society was an open one, which placed no restrictions on the amount of new information entering, nor on dissent from any idea. They based this assumption on the premise that all kinds and amounts of information are tolerable, if not good, since they contribute to the choices of the "free market of ideas," from which good will drive out bad in a competition that can only enrich the public. The progress of mankind comes from maximum increase of knowledge, which is due to free competition of ideas and openness to all sources of information. The price of closure is to stop progress, and hence limit the efficiency of the pursuit of happiness. Behind classic liberal theory is an assumption of the linear relationship between inputs and gain or loss in a system: The more good things (information) you put in, the more good things (truth, progress, happiness) you will get out. Yet, such a presumption that good things work to the benefit of a system at all levels of input does not seem justified either by everyday experience or modern systems theory. We know it simply isn't so that if a certain amount of fertilizer is good for a garden, twice that amount of fertilizer will be twice as good for the garden; that two steaks at a meal are better than one steak and three better than two; that if praising another person will make him like you, praising him twice as much will make him like you more.

In every systemic science, nonlinear relationships are found between input and output: economists call it the law of diminishing returns; chemists, phase change; biologists, metamorphosis; ecologists, population "crashes" when growth is too much. It is even more true where the whole (like a jigsaw puzzle or a meaning) is a pattern rather than a mere sum of its parts, the additional bits do not always lead to improvement. Nature seems to teach that we *can* have too much of a good thing. Why, then, should it be, that of all the inputs to systems, a special dispensation exempts information from the law of diminishing returns? On the contrary, meaning and communication systems can be glutted and thrown into crisis (too much entropy) by an overload of all kinds of information, or even of small amounts of certain kinds to which they are "allergic." The "open market of ideas" is no more invulnerable to crisis from overload than is the stock exchange to a very good rumor that dumps a thousand "sell" orders in the same day. The truth would seem to be that liberal theory of information is valid only within a certain range of information input; this is probably true even of science, which makes heroic efforts to keep open to new facts; it is almost surely true of societies whose symbolic balance depends on a complex interworking of communication cycles and homeostatic mechanisms for both groups and individuals. Nevertheless, the idea that a certain optimal input of change and challenge is good for society most of the time is not a bad conclusion to draw.

In Chapter 10 we shall consider fad and fashion as one of the ways in which modern society searches for new meanings and styles of life, making use of an idea that comes in part from liberal theory, namely, that modern society finds its new directions and styles by a kind of natural societal selection of competing novelties and information.

PART III

Collective Search

In this last part of the book we turn again to collective search, figured by metaphors such as the flowing river. "River" refers at the same time to flow in channels and overflow—the search for new channels. By another metaphor, a social movement puts out fingers of exploration, groping for various kinds of symbolic negotiations. Yet another

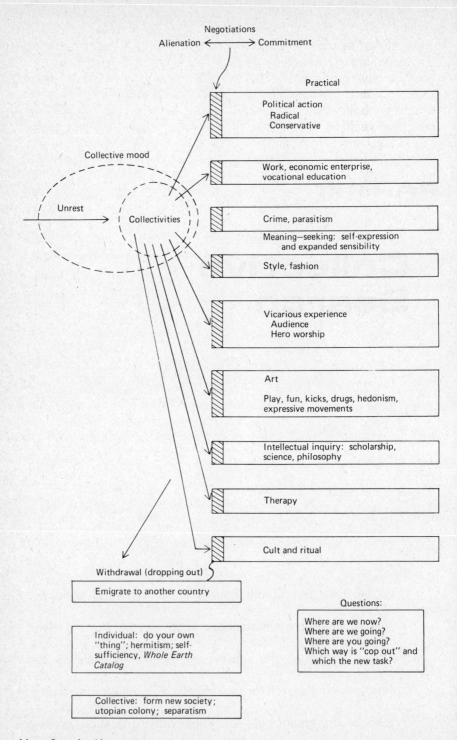

Mass Search: Alternatives—turning points.

metaphor is "sector," if you think of a battlefront. All are appropriate for describing what is going on in modern American life.

Collective groping may take various forms: expressive, stylistic, cultic, conflict, communal, political, vicarious. Each is a sector within which symbolic bargains can be made, battles won or lost, and meanings realized. When groping pays off in votes, power, protest, legislation, and so on, politicization occurs. But far more groping is going on today outside the political sector. One sees it most clearly in the early, so-called elementary, stages of movements. At this point in the search, a kind of "natural selection" is occurring among negotiations on a variety of fronts; and this is why one cannot easily say just where the river is going.

Two streams of such search are dealt with in this last part of the book. Search for style occurs through negotiations commonly called *fashion* and *symbolic leadership*. Search for meaning is seen most clearly in the early stages of a movement such as the "counterculture," which has not yet found political or other practical form. In both, one can see search for "we" in mass society, trying to form a stronger collective identity from diffuse and conflicting reference groups.

If collective search is viewed as negotiation along a "front," the preceding chart may give an idea of the main possibilities for people in unrest—negotiating through collectivities.

CHAPTER 10

Fashion and Fad
as Style Search

PUT HER ON. —These real hair put-ons are a new kind of make-out. At the very least, they're exciting, unexpected. They are definitely for the new breed of cat. Life is short—why not live it to the fullest. Who knows. MAYBE THE GUYS WITH THE BEARDS ARE RIGHT, AFTER ALL? Commodore moustaches and goatees are so real we defy anyone to tell them from the real thing—even close up. They're real hair: each strand handwoven into the finest of netting that looks like real skin pores when on the face. Colors are black-brown mixture or light brown (light brown goes with almost any hair color but jet black). Each kit comes with complete instructions and spirit gum adhesive in a handsome red and black alligator vinyl case. Inside face tray is for safe daytime storage after a nighttime of happiness. (Ad in *Playboy*, March 1969.)

Fads are usually taken as a sign of the progress of a dynamic free society. A mere list of some of the notable ones in the past fifty years should be sufficient to prove how prominent this kind of change has been in America. F. L. Allen (1931) painted the decade of the 1920s in lighter hues, largely by innovations like flagpole sitting, marathon dancing, bathing beauty contests, crossword puzzles, Mah Jong, *The Sheik*, trans-Atlantic flights, bobbed hair, and the Jazz Age. He concluded that after the crash of 1929, Americans were "just as susceptible to fads as ever." If they were buying nothing else in the gloomy summer of 1930, they still had money for miniature golf, of which 30,000 courses were operating at high profit (Allen, 1931: 392). Following this frenzied period came goldfish swallowing, bubble gum, Boop-boop-de-doop, jam sessions, bank nights, jitter-bugging, zoot suits, bebop, bobby socks, luminous socks, $64,000 questions, "A Tisket-a-Tasket," yogurt, "New Look" (Dior in 1948), Mickey Spillane books (in 1952), shaved heads (with Mohawk, Comanche, and Apache variations in 1953), hula hoops (which made their inventors $2 million in six months of 1958), fast-draw champion-ships (in 1961), the Twist epidemic (from 1961 to 1962), the hiking craze (in 1962), Beatle haircuts and long hair for men (in 1964), banjo fad, with old-fashioned mustaches and straw hats (in 1964), toplessness (Gernreich in 1964), painted knees (in 1965), the Mer-sey sound from England (in 1965), Batman (in 1966), discotheques (in 1967), psychedelic fashions (in 1967), "hot pants" and water beds (in 1971), to name a few. Four decades after Allen, the theme of fad and folly seemed to be continuing unabated (Sann, 1967). Some fads came back for repeat performances (Calypso in 1956; midget golf in 1961; "Gone With the Wind" in 1969; the "20's look" from 1964 to 1970). Bogardus (1950) surveyed over 3,000 fads adop-ted between 1914 and 1949; 54 percent were in women's dress and decoration, 16 percent in men's clothing, and 8 percent in recreation, accounting for almost four-fifths of the sample. Of these, 80 percent lasted less than a year (Bogardus, 1950:305–309). Women's dress, of course, is a flourishing area of fashion (Anspach, 1967), but to give women undue credit or blame for faddism seems a little unfair, since it seems to enter into almost every sector of life style where choices are not dictated by sheer necessity—vehicles, sports, beverages, smoking, art, politics, opinion, religion, philosophy, science, and even dogs and cats (whose fashions can be seen in pedigree regis-trations).

But some strange things were going on in fashion in the early 1970s. The most visible phenomenon was the active hostility of various parts of the public for each other's styles. Of course, bobbed hair had had a hard time in the 1920s; but in the 1970s, the greeting to style rebels was even more acrimonious: Vice-President Agnew felt called upon to comment on a "whole damn zoo" of "tomentose exhibitionists," an "effete corps of impudent snobs." There was a deep aversion of neat and clean middle-class and blue-collar members of the "silent majority" for long-haired "hippie" and "Easy Rider" types, which became more outspoken; billboards over the country showed a close-up photograph of a pimply-faced wild-haired hippie against a yellow background, with the message: "Beautify America, Get a Haircut." Leading rock-music groups published albums in questionable taste (such as a Rolling Stones' album showing a graffiti-covered wall of a toilet, or a cover view of a member of the Beatles nude, front and back side). Policemen and marines were forced to cut their hair or submit to discipline; a policeman was arrested and fired for smoking pot on the steps of the Hall of Justice, San Francisco. The general aim of fashion seemed to be not taste but impact: "Wham the outfit, hit them straight between the eyes," was a typical report. A fashion authority commented: "Gracious living no longer exists. . . . When I was a boy aesthetes and eccentrics were stared at. Now no holds are barred, nothing is ridiculous." Long hair, beards, dark glasses, Indian costumes, and so on, in public places gave a theatrical impression that was rather like that of a collection of Hollywood extras. But the dominant theme seemed to be not only theatricalism but also animosity. Blacks rejected White middle-class styles, even the name Negro. Women were putting off feminine customs for pants and karate lessons. In England, rowdies called "skinheads" bashed "hairies" (those with long hair or hippie clothing), homosexuals, and immigrants from Asia or the West Indies. There was a general tendency to confuse style with political position and ideology; hippies were recklessly accused of being radical activists and socialists. Fashion was more than a matter of taste, an almost philosophical commitment, which implied that one must endure knocks for it. "Keeping up with Jones" was no longer a race but a war.

Basic Concepts

How is one to understand all this? It will help to review the fundamental concept of *mores.* The presence of so much war in style tells the sociologist that fashion has left the range of tolerated freedom (taste) and is invading mores, nondiscussible social sentiments connected with the basic welfare of society. Mores are "always unconscious and involuntary" and "cover the great field of common life where there are no laws or police regulations." Laws and institutions formulate and implement mores, while fashions change them. But mores change much more slowly than fashions, and often resist them; "the masses are the real bearers of the mores"; they accept and imitate as they see fit in accord with these notions; fashions of the upper classes, or from foreigners, may take generations to change the mores (Sumner, 1906:46, 56). Today, fashion changes are challenging such vital assumptions much more rapidly and radically, bringing about a crisis to which defense is a homeostatic response.

In the staid old world of Dame Fashion and Beau Brummel, the normal function of fashion was to identify a person with his class or set (keeping pace with its changing norms), announce his status, and maintain the front appropriate to his position, with fads as a rather frivolous and expensive indulgence of taste on the periphery of what was allowed by fashion. In short, the main effect of fashion was to celebrate the sense of being "in" and that all was in place in the social world. Today, by fashion, people are often announcing outsideness (barbarism), defying categories, making "squares uptight," and producing a sense of topsy-turviness. This is illustrated by changes in dress fashions for the sexes: look-alike hairdos, women in pants, the identity crisis of males compounded by being offered in 1970 a midiskirt for men, which caused a fashion commentator to say that "in the circus that greets us every day on the street anything goes." Against such challenges of fashion, other institutions seemed to have a compensatory function: Western movies; the "rootin-rip-snortin-rompin-stompin-whoopin" rodeo; and John Wayne, seemingly indestructible, went on in one role after another. Thus, clashing life styles was the American predicament in the early 1970s—people were thrusting upon one another in ways never before experienced, even in the name of fashion. "Barbarians" and "freaks" turned out to be native White Americans. But when a native challenges mores, *his* deviance seems to be a betrayal of group standards and identity. The crisis in America in the 1970s was caused in good part by a feeling that fashion was threatening group identity.

Another concept needed to understand fashion, especially when there is so much conflict in it, is that fashion is a *symbolic negotiation* (Chapter 5), a process too complex to be explained by a simple model such as imitation of elites or monological input from mass media (Chapter 6); it is more a dialectical dialogical process in which new meanings and consensus are negotiated, possibly out of the bitter brew of conflict.

A third basic concept is that fad and fashion are part of the *balance sheet* of social systems. We have tried to show that all collective behavior occurs in the setting of a system in which individual tensions are paralleled by systemic strains (Chapters 5 and 6). The balance sheet of a system may shift, incited by collective behavior like contagions or expressive movements, without individuals being fully aware of a collective choice (Chapter 7). Fad and fashion have some part in the balance or imbalance of systems, the questions being: Which predominates—homeostasis? Breakdown from too much conflict? A search for new meaning and patterns, which is fundamentally negentropic* and creative? (We have seen in Chapter 9 that too fast an input leads to the strains of information overload.) The theory of natural selection will be used in an attempt to explain how fashion might be negentropic.

A fourth concept we shall need for understanding fashion is that of *meaning crisis* leading to a search for meaning (Chapter 9). According to this view, fad and fashion, while being a part of crisis, are also part of the collective search for meaning; indeed, they have a vanguard role in creating new life styles and meanings.

If these things are true, we deal with a very important collective process—not a trivial matter of whether madame's dress is longer or shorter, but life-style building as a form of nonverbal philosophy: philosophy being how a person thinks about life, and style in the sense of how he lives it. But the information inflow and abundance of an open society mean an unparalleled profusion of styles—how to eat, how to raise children, what to think. Modern man's position is like a revolving door through which fads go in and out. We have yet to find, from systemic study, whether constant life-style revision is privilege or price.

Before going further, let us make some distinctions. As anyone can see who visits an anthropological museum, cultures have distinctive styles that can be identified immediately; no one, for example, would have trouble telling Chinese from Navajo. All cultures have *style* (Kroeber, 1957), but only changing ones have fashion. Fashion is a flow of change in life styles, which gets going in societies that are relatively open to acculturation and invention (a static traditional society has zero fashion—a style so standardized that change could be measured only in centuries; closed totalitarian systems like the Peoples' Republic of China and Soviet Russia have minimal fashion because of restricted choice and class competition). Modernizing societies are entering the fashion race, and modernistic ones are so immersed in it that "keeping up" is a compulsion—a tendency to overvalue the new. Fashion does not occur equally in all areas of culture, but especially in those where taste rather than utility governs and where personal display of status symbols is possible; for example, fashion is more likely to be exhibited in an automobile body than in its battery.

---

* Tending to decrease disorder or "shuffledness" in a system.

Within the range of personal display of styles as status symbols, some distinctions should be made:

1. When style is devoted to maintaining a social position to which one has a reasonably valid claim, it may be called *front*. The majority of fashionable people try to maintain the front, that is, stay in the vogue, of their social set rather than get too far ahead or behind.
2. *High fashion* goes to extremes that express the bravura of an actual or would-be leader who feels sure enough of his position and fashion sense to move far in front with something daring; it is individualized and short-lived, the majority do not reach it.
3. *Fad* is like high fashion in being short-lived, extreme, and risky; but it is more frivolous and does not represent sure fashion sense—rather, it is an adventure in which one is being a little risqué or silly, even though "everybody is doing it." It is a capricious eddy of style change rather than the main wave. If fashion calls for a stuffed bird on a hat, the faddist will try a live one. The point is that fad is an experiment in identity (which may engage a whole peer group), going farther than maintaining position or front.
4. Style becomes *pose* when it is used for a riskier adventure in identity— a claim that is somewhat theatrical or illegitimate, far afield from what a person is entitled to by upbringing and competence (Klapp, 1969:75).
5. Another useful distinction is between *costume*—a "misrepresentation" that allows one to get away from oneself, as in pose and *uniform*, which firmly fixes and announces an appropriate identity (Stone, 1962:113).
6. Finally, *style rebellion* is a fashion whose aim is not just display of personal taste but, at least in part, an effort to shock conservatives and "put down" the established style (Klapp, 1969:84–95).

What Moves Fashion?

Motives

What starts fashion and keeps it going? Why do people stay in the "race" or battle, whichever it may be? Unless we postulate simply that humans are restless animals, we have to account for fashion by individual or systemic motives that make humans engage in that kind of activity. Such motives come into play more and more as societies move through the sequence of modernization: traditional, transitional, modern (Chapter 8).

The easiest supposition to make—and to disprove—is that fashion is useful; in other words, like tractors, fashions are welcomed by developing countries because they improve people's lives in some fairly obvious way. It is true that some useful inventions have had a faddish start, being adopted by a sudden contagious enthusiasm rather than clear public demonstration of their utility;

as examples we have television, hi-fi, zippers, even the horseless carriage. But it takes only a moment to place against these the countless fad and fashion items that have not only no clear utility but also extremes of frivolity and vanity—five-foot feathers on hats, green wigs, huge tailfins on automobiles, goldfish swallowing. How could one make a case for wasp waists, stiletto heels, meshed versus sheer nylon stockings, burning to a crisp in sunbathing? The epitome of the question is the gun game called "Russian roulette," in which a single cartridge is placed in the cylinder of a pistol, the cylinder is spun, the muzzle is held against the temple of a person, and the trigger is pulled. This deadly game of chance was responsible for a number of deaths in 1951.

Fads, by their very coming and going seem to indicate that most new fashions are not more useful than those they displace. Many writers have commented on the enormous expensiveness, waste, and nonutility of fashion (Veblen, 1899; Chase, 1925; Packard, 1960).

That fashion is more beautiful than what it displaces is hardly a valid argument; take for example the "Dior look" versus the shapeless short dress of the 1920s or the maxi skirt of the 1970s. Many styles seem strange and ugly when they come in, and equally grotesque after they have gone out. Whatever the public is seeking in fashion is probably neither utility nor beauty, though it may be rationalized as such.

In any case, a central question of fashion is about *image.* It is well known, for example, that what a person selects when he buys an automobile is not horsepower, economy, or such utilitarian qualities, but how it will increase his prestige as a social type or member of a class. A survey of university students (Klapp, 1965) showed different images associated with the drivers of four makes of automobiles:

Mustang: trying to show off, make an impression, status seeker; sporty, playboy, fun loving, youthful; fashionable, classy, up and coming, jet set, good taste; practical, middle-income status.

Thunderbird: middle-aged; playboy, sporty; financially successful, can afford the "finer" things; has arrived, suave, sophisticated, likes the best, fashionable, good taste, has class; trying to create an impression, flashy, showy, status seeker, status conscious.

Lincoln: wealthy enough to gratify his desires, successful professional or businessman; middle-aged to older person with conservative tastes; wants prestige car to show superior status, somewhat of a snob; likes luxury and comfort, expensive tastes, sophisticated, well educated, buys car for quality of performance.

Foreign sports car: youngish; sporty type; independent, intellectual, sophisticated, cosmopolitan, nonconformist, nonconservative; trying to impress the public; irresponsible, reckless, speed fiend.

Such images show something of what a person seeks in fashionable goods—clothing, housing, home furnishings, neighborhood, foods and beverages, sports equipment, and other elements of life style. The key to choice seems to be (beyond whatever utilities are involved): What will it do to one's look (social identity) and how will it affect one's status in relation to other people?

Most people are aware of the pressure of being in a *race*, however they may feel about winning. A survey of university women showed that most were willing to comply with fashion and would feel uneasy or uncomfortable if they did not. They felt little resentment of the pressure and would dislike to have it disappear as a regulating device (Cobliner, 1950). A survey of university men and women in 1965 showed that roughly 18 percent classed themselves as highly fashion-conscious, 55 percent as moderately, and 26 percent as little or not at all; women were more fashion-conscious than men; three-quarters said they tried to stay in the middle of fashion, neither behind nor too far out in front; three-quarters also said they tried to achieve "looks" by fashion (Klapp, 1969:74). An earlier survey of college women showed that the vast majority were followers rather than starters or nonfollowers of fads: 27 starters (bizarre, distingué, egregious, etc. started 52 fads; 232 conformers merely followed without originating any fads; 20 "obsolescents" wore outmoded clothing and resisted fashion (Janney, 1941).

Such figures show that most people are more or less involved in fashion without being either leaders or resisters; they go along in the race and would feel uncomfortable if they could not keep up; nor would they feel comfortable to stand too far out. A feedback and pressure to one's image reward those who lead and stay "in" and penalize those who fall too far behind.

Sumner (1906:194) held that fashion pressure was like that of mores, that there was no arguing with fashion, and that dissenters suffered punishment: "The authority of fashion is imperative as to everything which it touches; the sanctions are ridicule and powerlessness." Nothing one can say against a fashion stops it or changes it much. Indeed, many women's fashions have been established over the protest and resistance of the majority (K. and G. Lang, 1961: 468–469).

Fashion "Dictatorship?"

So, it is not surprising that the idea has grown up that there is a kind of dictatorship working somewhere in the fashion industry. Manufacturers may be suspected of conspiring to cause heavy turnover by making shoddy goods, exploiting consumer ignorance, and exerting monopolistic control over the market (Gregory, 1947). "If the styles weren't completely changed every year, there would be no reason for buying new things before the old ones are worn out," said Aldous Huxley (1964:138). The success of popular songs, plays, books, and products is commonly attributed to "plugging." Indeed, some leaders seem to have extraordinary power as "arbiters" of fashion or "taste-makers" (Lynes, 1954); typical of such leaders is perhaps Christian Dior, who, said *Time*, "at one stroke outmoded every dress in every closet in America. The public relations counsel E. L. Bernays (1965:389–395) claimed that he had created a "green fashion" to support Lucky Strike advertising.

Nevertheless, whenever the "dictatorship" of fashion is looked at closely, its power is found to be much less than supposed. Wiebe (1940), for example, studied the plugging of popular songs and found it had no effect on the liking, though it did help somewhat to keep a song from being forgotten. Considering the brevity of the season for fashions, best sellers, hit recordings, entertainment stars, and the phenomenal failure rate among aspirants who don't make it, it has been argued that there is very little ability of commercial oligarchies or anyone else to dictate fashion or even predict it. Surely, if there were such power, producers would use it to get a longer profit run on items they had gone to the expense of building up. For example, of the most promising actors groomed and built up by film studios, only a few became stars, and no one knew in advance who the stars would be (Klapp, 1964a:27–37). It is commonly known in the fashion world that of many designs, only a few succeed; and that "disasters" are possible with even the best-planned promotions, such as the Edsel of the Ford Motor Company; or, in 1970, the disaster of the "maxi" dress, even with the backing of the great Dior:

> In France the maxi dress is a disaster. The women simply won't buy it. Rack upon rack of maxi dresses have been returned to French ready-to-wear manufacturers, many of whom are facing ruin. Despite the increased backing of the maxi by the haute couture houses of Givenchy, St. Laurent, Dior, and Cardin, young French women regard long skirts as an attempt by some homosexual dress designers to hide sexy attributes of the female anatomy from male admirers. The truth is that large textile interests backed some of the haute couture houses to produce the maxi in the hope that longer skirts would provide them with higher profits. That hope has now been dashed. (Shearer, 1970:4.)

A shrewd fashion buyer said flatly, "We have no dictators of fashion." A manufacturer must watch his customers and ask women what their tastes are before he invests; the leaders are not the ten best-dressed women or the social arbiters of yesterday:

> The leaders are anonymous and their voices do not carry the authority of a Mrs. Belmont or a Mrs. Vanderbilt. Today these women of

taste who are the leaders of fashion are in the colleges, in offices, in homes, among all classes. . . . They obey no dictates of retailer or designer. They take ideas from both; they supply them with many. The merchant who is close to his business must watch for these signs of fashion experimentation by his customers. (Marcus, 1948:43–47.)

An other-directed society, unsure of its standards, leans on "taste-makers," but leaders *seem* to be dictators only as long as fashion is behind them. Well-known social psychological research shows that the leader does not make, but conforms to, group norms (Sherif, 1936; Merei, 1949). He is, rather, in the position of the crowd leader who, an apocryphal story tells, when he heard a tumult, rushed outside, saying: "The crowd is in the street; I must find out where it is going, for I am their leader." We have only to consider the downturn of popular heroes such as Lord Nelson or Ingrid Bergman (Klapp, 1964a:121–147) to see how fragile is the power of the leader, once he departs from the trend of popular norms. Suppose that the glamorous Jackie Kennedy-Onassis shaved her head; how many women, for all their admiration, would follow her? There *is* power in the fashion process, but it does not reside in particular leaders except when they are working with it.

Blumer (1969) positively denied that elites lead or start fashion, as Simmel held. Rather, they are as anxious as anyone else to find the center (wherever it is), to keep up with change in a "*collective*," not a class, process. Elites go out of date, and fail to start fashions even when they try. Fashion is an innovative collective process that develops "a pliable and re-forming body of taste to meet a shifting and developing world."

In this process members of a mass make a vast number of decisions about life style with the help of reference groups in response to a marketing system that pushes goods at them in variety and abundance. The trend of these decisions constitutes a "race," not only for followers but also for producers and sellers, who must exert themselves to keep up.* No one is in charge, and norms vary with one's place in the race, the choices of which are as tactical as plays in a poker game. The coercion of fashion is not so much *what* one must do, or *who* says one must do it, as it is the costs of withdrawing from the game without losing status. Thus, fashion today exerts a relentless but *not a uniform* pressure. The latitude is in choice among—not avoiding—fashions. For example, in 1970 a matron could contemplate with propriety for street wear: mini, midi, or maxi skirts; or trousers, narrow or bell-bottomed; or, for the more venturesome, psychedelia, pseudotribal and peasant designs, or heavy hippie "swaddling" robes. Hardly regimentation, whatever else

---

* A closer look at the organizational side of fashion selection during production and promotion has been furnished by Hirsch, 1972.

one called it. The feelings of most fashion participants were mixed, between being forced into a race to buy what they didn't need, and the pleasures of expressing themselves by a widening variety of choices.

Anonymous Interpersonal Communication

If neither economic forces nor leaders dictate the fashion process, then what are its followers, victims or willing slaves? We cannot ignore *suggestion and imitation* as sources of the contagious character of fashion, its rapid and seemingly irrational adoption. Nor does this commit us to emphasize the power of mass media. The most elusive kind of communication in our mass society is that which does not come from established channels but flows, largely unwittingly, among persons who do not know one another. It is the hardest source to trace, study, even be aware of. It is hardest to control because, unlike media communication, its sources and channels are unknown. One kind of such communication consists of emotional contagions, already dealt with in Chapters 3, 4, and 6. Another kind consists of stories, songs, sayings, catchwords, slogans—verbal messages of a repeatable sort coming from everywhere and nowhere, treated in Chapter 8.

A subtle kind of communication, which may be called vicarious, consists of taking roles of (identification with) strangers. This goes on all the time in daily life, but is conspicuous in fashion, audience response to dramatic heroes and victims, and orientation of fans to popular heroes. In vicarious learning, even though one does not *act out* patterns, nevertheless he absorbs something in terms of attitudes and latent roles. (Faris identified it as "slow unwitting" imitation; 1937:75.) It is true for all the main forms of anonymous interpersonal communication (contagion, rumor, vicarious learning, and fashion imitation) that we usually do not know where they come from, who influenced the person who influenced us, or by what "channel" they came. It would be a mistake to suppose that mass media are wholly, even chiefly, responsible for the spread of such influences, though obviously they have a part. In the case of fashion, we have noted that the media are constantly searching for "trends" in mass tastes, such as what music to record, for example, what people are humming and listening to. Second, though one may have been exposed to something via the media, there is still the impact of uncounted numbers of people on the street and their feedback in daily life, which gives rise to the feeling that that particular car body or dress style is "for me," "chic," "in." It is characteristic of our technological society to overstress the power of mass media (in spite of the warnings of Schramm, 1960; Klapper, 1960).

We also underplay the interaction that goes on within and outside established networks.

To all such forms of anonymous interpersonal communication, epidemic (S-shaped) diffusion curves are appropriate, and the higher the tension, the more appropriate they are because at such points they spill out of the channels that might be controlled by gatekeepers (Chapter 6).

In sum, anonymous interpersonal communication leading to unwitting formation and change of social norms is an important, though as yet uncharted, part of the fashion process. But sociology has more to say, especially on how the status system generates fashion.

Status Theory

Three important theories developed by sociologists help explain how a status system helps generate the fashion process. One is that *status aspirations, obligations, and anxieties* favor fashion. In a mobile, striving society, many people make claims to status that are fragile, perishable, even illusory. The middle classes are subject to "status panic" (C. W. Mills, 1951); likewise, blue-collar workers— any upwardly or downwardly mobile group—can get "uptight" about competitors who threaten their status (Hofstadter, 1955:131–173; Bettelheim and Janowitz, 1950). Mills described how status panic is connected with the "illusionary" character of status symbols in modern society: White-collar workers in bureaucratic hierarchies have minutely graded ranks and fragmented skills. The difference, for example, between supervisor-2 and supervisor-1 may be hardly visible, and the content of the work not much to talk about. So, prestige based on rank or skill is precarious. Workers seize, therefore, on small distinctions for status claims. In doing so, they not only compete more intensely with their fellows but are also alienated from solidarity with them and the work because they so eagerly look forward to the *next* rank they will hold. However, the next rank will not really give them much better basis for status claims. So, success is "illusionary":

> Status ascent within the hierarchy is a kind of illusionary success, for it does not necessarily increase income or the chance to learn superior skills. . . . If the status struggle within the job hierarchy is lost, the status struggle outside the job area shifts its ground: one hides his exact job . . . among anonymous metropolitan throngs, one can make claims about one's job, as well as about other bases of prestige. . . . Anonymous and the just-known strangers, who cannot so readily "place" one, may cash in one's claims . . . the first, often the only, impression . . . may permit a brief success in status claiming, sometimes as a sort of mutual deal. . . . The leisure of many middle

class people is taken up by attempts to gratify their status claims. . . .
It takes money to do something nice in one's off time. . . . But in a
mass society without a stable system of status, with quick, cheap
imitations, dress is often no talisman. . . . People in a lower class
and status level . . . act like persons on higher levels and temporarily
. . . get away with it. . . . Urban masses look forward to vacations not
"just for the change" . . . for on vacation, one can *buy* the feeling, even
if only for a short time, of higher status. The expensive resort . . . the
cruise first class—for a week . . . the staffs as well as clientele play-
act the whole set-up as if mutually consenting to be part of the successful illusion. . . . A holiday image of self, which contrasts sharply
with the self image of everyday reality . . . permitting him to cling to
a false consciousness of his status position. . . . Fashion has become
a rational attempt to exploit the status market for a greater turnover
of goods. (C. W. Mills, 1951:164, 254–258.)

Anxiety, we know, makes people more suggestible: Insecure
people trying to win the approval of superiors, climbers trying to
change life styles, other-directed people (Riesman, Glazer, and
Denney, 1950) leaning on taste-makers and peers because they are
not sure of themselves. So, in status anxiety we have one explanation for why people should be searching in the fashion market.

Behind this is the mass as a *milieu* of status anxiety, rootlessness, anonymity, and monological communication (as explained in
Chapter 7) which, depriving the individual of balanced feedback of
the oral system, contributes to anxiety about who one is.

Thus, the hypothesis is, Other things being equal: the more
anxiety in a system, the more fashion changes.

A second sociological theory helping us to understand fashion
is that *opinion leaders* have more influence on their peers than do
people at large or the media. *They* select—from the media, markets,
and public at large—styles and ideas toward which they influence
their peers by talk and personal exchange; hence, they play a role
as intermediary leaders or gatekeepers. Such opinion leaders are
not easy to identify because they are by no means necessarily
formal leaders or highly visible celebrities; rather, they are ordinary people with higher than average exposure to media, more vigorous personal impact on associates (because extroverted, talkative, dominant, well informed, and so on; and because they get
about more and see people more often), and with more than average prestige and standing in local groups (Katz and Lazarsfeld,
1955; Rogers, 1962; Katz, Levin, and Hamilton, 1963). So, the opinion
leader is both a filter or threshold for a fashion to pass in reaching
the majority, and a lever to pass it on by embodying it and, so to
speak, twisting the arm of his followers.

A third contribution of status theory is the powerful concept of *class differentiation* by fashion. The wish of status groups to separate themselves from the emulation of other groups keeps the fashion race moving. This explains why elites are so eager to innovate and why a fashion, once started, marches to a quick death. Fashions cannot spread widely as long as styles are imitated only within an elite set (restricted by custom or even by legislation prescribing what a person may wear). But when the common man feels free to imitate elites, this increases status anxiety and competition in both imitation and innovation. It sets waves of fashion spreading through the entire society, which become weaker and die about the time that everybody "gets into the act"—that is, joining the bandwagon is the end of the fashion game, for it can no longer pay off by distinctive status, which was the reason for innovating and imitating in the first place. The inherent limitation of fad and fashion (unlike general culture) is that they cannot be universalized, cannot pay off to everybody, because differentiation is their prime function. Thus, only an open class society (neither traditional, caste, totalitarian, nor equalitarian) can generate such movement, since a kind of conflict between aristocratic innovation and equalitarian imitation is required. This idea, sometimes called the "percolation" theory, comes from Tarde (1903), Veblen (1899), Sapir (1931), but mainly from Simmel (1957), who summarized it as follows:

> The fashions of the upper stratum of society are never identical with those of the lower; in fact, they are abandoned by the former as soon as the latter prepares to appropriate them. . . . Just as soon as the lower classes begin to copy their style, thereby crossing the line of demarcation the upper classes have drawn and destroying the uniformity of their coherence, the upper classes turn away from this style and adopt a new one, which in its turn differentiates them from the masses; and thus the game goes merrily on. . . . The very character of fashion demands that it should be exercised at one time only by a portion of the given group, the great majority being merely on the road to adopting it. As soon as an example has been universally adopted . . . we no longer speak of fashion. As fashion spreads, it gradually goes to its doom. (Simmel, 1957:543–547.)

It would be hard to imagine such a process operating in the Massachusetts Bay Colony, where the finery even of elites was rather severely restricted. It seems to apply to such things as the switch of wealthy women's taste in furs to chinchilla and sable when mink became easier to get, or the movement of the middle classes from urban areas to "nicer" neighborhoods, or a society woman giving an "exclusive" dress to her maid after she had seen a copy on a store clerk. The model of fashion marching down the terraces of social structure fits best into a simple, open class hierarchy where one elite sets the style that others follow if they can. An example is England in the 1920s, with the aristocracy faithfully watching the Prince of Wales and the middle classes watching both for cues as to what to do, wear, and say.

However, it seems plain that such a model fits the American scene rather poorly today, and England, too, for that matter. The main reason is that though differentiation still functions, there is no single hierarchy, no authoritative center from which styles come; all kinds of groups seem to be differentiating themselves from each other for various reasons, which cannot be fitted into a single scheme of values. Heterogeneity and extreme individuation seem to be the keynote of modern fashion; as one writer put it, "Wherever you go these days, there's usually an 'in' look" which it is "maddening" not to be able to promptly apprehend. And beside the "in" looks, there are various "out" looks, which speak of fragmentation between generations, ethnic groups, "hard hats" versus hippies, and "publiciety" versus the "old guard" (Amory, 1960). Amory held that the taste standards of the old "high society" were giving way to those of racetrack crowds, nightclub singers, and other flashy types among the *nouveaux riches*. But this is only part of the range of tastes forming fashion today; it seems to be virtually true that no class is incapable of being a fashion leader, that styles can come from "anywhere" and be doing many more things symbolically than announcing the superiority of one class to another (Klapp, 1969:73, 115). Style might be used quite as much to set oneself *off* from, as well as "in," the Establishment. A Black fashion writer noted—

> Recently I observed some young people shopping in a local second-hand clothing store. As is chic today, they were junkin' to dress themselves as unlike "The Establishment" as possible. I was amused and reminded of the days when a girlfriend and I junked, as a means of being like "The Establishment." Being the only black and chicano (they didn't use those titles then) in a white upper-middle-class school, we needed nothing more to make us "unlike" our classmates. . . . We wore second-hand clothing because we didn't have the money to buy new, expensive clothing and we wanted to go to school nicely dressed. . . . Well, times have changed, and it is Middle America's young who haunt the junk store scene now. They junk as an "out"—we junked as an "in." (Haggerty, 1970.)

Indeed, the profusion of styles by groups trying to set themselves apart, combined with the ease of imitating any style, threatened to blur social categories rather than distinguish them—not only the classes but other status roles that, functionally different, had a greater need for explicit role signs (Banton, 1965:70–71).

Banality as a Source of Fashion

Is there not something else in the fashion process (perhaps more important as the class function declines) working to speed the pace of faddism? While the jet set cannot hope to have fashions much more colorful than those of thousands following them with knapsacks on jumbo jets, is there not some other reason than class leadership which makes their search for life style more urgent than ever today?

A clue to this process lies in the fact that so much radical style creation seems to be a reaction to boredom, a feeling found in any class but especially acute among the young.

> Why wear the dreary clothes of the decade, ties and clean white shirts and suits and carefully polished shoes? All so careful and uninteresting. Why not wear a Roman toga on Monday, a nineteenth century English Army officer's uniform on Tuesday, a Japanese kimono on Wednesday, dress like an American Indian on Thursday, an Indian Indian on Friday, Marlon Brando on Saturday, and anything you please on Sunday? Why not? What is stopping us? Only the fear that we might be different, that our decade might think us strange. (Westbrook, 1969.)

> Those American Indian outfits are being traded in for the current craze of the moment in men's wear for the young: The Depression Look. . . . The other world is considered plastic. . . . Poverty is a big thing with the young and in their fashion choices. As one says, "I don't want to look like the good little gentleman who follows everyone. . . . We aren't escaping reality. We see it. But we are rejecting the theory that life has to be dull. These are life clothes and anything is possible." (Cartnal, 1970.)

An art critic (W. Wilson, 1970) commented on faddish trends in recent shows (smashed rusty metal, junk assemblages, streamlined constructions, leathery fetishes, Pop works, fluorescents, walk-ins): "There is a . . . kind of human tiredness that needs art, the tiredness that results from sameness, routine, the feeling that life is drearily solved." A similar theme is found in this despairing note sounded by a teacher of English literature:

> Teachers of literature are fighting a losing battle against the indifference of their students. . . . Anything not hot from the press is, as they say, irrelevant. . . . Shakespeare, Coleridge, even Eliot . . . are all so many bores to be dragged through in a kind of impatient despair for the sake of grades and examinations. In comparison, real literature is what comes at them through a PA system and a haze of pot smoke, to the sound of finger bells and guitars. (Alvarez, 1970:27.)

The "Yippie" leader Abbie Hoffman tried to explain what he was rebelling against and came up with boredom, not political repression:

> Most of the trial (of the "Chicago Eight") was kind of boring. It's not all that Perry Mason stuff. It's pretty boring, and we recognized that. We recognized that America is boring—that all its institutions are boring. Therefore, you work to build a kind of drama in which the defendants represent the forces of life, and the people who are putting you on trial represent the forces of death. That's why we had a Festival of Life in the park when we came to Chicago, and we called theirs the Convention of Death. That's why "cultural revolution" means the development of new myths, new symbols, a new language, a new style of living that represents life. . . . It's fun. We don't work, we struggle; and we yearn for the society where work and play are the same. Where cutting sugar cane and dancing in the streets are the same thing. The society where you live your dreams. We live our dreams right now. And that makes trouble for the parent culture because they have no dreams. (A. Hoffman, 1970.)

Here we see that a kind of protest, which most regard as political, is part of a style rebellion—as in art, literature, and clothing—reacting to boredom. The romantic rebel, however, talks about not only creating a style but a "dream"; therefore he gets into utopianism and much more trouble than if he simply wore a midi skirt and toe rings.

Style has always been concerned with making oneself; the American woman, said Wax (1957), "tends to view her body as a craftsman or artist views his raw material." But in the early 1970s this had become much more explicit as a new romantic right to make oneself as one pleases, far beyond what the "self-made man" (epitomized by Horatio Alger) would have dared (Klapp, 1969). An article in *Life* (1970) featured a picture of a scraggly-haired male in dark glasses, bare above the waist except for a black vest, holding a pipelike instrument and vaguely resembling a faun:

> The important thing is to express yourself. Depending on your talents you can do it with a 25-key soprano Melodica or a long cool stare. You choose. The New York look is a daily celebration of the self.

To provide materials for making new styles, artifactories were established under ancient Tibetan and other exotic symbols, where people could work in leather, jewelry, candles, pottery, silk screening, metal, wood and so on; whether in home design, jewelry, or dyeing one's own shirts and skirts, fashion was becoming more a matter of "do it yourself."

The bursting-out in American men's fashions began in 1965 when, stimulated by Beatlemania, the "big sprout-out of mop-tops" replaced crew cuts; by 1966, as "mod" dandyism entered the United States from England, *Life* announced: "The guys go all-out to get gawked at." By 1968, the pace of faddism had become so frantic that it seemed to enter the realm of fantasy theater:

Fashion this fall seems to be the work of the Madwoman of Chaillot. Plus elements of a rummage sale, a fancy-dress party, and that haphazard art form based on "found objects." (*Time*, Oct. 25, 1968.)

But, for those with verve, the challenge of "instant individualism" had never been more exciting, said a fashion designer; after all, "no two people can really come out with the same combination, even if they use the same six or seven components."

The connection of boredom with increasing pace and stridency of the fashion race seems plain enough: New styles are one way to make life more interesting—a toe ring or Indian costume, "bending one's mind" with psychedelic drugs, even a desperate fad like Russian roulette. Behind such symptoms, social scientists, philosophers, and artists were making a background plain: Modern affluent society was generating boredom at an appalling rate. The fault seemed to be not in abundance *per se* but a kind of sameness, which, when encountered in a work of art, is called *banality*. The essence of banality is superficiality, repetitiveness, lack of surprise. One can encounter banality when a politician speaks, reading a newspaper, at the desk of a bureaucrat, in a welfare office, in a television show, adding a grocery bill. Many good and practical things are banal for the simple reason that they are so useful they have been repeated again and again. Man is the only animal who can be bored in the midst of abundance because he demands meaning, fillip to imagination, and connection with his deeper side, in addition to sensory satiation.

It is not hard to see that a mechanized society is prone to banality because of its very success at reproducing many standard units of things. Critics are constantly deploring the sameness of television shows and other shoddy, imitative products of mass culture. Even play comes in standardized packages. Huizinga (1955:192–193, 199) said that the spirit of play was threatened with extinction by the very success of technical organization and scientific thoroughness in the nineteenth century, and that the banality of these forces denatured and dulled men's fashions. If this is correct, then the 1970s have shown that this is not the last word that men will have to say in the matter. The very massiveness of the banality of standardized experience, monological input, "pizza-burger" culture, the limited existence of "one-dimensional man" (Marcuse, 1964) seems to have produced a rebellion of color and variety of style against the "plastic" values.

The human, being an imaginative animal, is capable of several stylistic reactions to banality. One is to seek novelty, frivolity, sheer fun. A second is to become creative. A third is to use something that is banal, cheap, gimmicky in a bravura way for a comic or extravagant effect—the tactic of "camp" fashion and "pop" art in the 1960s. Another reaction is to achieve dramatically a contrary, rebel look that is shocking and smashes the old image—stylistic iconoclasm.

Thus, we see some kinds of style as a response to banality in a system, which for various reasons is failing to give its members enough meaning. Some of the sources of meaning gap have been explored in Chapters 8 and 9. Boredom, as a type of dissatisfaction, breeds *extremes* in searches and swings of fad. An unhappy society is constantly breeding new social types in *opposition* to those that have failed for some; for example, the hard work, materialism, and residual Puritanism of a Babbitt gives way to hippie hedonistic poverty, or flamboyant style and sensation seeking of rock musicians. But it should be recognized that fashion, in even its most frivolous and desperate searches for novelty, is not mere sensationalism but a *search for meaning.* Style—like rumor—supplies a pattern, a meaning. Fashion has a mystique, as we may call the more intangible elements of meaning; it is not only a different color, shape, or sound, but also an image of the life of, say, the "beautiful people." Likewise, when places like San Francisco become fashionable, the reason should not be sought in their climate and skylines but in their mystiques (F. Davis, 1970). Thus, fashion, starting as a reaction against banality, is more than novelty; it is part of a collective meaning search, in the direction of style and mystique, rather than politics.

Style Search as Dialectical Transaction

From what has been said, it is evident that fashion cannot be explained by a simple imitation, contagion, or diffusion model. In our complex society, fashions do not spread uniformly like ripples in a pool, or march rhythmically down the steps of a clear status hierarchy. Since the discovery of opinion leadership, sociologists have believed that fashion is a complex interactive process at each of several stages (Meyersohn and Katz, 1957). R. H. Turner (1964: 123) said that collective behavior should not be viewed as a simple process, whether of contagion or stages, but as "the resolution of competing and often contradictory processes which are in continuous operation," from which comes "a highly variable set of outcomes." One reason for this is that no part of the formation and interpretation of symbols—symbolic interaction—is mechanical (Blumer, 1969a). This means that the difficulty of predicting fashion is rather like that of weather: Many observations in different places are required to put a heterogeneous picture together. In another perspective, predicting fashion is like trying to predict a very large and unskillfully handicapped horse race starting from different places. Jet-setters, "Mr. Jones," "hard hats," the hip young, "Easy Riders," surfers, and Southern rednecks—how do they relate to one another? One saw an uneasy relationship, *including* imitation, competition, defiance, dialectical symbol formation, in the 1970s. How would it come out? That was the question.

To say that fashion is a dialectical transaction means, first, that parties shift their relationships to one another during a transaction and do not know at the beginning how they will eventually come out. In a simple dialogue it can be diagramed as a shift of A's position from A_1 to A_2 to A_3 while B goes from B_1 to B_2 to B_3. With several parties in the interaction, of course, the shifts are more complicated. There are two main reasons for this shifting of positions. One is that all meaningful social behavior involves pragmatic construction; that is, a person takes a view of a situation, which he tests and changes in action (Dewey, 1922; G. H. Mead, 1934). Any definition of a situation, any opinion offered to others, is such a pragmatic construction. The second reason is that, apart from changing their own constructions, parties change positions tactically in response to each other by *negotiation* in which tact, diplomacy, bluff—all the elements of gamesmanship—are relevant, the outcome of which is not determined by the view of either side—even in the extreme case of physical mastery. Everyone knows the slave has his view and strategies too. A. K. Cohen's (1955) famous description of "sticking one's neck out" is an illustration of collective negotiation of deviant subcultures. People with status problems "shop around" for others who are "congenial":

> . . . The innovation occurs by increments so small, tentative and ambiguous as to permit the actor to retreat, if the signs be unfavorable, without having become identified with an unpopular position. . . . If the probing gesture is motivated by tensions common to other participants it is likely to initiate a process of *mutual* exploration and *joint* elaboration of a new solution. . . . By a casual, semi-serious, non-committal or tangential remark I may stick my neck out just a little way, but I will quickly withdraw it unless you, by some sign of affirmation, stick *yours* out. I will permit myself to become progressively committed but only as others, by some visible sign, become likewise committed. . . . Each actor may contribute something indirectly by encouraging others to advance . . . the product cannot be ascribed to any one of the participants; it is a real "emergent" on a group level. (A. K. Cohen, 1955:chap. 3.)

This might be applied to anyone trying out a new costume with his peer group. It is applicable even to the general public, though the responses are more diffuse and somewhat different; for example, a stare might indicate that one is attracting favorable attention or making a fool of oneself. In any case, success of the negotiation becomes a solution to others' style problems, while conferring leadership upon the innovator. He knows he is a leader because positive feedback such as applause, envious stares, favorable gossip tells him so and because of others' adoption and diffusion of the fashion. Also, a new fashion may "invite the hostility of outsiders," thus giving *them* the opportunity to get into the act of forming the new culture.

Celebrities as Symbolic Leaders

Entering a restaurant, John Wayne pointed to a man with an eye patch and laughed, "That man is imitating me." Fashions seem often to explode into popular adoption from a hit show or other dramatic or literary event—"Woodstock," Arlo Guthrie's song "Alice's Restaurant," Peter Fonda as "Easy Rider," "Hello, Dolly," "West Side Story" songs and mannerisms, Beatlemania (including 20,000 wigs a week sold in New York City); James Bond, Ian Fleming's hero, who spread the style of 007, the secret operative playboy, who could do anything on or off duty; back to Rudolph Valentino, whose smoldering love techniques, vaselined hair, long sideburns, and tango dancing filled the country with "lounge lizards." Some celebrities speak for so many they seem to sum up an entire epoch. A literary critic (Parker, 1970) said: "In a way, Zelda and Scott Fitzgerald invented Flaming Youth and the Jazz Age. . . . Did art imitate life or life art?"

But the array of celebrities does not produce uniformity of popular style but increases the alternatives. By competing styles, they intensify the dialectic. For example, Norman Mailer versus William Buckley, each with his own enthusiastic following—in this case a wild, exhibitionistic rebel, an *enfant terrible* versus a smooth, elegantly wisecracking conservative. Or take the interesting contrast between Peter Fonda on his sweptback, Stars-and-Stripes decorated motorcycle and John Wayne on his horse as Duke, hero of the silent majority.

Such contrasts show that a hero does not *cause* fashions in the way a stone cast into a pool produces ripples; he merely finds styles for which he must negotiate with rivals and support by public roles with audiences through feedback until some people start to "tune in" on his vibrations. A public person is in a strategic position to get his style noticed *if* he has something people are interested in. But he does not know what people are interested in until he negotiates; if he tries to introduce something totally foreign to what his followers want, he will find out quickly how strong is the pressure on him to play desired roles. Nor is it followers only who expect him to stick to his style. Opponents do, too. The public demands wildly eccentric manners of some and smooth good taste of others; of some, a "great lover," and of others, the moral austerity of a saint. Each has his part to play for his own time and public (Klapp, 1964a). Some celebrities (for example, Frank Sinatra, the Beatles) go through an *evolution* of styles, none of which could be easily predicted, each of which had to be negotiated. Thus, we see that though celebrities seem to set fashions, to diffuse them, they are better described as signalers, catalysts, not makers of style. They are only the most visible and agitated part of the fashion process; one might say the "funnel of the tornado."

The key for someone wishing to be a leader of style, aside from sensing in general what response people will make, is to try to introduce something that people at the moment need for their *identities*, to feel good about themselves. Esthetics and utility are not primary considerations. For example, when the Beatles made their sensational hit in 1964, it was not because they had made a great contribution to music (dozens of Liverpool groups had been playing that way for years), but because a *look* and *personal style* was inspired by their manager, Brian Epstein. A certain flippant humor—along with long hair, Edwardian dress, and the music—was what adolescents at the time appreciated most. In other words, it was not primarily a musical phenomenon. Epstein (1964) himself noted, "the Beatles don't have to sing a note to arouse mass interest," the "look" does it. Later they developed remarkably as musicians. But this did not explain the success of their image. The majority of adolescents did not wish to be musicians, even to sing their songs, but they did gain much for their identities from the expressive life which the Beatles lived, on and off stage. Similar formulation of identity images is seen in the sudden popularity of Vice-President Spiro Agnew because (as a Gallup poll of June 21, 1970 showed), he "called a spade a spade" and said "what a lot of people are thinking and are afraid to say"; or by the dialectical development of the role of Will Rogers as "court jester" and "ambassador" of America (Klapp, 1954). These people were enacting in their public roles what their followers wanted to be, do, and say.

So we see that the function of a symbolic leader is to *crystallize* a *social type*: embody it, dramatize it as a role, give it a name (often his own), and provide a model for others to imitate, if they are so inclined.

Intermediate Leadership

But, as already implied, whatever a celebrity does to introduce a fashion is only the first step of the style transaction. After he passes the threshold of dramatizing something people want for augmenting their identities, his style reaches the second threshold—intermediate leaders who, selecting it, will pass it on to groups they personally influence. Such less visible leaders, said Katz and Lazarsfeld (1955:331, 452), are not distinguished by formal or media status; most of their impact comes from the fact that they are highly gregarious and effective in day-to-day interpersonal relations. Youth has some advantage over age for women's fashion leadership, since social energy, mobility, and number of children are important factors in how influential one can be outside the home. Higher exposure to media plus greater effectiveness of personal input into social relations gives fashion leaders their advantage in leverage; they are influenced more by mass media and less by other people than are nonleaders.

To visualize the threshold that must be passed at this second stage of fashion negotiation, let us suppose that an enthusiast has bought some sports equipment, clothing, an idea, or a hairdo, which he or she brings home. He has yet to face his family, friends, and associates. What will it do for his status with *them*? For one thing, will he dare to wear it, display it? Or will he, after one encounter of jest or reproof, quietly lay it away forever or until a more propitious time? Much depends on his flair, wit, and popularity already earned as opinion leader. If members of his group become interested in the same thing, look at it, buy it, imitate him, the second threshold has been passed. But his friends have the power to stop or transform it. One testing at a party is enough to make or break an item of high fashion, as far as one's personal use is concerned.

In this second stage, fashions may be differentiated through networks, as each group selects and forms what it wants from what was uniformly presented in mass media. For example, groups of teenage girls in nearby areas of Chicago chose different kinds of popular songs as favorites from among those played to all of them in the media (Johnstone and Katz, 1957). The adoption and diffusion process may be a differentiated series of steps as different categories of the public respond selectively to media and to their own opinion leadership (Rogers, 1962; see Chapter 8).

For those in the "middle" of the race of fashion, success means merely to "look nice," to be accepted, not be noticed as standing out. For a leader of high fashion, however, the feedback is much more active and risk is proportionally higher. A new costume at a social affair becomes a dramatic event, duly reported and photographed in social columns; a line of comment is read as avidly by the star, her friends, and competitors as would be a critic's review of a stage play.

Then there is the continual daily encounter with business contacts, secretaries, doormen, headwaiters, clerks, strangers on the street, all adding silent signals to the interpersonal testing of the fashion.

Opposition Processes in Fashion

A third stage—more properly called a battle sector—of fashion negotiation is interaction between groups whose styles do not agree; here the feature of conflict and protection of collective identity become uppermost. Much of the fashion scene in America during the early 1970s was conflict. Symbols were being "pushed" aggressively by style rebels, by deviant groups, or by equally established groups trying to put each other down. Styles polarized and differentiated as result of such dialectic. But that was not all. One also saw established classes *imitating* some of the very styles they deplored; for example, fashionable beatniks of the 1950s or the "rich hip" look imitating the hairy hippie look in the 1960s. Such co-optation drove rebels wild, who tried to differentiate themselves by looking even poorer, or wilder, perhaps flaunting Che Guevara or Viet Cong symbols. In short, the fashion process showed itself to be not an orderly flow through networks, but a *melee* of cross currents and oppositions. Some of these influences are distinguished in the eight following sections.

1. *Style rebellion* is use of a fashion more or less deliberately as symbolic protest, an effort to shock or "put down" an established style by another that negates it. For example, the Dennis Hopper look, the Che Guevara look, the Afro look, the Rolling Stone look, the acid rock sounds, the Joan Baez look—all had in common the purpose of repudiating the style of the middle class in a way so pointed that it could not be taken as mere difference but as a rebuke. Hippie style perhaps sums it up: The uncouthness of this group offended middle-class cleanliness and respectability; their scrounging, carefree existence offended the belief that it was good to work hard for one's own living; "flower power" was a flippant rebuke to militarism and the authority of the state; free love was a threat to the monogamous ideal and responsibility of parents; the use of drugs seemed (to vestigial Puritans) selfish, sensual indulgence, threatening morality and the work structure of society; their hair, unkempt, indistinguishable between males and females, was offensive to middle-class ideals of neatness and masculinity. "We want to be free as hair," said the Yippie leader Abbie Hoffman; but that was a freedom that happened to be unacceptable to the middle classes, who also said they liked freedom. An infuriating twist of freedom was the display of the American flag in unusual ways, such as upside down, patches on pants, or decor for "Easy Rider"

motorcycles—practices that caricatured what the middle class it-self was doing in using automobile flag decals or packaging prod-ucts with the stars and stripes.

2. The most obvious response to style rebellion was *attack on deviant style*. People were refused permits to assemble, were ar-rested, were assaulted by onlookers, even police, sometimes for no reason other than display of symbols of style rebellion. Particularly in the South, violent reactions to these styles were likely. As we learned earlier, persecution of style rebels is not just gratuitous intolerance but an alarm response when one's own collective iden-tity is threatened.

A similar attack on style rebels occurred in the Communist world. China peremptorily imposed what amounted to a uniform on all citizens. In Bulgaria and Roumania in 1970, on-the-spot hair clipping, tailoring, and ripping of bell-bottom trousers, maxi skirts, or any costume that was deemed "decadent" were administered by police. Only Czechoslovakia and Yugoslavia could be called lenient (the latter even allowing production of the musical "Hair").

3. *Polarization*, a widening of differences, escalation of responses, and a group of like interests resulted from the interaction of con-servatives and rebels. Increasingly, heated rhetoric and provocative symbols came to be used: "pigs" faced "weirdos"; Blacks and other ethnics faced "honkey" or "Whitey." Juveniles joined the battle. John Lennon, in dismay at what was happening, warned rebels against allowing escalation to progress from symbols to physical violence, which he saw as a defeat to the spiritual message of style rebellion.

> The students are being conned! It's like the school bully: he aggra-vates you and aggravates you until you hit him. And then they kill you, like in Berkeley. Establishment, it's just a name for . . . evil. The monster doesn't care . . . the blue meanie is insane. We really care about life. Destruction is good enough for the establishment. The only thing they can't control is the mind, and we have to fight for sanity and peace on that level. But the students have gotten conned into thinking you can change it with violence and they can't, you know, they can only make it uglier and worse. (Sander, 1969a.)

Style polarization was not always so grim; but it was plainly part of what sociologists call the vicious circle of deviance (Parsons, 1951:255), or deviance-amplifying feedback (Maruyama, 1968).

4. *Reaffirmation* or *revival* of style occurs when a group asserts its symbols more vigorously in the face of challenges. Anthropolo-gists call such nativism among traditional peoples threatened by acculturation (Linton, 1943) or revitalization (A. C. Wallace, 1956). But it could be found in American life, too, as the following news article shows—

FLAG PINS SELL LIKE HOTCAKES. The St. Louis Globe-Democrat says it has sold 42,575 American flag pins in the past three weeks and it expects orders for as many as 40,000 more. The 18-carat, gold-finish pin is being sold for 25 cents over the counter and by mail. (*Associated Press*, June 25, 1970.)

Bumper stickers and decals on automobiles said: "Love it or leave it; if your heart isn't in it, get your ass out of it; the flag, defend it, silent majority; Agnew tells it like it is." A Manhattan clothier, in six months prior to July 1970, had sold 36,000 flag shirts to retailers across the nation. "Honor America Day," the biggest Fourth of July ceremony in years, took place before the Lincoln Memorial and featured Bob Hope, Billy Graham, and other celebrities. Such events, obviously, were part of a positive reaffirmation of patriotic style in the face of prolonged dissent and growing alienation. Such style revivals represent a homeostatic response of a system by counter-asserting a style against the imbalance or dissonance introduced by a new one.

5. *Invasion* of style occurs when a group takes over another group's identity symbol, as when White Americans wear Indian headbands, moccasins, and imitation buckskin jackets; or when Japanese play American jazz and manufacture Scotch whisky. Invasion becomes a threat to the original group's identity when the invading group is felt to be inferior, presumptuous, and degrading to the style; or the number of new adopters threatens to swamp the original group and wipe out its boundaries. We can see that style invasion had much to do with troubles of immigration restriction. Also, according to the Simmel theory, it is the heart of the fashion process.

Invasion can go downward, too. The history of jazz shows how Whites have continually invaded Black style. Benny Goodman, the Dorsey brothers, Harry James, and other White stars of "swing" used to "jam" in Black nightclubs of Chicago's South Side after working in downtown hotels. In originating "swing," Goodman was helped greatly by Black arranger Fletcher Henderson. White "cats" hung around Black clubs. Louis Armstrong had an enormous influence on the style of White musicians such as Eddie Condon, Bobby Hackett, and Jack Teagarden. This was true also of the influence of Charlie, "The Bird," Parker. Blacks showed a subtle resentment of Whites copying Black style, which *Downbeat* magazine called reverse Jim-Crowism. Some Black artists, such as Coltrane, Davis, Monk, Hodges, and Hawkins, had styles almost deliberately baffling to Whites. Rock-and-roll and rhythm-and-blues carried on White imitation of Black styles, even voices. When the Black Power movement broke out, "soul" became the rallying symbol of the essence of a style that Whites could not imitate. Of course the other side of the story was that some Blacks took up White middle-class styles, including the posture of looking down on jazz and being ashamed of "soul" food and music.

Yet another example of style invasion was that of the hippies and university students following the jet-set around the world with sleeping bags. In a sense, appropriating other people's styles is what fashion is all about.

6. A natural response to style invasion is *differentiation*, effected by changing the symbols of one's own group to make them more exclusive, as we have seen in Black resistance to invasion of "soul" by Whites or upper-class expensiveness and cultivation of accent differences.

7. *Legitimation* is the opposite of style invasion in that the group of less prestige, instead of copying the higher group, struggles to get its own style accepted by the majority, ultimately perhaps to have elite prestige. Such a triumph was achieved in the case of women's smoking and bobbed hair in the 1920s. Jazz, too, finally became highbrow when popularized by artists such as Ellington, Gershwin, and Whiteman—especially when David Brubeck took it onto university campuses as concert music, Leonard Bernstein gave it his blessing, and music schools began to offer courses in jazz. At such points, a Black jazz artist was invested with the aura of a European concert pianist. A similar legitimation occurred for the Beatles' music when Bernstein and other critics discovered its "polyphony" and began to compare it with Bach. However, mere appropriation of deviant or lower-class style by an upper-status group (for example, swearing, slumming) is not legitimation until a public blessing is given to it, which feeds back to the status of the originators so that they are able to enter the dominant group on more equal terms.

The struggles of Gay Lib, nudists, pot smokers, in the 1970s tell some of this story. New claims broke out after legitimation seemed completed, as Women's Lib carried on a struggle that some males supposed they had already won.

8. Lacking or failing legitimation, minorities may develop life styles that are *tactical reactions to exclusion and underprivilege* and which are adaptive in a ghetto, "Casbah," or underworld situation. These styles, while not respectable or even legal, are ways of carrying on a measure of opposition to the legitimate order. A study of American Black ghettos (especially Houston, Watts, and Oakland) identified seven such styles: (a) the "stoic," who is outwardly apathetic and accepting, finding some happiness perhaps in joining a traditional Black church or simply resigning himself to being an "invisible man"; (b) the "defeated," who has been crushed by life and may escape into a world of drugs, alcohol, or psychotic hallu-

cinations; (c) the "exploiter," who is perhaps a "blockbuster," numbers man, mortician, or local landlord who has a stake in maintaining the *status quo* of the ghetto; (d) the "achiever," who tries to better his own lot, with little concern for the collective condition of American Blacks; (e) the "rebel without a cause," who rejects existing society without any program of reform, and expresses his rebellion through delinquent behavior; (f) the "activist," who hopes to change society by reform measures; (g) the "revolutionary," who rebels militantly against American society and hopes to bring about a total change in the Black way of life (McCord et al., 1969).

Opposition processes give thrust and bite to encounters that involve fashion transactions and keep them from being simply flow or convergence of tastes represented by one symbol. They accentuate challenges; groups feel their life styles threatened; defensive response polarizes fashion further—perhaps drives it in political directions. Styles become more shocking and deviant when conflict predominates in the fashion process; and tastes may shift from prettiness, pleasantness, smooth good taste to defiance and ugliness because the objective of the stylist is not to please himself but to infuriate Mr. Jones, or perhaps to announce the separateness of his class from that of Mr. Jones.

Natural Selection of Fashion

After considering the struggle in fashion, we see more clearly why it is a process of natural selection—survival almost in a biological sense: styles live, grow, reproduce themselves, and die, partly because they help living groups to do the same. If the only process in fashion was imitation, there would be a question of selection and survival. With opinion leadership and all these opposition processes working, there is more complex interaction and greater question; not only the uncertainty about what will "sell" and who will "buy," but also what tactics competitors will use on one another and what will come out.

To say that style is subject to natural selection is to say that competition and conflict of various patterns eliminate some and allow survival of others that are somehow better. The choice of alternatives is not an intentional outcome any more than market price is. Economic theory has long used the notion that competition of products in a market leads to results that are not the rational decision of participants—for example, Gresham's law, driving "good money" into savings and leaving less reliable money and credit paper in the market. Sociologists fell into fallacies of "social

Darwinism" (Hofstadter, 1944) by failing to treat culture as a symbolic rather than a biological process; but some are now moving again to apply natural selection, for example, to cultural forms (Gerard, Kluckhohn, and Rapoport, 1956; Campbell, 1965b), to rumors (Shibutani, 1966) and social systems generally (Buckley, 1967:64). For all such theory, there must be an account of three basic processes: *variation*, an input of variety (new forms, mutations, "noise," alternatives) to the system; *selection*, competition of old with new forms and screening those which better meet the criteria or conditions of an ecological or social niche; and *preservation*, a means of propagating or perpetuating the new forms over a longer time (in biological terms this means successful breeding; in sociological terms it might mean communication, recruitment, socialization, culture-making), commonly called viability. The reason for calling fashion selection "natural" is that no one is in charge of such a process, the outcome of negotiations such as we have reviewed is no more intended than is the success of a species in finding an environmental niche.

Viability

Just how a fashion proves its viability is far from clear. Viability is passing the test of survival. What does a living thing need or do to survive? Watching dinosaurs crawl about amidst the tar pits, biologists would have been hard put to predict their fate, or what would replace them. One thing we learn from natural selection is that its outcome is *not* predictable from a mere inventory of input and conditions—that is, we do not know which particular features of environment will select which particular features or patterns of living forms. The game must be played to find out. This is why fashions are so hard to predict. Some of our styles today look pretty good, but they may be "dinosaurs"—the question is, which? And which of the freakish creatures running away from the dinosaurs are the birds of tomorrow?

Moreover, the "environment" to which fashions adapt is not a matter of habitat conditions like coldness; it is far less easy to define—vague functional needs, moods, conflicts, strains, and other conditions, permanent or transitory we cannot be sure. So the death rate of fashions is high and emergence of new forms sudden.

One may see the goals of societal selection as a better fit or more successful form of culture for the conditions of modern life *after* competitors have fallen by the wayside. But even looking back it is sometimes hard to tell; what, for example, were people seeking in the Kewpie doll? And did they find it? One may view such fads as rather like arrows shot at a mark, some of which hit but most miss—

as society searches for new styles and institutions. But the trail of misses gives little indication of what is coming.

The question is complicated by the fact that most radical innovations meet with some hullabaloo of opposition, and seem strange and freakish at first. Freakishness is no indication of the survival value of a style. Another difficulty is that new fashions are not obviously useful in the ordinary sense (though useful things can become fashionable). Their value to society is better expressed as a function, or meaning, which may be not at all obvious; sociologists use the term *latent* for functions that are not manifest as purposes (Merton, 1968:105). So, to determine the viability of a fashion, we need to know its meaning as a life style in context, including what it does for people psychologically and socially, a matter requiring intensive case study, which has been applied to very few fads, fashions, or social types. Then, on a broader scale, an ecological study should be made of the scene over a period of time in which styles interact.

An example of the difficulty of understanding fashion functions is the bigness of American automobiles. When the Model T Ford came out in competition with Buick, Cadillac, Hupmobile, and Stutz, one might have supposed that the trend of American fashion in automobiles was toward economy (Ford said, "They can have any color they want, so long as it is black."). But automobiles, including Fords, got bigger and more powerful until they became unwieldy boats with huge tailfins. Then the Volkswagen invasion showed a strong trend toward compactness and economy; but, almost immediately, the American compacts offered in competition grew bigger and more powerful. Then, in 1970, came a wave of "mini" models. One could hardly tell what was going on here, what was doing what for whom, unless one had a better insight of something beside horsepower and mileage—mainly, latent functions concerning status and image and interactions such as style rebellion and polarization (a little car, perhaps, driving another American to an even bigger one). We may suppose that the kind of competition going on among automobile styles is not merely economic, even though registered in sales and prices; any account of the "success" of a model evidently depends on latent functions that are not yet understood and therefore require careful sociological and symbolic analysis.

Popular Moods

One of the subtlest of latent functions complicating the problem of predicting fashion evolution is how fashions meet *popular moods* that drift through public opinion. There is as yet no classification of

popular moods, nor is there a pattern by which to follow their con-
tours, dynamics, and precipitation points. Opinion polling does not
usually catch either the nuances of feeling and imagery or the con-
tours of popular moods; such things are mercurial, a mystique. For
example, there was something in the air, perhaps a feeling of guilt
about "getting soft," that caused Americans to respond so vigorously
to a suggestion of President Kennedy that they ought to walk more;
this led to a fad of fifty-mile hikes. Again, the late Senator Joseph
McCarthy sensed and caught a mood in the 1950s—it happened to
be an ugly one. He picked it out of the air, tuned the sound of the
wind to a certain pitch, and the nation resonated. Why one kind of
mood follows another, or why particular "looks," "sounds," and expressive movements catch on remains mysterious. Hard though the
stock market may be to predict, its trends are either up or down; but
fashions can go in many directions, and we have no collective
weather stations better than price indices in economics. So contagions come and go: booms and panics, carnivals ("anything goes")
and austerity, sentimentality, friendliness, witch hunts, gay and dark
colors, dances energetic or sedate, futurism and nostalgia, politics
to the right or the left. Of all these mass trends, the least compulsive are those we call fashions, and the most compulsive are those
we label as contagions and hysterias (Chapter 6).

Conclusion

In this chapter we considered fad and fashion as types of anonymous interpersonal communication which require considerably more
than imitation to explain. We considered what makes fashion move,
and rejected the ideas that either useful invention or a kind of dicta-
tion by the economic process is sufficient to explain the innovation
and turnover of styles. Status theory gives us three important ideas
that help us to explain why the fashion process moves: the generation of status anxieties, the role of opinion leaders, and class differentiation. But even those do not seem sufficient. We add the factor
of banality as a source of boredom, and show how it leads to fashion
as a search for meaningfulness, an effort to build a fuller life.

By looking at fashion as a dialectic, or negotiation, in which
oppositional processes have a large part, we get more insight into
what is going on in fashion and where it may be going. Natural selection is a reasonable model into which to fit oppositional processes,
especially when class maintenance (the Simmel model) seems not
so relevant. But natural selection helps little in predicting which
style will prevail, and therefore cannot forecast where the whole
process is going.

Nevertheless, fad and fashion cannot be depicted as mass disorder. Rather they represent a collective search for a pattern known as life style, a distinctive expression of mass identity. In this sense, fad and fashion are not just sporadic caprices; they are selected trends toward an ultimate societal image, i.e. a search. These trends have a dialectical (negotiative-oppositional) character that makes them seem more disorderly than they actually are.

Natural selection brings order to conflicts and failures. The goals of the search are adoptions of styles that hit the bull's-eye in latent functions and meanings and prove their viability in competition with alternatives. Such a process is presumably negentropic (pattern and meaning seeking, organizing), aiming toward a quite possibly better pattern as part of a larger systemic balance sheet.

But one reason for withholding undue optimism from fashion search is that the *rate* of innovation cannot exceed a certain point (which was described in Chapter 9 as information overload) before the search begins to suffer strains that raise a question whether it can at these levels of variability achieve negentropy. The battle of order against disorder is not always won. Just such a diagnosis of overload by novelty—society going to pieces in a mad race of "keeping pace with pace"—was made in 1970 by one writer for England and presumably for America, too (Booker, 1970), something, at least, to weigh against the optimism of the "greening of America" (Reich, 1970).

Let us look at this within the context of meaning-seeking movements.

CHAPTER 11

Meaning-Seeking Movements

Parties may come and parties may go, but you and I must march on together! (The Universal Party, Berkeley, California, 1971.)

Social movements are commonly defined as "collective enterprises to establish a new order of life" (Blumer, 1946: 199); or "socially shared activities and beliefs directed toward the demand for change in some aspect of the social order" (Gusfield, 1970:2). The essential points are (1) activities usually involving struggle, by (2) collectivities over (3) a period of time—at least a few years, maybe centuries—on (4) a large scale (often clusters of collectivities working together, whether or not fully aware of it) to bring about (5) change, including the adoption of new organizations and symbols, whether by destroying or adding to old ones. The typical end of a movement, said Park (1939) is an institution.

> Every social movement may . . . be described as a potential institution. And every institution may in turn be described as a movement that . . . has settled down to something like routine activity. . . . when the community and the public in which and for which it exists claim as a right the services to which they have become accustomed. (Park, 1939:7.)

This chapter focuses on one kind of movement—meaning-seeking—using as an example the romantic quest of the early 1970s, known as "the movement." In so doing, it skirts a vast field of political, economic, and other kinds of movements, recognizing that to treat them satisfactorily is beyond the scope of this book. But the "counterculture" is sufficient to illustrate points about collective search being a flow of symbolic negotiations, seeking (in this case) new *meaning* rather than merely practical objectives. Fashion, treated in Chapter 10, is one form of such search for symbols adding to a person's social identity. In the "counterculture," we see a larger sector and more prolonged course of negotiation, sometimes politicized but by no means primarily concerned with this. Indeed, the thesis presented here is that a prime cause of modern unrest is not the distribution of economic goods and political rights but banality, a shortcoming in meaning to which modern systems are prone (as suggested in Chapters 9 and 10). For developing societies, and for minorities in developed societies, distribution of goods and rights is still a prime concern; but for the urbanized and suburbanized masses of modern industrial society, something is "eating" them besides what and how they are eating.

So, this chapter focuses on the problem of meaning as a new kind of unrest in modern societies, closely associated with boredom, a spiritual or psychological rather than material deprivation. In such a context, the symbolic task of the movement is to construct new meanings and values, rather than go on doing the same kinds of things.

All movements have a problem of building appropriate meanings. Mass migrations and rushes usually have highly romantic images of what is at the end of the rainbow. The Crusades were inspired by a holy zeal combined incongruously with romantic and sordid images of what they were going to get. The Pilgrims came to America with a utopian vision of a society of saints; the American Revolution had an elaborate ideology of natural rights and social contract theory, which it proposed to realize by building a society to match.

But these are not the main meaning problems of today. Abundance has its own troubles. This book treats social movements as efforts to rebalance or change a system. When major movements develop, we postulate a lack of something. In Chapter 10, we analyzed banality as a deficit that might contribute to style search. Ten vital relationships were mentioned in Chapter 7 as part of a systemic balance sheet, suggesting lines along which movements might be expected to occur. But even if we know what is lacking, we have no guarantee of the direction and outcome, for a movement is not a mechanical process but a flow of symbolic negotiations requiring meanings to be built. It involves dialectical interchange and shifts of position along the way. Such a view avoids fallacies, such as that there is some kind of linear thrust or cyclical swing in history which does not involve the actual working out of the varying struggles of people to find and negotiate meanings.

Certain theories advanced by sociologists are especially helpful to us in seeing what the symbolic tasks of a meaning-seeking movement could be. One is the idea of Max Weber (1946) that history may be regarded as a trend toward greater rationalization of institutions, with the charismatic leader as often a rebel against legalism and bureaucracy, an agent of radical change by religious and political movements that he stirs up. Thus, the charismatic leader is a bringer of new meaning, which the establishment often defines as irrational.

Another theory of great importance for the study of meaning-seeking movements is that which sociologists have developed of a religious sectarian cycle, of heating up and cooling off of fervor as religious movements go from reform to institution. Park and Burgess (1924) called this the evolution from sect to denomination:

A sect is a religious organization that is at war with the existing mores. It seeks to cultivate a state of mind and establish a code of morals different from that of the world about it, and for this it claims divine authority. In order to accomplish this end, it invariably seeks to set itself off in contrast with the rest of the world. The simplest and most effective way to achieve this is to adopt a peculiar form of dress and speech. This, however, invariably makes its members objects of scorn and derision, and eventually of persecution. . . . A sect in its final form may be described, then, as a movement of social reform and regeneration that has become institutionalized. Eventually, when it has succeeded in accommodating itself to the other rival organizations, when it has become tolerant and is tolerated, it tends to assume the form of a denomination. (R. E. Park and Burgess, 1924:872–873.)

Troeltsch (1932), a student of Weber, analyzed such change through the generations of members as an ascetic sect, which by compromise with the world moves toward the more easy-going church as an institution; development such as this has been followed up by scholars like H. R. Niebuhr (1957), S. D. Clark (1948), Dynes (1955), and B. R. Wilson (1961). When sacred values are watered down by compromise with the world, this is usually called *secularization*, accompanied by loss of fervor and idealism. This effect might be found also in a crusade or a political revolutionary party that reaches institutional status after a struggle.

The other side of this coin, the sectarian cycle, is a collective effort to return to the fullness of values and fervor of belief in a system that for some reason has become empty and unsatisfying. A. C. Wallace (1956) called this a *revitalization movement*, of which examples might be found in the "cargo cults" of Melanesia (in which people entertained a belief that their ancestors were coming in a great ship filled with wealth and that the Whites would be driven away), the ghost dance of the North American Indians (involving belief that dancing would renew their world and drive away the White man in a coming holocaust) or in the reformations of leaders such as Luther, Mohammed, Gandhi, or Martin Luther King—great liftings of the spirit.

> The emotional atmosphere of such movements is . . . ecstatic, particularly in the early phases, for the goal to which the movements strive is not just rational, technical improvement, but [and this is an invariable rule] an improvement in the self-respect of the people. The members of a revitalization movement are seeking to achieve new identities; they hope to be reborn . . . . (A. C. Wallace, 1956:54.)

Revitalization movements include *nativism*, "any conscious, organized attempt on the part of a society's members to revive or perpetuate selected aspects of its culture" (Linton, 1943); and *millenarism*, movements that reject the present as evil and look forward to a marvelous future apocalypse and perhaps arrival of a Messiah (N. Cohn, 1957; Lanternari, 1963; Talmon, 1962).

By putting revitalization movements alongside the running down of sectarian fervor traced by Park and Troeltsch, we get a picture of the balancing of society by two directions of flow of social energy and information in social systems, toward greater rationality, technology, compromise; and by movements with fervor seeking faith, fulfillment, utopia, by seemingly irrational images.

Mannheim (1936:173–174) traced these two directions of symbolic development as, on the one hand, *ideology*—building arguments, beliefs, and images to make society seem reasonable the way it is; and *utopia*—building an image of a future fulfillment that requires transcending, possibly destroying, the *status quo.* To illustrate, Christianity might be utopia if its beliefs of brotherhood actually led people to challenge inequalities and relate to each other in a close way; otherwise, it would be ideology if it made people content with things the way they are now (as it was used to defend the divine right of kings), by a picture of heavenly rewards later, acting as what Marxists call an "opiate."

Such concepts—of the rebellion of charismatic leadership against bureaucracy, the sectarian cycle, and the building of utopia —help us to see in sociological perspective that a meaning-seeking movement such as the "counterculture" of the 1970s might be a "river" of symbolic negotiations. It seemed to be trying to revitalize modern life, approaching sectarian fervor, building some kind of utopia, though it had not a clear ideology to state and justify what it wanted or what it would be after it became what it wanted to be.

We can sketch this movement under four headings: (1) banality as a systemic product, generating boredom intense enough to stimulate a social movement as a collective search for meanings; (2) the seeding of collectivities searching for meaning in a common mood; (3) negotiations by which movements develop meaning; and (4) the dialectical growth of a movement against opposition.

We must give considerable attention to banality because it is the heart of the theory of meaning-seeking movements, and is not at this time readily perceived as a systemic problem.

Romanticism and Other Responses to Banality

Something hung heavily over the spirit of youth and many older persons in the early 1970s. Whatever it was, pervasive symptoms were boredom and a wish to reject or escape the established order by romantic or other impractical means. Chancellor William McGill, University of California at San Diego, said—

> It is clear it is an attempt by these young people to establish an impression of romantic vagabonds and to show solidarity with the ostracized and downtrodden. One need only look at their hands to recognize that this is a charade, but the need and the longings underlying such stylistic affectations, are almost an expression of hunger. [They seek liberation through] transcendental experiences. . . . It is a form of modern mystical romanticism and it has captured the youth culture. (McGill, 1970:B–6.)

Such movements seemed less interested in practical reforms than in "far-out" or "mind-bending" experiences: freakouts, sensory awakening, trips on a "yellow submarine." In view of the level of abundance and recreational opportunities, it was surprising to find so many people trying to escape from boredom. Men were bored with jobs, women with housework; "pot" became a major problem among soldiers on military posts; one said he was "perpetually stoned" for three months—"we'd try any pill we could get, even if we knew nothing about its effects. They were free, so we thought, why not?" (*Christian Science Monitor*, July 22, 1970). Girls working in Manhattan, asked why they were smoking pot on their lunch hour, said—

> Look around. It's part of the scene. It's the times. As long as nobody gets too high, and it doesn't bother anybody else, who cares? . . . We've got these stupid jobs, clerical jobs in a couple of brokerages. We either work our fool heads off, nights and Saturdays included, when they're busy, or they talk about laying off girls—us, because things are slack. . . . We've had it. What we do is come out here to relax. Two or three joints and we feel good. We don't care if it might be our last week on the job. We don't care if the work is stupid, we can stand it then. When we go back, it wears off after awhile and we go down again, but we've had it. We've been up. (Townsend, 1970.)

Even leisure, for some strange reason, was boring. (See Fig. 11.1.) A former marketing director of Disneyland said the development of this ingenious enterprise was in response to—

> a kind of mass groping. . . . they felt awkward about all that leisure time thrust onto them and they weren't sure what to really do with it. Sure, they had their two cars, their pool and their golf and all that— the great American dream. But they were still bored and they weren't sure why. (Wong, 1970.)

John Ciardi, the poet, said—

> Inured as we are to both the malice and the miracle of our technology, we walk through our incredible lives, separated from them by a dull habituation. The hydrogen bomb is a bore. The pollution of the planet is old hat. Half of my friends confess they did not tune in to watch the second moon landing. They had watched the first, hadn't they? Once you've seen one moon landing, you've seen them all, haven't you? (Ciardi, 1970:6.)

Boredom is not a very good word by which to describe what is wrong, because most Americans think of it as a temporary state that is easily remedied by recreation (if not by work). The trouble is rooted in a semantic difficulty. American society is reluctant to

"I've been bored before, but this is the first time I've ever been bored in living color!"

FIGURE 11.1.   The boredom of leisure. (From *Christian Science Monitor*, Oct. 16 1970.)

face boredom, however deeply afflicted by it. Why is this so? There are two main reasons. One is that the lingering Puritan work ethic has no concept of boredom except as a moral fault: the curse of idleness and luxury; lack of piety; shallowness, frivolity of a person with no serious aims; or sheer stupidity. The second reason is that a free society—enjoying a high GNP (gross national product), dedicated to the pursuit of happiness, with burgeoning amusements (some in reaction against Puritanism)—cannot find evidence of a lack of "fun," "the good things of life"; therefore, it cannot logically be bored. By definition, boredom can be only a temporary state, since leisure waits; get a machine to do the boring part of your work. All-encompassing, chronic boredom is incomprehensible within the American ethos, either in the Puritan or the playboy sector—yet we have it! What, then, is it to be called? Rather than fight the semantic battle, perhaps we need another name. There is a term that helps us designate the features of a social system that generates boredom and a need for imaginative escapes; namely *banality*. Webster's dictionary defines it as "commonplace, trite; used until so common as to have lost novelty and interest; hackneyed, stale; stereotyped; vapid." In other words, banality is the inability to give a lift to the spirit and imagination from fresh insight; inability to "turn you on."

Banality as Variously Experienced

Artists are sensitive to banality as a failure of creativity; and they, perhaps more than others, use the term. Most people experience it as endless miles of paving, "motel modern" style, pizzaburger culture, streams that run straight, the hundred-thousandth horse opera; the predictable pitch of a preacher, salesman, or politician; billboard ads like "Suzuki Conquers Boredom." A plastics-producing company, trying to be fetching in its advertising, said—

> Beneath this soft and warm exterior there lies a heart of plastic. So far, it's only a [heart] valve. . . . Right now, we've got you surrounded by our plastics. We were in plastics before most people knew the word. We make more plastics than anyone else. We haven't scratched the surface yet.

Surrounded by plastic wherever one goes is perhaps the message one is supposed to get from this.

Banality is not inherent in any cultural product—art, religion—but a way of living with it. Thoreau, who could be called a patron saint of the counterculture, rebuked his fellow New Englanders:

> It is remarkable that, notwithstanding the universal favor with which the New Testament is outwardly received, and even the bigotry with which it is defended, there is no hospitality shown to, there is no appreciation of, the order of truth with which it deals. I know of no book that has so few readers. There is none so truly strange, and heretical, and unpopular. To Christians, no less than Greeks and Jews, it is foolishness and a stumbling block. There are, indeed, severe things in it which no man should read aloud more than once.—"Seek first the kingdom of heaven." "Lay not up for yourselves treasures on earth." "If thou wilt be perfect, go and sell what thou hast, and give to the poor, and thou shalt have treasure in heaven." "For what is a man profited, if he shall gain the whole world, and lose his own soul? or what shall a man give in exchange for his soul?"—Think of this, Yankees! . . . Think of repeating these things to a New England audience! . . . Who, without cant, can read them aloud? . . . They never *were* read; they never *were* heard. Let but one of these sentences be rightly read from any pulpit in the land, and there would not be left one stone of that meetinghouse upon another. (Thoreau, "Sunday," from *A Week on the Concord and Merrimack Rivers*, Boston, 1849.)

The very words that lifted early Christians into sublimity put nine-teenth-century New Englanders to rest in complacency with "things as they are."

Thoreau was a man who refused to be banal. We may use him as a model of the problem and its responses—paralleled by the life of any saint or seer, such as St. Francis, Gautama, or Ramakrishna:

> Where I lived was as far off as many a region viewed nightly by astronomers. . . . My house . . . had its site in . . . a withdrawn, but forever new and unprofaned, part of the universe. . . . I got up early and bathed in the pond; that was a religious exercise. . . . The morning . . . is the awakening hour. . . . For an hour, at least, some part of us awakes which slumbers all the rest of the day . . . little is to be expected of that day . . . to which we are not awakened by our Genius . . . to a higher life than we fell asleep from. . . . That man who does not believe that each day contains an earlier, more sacred, and auroral hour than he has yet profaned has despaired of life, and is pursuing a descending and darkening way. (Thoreau, *Walden*, chap. 2.)

So speak "romantics" and "mystics" who reject the world as given in the practical terms of their cultures.

An American Zen student expressed feelings about banality in this way:

> I had some feeling that everyday life as most people are living it is not enough—it's not fulfilling. Desires that we have and satisfy—that's not enough. That isn't what I really want. All the things that I wanted, they weren't what I wanted. Something more basic, something deeper—it wasn't a woman, a family, a car, or education, or money, or anything like that. And . . . when I had those things, that wasn't it. (Needleman, 1970:50.)

A psychological definition might be that banality is a *restriction of awareness*, of which a main symptom is boredom as a kind of frustration. It is not a material deprivation (the most abundant so-cieties suffer from it) but a shallowness of meaning, a lack of payoff to imagination, hope, identity, the human spirit. Many humans feel a need for something "more" in their environments—more than meets the eye, that will go on when they die. Awareness that there is "nothing more" is the essence of banality, whether in steak and fried potatoes or in education, entertainment, even religion—home of mysteries.

To be aware of banality is to realize the restriction—that one has been denied a living experience by a barrier between oneself and nature or real contact with others—like a glimpse from a tourist bus of an interesting scene one will never fully see. One may be unaware of banality and merely be bored, as perhaps most of us are. Artists are sensitive to it because it is their business to outwit the enemy,

which they may call "commercialism" or other names. Psychologically, a banal situation is like a prison cell with four walls and nothing
else. It may be argued that no one need be bored in any situation if
he is imaginative enough; but the fact remains that some situations
make it *more difficult* to be creative. Indeed, a whole society can
be more or less like that for a large part of its members.

Toward a Definition in Systemic Terms

It is beyond our scope to trace all the causes of banality except to
point out that it is *systemic* and not an accident. Further, it is a
communication problem, and not to be solved except by symbolic
analysis. It seems to arise wherever communication networks and
social experiences are (1) unduly repetitive, offering nothing new—
"I've heard all that before"; (2) artificially fabricated and packaged,
with arbitrary exclusions—"pseudo-events," Boorstin (1962) called
them; (3) shallow in various senses—not permitting depth exploration, meditation; too impersonal; too rapid change; unimaginative
matter-of-factness; (4) stereotyped, false as images; (5) hypo-
critical; (6) low in personal input: requiring little involvement, giving all the answers and leaving nothing to do. Many have thus described the organized technological world—as Jacques Ellul (1965)
put it, a velvet-lined concentration camp.

The artist rebels against banality endlessly. One tactic is to
blow it up so everybody can see it, as in the "soupcan and comic
strip" art of Andy Warhol—a tour de force of "camp," extracting
esthetic statement from banality itself.* An advertisement perhaps
unwittingly copied Warhol by producing what is probably the utmost
of banality—a full newspaper-page picture of a stairway ascending
into heaven, represented by a plate of Sarah Lee Cheesecake: "Go
Where No Man Has Gone Before."

---

  * Other voices against banality have been heard: "For all of us, the automobile talks back to boredom and emptiness, promises escape, even if it
never delivers" (Peter Schrag, "White Man in Harlem," *Saturday Review*,
Aug. 3, 1968:12). "The banality and triviality of the curriculum in most schools
has to be experienced to be believed" (Charles E. Silberman, 1970). ". . .
the testimony of the arts. . . . The banality of the age turned to impotence
and numbness and paralysis, a total anesthesia of the soul" (Archibald
MacLeish, "The Revolt of the Diminished Man," *Saturday Review*, June 7, 1969:
19). "The denial of metaphysics" in modern societies means "the triumph of
triviality. . . . a profound impoverishment" (Peter Berger, *A Rumor of Angels:
Modern Society and the Rediscovery of the Supernatural*, New York: Doubleday). Jessica Mitford, in the *American Day of Death*, amusingly describes the
banality of funeral practices. Harrison Brown, a geochemist, said: "Just
imagine the thrill of flying from Los Angeles to New York and having the
landscape look like Los Angeles all the way" ("After the Population Explosion," *Saturday Review*, June 28, 1971:13).

Who is most sensitive to banality? Presumably those who are most educated and exposed to the cultural side of affluence; and particularly among these the types of people one would describe as antic, creative, mystical, or romantic in their response to life, as we shall describe.

Yet, the trouble is that there is a kind of person who seems content to pave everything over, as it were: convert everything to the clichés of materialistic culture. There is an unending—possibly endless—dispute between those happy with things-as-they-are and those whom William James called "tender minded" or "sick souls," who feel the need for "more"—hidden meaning, immortality, fulfillment, rebirth. A contemporary writer states it nicely:

> It is . . . disconcerting for me to realize . . . that half the world feels no need whatever to "escape from time," has no sense of being imprisoned in a three-dimensional prison, is, in fact, perfectly content with Reality as defined and limited by the five senses, extended, of course, by all the resources of modern technology; and wishes for nothing better than to go on exploring the exciting possibilities within this ample framework. To the other half of the world—my half—such an attitude is as inconceivable as for an embryo to be content to live and die within the womb.
>
> The other side, of course, will not accept this simile, and tells me my trouble is that I cannot face up to Reality. . . .
>
> The devil of it is, *he may be right.* There are as many of him as of me . . . I should hate to risk a vote on it. . . . But . . . I will not let him get away with this story that I "can't face up to reality." . . . The whole point is that his Reality is different from mine. If his Reality is the more basic, then I am . . . "an escapist"; if mine is, then he is spending his life in a locked room without bothering to look for the key. (McGlashan, 1967:126.)

All one needs for a meaning-seeking movement, of course, is that *enough* people feel this way keenly enough to get involved in a collective effort to transcend the ordinary—by some means, political, ideological, recreational, artistic, or cultic. Which is what this book is saying about modern society: Communicative side effects of abundance are driving more and more toward effort to transcend the established order. So, the world seems divided between those who are content with the communication system in which they live, and those who regard it as a prison to be transcended by various means.

By summing up under the term "banality" the shallowness and dulling of experience in a culture, we reach the formulation that (1) nature is never banal—only relationships, communication, concepts are; (2) mere increase in communication does not necessarily cure banality—indeed, it may grow worse (Chapter 9); (3) *generation of too much banality by a social system leads to meaning-seeking movements* because it creates strain. Resentment of banality with high expectations of meaning and fulfillment reaches a supersaturation of tension (Chapter 6), which can finally lead to explosive results. Eric Hoffer said: "There is perhaps no more reliable indicator of a society's ripeness for a mass movement than the prevalence of unrelieved boredom" (1951:50).

But a movement, once it leaves the confines of conventional reality, has the burden of constructing a whole set of countermeanings to combat the clichés of the system—another world, whether in the temporal future (utopia, chiliasm) or outside "reality" (heaven, nirvana).

Responses to Banality

What, then, are the main modes of defiant response to banality? How does the bird of imagination escape from his plastic cage? Primitive society was rescued by myths and rituals, emphasizing wonder and mystery (Langer, 1942; Eliade, 1958, 1964). Unfortunately, modern man seems to be reduced to comic strips, with science perhaps the best wonder going. But four major ways out of the cage are available to imaginative people, all copiously illustrated by the movement known as the "counterculture."

1. The first is *revelry*: expanding sensory horizons by "fun." The yawn of boredom leads quickly to activities like horseplay and high jinks, which are essentially gropings of people trying to "swing," make things "happen," "turn on" with "groovy" things. *Mad* magazine made a pyrotechnical display of satire against established culture. The range of expressive activities that broke out in the late 1960s is indicated by phrases like "it's happening" (Simmons and Winograd, 1968), "freaking out," the "Age of Aquarius" (W. Braden, 1970), all of which showed what people were up to in their fight against boredom. The underground press furnished recipes for "cooking with grass":

> The easiest way . . . is to begin with "electric butter." This is made by adding approximately one-half lid of grass or one gram of hash to one pound of butter or margarine and sauteeing over a *low* heat, stirring occasionally, until the mixture obtains a noxious olive-green-chartreuse color. . . . When the proper color has been reached, and the butter has separated into a bubbly froth on top and all grass particles below, strain out the dope, if it's grass (hash will dissolve) and throw it away. You've gotten all the goodies out of it. Pour . . . into some sort of container and store in your refrigerator . . . Corn bread made with electric butter will blow your mind. Cookies don't taste green . . . and, best of all, when the cops come to bust you, you'll be reasonably

safe, unless they taste everything in the fridge (ho ho). (*Quicksilver Times*, May 8, 1970.)

Ken Kesey's merry pranksters came on the scene (Wolfe, 1968). A rebirth of festivity was noted by Cox (1969b):

> Festivity—the capacity for genuine revelry and a joyous celebration; and fantasy—the faculty for envisioning radically alternative life situations. . . . in very recent years, industrial man has begun to rediscover the festive and the fanciful dimensions of life. . . . We may be witnessing the overture to a sweeping cultural renaissance, a revolution of human sensibilities in which the faculties we have starved and repressed . . . will be nourished and appreciated again. (Cox, 1969b:25.)

2. A second likely response to banality is *creativity*. The whole history of music, art, literature, and thought is, in some sense, a testimony of the struggle against banality. The output of rock song and music, psychedelic art, and a political position identified as "new left," in the 1960s and early 1970s were creative breaks with tradition. But perhaps the most pointed intellectual theme was existentialism, whose fierce rejection of clichés and radical insistence on freedom swelled to a major movement in the 1950s (from writings of Sartre, Camus, Kierkegaard, Jaspers, and Heidegger) and continued as a premise of the counterculture in the 1970s.

3. A third response, less demanding on abilities, is *mysticism*, a search beyond rational thought, through intuition or revelation, for a reality beyond the surface of things and the clichés of ideology and dogma. Needless to say, cultism and occultism have burgeoned in the "Age of Aquarius." The rush to soothsayers, gurus, and prophets has been strong. Mystics like Krishnamurti and Maharishi, and expositors like Alan Watts, have had vast followings. People have sought here and there for meditation techniques, mantras, chants, and messages by which to reach truth beyond the appearance of things. "Jesus freaks" are teaching a form of primitive Christianity on street corners that is disturbing to the churches. The age is awash with a tide of religious seeking unmeasured— but many churches are half-empty.

4. A fourth response to banality, far easier for ordinary people to participate in, is *romanticism*. And, because it is so easy to share, it looms larger in meaning-seeking movements. To some people, romanticism means something like "Romeo and Juliet" or "The Sound of Music"; but there is another side, far more disturbing. Romanticism is not a clear concept, and scholars despair of confining it to a simple definition (Babbitt, 1919; Barzun, 1943; Halsted, 1969), although some of its themes are plain enough: (a) idealistic, dreaming, chivalric but impractical (like Quixote); (b) freedom from external obligations, roving, vagabondage; (c) "far out," tran-

scending, questing for something more; (d) self-expression versus conformity or reason, letting oneself go, dionysian (versus apollonian or classical); (e) naturalness, wildness (versus culture, government); (f) trusting the heart (versus the head), sentimentalism, trust the (great heart of the) people, "Love will find a way"; and (g) immediate action, activism, impatience, wipe the slate clean at one stroke, perhaps by cataclysm. Now, a romantic may not be committed to all of these things, but stressing many of them places him in the perspective. The following quotations express some of them:

> I see an animal . . . satisfying the calls of hunger under the first oak, and those of thirst at the rivulet; I see him laying himself down to sleep at the foot of the same tree . . . and behold . . . all his wants are completely supplied. . . . He knows no goods but food, a female, and rest, he fears no evil but pain and hunger. . . . His moderate wants are so easily supplied with what he everywhere finds ready to his hand, and he stands at such a distance from the degree of knowledge requisite to covet more, that he can have neither foresight nor curiosity . . . . (Rousseau, "Discourse on Inequality.")

> I would have every man so much like a wild antelope, so much a part and parcel of Nature, that his very person should thus sweetly advertise our senses of his presence . . . the trapper's coat emits . . . a sweeter scent to me than . . . the merchant's. . . . How near to good is that which is *wild*! . . . The most alive is the wildest. . . . Hope and the future for me are not in laws and cultivated fields, not in towns and cities, but in the impervious and quaking swamps. . . . (Thoreau, 1862.)

> I think I could turn and live with animals, they're so placid and self-contained . . . they do not sweat and whine about their condition. . . . scent of these armpits . . . spread of my own body. . . . I dote on myself. . . . I wear my hat as I please. . . . I am the poet of my body. . . . through me forbidden voices. . . . I believe in the flesh and the appetites. (Whitman, "Song of Myself.")

A hero of the rock musical "Hair" sings that he is "just a hairy guy" who wants his hair as long as it will grow, to be a home for fleas and bees, and a nesting-place for birds. "There ain't no words for the beauty, the splendor, the wonder of my hair." He notes that his hair is biblical "like Jesus wore." Mary loved her son, so why didn't his mother love him? (Ragni and Rado, 1969:63–66.)

One strand of romanticism, with political implications, is anarchism, a wish to do away with repressive government and live naturally, relying on the good potentialities of human nature.

Such has been the emotional source from which hippies and many activists of the New Left have drawn their inspiration, said

Roszak (1969:91)—not from Marx, who had abandoned the German romantic tradition; still less from Lenin, who was hard-headed, severely antiromantic; he would have had little to do with the expressive counterculture:

> We are not Utopians, we do not indulge in "dreams" of how best to do away *immediately* with all administration, with all subordination; these Anarchists' dreams, based upon a lack of understanding of the task of proletarian dictatorship, are basically foreign to Marxism, and, as a matter of fact, they serve but to put off the Socialist revolution . . . . (Lenin, 1932.)

By contrast, the revolutionary spirit of "the movement" in 1970 has been closer to millenarianism than hard-headed, practical revolution. Its underground press said—

> The contemporary theater is decadent because it has . . . broken away from the spirit of profound anarchy which is at the root of all poetry. . . . The Living Theater—doesn't want to perform for the privileged elite anymore . . . we don't want to perform in theaters anymore. Get out of the trap; the structure is crumbling. The Living Theater . . . is dividing into five cells. One cell is currently located in Paris, and the center of its orientation is political. Another is located in Berlin, and its orientation is environmental. A third is located in London, and its orientation is cultural. A fourth is on its way to India, and its orientation is Spiritual. A fifth cell is now forming in North America, and its orientation is political, environmental, cultural, and Spiritual. If this structure is to be transformed, it has to be attacked from many sides. This is what we are trying to do. (*Sunrise*, July 8, 1970.)

Millenarian movements have three classic characteristics, said Hobsbawm (1959): (1) "Profound and total rejection of the present, evil world, and a passionate longing for another and better one; in a word, revolution"; (2) chiliastic belief (that the world as it is will come to an end and be utterly remade, perhaps by a messiah); (3) "a fundamental vagueness about the actual way in which the new society will be brought about."

Millenarians are "not makers of revolution," but they expect it to come about by itself, and so they gather and watch "signs of the coming doom" (Hobsbawm, 1959:57–59). It is on point three, above, that contemporary romantic revolutionaries most resemble millenarians. They do not care much for the pedestrian machinery of practical politics. Their press comments disparagingly on a Fourth of July antiwar march:

> All the elements . . . were present again this time—marchers, picket signs, monitors, chants, cops, rally, speeches, tired feet and then back home. There was nothing the man in the street could label

"revolutionary politics." Nothing you might say was "exciting" or "heavy" or "moving" or "violent." It's all become ritualized and institutionalized. (*Sunrise*, July 8, 1970.)

In this context, romanticism reveals its reluctance to face up to banal political necessities. By contrast, Gandhi, for all his spirituality, was no romantic; he knew too well what had to be done, in terms of tired feet.

The romantic tactic is to reject prosaic means and either thrust at an enemy with hope of dramatically defeating him, or break with the frustrating scene and seek a better world. So, rebels of the 1970s have crusaded against various enemies—technology, bureaucracy, the "Establishment," racism, sexism—hoping for fulfillment by defeat of psychic repression as described by Marcuse (1964), Laing (1967), Roszak (1969). A picture of the enemy is provided by the following statements from the literature of the movement:

> We've all been brought up on *Tootle*, the children's tale in which baby locomotives are told to stay on the tracks no matter what; don't go off to look at the buttercups, don't take shortcuts to race with the stallions. The struggle is for each man to live up to his own conscience, even if it is under continual pressure to go to sleep. The whole world is being divided into those that are participating in the waking up and those that would massage and tranquilize. (Shapiro, 1968:44.)

> The entire pig punitive system is designed to rechannel your life energies along lines supportive of the prevailing, joy inhibited consumer oriented social system. (*Street Journal*, July 24, 1970.)

For those who felt discouraged about defeating banality in the system the alternative seemed to be escape. If one cannot build utopia, perhaps the next best thing is to "split":

> I'm planning to go around the world. . . . First, I'd like to reenact the Mayan sacrificial ceremonial rites of Chichen Itza in Mexico. Not that I want to be killed, but I'd like to know what it was like in one of those enormous wells that the maidens were thrown into. Also, I'd like to parachute into the jungles of the upper Amazon and work myself out, talking and living with the tribes along the way. Then I want to swim the Wedding of the Waters, where the Amazon and the Rio Negro join forces with such strength that for several miles they don't actually flow together. . . . Instead of just looking at people, I relate to them as I travel. . . . I become a part of the area in which I find myself. When I first began, my family and friends thought I was out of my head, that I was a "hippy" or a bum. Now that I make a living out of it—that I appear on television talk-shows and get written about—they see it differently. . . . What I hope is that it'll prove to people to do what they want, not what other people want for them. (Dennis, 1970.)

David Smith, quoted above, was in tune with the "Age of Aquarius." An unabashed romantic, though aged thirty-two, he was roaming the world, rapping with people, turning on, "doing his thing." He had already swum the Hellespont in forty-three minutes, cutting Lord Byron's time by half. He was engaged in a fight with banality, searching for personal meaning. Thousands were joining him, in one way or another.

All responses to banality, such as those noted above—sensory exploration by revelry, creativity, mysticism, and romantic crusading or escape—are likely to be found in a meaning-seeking movement, either concurrently or as tactical alternatives. Mysticism is politically significant only in the negative sense, of what it does not do, its refusal to "render unto Caesar." Romantics usually despise mystics for their passivity—belief in Tao rather than struggle, denial of self and will. Neither can agree with practical militants on such questions as whether to join the fight, work hard, emphasize style, take drugs, seek mystical fulfillments and shun action altogether. So, Abbie Hoffman was rebuked for being too politically oriented at a rock concert, by an acid head who struck him with a guitar for trying to take over the mike to give a political speech (W. Braden, 1970:276).

Though tactics cannot easily be predicted, meaning-seeking movements do begin their symbolic negotiations with the seeding of collectivities in a common mood. Let us look at such negotiations.

Moods and Seeding of Collectivities

A meaning-seeking movement takes shape out of the ground of unrest of collectivities searching for new experience—in this case moved by a feeling of oppressive banality and irrelevance, a tension of feeling that the clichés of present society must be transcended. It does this by wandering, by milling, by sensory exploration, by revelry and disorder, by fantasy together and separately, by romantic visions, by mystical and cultic experiences.

For one thing, there has been a "participation explosion" (Sennett, 1970a), a vogue of encounters and confrontations of all kinds. People have been talking more, doing more, moving more. Hitchhiking has become an enthusiasm among students: A veritable flood tide of young people poured into the roadsides in 1970, 25 percent more than the preceding year, according to a California Highway Patrol estimate. Reasons given were: a way to get in close touch with interesting people, seeking peace and a good time in ruggedly beautiful places, to get away from the "whole social garbage" of the older generation's world, and even a kind of evangelistic spirit about hitchhiking's being a way to "help mankind." Films like "Five

Easy Pieces" (1970) repeated the story of the homeless hero on the road looking for an elusive something. All this participatory activity expressed a mood; but people had yet to find out where they were going.

Various kinds of collectivities formed—crash pads, communes, cooperatives such as the Berkeley Food Conspiracy, and, of course, gatherings, "be-ins," and demonstrations. Gatherings of "the movement" were festive and disorderly. A university student newspaper reported—

> Extreme rowdiness, drinking and throwing firecrackers have caused State's summer movie program to be rescheduled. Movies, free of charge, and open to the public, had been shown every Sunday evening. . . . The decision came after the movies were bombarded by firecrackers, wine bottles were broken on concrete seats, beer cans were thrown at the stage, and the screaming of dozens of youths that sometimes drowned out the sound of the movie. . . . [The manager said] "people broke water mains and tore up storm drains. People were also there with chains and knives." Several near fights had started . . . most incidents were caused by people throwing firecrackers, and breaking bottles kept people from trying to watch the movies.

The rock musical "Hair" (Ragni and Rado, 1969:ix, 2.) told that the "tribes" were forming, establishing their own morality, ideology, way of life—dress, behavior, including the use of electricity and drugs. For costume they would use sandals, saris, loin cloths, beads, old military or band uniforms, flowers, incense, candles, oriental rugs. For drumming they would use pots, kettles, spoons, paper bags, or whatever. The "Tribe" was gathering to make its own new kinds of rhythm and harmony.

A new cultural mood was forming, which was partly hostility to established clichés, partly festivity (Cox, 1969b), and partly a kind of oceanic love about to swallow up those who were willing. It was, said "Hair" (Ragni and Rado, 1969:3): the dawning of an "Age of Aquarius" where there would be harmony, understanding, trust, sympathy, no more falsehoods, golden visions, the mind's true liberation; "then peace will guide the planets and love will steer the stars."

People were looking to crystal balls, soothsayers, and clairvoyants for spiritual clues.

Woodstock (discussed in Chapter 2) in 1969 was a signal gathering. Its songs told of:

> handsome Johnnie . . . marching to the Dunkirk War. . . . Korean War. . . . Viet Nam War. . . . Birmingham War / where we're going I cannot say, but we might even leave the U.S.A. / Speak out, you've got to speak out against the madness. . . . But don't try to get yourself elected. If you do you had better cut your hair. / Guess I'll set a course and go.

. . . Take a sister . . . by the hand. Lead her away from this foreign land. / People say because my daddy did these things . . . I must wear a tie and be the same. I gotta treat my brother wrong and kill him. . . . There's gotta be a change / I'm a thief—and I dig it! / I keep movin' on but I never found out why. . . . Don't expect any answers. / I get high . . . I get by with a little help from my friends. / Don't touch my bags if you please, Mr. Customs Man. / You must think Santa Claus weird, he has long hair and a beard; giving his presents for free. . . . A red suit, he's a communist. / . . . Why do police guys beat on peace guys? Well, come on mothers throughout the land, pack your boys off to Viet Nam. . . . Be the first one on your block to have your boy come home in a box. / You will see that all that's bright is not what's right. Look around. / . . . I want to take you higher. / I got a message that says "All the squares go home." / STAND, there's a cross for you to bear, things to go through if you're going anywhere, STAND, for the things you know are right; it's the truth that the truth makes them so uptight. (*Woodstock*, 1970.)

Here we see most of the themes of romanticism: rejection of a banal establishment, standing up to fight against the rest of the world, escaping to a better world, mind-expanding experience.

Countercollectivities in the early 1970s were, of course, also forming from the provocation of the newly visible strange collectivities. This was mentioned in Chapter 10 in connection with style rebellion. This is called the "seeding" of collectivities. Other writers call it "crystallization" (K. and G. Lang, 1961:44). From interaction, stimulated by catalyzers, moods and images form and symbols grow.

A metaphor from meteorology helps us here. Rain is not just a matter of cooling of air. The basic picture is that rising moisture-bearing air, if it cools enough, becomes saturated; if it cools beyond that point, it has reached the dewpoint, at which water condenses into tiny particles, usually called clouds or fog. With more cooling, the particles unite into drops so heavy that they fall as rain. But floating dust particles in the air help raindrop formation because vapor condenses more easily on them. So rainmakers "seed" the clouds with particles such as silver iodide, especially attractive to moisture. The particles are carried up into the clouds by smoke from generators moving along the ground. Now, applying this to systems, let us go back to Boulding's idea of supercooling (Chapter 7): Systems can be overloaded without going into a phase change. Moods, in our scheme, may represent the state of a system that is heavily strained, waiting for a crisis (trigger) or a "particle" to start things moving.

Popular leaders are the most obvious examples of "particles" that catch a mood at just the right time. For instance, Lindbergh turned a whole nation into a collectivity of fervent fans. Likewise,

Martin Luther King seeded the Black mood ("Now is the time") by the Montgomery bus boycott of 1955. At the "supercooling" stage, a feeling is present, but nobody comes out and says what it is or knows what to say. The leader who finally tells people what they feel may seem like a savior.

Seeding depends on a kind of match between the mood and leaders—an expression of ideas or programs that "catches on." At this time, groups and leaders seem to choose each other; thus, Erikson (1969:409) described the people who gathered about Gandhi. Agitators do not usually create moods, but draw on them; they find it easy to get results if a mood is already there. Alinski (1965), who is described as an "urban populist" and professional radical, said—

> When people talk about Back of the Yards today, some of them use lines like "rub resentments raw" to describe my organizing methods. Now, do you think when I went in there or when I go into a Negro community today I have to tell them that they're discriminated against? Do you think I go in there and get them angry? Don't you think they have resentments to begin with, and how much rawer can I rub them? . . . What happens when we come in? We say, "Look, you don't have to take this; there is something you can do about it. . . . But you have to have power to do it, and you'll only get it through organization. Because power just goes to two poles—to those who've got money, and those who've got people. You haven't got money, so your own fellowmen are your only source of strength . . . . (Alinski, 1965:45–46.)

At the right time, there is a sensitivity or leaning, perhaps generated by systemic strains. Collectivities grow. One laughs a little louder, applauds and contributes more, stays longer. Selective recruitment begins. If the mood persists, one comes again. *That* kind of collectivity draws bigger audiences, has more synergy for whatever task it undertakes. High points of synergy are expressive happenings (such as the Woodstock Festival, 1969) when an overflow of payoff occurs, sometimes also called "halo" effect, "group surplus," or conversion and religious grace. This is the moment of the sprouting or bursting of the seed (if we may change from meteorological to biological metaphor).

All of the seeding does not occur in one collectivity or occasion, of course, but again and again, with various inputs. Intellectuals, artists, and writers respond to the mood. Ideas "in the air" are picked up by sensitive and creative formulators (as we call innovators who give shape to moods), who pass them on to opinion leaders (highly exposed to media, with personal influence in peer groups). The point is that a mood is not merely an emotion condensed at one time—it is a *symbolic formation*, a complex of images and symbols, which spreads and grows through communication nets. For example, Paul Goodman's utopianism caught on in the 1960s, though his major utopian works (*Communitas* and *The Empire City*) were written in 1947, but the network was not ready to pick him up. In the 1960s he emerged as a middle-aged spokesman for the young. Without derogation of his contribution, one might say the mood picked him up. Do books make moods or do moods make books? In cases like Harriet Beecher Stowe's *Uncle Tom's Cabin* or the writings of Paine and Rousseau, books made the wheel spin visibly faster (though they would have had little influence if the wheel were not spinning in the first place).

Of course the kinds of collectivities seeded depend upon the mood and the kinds of "particle" that join with them: perhaps crowds gathering for riots and episodic protests (Rudé, 1964; Gusfield, 1970:108–120); the "love feasts," confession, and revivalism like those of early Methodism or the Oxford movement; the guru coming to the universities to draw students into attentive gatherings; the rapid formation of encounter groups, which were suddenly seen in 1970 to be "all over the place"; a novel, like *The Harrad Experiment* (Rimmer, 1966), exciting students of the Ivy League into thinking of new possibilities for group love. "Varoom!" said a magazine article in 1970, "the voice of the motorcycle is heard in the land," speculating as a motorcycling movement leaped into life, forming groups from teen-agers on minibikes to clubs of middle-class people on Harley Davidsons, and sustained by a series of inputs such as films with Steve McQueen in "The Great Escape" and Peter Fonda in "Easy Rider."

So, a ferment of various group activities made up that collectivity known as "The Movement" in 1970. A feeling for the activities is gained from this list in a street journal: feast fund raiser to help Black and Brown students go to Cuba; community meeting with the staff of the *Street Journal* to help get reinforcements; benefit dinner for Peace and Freedom Party; Women's Liberation rap groups; 25¢ lunch at the Wesley Foundation; judo classes at the Jewish Community Center; Free Clinic open every Monday; Ocean Beach Ecology Action at the Recreation Center; legal counseling at the Crisis Center; 25¢ spaghetti dinner at the Lutheran Center; draft counseling and workshop; draft coffee; military coffee; everyday felony arraignments, San Diego County Courthouse, treat yourself to a real experience; everyday Kundalini Yoga classes; film "An Inner Journey," with Fritz Perls; military counseling; DARE (drug counseling); Huelga-Grape Boycott; abortion counseling; Youth Lifeline; The Bridge (for runaways); Movement for a Democratic Military; GULF (information center for homophile community); Non-Violent Action Center; 5¢ dinners at Munchies:

A rookie checking a "noise complaint" at Munchies apparently got freaked and radioed for some help and for the supervisor. More cops came and sat around telling Moffet that the music was too loud and they had had many complaints so they were going to impound the amplifier that was sitting in front of Munchies. Supervisor Cambell cited ordinance 56–35 1b which says that one cannot play a musical instrument, radio, phonograph, etc., in such a way to disturb the peace of the neighboring inhabitants or play music with a louder volume than necessary for convenient hearing of voluntary listeners.

A lot of mumbling from the crowd about that, but the cops started to split. Cambell went to his car which was standing unattended in the alley and discovered someone had tampered with the valve stem on the tire and some air got out. Cambell marched back to Munchies, entered, and arrested Moffet. He wouldn't state the charge until people started becoming hostile and then he rattled off the perennial "disturbing the peace" bit.

Some of the cops . . . seem to be alright; . . . . But the rookies and dudes . . . act like pigs and treat people like pigs. They think they can hassle people until the problem goes away, but what they don't understand is that they are part of the problem. The more they come around, the more pissed people are going to be until talk becomes action for that is our only protection from pigs. When cops act like pigs they will be treated like pigs. (*Street Journal*, San Diego, 1970.)

Our conclusion at this point is that we can tell something about the mood of a movement from the collectivities that form in its early stages, but the goals and course remain ambiguous because movements are pluralities of collectivities that have certain problems to work out through dialectical and practical relations. At such a stage, movements flow; they do not have fixed characteristics or course, but can become, within broad limits, "anything." It would be difficult to say, for example, that the movement described above would be ultimately politically revolutionary, or religiously cultic, or merely expressive gatherings concerned with the kicks of the moment.

It is useful here to list some of the main kinds of collectivities that might be formed in the early seeding stages of a movement. *Crowds*, including mobs, riots, protests, panics, and expressive crowds have already been treated in Chapter 3; likewise, *contagions* (hysterical, hostile, enthusiastic) in Chapter 6; *publics*, as collectivities focused on news and united by talk processes, in Chapter 8.

Audiences might be defined as collectivities engrossed in vicarious experiences—sometimes called shows, dramas, meetings—which (unlike the talk processes of the public) have the character of a collective dream, a dramatic role or fantasy in which people are participating together. *Followings* are collectivities of people

with enthusiastic interests, commonly called *fans*, who can be relied on to turn out for events, meetings, and persons when their
interest is involved. Followings merge almost imperceptibly into
cults when the interest of followers becomes so serious that it
may be spoken of as devotion; relationships become more intense
along lines, such as commitment to a belief or cause, conversion
(deeply changed personality), loyal fellowship, ritual, and the role
of the devotee (Klapp, 1969:138–210). Followings gather around
celebrities and leaders, and there is a point of devotion at which
the following becomes a cult and its object a *hero*, as we may
designate an idealized personage with many devoted admirers who
identify with him; or another way of defining hero cult is to say it
is a group that gets its meaning from one man.

A number of collectivities in social movements may be called
conflict groups because they get their meaning from a fight against
an enemy. Chief among these are: *rebellions*, collectivities that
defy established authority; *secret societies*, which because of conflict with the dominant group go underground and build their morale
on the sharing of a secret and a certain amount of conspiracy (Simmel, 1950:345–376); *sects*, collectivities whose fight with the rest
of society is largely in the realm of cult (faith, ritual); and *crusades*,
collectivities that have a sense of militance, righteousness, uphill
struggle, fighting evil, unwillingness to compromise, and evangelism
(Klapp, 1969:270). Sometimes it is difficult to draw the line between
a crusade and a sect, as can be seen by comparing groups like
Jehovah's Witnesses, Black Muslims, and the John Birch Society;
however, the sect has an other-worldly orientation, whereas the
crusade finds in this world the evils it wishes to fight. In any event,
social movements have to form what sociologists call *voluntary
associations*. These are the groups that people form to share and
achieve common interests and which range from recreational clubs
to labor unions and political parties. Such associations can, of
course, become cultlike, sectarian, crusadelike, take on the features
of audiences, and so on, depending on the negotiations they go
through.

Because popular moods are the emotional weather favoring what
collectivities are likely to do, we need to study such "tides in the
affairs of men." Expressive behavior often signalizes the mood
people are in: kinesics of daily life, such as temper outbursts, facial expressions, clowning. Lasswell (1966) proposed content analysis of often-sung hymns as a clue to the international "climate" and
what political actions are likely to occur. Likewise, styles coming
in and out of fashion (Chapter 10) are important indicators. Words
may have the advantage of explicitly stating moods in symbols such

as slogans, lyrics, prayers, mantras; but what people *do*, rather than what they say, will probably tell us more about moods—once we can interpret the actions they portend.

How Movements Find Meaning

The symbolic task of a meaning-seeking movement is to transform a mood, into a symbolic reality (Chapter 5). The transformation occurs by negotiations in which activities, experiences, gestures, names, and concepts are put to people as proposals, selected and reinforced by feedback that repeats and forms them through networks as reliable communication events. The growth of the network and its communication events is the growth of the movement. Institutionalization of such a network transforms the old society or creates a new one. Because so many of such negotiations in the mass are anonymous and interpersonal (rather than objective media content), it is hard to trace them until they emerge as a structure (ideology, organized force, party, underworld system, etc.) that can be dealt with politically. But politics tends to be late in recognizing symbols.

Negotiations of a meaning-seeking movement have purposes different from those of a practical movement, the main difference being that they aim at construction of *images* and realizing *experiences* rather than physical results. The focus is on meaning, spirit, personal fulfillment. An important distinction here is that a practical movement may focus on an image to manipulate it, but a meaning-seeking movement does so for its own sake.

We can here distinguish briefly some of the main general lines of symbolic negotiation: (1) ideology building, (2) expressive activities, (3) symbolic formation of mystiques, (4) building morale and "we" feeling, (5) growing special languages, (6) creative interactions and encounters, (7) finding heroes, (8) public drama to draw in the mass, (9) conflict as negotiation of morale, and (10) ritual and cultic development.

The most obvious negotiable development is *ideology building*. When intellectuals spin out an idea that provides a picture of reality for many people, it becomes an "ism." Philosophy may be abstruse, but a simplified version can become ideology. Historians have noted such a development in many theories that became a vehicle of life's meaning to their followers: scholasticism, Freudianism, Marxism, natural rights, laissez-faire, Darwinism, positivism, existentialism (to mention a few) are notable examples. As a movement takes over the theory, a kind of theology grows up; followers claim expertness in an abstruse philosophy that perhaps the originator never thought of. Often there comes a point at which, if the author could be brought back, he would repudiate the doctrine that has grown up in his name.

We are concerned here, however, mostly with the less rational and verbal tasks of meaning-seeking, such as *expressive activities* in the early 1970s. The "Age of Aquarius" was awash with festivals, dances, clowning, and "revolution for the hell of it" (Free, 1968). Costumery had become psychedelic; fashion designers and stage directors, said *Life*, had "switched on the footlights, and all the world became a hippie stage." Audience participation became the thing in entertainment. At a theatrical production called "Paradise Now," a drama critic in the audience, caught by the enthusiasm, astounded the nearly nude cast by totally disrobing and joining them. We can understand, however, that besides the sheer fun of letting go (catharsis), there is for expressive movements the symbolic goal of "realizing Paradise" and embodying it in visions (however incompletely expressed in concepts) and repeating it in performances that can become ritual (Klapp, 1969:116–137).

An important question arises at this point: Does a given form of expressive activity *move* a movement to new stages, or does it drain off its energy by a safety-valve function (Chapter 7)? For example, the "free universities" that burgeoned during the 1960s, offering an outlet from the psychic restrictions of the bureaucratic curriculum, seemed to be dying by the end of the decade because they had become legitimized, accepted by the universities, supported by grants, and because administrators were channeling students into "constructive" study programs. A national vice president of STS commented—

> At best, they had no effect. But it is more likely that they had the effect of strengthening the existing system. How? First of all, the best of our people left the campus, enabling the existing university to function more smoothly, since the "trouble makers" were gone. Secondly, they gave liberal administrators the rhetoric, the analysis and sometimes the manpower to co-opt their programs and establish . . . "experimental" colleges inside of, although quarantined from, the existing educational system. (Lauter and Howe, 1970:93.)

A similar question arises in the history of religious revivalism. Does the revivalist provide a true awakening of faith, perhaps a sectarian movement; or do his Jeremiads and calls to repentance merely drain off discontent and become co-opted and embraced by the religious establishment? (Goen, 1970.) Such a view, putting "free universities" into a category with college "pep" rallies, revivalism, and the "churches of the oppressed" (Pope, 1942; Lanternari, 1963) suggests that expressive activity might work as the "opiate" theory that Lenin supported—to retard rather than help movements change a society.

However, the proper task of expressive activity in a movement, beyond sheer catharsis, is to *build mystiques*: symbolic formations of images, sentiments, and symbols by which the vision of the movement can be brought to life, whether in ritual (mystic symbols, horoscopes, mantras, and so on) or eschatology (picture of the future). We see the romantic eschatology of the "Age of Aquarius" brought into being on the stage: "Hair" invites us to take a spaceship to another galaxy, the planet, "Exanaplanetooch":

EXANAPLANETOOCH*
A PLANET IN ANOTHER GALAXY . . .
A PLACE WHERE ALL THE PEOPLE LOOK LIKE ME
A PLANET WHERE THE AIR IS PURE
THE RIVER WATERS CRYSTAL BRIGHT
THE SKY IS GREEN
AND IN THE NIGHT
TWELVE GOLDEN MOONS
PROVIDE THE LIGHT . . . .
SWIM IN THE WATER
DRINK FROM THE RIVERS
TOTAL BEAUTY TOTAL HEALTH
EV'RYMAN'S AN ARTIST
    AND A SCIENTIST-PHILOSOPHER
NO GOVERNMENT AND NO POLICE
NO WARS NO CRIME NO HATE
JUST HAPPINESS AND LOVE
FULFILLMENT OF EARTH MAN'S POTENTIAL
AND AMBITION
WITH EVER-WIDENING HORIZONS
EXANAPLANETOOCH . . . .

Sheila, I'm not going into the Army tomorrow. My people are sending a space ship for me and I'm going back to my home. Will you come with me? (Ragni and Rado, 1969:191–192.)

Cox (1969a:113) compares the wish image of the new militants for a "participative society" to the messianic hopes of Israel and early Christianity. The need is not so much to intellectualize as to construct vivid images that will overcome meaningless banality and negative utopia (Keniston, 1963), to help the movement see where it is going. Thus, Black nationalists sought to visualize a "separate, free, independent nation for Black people" in five Southern states, starting with purchasing land somewhere in Mississippi on which to build a city for Black people and encouraging them to emigrate there, according to announcement of the Third National Conference on Black Power, 1968. Sooner or later, an expressive utopia-building movement reaches a fork in the road between practical politics and millenarian eschatology, the latter being especially the symbolic burden of cultlike groups. Quick arithmetic will show that there are, broadly speaking, nine possibilities for locating the image of the grand fulfillment.

1. It may be conceived as possible and imperative to build a new society now (soon) or return to a golden age of the past or seek a distantly future utopia, requiring hard work or a historical trend (historicism; Popper, 1952) to take us there.

2. Then there is the choice between an earthly or an other-world plane of fulfillment.

3. If earthly, there is the choice between having the fulfillment here or somewhere else geographically (emigration).

4. A fourth classic line of symbolic negotiation for meaning-seeking movements is to develop—through images and through interaction—*morale* and *"we" feeling.* Somehow or other, scattered collectivities must reach collective self-awareness as a movement, as happened at the Woodstock Festival, already mentioned. It was the aim of energetic agitation by Women's Lib in the early 1970s to make females aware of a common grievance against males. Beyond mere "we" feeling is morale, the loyalty and commitment to cause, which helps the movement to carry on, as in the fanatical commitment to "La Causa" in the grapepickers' strike. Cesar Chavez said—

> We're an action movement. We keep moving night and day. I'd feel complimented if you called me a fanatic. The only ones who make things change are fanatics. If you're not a fanatic around here, you can't cut it. (*Newsweek*, Aug. 10, 1970:59.)

Here, however, morale has a practical value, rather being—as it so often is—for its own sake.

5. Aiding the symbolic task of morale and "we" feeling is the *growing up of special languages* (lingos, argots) that crystallize esoteric and ecstatic meanings into concepts making visible worlds of experience for new recruits and becoming a memory for the members. A meaning-seeking movement needs a richer and more expressive language than does a practical movement, which can be content with terms used in established society. The former must capture elusive experiences and goals, build a fabric of togetherness, and also possibly have secrecy of language to act as a barrier to outsiders. Live as the lilies of the field, said early Christian leaders; let "thine eye be single." What strange words! Likewise, the counterculture has a strange new lingo: relate, turn on or off,

grooving, one's thing, blow one's mind, vibrations, cultures of life and death; trip, bummer or good; split, freak out, cop-out, hassle, busted. So, in a changing world, many kinds of lingos are needed to share new realities: ethnic, underworld, "gay," "hip," surfing, motorcycling—here is how a "chopper" (a motorcycle with a small front wheel on a long raked fork, made popular in the film "Easy Rider") is described in chopper language:

> A chopper is a hog or other garbage wagon stripped, chopped, and fitted with a springer, a knuckle head engine, and a sissy bar.

Only the cognoscenti, knowing such language and the world it represents, can draw together with the "we" feeling of potential comrades in a social movement.

6. Another source of meaning for movements is creative *interaction and encounter*, as people realize intense experiences of comradeship, proving themselves in the eyes of others, in group confessions, "love feasts," disciples' relationships, and other kinds of interactions not easy in ordinary life. Such was provided by the Encounter Group (Human Potentials) Movement, which, introduced as sensitivity training in 1947, grew rapidly into a middle-class movement during the period 1967–1970, spread as new therapy and parlor game coast-to-coast—but mostly in California and particularly at Esalen, the headquarters. It offered a cafeteria of interpersonal experiences—by discussion, sensory awakening, gestalt awareness training, touching and hugging one another, and so on, which to some outsiders looked like people wallowing in their own emotions. Peripatetic gurus went from one center to another like circuit riders; converts became leaders and set up their own encounter groups. By 1970, it had become a national pastime, and for some a passion. A typical experience was for people to break down and confess the emptiness of their lives and receive consolation from others. It seemed a commentary on the "joyless way of life" of American institutions. It gave personal meaning, though there was doubt whether its contribution was that of therapy, religious cult, or merely another fad that would perhaps make Americans more mobile and impervious to intimacy than ever (Howard, 1970; J. Mann, 1970; Shepard and Lee, 1970). However, such interaction, though it resembled that of the primary group, was basically anonymous and offered some of the freedom to abandon identity, a characteristic already discussed in relation to individuals in a crowd.

7. It is possible also for a movement to get meaning from a leader. A seventh line of negotiation is *making heroes*, not just leaders but individuals so admired that the mass draws inspiration and meaning from their image. A meaning-seeking movement uses a hero as a symbol of its style and role, and as a vicar of its busi-

ness. Enacting such images is the hero's work. The movement may need a splendid performer or other exemplar of its life style (as, for example, the rock movement's Jimi Hendrix, Janis Joplin, Jim Morison, Beatles, Rolling Stones), a defender or champion to push and protect the cause; martyrs if need be (such as Angela Davis or Timothy Leary), or possibly a clown or jester to liven the activity with revelry and put down enemies comically (Abbie Hoffman, Jerry Rubin, Ken Kesey). Feedback from such performances builds morale, aids clarity, and solidifies commitment to goal and style.

Perhaps the crucial function of a hero for movements is to boost the following from small "seeds" (such as leaders and agitators usually create) *to a large public following* attracted by his colorful image.

Figures such as Joan of Arc or Sacco and Vanzetti can raise small collectivities to enormous mass followings. The hero's role embodies a value realization that is a vague mystique until everybody can see it and join by public identification: "I am a Gaullist . . . Castroite, etc." From the public following, new "seeds" (fan clubs, parties, and so on) are formed by the actions of the hero in a continuous interaction. The mass behavior of hero worship has been described elsewhere (Wecter, 1941; Klapp, 1949b, 1969). The main symbolic contributions of the hero to movements are morale for the cause (from loyalty to the hero) and the vicarious identity that followers get from the hero's role. Without heroes, a movement is practically and meaningfully weak; with the right kind of heroes, such as martyrs, it is hard to say where it will stop. The hero's input is like a rolling snowball: He finds himself in a critical role; then his followers find themselves in him. Their devotion pushes him on to further roles.

8. To understand the impact of heroes, one must consider the eighth factor, drama. *Public drama* has an enormous capacity to confer meaning on social movements, through identification, which is not quite the same as information ordinarily conceived. By their dramatic roles, heroes and martyrs get sympathy—and villains, hatred—which are mystiques in the minds of their followers, not simply rational conclusions from facts and issues. So, Lincoln and Booth acquired a powerful mystique from the drama of assassination, especially the fact that it happened on Friday (Basler, 1935). A humbling drama can give a leader a democratic mystique. Others might earn sympathy by being regarded as the "underdog" hero, "stabbed in the back," Promethean genius, "great man" in tune with destiny, and so on. Martin Luther King expressed some surprise at what took shape from the fact that in Montgomery, Alabama, a Black woman had tired feet on December 1, 1955, and refused to stand up on a bus so that a white could sit down:

If you had asked me the day before our protest began whether any action could or would have been taken by the Negroes, I'd have said no. Then all of a sudden, unity developed. (*Time*, Feb. 18, 1957:18.)

Powerful dramas can bring about role reversals in which "villains" become "heroes" and powerful people seem fools, and so on, in an alchemy that has been analyzed elsewhere (Klapp, 1964b). Therefore, movements trying to grow—especially meaning-seeking ones—want publicity; but what they really need is not just attention to their movements but also *dramas* of appropriate kinds that will confer hero roles on them, villain roles on their enemies, and a plot pattern on the action in which followers can believe and the public at large can perceive.

9. Finally, we consider *conflict as negotiation of morale.* It is regrettably true that conflict creates meaning, that is, it is not merely entropic. Collectivities can derive their meaning from the image of an enemy. The villain, not the hero, is the star of this process. As we all know, introducing a threatening outsider or pitting people against one another makes life more interesting. Professional sports seem to thrive when players and crowd become boorish, bad-tempered, unsporting; players foul one another; fans scream and call names, and players return the compliment. A basketball player said in Madison Square Garden, after the game ended with thousands of fans chanting obscenities at him: "That's cool. I got fined this year for making one obscene gesture at a crowd. Tonight I had 10,000 animals making obscene gestures at me." Such an example illustrates how conflict gives meaning to a collectivity. Eric Hoffer (1951) said—

> Hatred is the most accessible and comprehensive of all unifying agents. It pulls . . . the individual away from his own self . . . . Mass movements can rise and spread without belief in a God, but never without belief in a devil. Usually the strength in a mass movement is proportionate to the vividness and tangibility of its devil. (Hoffer, 1951:89–90.)

What the image of an enemy contributes is not just interest in a cause, of course, but morale—a clearer conception of the goal and importance of winning—and enhanced sense of self as part of "we" (courage, self-sacrifice, virtue in fighting for the group). A collectivity that derives most of its morale from such a process is called a *conflict group* (Park and Burgess, 1924:50). The Ku Klux Klan, said Allen (1931:82–86), lacked heroes in its early days, but had plenty of villains from the beginning. The late George Lincoln Rockwell, American Nazi leader, was not much of a hero, but he had lettered on the back of his bus: "We *DO* hate race mixing. Lincoln Rockwell's HATEBUS." Lowenthal and Guterman (1949) analyzed themes used by agitators in developing conflict movements. *Crusades* are perhaps the most important kind of conflict movement connected with social reform, the crusaders conceiving themselves to be in a righteous struggle to defeat an enemy for a noble cause (Klapp, 1969:257–311). Even a religious movement such as Christianity has been unable to get through history without the image of crusade against a Satanic adversary (Rudwin, 1931). Gladstone (1959) described the (dubious) advantages to America in morale of a "cold war" crusade aaginst Soviet Russia as the enemy.

Needless to say, our main example of the counterculture—the present meaning-seeking movement—has had much to stimulate its growth: images like repressive bureaucracy and police action, the Chicago Democratic Convention of 1968, the Kent State and My Lai massacres, defoliation and pollution of environments, all have given it impetus. It has carried on its fight both within and outside the political process, building images that have influenced changes in, if not reversed, the established definitions.

Finally, among the time-tested lines of meaning development for movements are *ritual and cult*. Cult uses ritual to heighten the intensity of a social value until it becomes almost, if not quite, religious. But cult, as defined here goes beyond religion as ordinarily conceived, taking in play, work, education, food, war, science— almost anything that people get serious enough about. Six criteria help us to decide whether a movement is becoming cultic.

1. How intense is the enthusiasm toward the central value or purpose—is it reverence, piety, devoutness, faith, loyalty, all-out commitment?
2. Is there mystique—mysteries, esoteric knowledge—which only initiates or advanced members can share?
3. Are such feelings and mystiques shared and celebrated by ritual?
4. Is the member's life devoted to the central value by the regular performance of ritual?
5. Is there in the movement emphasis on identity change or a redemption —satori, nirvana, enlightenment, salvation, rebirth, conversion?
6. Does the movement have the solidarity of a fellowship or brotherhood?

The more such qualities are developed, the more cultlike a movement is. Having listed such characteristics, it is hardly necessary to say how deep and rich the meaning given by a cultic movement can be, supplying (as it often does) the key to life's mysteries and purpose and an identity to the individual that is so deep it may be believed to survive even death (Klapp, 1969:116–210).

With regard to the counterculture, it is plain that cultic development plays a large part in this movement. To transcend banality by ritual seems to be the main reason for the boom of occultism, spiritualism, astrology, ESP, tarot-card reading, palmistry, graphology, phrenology, numerology, witchcraft, satan worship, Hare Krishna chanting, yoga, Zen—and a proliferation of gurus, domestic and imported. Jasper zodiac plates sell for $25.00; across the counter a horoscope portrait and six months' forecast sells for $5.00; two hundred or more new books on astrology are being published each year, some selling as many as eight million copies yearly; an estimated 10,000 full-time and 175,000 part-time astrologers practice their art; and 1,750 daily newspapers carry horoscope columns (Dennis, 1969). Scientology (dianetics) offers to explore your unconscious mind by a gadget resembling a simplified lie detector. Such esoterica put a meaning-seeking movement at the opposite end of the scale from rational, practical search, which pays off in more prosaic currency. Meaning-seeking movements have a different kind of work and different kind of payoff in the social order than do practical movements. They function not for political and economic goals but to reduce systemic banality; or, as Ayn Rand (1971:75) said of romanticism, to make life more interesting. Perhaps this is the meaning of the advice of Norman O. Brown, "that the real fight is not the political fight but to put an end to politics" (Roszak, 1969: 118).

So a meaning-seeking movement can assess its gains in various sectors—ideology, expressive catharsis, mystiques, morale and "we" feeling, special language, creative encounters, heroes, public drama, negotiation of morale by conflict, and ritual and cultic development—in terms that may, or may never, become political.

Dialectical Negotiation of Movements

Like style search, the symbolic negotiations of meaning-seeking movements are dialectical, that is, involving interchange of views and shifting of positions and tactics by parties who are communicating, cooperating, competing, or opposing one another. The "seeding" of collectivities is a dialectic with the highly problematic responses of mass audiences. Later stages of movements, though more political and concerned with organizational development, still consist of efforts at communication, offers and deals, sorties and retreats, coalitions and betrayals, thrusts and counterthrusts, the outcome of which is highly contingent—that is, depend on circumstances of the moment and what the other just did. New conceptions of reality and rules of the game are continually evolving (Chapter 5). So, it is plainly not easy—perhaps it is impossible—to chart movements into regular stages. Surely a conception such as Marx's—of a dialectic between a ruling class "thesis" and a working class "antithesis," making possible distant predictions—is crudely unrealistic (Mills, 1962:129–131; Popper, 1952). Nor have later social scientists such as Brinton (1952) or Hopper (1950) had much better luck. Once one sees that the growth of a movement is dialectical in the negotiative sense, one sees that it can be neither a linear thrust (of input) nor a programmed growth like that of a seed.

Tactical Give and Take

We can illustrate from the cultural rebellion of America in the early 1970s some aspects of thrust and counterthrust which offer tactical options for the course of a movement.

1. New collectivities—especially those that seek meaning—are likely to make pressures and demands that are irritating, even offensive, to the *status quo.* Rock music, from the time of Chubby Checker and Elvis Presley to the mammoth concerts overwhelming communities in the 1970s illustrates this.

2. Unfriendly reaction by the *status quo* to the activities of the new collectivity toughen it, give it morale in the sense of a cause, and help it to develop tactics. So, the advocates of rock saw the "sonic boom" of electronic music as an "armor" against criticism. The lyrics of the musical "Hair" advised turning the amplifiers up higher, to encase oneself in "sonic armor" against being enchained and brainwashed by straight society (Ragni and Rado, 1969:123–25). Unfriendly authorities come to be seen as enemies. Followers of the unwelcome new life style develop warm, close feelings among "brothers" with common cause. Members say—

> They don't dig us outside, and they send the pigs down to impose an alien culture on us. . . . It makes you feel bad, you know, to have some pig shining a light in your eyes. . . . Like I had a burglary, I wouldn't call the cops. They'd be looking around. Maybe they'd drop a joint on the floor and then take me in. Cops are the enemy. . . . "Let's go hassle the pukes," they say. That's what they call us. "The pigs versus the pukes," a deputy who busted me kept saying. He was grinning. It was like a game. (Nevin, 1970:45.)

"Hassling" the authorities develops standard tactics. Rioting and other violent activities escalate and develop in patterns of tactics that are clearly negotiative (Janowitz, 1969; K. and G. Lang, 1970). Dramatic confrontations pay off in morale and style for the movement (Klapp, 1964a:66–100). Michael Lewis analyzed how American Blacks developed patterns of protest in response to "denial of the dream," helping them to find themselves as a political group (Gusfield, 1970:155–189). So, movements, as it were, find themselves by how they respond to the responses made by the *status quo.*

3. *Countermovements* are also sharpened by vigorous activity disturbing the *status quo*. Hardly had the movement against pollution gained momentum before "backlash" views were being expressed by groups like the D.A.R. against ecoactivism, "One of the subversive element's last steps," which, having "gone after the military and the police . . . now they're going after our parks and playgrounds" (*Time*, Aug. 3, 1970:42). On university campuses, left wing followers of SDS sometimes found themselves neatly balanced by YAF (Young Americans for Freedom). Thus, the "conversation" of a new movement with the *status quo* becomes a conversation also with countermovements, which add to the uncertainty of the outcome (as when that strange hybrid called National Socialism answered the challenge of the left in Germany).

4. *Acculturation* is part of the give-and-take. The "establishment," in the 1970s has readily taken up the psychedelic colors of the hippies. A curious part of this dialectic is that even some conservatives accept labels put on them by rebels and attempt to laugh them off or make countersymbols of them, as when police in some communities accepted the name "pig," adopted porcine mascots, and reinterpreted the letters to be an abbreviation for "pride, integrity and guts"; or in Los Angeles, a conservative publisher put out a magazine called *Square,* measuring 11 by 11 inches, speaking out for patriotism and law and order.

Another form of acculturation has been commercial exploitation of the counterculture in films and the like, which purport to interpret the new values to audiences. Roszak (1969:70) found a threat to the counterculture in such co-optation by the establishment—middle-class swingers imitating "flower children" and frequenting rock clubs, a "flirtation with the offbeat that inevitably distorts the genuineness of the phenomenon." Thus, many kinds of communication have been occurring among opposing movements. What message is sent when hippies respond to invective with song and bedecking opponents with flowers, beads, fruit, and gifts; or protesters try to levitate the Pentagon by magic?

5. Perhaps these trends indicate accommodation, a growing recognition by both sides of *rules of the game*. Even riots, crime, and arson became more predictable as a riot-making subculture grew up in America (McCall, 1970). Guidelines for protest were drawn up, and Americans began to learn what was permitted in street demonstrations (helped by Supreme Court decisions that clarified points, such as no permits are required for street-corner speeches). Among the long-haired types viewed as troublemakers, police tolerated— even liked—"Jesus freaks," who called to hippies for repentance on street corners. They could do their thing without interference.

Thrust against Safety Values

A considerable part of such negotiation may be called *thrust* against the safety valves of the system. (See Chapter 7.)

One example is the soothing impact of media versus irritations of the counterculture. This concerns the relative effect of soap opera, love stories, athletic entertainment, comedy, and the like on audiences of magazines, film, radio, and television—whether, for example, the media keep their audiences glued to the message or send them muttering to write protest letters or attend meetings.

Another example is the way in which the member of a counterculture is continually being "courted" by established institutions, which would "buy him off" by entertainment, careers, promises of political participation, church membership, marriage, rewards of one kind or another, if they could. The presidential commissions on student unrest and on pornography in 1970 were examples of such bargaining—the latter plainly unsuccessful, since the Administration repudiated its findings. The rebel may feel that he has to resist the blandishments of institutions to keep his meaning or the integrity of his search. For this reason, Jerry Rubin rejected legitimate economic rewards of the system by adopting a romantic philosophy of looting:

> All money represents theft. To steal from the rich is a sacred and religious act. To take what you need is an act of self-love, self-liberation. While looting, a man to his own self is true. (*Time*, June 22, 1970: 52.)

The romantic rebel feels that accepting the terms of the establishment is a kind of psychic repression, which Marcuse (1964:71–79) called "Happy Consciousness." Roszak (1969:250, 252–253) saw a danger in the programmed comfort of technology. The meaning-seeking movement thrusts against the safety valves of the system, which act like a net to capture its wildness and protest. The rituals of established culture are constantly buffering, cushioning, in a sense seducing the romanticism, mysticism, and creativity of meaning-seekers—seducing them into comfortable arrangements with things as they are: for example, an angry writer doing TV scripts, commercialism threatening the artist, the guru leaving the austerity of his hermitage to become a celebrity, yoga becoming an adjunct to a health and beauty spa, occultism becoming Freemasonry, "Jesus freaks" being invited into church, romantic revolutionaries being called on to support candidates and take part in electoral rituals. So, banality threatens to triumph over the Movement.

Since a large part of mass media today functions as safety

valves, a meaning-seeking movement has to meet this continual input, which, like waves crashing on a beach and leveling sand
castles, batters the fragile meanings of the counterculture.

We need to know more about how media images are negotiated
with mass audiences, especially in that elusive area of vicarious
experience. For example, what proportion of an audience sees char-
acters of a drama as heroes or villains? With which figures are
viewers closely identified? (Klapp, 1948, 1965.) TV commercials do
sell products, but no one knows how many viewers are put off and
alienated by these same messages. What proportion of images are
tension and unrest producing/reducing? How many outbursts or
other expressive activities can be attributed to images generated
by media? What is the credibility of media images? What proportion
of image output by the media is experienced as banal? And by what
parts of the public? If we knew answers to some of these questions,
we might then know which images are serving on the whole as
safety valves, diversive, cathartic, aggressive. The truth, it seems,
is that we often do not know whether the symbols being negotiated
by mass media are serving as safety valves or are driving people to
desperation.

Major Response Strategies

Sooner or later a growing movement reaches the major threshold of presenting its message to the public in a systematic way and
developing the secondary group organization to coordinate its large
membership. Students for a Democratic Society, for example, found
itself by 1969 with over 7,000 dues-paying members on 300 campuses, publishing *New Left Notes* with monthly circulation of 30,000;
yet its formal organization was vague and it did not really know
who its members were. A leader said—

> What's a member? You don't take a pledge . . . You just act accord-
> ing to your personal convictions. Maybe we've got 60, give or take 40.

Another, denying that there was any conspiracy in radical student
action, said—

> It's like flying saucers. Everybody wants to believe they exist, but
> the proof is hard to come by. More than anything it's their outrage that
> holds radical students together.

But organization remained formally leaderless, and meetings were
often chaotic examples of "participatory democracy" (Holmstrom,
1969). Even less organized was the larger movement, which relied
mainly on hundreds of underground newspapers to inform and co-

ordinate the fluid activities of its members. But a political party, or any organization to represent it as a whole—beyond momentary coalitions—"the movement" did not have.

Politicization refers to greater use by a movement of organized political and economic means and greater involvement with the control machinery of society in order to achieve its goals. This covers a broad range of activities: legitimate, such as votes, lobbies, petitions, protests, boycotts, strikes; and illegitimate, such as rebellion, civil disobedience, and guerilla tactics.

For a practical movement such as the consumer crusade of Ralph Nader, choice of means is merely a tactical question. But for a meaning-seeking movement, it can be a major turning of the road. The celebrated break in 1971 between Eldridge Cleaver, as a leader of Black Power, and Timothy Leary, psychedelic guru, showed the sharpness of such a turning. In effect, Cleaver said: We activists do not want the mind-expanding experiences of your drug culture. But Leary proposed to withdraw from the "games" of money and power seeking, including those of proletarian revolution; drugs were one nonpolitical means. Though both groups were "against the establishment," they simply could not harmonize their methods and goals: Leary wanted peace of mind; Cleaver wanted a piece of the action.

Many members of a meaning-seeking movement prefer to stay out of politics and devote themselves to expressive, romantic, or mystical activities requiring little political power—at most, toleration and the legal right to be let alone. Their battle is with banality in some form. They may fear that the prosaic machinery of politics will involve them in the very banality they are trying to avoid. Within the movement, debate persists between activists recommending politicization and mystics and style rebels who favor dropping out and avoiding politics altogether. Marxists rebuke dropouts for shunning the revolutionary task.

So in the early 1970s the Movement flowed and eddied, without fixed course, without political commitment—like water from a hose lying on the lawn. It flowed and paused, not knowing quite where to go.

> Underground writing stews in its own underground these days—an underground of self-examination . . . a mood of uncertainty seems to hang. . . . The Movement—the young extrovert of the '60's—is going introspective in the '70's: trying to get its bearings, trying to find where it's at. . . . The Movement doesn't know what's happening now . . . some mysterious momentum—some excitement so intense as to pass for purpose—has come to an end. The Movement has gone about as far as spontaneity and revolutionary gameplaying will take it. Saying "Right on!" doesn't make everything work any more.

> Trashing and flowers, peace symbols and clenched fists, oom chants and Rubin and Hoffman—the novelties of guerilla theater are wearing off. The ultimate crisis of the official culture, the crisis of boredom, has fallen upon the counterculture as well. (Maddocks, 1971.)

The main concern remained to find and do their "thing," and not to be captured or co-opted by the establishment.

For a movement that chooses to grope—or, it may be to beg—outside the gates of the Citadel without either attacking politically or entering as workers and traders, the main options seem to be (1) *style rebellion*, using symbols and gestures for self-assertion, defying authority and established taste; (2) a *parasitic* or *symbiotic modus vivendi* within the system, such as vagrancy and begging; and (3) *withdrawal* or *separatism* as a collective move.

An argument for radical turning away was given by a member of the Movement:

> Today, I became one of the New People. I've had it with your cities. An article I read today did it. Seems a federal survey found that toxic mercury is poisoning the water of fourteen states. That's all they've looked at so far . . . besides the mercury, there are detergents in all the rivers . . . the air in Southern California is so bad that trees are dying and people are starting to. Sixty top doctors and scientists at UCLA have told residents to move out of the smoggiest parts of L.A. So, as soon as I can get some friends together, it's back to the earth. We won't contribute to the pollution scene anymore. We'll be far away from the cities, where there's still fresh air and water. My parents are against this commune idea, of course. They are Old People. They live in the suburbs; they drive the cars that cause the smog. . . . I hope you print this, so that other kids will take off and form communes like we're going to. (Letter to Editor, *Los Angeles Times*, Aug. 2, 1970.)

For some, a failure of human relations was felt to justify leaving the established structure (Otto, 1970). Reflecting such thinking, there was rapid growth of a movement trying out radically new forms of communal, monastic, and family living. The movement developed its own journal, *Modern Utopian*, listing hundreds of new communes in the United States. Of course, such experiments are not new in America (Nordhoff, 1875; Holloway, 1951; Hine, 1953; Webber, 1959; Carden, 1965; Kanter, 1968). But the reasons for forming and the scale of involvement in today's communes *are* new.

The Problem of Viability

"They're going into communes, but how many will stay there?" asked a middle-class woman. It was easy to suppose that experimental communes would be wrecked on the reefs that had stopped

so many voyages in the past: rivalry among leaders, disenchant-
ment with hardship, sexual tensions, even prosperity. Moreover,
movements transform their character and objectives, even with the
best intentions (Messinger, 1955; H. R. Niebuhr, 1957; Zald, 1966).
But the unanswered question was viability, and, to answer it a game
called *natural selection* had to be played. One thing seems plain:
Common sense or obvious practicability does not always tell us
whether a movement or its strategies will succeed. By such a
criterion, the future of Christianity would have looked dim indeed.
A movement may make its members suffer, yet draw them closer so
that they become more dedicated to the cause (Riddle, 1931).

A helpful sociological study focuses on just this matter, how
members are committed to the goals, work, and fellowship of communal groups. Of about a hundred utopian communities in nine-
teenth-century America, some, such as the Shakers, lasted as long
as 180 years; while others managed for only six months. Using a
life span of twenty-five years as a criterion of success, Kanter
identified nine successful and twenty-one unsuccessful utopian
communities for intensive study. The commitment mechanisms of
these communities were sorted into three main categories: those
that bound a person to continued participation (for example, sacrifice, vows, investment); those that helped cohesion (such as renunciation of other relationships, group communion, experience of
persecution); and those that followed commitment to control (such
as mortification, confession, self-surrender). This study cannot be
fully reported here but Table 11.1 lists some of the mechanisms
that were most often present in successful utopias and least often
in unsuccessful. They give an idea of the kinds of things that
utopia designers might try if they wish to build a new communal
world that has much chance of lasting.

These findings give us some insight into the problem of viability
of communes; that is, the most successful ones did some of the
things listed in the table, to bind their members more firmly into the
group and make them participate more whole-heartedly in the activities. A community that used such devices might be expected to
maintain its discipline and resist invasion from conflicting values
of the outside world. We cannot, of course, conclude that a community, to be successful, must use all, even any, of these things.
There are presumably other ways of getting commitment, some of
which have not yet been discovered. Such findings merely tell us
what past utopian communities did to preserve themselves—as it
proved, not for very long, historically speaking.

Other organizations—for example, churches, armies, and political parties—use some of these methods. Their survival and discipline suggest that early death need not be the fate of utopias—

unless, indeed, integration with the prevailing power structure becomes necessary for survival.

We might distill from Table 11.1 a hypothetical recipe for a successful commune: Make the members contribute property and labor without reimbursement. Require sexual abstinence or at least renunciation of dyadic claims. Insulate the group by boundary control, special language, and a uniform. Recruit members from a

TABLE 11.1.
Some Commitment Mechanisms*
of Utopian Communities

	Percent difference successful and unsuccessful communities†
Investment (continuance commitment)	
Financial investment: property signed over at admission	55
Defectors not reimbursed for labor (in practice)	53
Sacrifice (continuance commitment)	
Abstinence: Celibacy	80
Renunciation (cohesion commitment)	
Insulation by special term for outside world	57
Insulation by uniform worn	59
Cross-boundary control: Average member never left community	100
Dyadic renunciation	
Free love or celibacy	71
Controls on free love, celibacy, or sexual relations	73
Communion (cohesion commitment)	
Homogeneity: common ethnic background	52
Communistic sharing: property signed over at admission	55
Communistic labor: no compensation for labor	59
Communistic labor: no charge for community services	53
Communistic labor: communal work efforts	50
Regularized group contact: group meetings held daily	50
Ritual: songs about community	49
Mortification (control commitment)	
Confession upon joining	50
Mortifying sanctions: public denunciation of deviants	48
De-individuating mechanisms: uniform worn	59

TABLE 11.1 (Cont.)

	Percent difference successful and unsuccessful communities†
Surrender (control commitment)	
Institutionalized awe: power to be invested in persons with special, magical characteristics	58
Institutionalized awe: special, magical powers imputed to members	74
Institutionalized awe: possession of special powers taken as evidence of good standing	65
Institutionalized awe (power and authority)	
Top leaders named or groomed by predecessors or founders	50
Special leadership prerogatives	62
Separate, special residence for leaders	68
Special forms of address for leaders	57
Programming: detailed specification of routine	54
Ideological conversion	
Recruit expected to take vows	59
Tests of faith for community children to receive adult membership status	54
Tradition: prior organization in existence at least 10 years before community began	51

* "Commitment mechanisms" refer to "structural arrangements and organizational strategies which promote and sustain commitment," which mean "the willingness of social actors to give their energy and loyalty to social systems." Continuance mechanisms help the individual to see maintenance of the system as rewarding: By sacrifice he gives up something as a price of membership, and by investment he gains a stake in the current and future payoffs of the organization. Cohesion commitment involves the individual emotionally in the group; for example, by renouncing outside relationships and insulating the group from the outside world, and by communion that generates "we" feeling. Control commitment mechanisms make the individual more obedient to authority and inclined to see the system's demands and rules as right; for example, by mortification, which makes the individual feel as of little worth except as part of the group, and surrender, which inclines him to give up decision making and accept direction from the group.

† "Percent difference successful and unsuccessful communities" refers to the greater frequency of the mechanism among successful than unsuccessful communities; for example, if 50 percent of successful communities used confession upon joining, and none of the unsuccessful did, then the difference is 50.

SOURCE: This table contains all differences of 49 or greater from Tables 1, 3, 5, 7, 9, and 11 of the source article. All information and quotations are from Rosabeth Moss Kanter, "Commitment and Social Organization: a Study of Commitment Mechanisms in Utopian Communities," *American Sociological Review*, vol. 33, August 1968, pp. 499–517.

common ethnic or cultural background and emphasize group contact and communion. Require vows and tests of faith for membership. Subdue the individualism and pride of members and denounce deviants. Cultivate the idea that leaders have special, magical, or religious characteristics (charisma) and that members can share in these by belonging to the group. Keep the members busy by a detailed program of work, worship, and leisure.

Psychedelic drugs have become a new factor in commune viability. We have no evidence of the viability of communes that give an important place to such methods, though the outlook has been hardly encouraging. A "rock doctor" told of "bad trips" at two rock festivals:

> At Woodstock everybody was determined to make it a peace and love thing. . . . So Woodstock was a benign, gentle drug scene. We had 800 bad trips there, but that many among a half million kids was small. At Powder Ridge with only 35,000 kids, we treated 985 bad trips, 400 of them on Friday night alone. The acid was heavily laced . . . with dangerous chemicals . . . which give a faster and better high. . . . It's truly a miracle that we didn't have any deaths. At one point we had 150 kids freaked out simultaneously. I'm not talking about the kid who is a little spaced out and saying, "Look, baby, I don't know where I am." I mean the horrendous kind, the paranoia, muscular activity, hostility, aggression, kind of frightened-out-of-their-minds scene that is unbelievable unless you've seen it happen. (Abruzzi, 1970:57.)

This is plainly not a very successful strategy of response to a banal and frustrating environment. It is hard to see how a commune can get its work done, even survive physically, with many members on such trips, without an extraordinarily (utopianly?) easy, indulgent, and therapeutic environment.

Conclusion

This chapter examines the counterculture as an example of a meaning-seeking movement in early stages of negotiation, showing its tendencies to avoid practical politics, to seek different kinds of reality, and to solve the problem of viability, which all new life styles and world views must face.

A meaning-seeking movement does not—as do practical movements—accept the world on its own terms and use the methods given. It has to make a different kind of reality from what it experiences as banal and useless in the world of today.

When attending a union meeting, one would never be under the impression that a kind of reality different from that on the street was being negotiated: "Bread and butter" practicality dominates both places. On the other hand, it would be a failure of a meaning-seeking movement if it were talking about the same reality as that on the street. Such seekers demand redefinition of the world and spend considerable time in expressive and other "realizing" activities, groping toward a new experience which must, to members of the *status quo*, seem impractical at the very least. So, meaning-seeking movements focus more on images, feelings, mystiques, ritual, drugs, kicks, personal encounter, communitas (V. Turner, 1969), style, and identity than do practical movements. They are concerned with images (dreams, myths, utopias, ecstasies), which help make life worthwhile. They give their members not just a job or material reward but a new role with dramatic qualities (such as that of the crusader; Klapp, 1969:257–311), answers to the question "Why?," and a better world than the one we have. So Women's Liberation fits the definition of a meaning-seeking rather than only a practical movement. This does not, of course, rule out a movement combining meaning-giving and practical activities. Gandhi's, for example, had two sides: People found meaning for themselves and India in him; the other side was achieving political objectives such as abolishing caste, emancipating women, and ending British domination through the strategy of *Satyagraha*. He was, so to speak, a combination of generalissimo and soul saver. He drew religiously oriented people out of withdrawal; after his meetings, workmen would form processions, marching through towns singing newly improvised songs (Erikson, 1969:297–342). His miracle was to put the quietistic mysticism of India into action.

We have barely touched on the variety of social movements in the economic, political, educational, welfare, recreational and other sectors, having brought into highlight only one kind, or aspect, of movements: symbolic negotiation of meaning, which is the central theme of this book. For a balanced view of movements, the reader is referred to sociological treatments such as Gusfield (1970), Cameron (1966), Toch (1965), Killian (1964), R. H. Turner and Killian (1957), King (1956), Nordskog (1954), or Heberle (1951), and for those who want action, there is Alinsky's (1971) practical handbook on organization and politicization of democratic action.

REFERENCES

Abruzzi, William, M. D., "The Rock Doctor Tells About 985 Freakouts," as told to Robert Stokes, *Life*, August 8, 1970, p. 37.

Adorno, T. W., et al., *The Authoritarian Personality*, New York: Harper & Row 1950.

Albee, Edward, *Who's Afraid of Virginia Woolf?*, New York: Atheneum, 1962.

Albig, William, *Modern Public Opinion*, New York: McGraw-Hill, 1956.

Alexander, Franz, *Our Age of Unreason, A Study of the Irrational Forces in Social Life*, Philadelphia: Lippincott, 1942.

Alinsky, Saul, Interviewed by Marrion K. Sanders, "The Professional Radical," *Harper's*, June 1965, pp. 45–46.

———, *Rules for Radicals*, New York: Random House, 1971.

Allen, Frederick Lewis, *Only Yesterday, The Fabulous Twenties*, New York: Grosset & Dunlap (Bantam Books), 1946. (Originally published by Harper Brothers, 1931.)

Allport, Gordon, *ABC's of Scapegoating*, New York: Anti-Defamation League of B'nai B'rith, 1948.

———, *The Nature of Prejudice*, Cambridge, Mass.: Addison-Wesley, 1954.

Allport, Gordon, and Postman, Leo, *Psychology of Rumor*, New York: Holt, Rinehart and Winston, 1947.

Almond, Gabriel A., *Appeals of Communism*, Princeton, N.J.: Princeton University Press, 1954.

Almond, Gabriel A., and Verba, Sidney, *The Civic Culture*, Princeton, N.J.: Princeton University Press, 1963.

Alvarez, A., " 'A Tale of a Tub' for Our Time," *Saturday Review*, June 13, 1970, p. 27.

Amory, Cleveland, *Who Killed Society?*, New York: Harper & Row, 1960.

Anderson, Gloria Brown, "Young Wanderers Trip on 'Vag' Laws," *Christian Science Monitor*, Sept. 12, 1970.

Anderson, Walter (ed.), *The Age of Protest*, Pacific Palisades, Calif.: Goodyear Publishing, 1969.

Angell, Robert Cooley, *Free Society and Moral Crisis*, Ann Arbor: University of Michigan Press, 1958.

Anspach, Karlyne, *The Why of Fashion*, Ames: Iowa State University Press, 1967.

Aranguren, J. L., *Human Communication*, New York: McGraw-Hill, 1967. (Translated from Spanish by F. Partridge.)

Ardrey, Robert, *The Territorial Imperative*, New York: Atheneum, 1966.

———, *The Social Contract*, New York: Atheneum, 1970.

Arendt, Hannah, *Eichmann in Jerusalem, A Study in the Banality of Evil*, New York: Viking, 1963.

———, *The Origins of Totalitarianism*, New York: Harcourt, 1966 (1951).

Argyle, Michael, *Religious Behavior* (London: Routledge, 1958); excerpted in Jahoda and Warren (eds.), *Attitudes*, New York: Penguin, 1966, pp. 100–101.

———, *The Psychology of Interpersonal Behavior*, New York: Penguin, 1967.

Armer, Paul, "What Will the Computer Do Next?," *New York Times*, April 24, 1966, pp. 16–17.

Arnold, Thurman W., *The Symbols of Government*, New Haven: Yale University Press, 1935.

————, *The Folklore of Capitalism*, New Haven: Yale University Press, 1937.

Asch, S. E., *Social Psychology*, Englewood Cliffs, N.J.: Prentice-Hall, 1952.

Ashley-Montagu, M. F. (ed.), *Man and Aggression*, New York: Oxford University Press, 1968.

Attneave, Fred, *Applications of Information Theory to Psychology: A Summary of Basic Concepts, Methods and Results*, New York: Holt, Rinehart and Winston, 1959.

Babbitt, Irving, *Rousseau and Romanticism*, New York: Meridian, 1955 (1919, 1947).

Bagdikian, Ben H., *In the Midst of Plenty: A New Report on the Poor in America*, Boston: Beacon, 1964.

Baier, Kurt, and Rescher, Nicholas (eds.), *Values and the Future, The Impact of Technological Change on American Values*, New York: Free Press, 1969.

Bales, R. F., *Interaction Process Analysis*, Cambridge, Mass.: Addison-Wesley, 1950.

Bandura, Albert, "What TV Violence Can Do To Your Child," *Look*, Oct. 22, 1963, pp. 46–52. (Also in Larsen (ed.), 1968, pp. 123–130).

Banton, Michael, *Roles, An Introduction to the Study of Social Relations*, New York: Basic Books, 1965.

Barnett, H. G., *Indian Shakers, A Messianic Cult of the Pacific Northwest*, Carbondale: Southern Illinois University Press, 1957.

Barnett, James H., *The American Christmas: A Study in National Culture*, New York: Macmillan, 1954.

Barnlund, Dean C. (ed.), *Interpersonal Communication: Survey and Studies*, Boston: Houghton Mifflin, 1968.

Barringer, H. R.; Blanksten, G. I.; and Mack, R. (eds.), *Social Change in Developing Areas*, Cambridge, Mass.: Schenkman, 1965.

Barrymore, Ethel, "Memories," *Ladies Home Journal*, April 1955, p. 208.

Bartlett, F. C., *Remembering*, Cambridge, England: Cambridge University Press, 1932.

Barton, Allen H., *Communities in Disaster, A Sociological Analysis of Collective Stress Situations*, New York: Doubleday, 1969.

Barton, Allen, and Anderson, Bo, "Change in an Organizational System: Formalization of a Qualitative Study," in Etzioni (ed.), *Complex Organizations*, New York: Holt, Rinehart and Winston, 1961, pp. 400–418.

Barzun, Jacques, *Romanticism and the Modern Ego*, Boston: Little, Brown, 1943.

————, *Science: The Glorious Entertainment*, New York: Harper & Row, 1964.

————, "The Man in the American Mask," *Foreign Affairs*, April 1965, pp. 426–435.

Basler, Roy P., *The Lincoln Legend*, Boston: Houghton Mifflin, 1935.

Bateson, Gregory, et al., "Toward a Theory of Schizophrenia," *Behavioral Science*, vol. 1, 1956, pp. 251–264. (Also in Bennis et al., *Interpersonal Dynamics, Essays and Readings in Human Interaction*, Homewood, Ill.: Dorsey Press, 1964, pp. 141–161.)

Bauer, Raymond A. (ed.), *Social Indicators*, Cambridge, Mass.: The M.I.T. Press, 1966.

Bauer, R. A., and Gleicher, D. B., "Word-of-Mouth Communications in the Soviet Union," *Public Opinion Quarterly*, vol. 17, 1953, pp. 297–310.

Baynes, John C. M., *Morale: A Study of Men and Courage; the Second Scottish Rifles at the Battle of Neuve Chapelle, 1915*, New York: Praeger, 1967.

Beal, George M.; Rogers, E. M.; and Bohlen, J. M., "Validity of the Concept of Stages in the Adoption Process," *Rural Sociology*, vol. 22, 1957, pp. 166–168.

Beal, George M., and Rogers, Everett M., *The Adoption of Two Farm Practices in a Central Iowa Community*, Ames, Iowa: Iowa Agricultural and Home Economics Experiment Station, Special Report 26–RS, 1960.

Becker, Ernest, *The Birth and Death of Human Meaning: A Perspective in Psychiatry and Anthropology*, New York: Free Press, 1962.

Becker, Howard S., *Outsiders: Studies in the Sociology of Deviance*, New York: Free Press, 1963.

———, *The Other Side, Perspectives on Deviance*, New York: Free Press, 1964.

Beckett, Samuel, *Stories and Texts for Nothing*, New York: Grove, 1967.

Bell, Daniel, *The End of Ideology, On the Exhaustion of Political Ideas in the Fifties*, New York: Free Press (Collier Books), 1960, 1961.

———, *The Radical Right*, New York: Doubleday, 1964.

Belz, Carl, *The Story of Rock*, New York: Oxford, 1969.

Benedict, Ruth, *Patterns of Culture*, Boston: Houghton Mifflin, 1934.

Bennett, John W., et al., *In Search of Identity, The Japanese Overseas Scholar in America and Japan*, Minneapolis: University of Minnesota Press, 1958.

———, *The Hutterian Brethren*, Stanford, Calif.: Stanford University Press, 1967.

Bennis, Warren G., and Slater, P. E., *The Temporary Society*, New York: Harper & Row, 1968.

Bennis, Warren G., et al., *Interpersonal Dynamics, Essays and Readings in Human Interaction*, Homewood, Ill.: Dorsey Press, 1964, 1968.

Berelson, Bernard, and Janowitz, Morris (eds.), *Reader in Public Opinion and Communication*, New York: Free Press, 1966.

Berelson, Bernard, and Steiner, G. A., *Human Behavior, An Inventory of Scientific Findings*, New York: Harcourt, 1964.

———, *Human Behavior, A Shorter Edition*, New York: Harcourt, 1967.

Berger, Peter L., and Luckmann, Thomas, *The Social Construction of Reality: A Treatise in the Sociology of Knowledge*, New York: Doubleday, 1966.

Bergson, Henri, *Laughter*, New York: Macmillan, 1911.

Berkowitz, Leonard, et al., "Film Violence and Subsequent Aggressive Tendencies," *Public Opinion Quarterly*, vol. 27, 1963, pp. 217–229.

Berkowitz, Leonard, (Participant in) "Violence in Mass Media," Governor Nelson Rockefeller's Conference on Crime, New York, April 22, 1966. (Also in Larsen (ed.), 1968, pp. 273–293.)

Berlo, David K., *The Process of Communication, An Introduction to Theory and Practice*, New York: Holt, Rinehart and Winston, 1960.

Berlo, David K. (ed.), *Mass Communication and the Development of Nations*, East Lansing: International Communications Institute, Michigan State University, 1968.

Bernays, Edward L., *Biography of an Idea*, New York: Simon and Schuster, 1965.

Berndt, Ronald M., *Excess and Restraint, Social Control among a New Guinea Mountain People*, Chicago: Chicago University Press, 1962.

Berne, Eric, *Games People Play*, New York: Grove, 1964.

Bettelheim, Bruno, *Love Is Not Enough*, London: Collier-Macmillan, 1950.

Bettelheim, Bruno, and Janowitz, M., *Dynamics of Prejudice: A Psychological and Sociological Study of Veterans*, New York: Harper & Row, 1950.

Biderman, Albert D., *March to Calumny, The Story of American P.O.W.'s in the Korean War*, New York: Macmillan, 1963.

Birdwhistell, Ray L., *Kinesics and Context: Essays on Body Motion Communication*, Philadelphia: University of Pennsylvania Press, 1970.

Blum, Richard, et al., *Utopiates: The Use and Users of LSD-25*, New York: Atherton Press, 1964.

Blumenthal, Albert, *Small Town Stuff*, Chicago: University of Chicago Press, 1932.

Blumer, Herbert, "Morale and the American War Effort," in W. F. Ogburn (ed.), *American Society in Wartime*, Chicago: University of Chicago Press, 1943.

——, "Collective Behavior," in A. M. Lee (ed.), *New Outline of the Principles of Sociology*, New York: Barnes and Noble, 1946; first published 1939.

——, "Public Opinion and Opinion Polling," *American Sociological Review*, vol. 13, 1948, pp. 542–554.

——, "Collective Behavior," in Gittler (ed.), *Review of Sociology, Analysis of a Decade*, New York: Wiley, 1957, pp. 127–158.

——, "Society as Symbolic Interaction," in A. W. Rose (ed.), *Human Behavior and Social Processes*, Boston: Houghton Mifflin, 1962.

——, "The Mass, the Public, and Public Opinion," in Berelson and Janowitz (eds.), *Reader in Public Opinion and Communication*, New York: Free Press, 1966, pp. 43–50.

——, *Symbolic Interactionism, Perspective and Method*, Englewood Cliffs, N.J.: Prentice-Hall, 1969.(a)

——, "Fashion: From Class Differentiation to Collective Behavior," *Sociological Quarterly*, vol. 10, 1969, pp. 275–291.(b)

Bode, Carl, *The Anatomy of American Popular Culture, 1840–1861*, Berkeley and Los Angeles: University of California Press, 1959, pp. xiii–xv.

Bogardus, Emory S., "A Race Relations Cycle," *American Journal of Sociology*, vol. 35, 1930, pp. 612–617.

——, *Principles of Social Psychology*, New York: Appleton, 1950.

Boguslaw, Robert, *The New Utopians, A Study of System Design and Social Change*, Englewood Cliffs, N.J.: Prentice-Hall, 1965.

Bond, Ruskin, "The Charm of Elephants," *Christian Science Monitor*, Nov. 17, 1969.

Booker, Christopher, *The Neophiliacs*, Boston: Gambit, 1970.

Boorstin, Daniel J., *The Image, Or What Happened to the American Dream*, New York: Atheneum, 1962.

Borrow, George, *The Zincali, An Account of the Gypsies of Spain* (London: J. M. Dent and Sons), New York: Dutton, 1914.

Boulding, Kenneth E., *The Image*, Ann Arbor: University of Michigan Press, 1956.

————, *The Skills of the Economist*, Cleveland: H. Allen, 1958.

————, *Meaning of the Twentieth Century, The Great Transition*, New York: Harper & Row, 1964.

————, "Towards a Theory of Protest," *Bulletin of the Atomic Scientist*, October 1965. (Also in Walter Anderson (ed.), *The Age of Protest*, Pacific Palisades, Calif.: Goodyear, 1969, pp. vi–viii.)

Braden, Charles S., *These Also Believe, A Study of Modern American Cults and Minority Religious Movements*, New York: Macmillan, 1949.

Braden, William, *The Age of Aquarius, Technology and the Cultural Revolution*, New York: New York Times (Quadrangle Books), 1970.

Brean, Herbert, "Wrestling Script Gone Awry," *Life*, Dec. 2, 1957, pp. 165–166.

Bright, J. R. (ed.), *Technological Planning at the Corporate Level*, Boston: Division of Research, Harvard School of Business, 1962.

Brillouin, L., "Life, Thermodynamics, and Cybernetics," in Buckley (ed.), *Modern Systems Research for the Behavioral Scientist*, Chicago: Aldine, 1968, pp. 147–156.

Brinton, Crane, *The Anatomy of Revolution* (rev. ed.), Englewood Cliffs, N.J.: Prentice-Hall, 1952.

————, *The Shaping of Modern Thought*, Englewood Cliffs, N.J.: Prentice-Hall, 1963.

Brodbeck, May, "Roles of Small Groups in Mediating the Effects of Propaganda," *Journal of Abnormal and Social Psychology*, vol. 52, March 1956, pp. 166–170.

Brogan, D. W., *The American Character*, New York: Time, Inc., (1944, 1956), 1962.

Brown, J. A. C., *Techniques of Persuasion, From Propaganda to Brainwashing*, New York: Penguin, 1963.

Brown, Roger W., *Social Psychology*, New York: Free Press, 1969.

Bryson, Lyman (ed.), *The Communication of Ideas, A Series of Addresses*, New York: Cooper Square Publishers (1948), 1964.

Buber, Martin, *I and Thou*, Edinburgh: T. and T. Clark, 1950.

Bucher, Rue, "Blame and Hostility in Disaster," *American Journal of Sociology*, vol. 62, 1957, pp. 467–475.

Buckley, Walter, *Sociology and Modern Systems Theory*, Englewood Cliffs, N.J.: Prentice-Hall, 1967.

Buckley, Walter (ed.), *Modern Systems Research for the Behavioral Scientist*, Chicago: Aldine, 1968.

Buckner, H. Taylor, "A Theory of Rumor Transmission," *Public Opinion Quarterly*, vol. 29, 1965, pp. 54–70. (Also see R. E. Evans, 1969, pp. 120–136.)

Burke, Kenneth, "Permanence and Change, An Anatomy of Purpose," New York: New Republic, Inc., 1936.

Burr, George Lincoln, *Narratives of the Witchcraft Cases, 1648–1706*, New York: Scribner, 1914.

Cadwallader, Mervyn L., "The Cybernetic Analysis of Change in Complex Organizations," *American Journal of Sociology*, vol. 64, 1959, pp. 154–157.

Cameron, N., "The Paranoid Pseudo-Community," *American Journal of Sociology*, vol. 49, 1943, pp. 32–38.

Cameron, William B., "Social Roles in a Jam Session," *Social Forces*, vol. 33, 1954, pp. 177–182.

————, *Informal Sociology*, New York: Random House, 1963.

————, *Modern Social Movements*, New York: Random House, 1966.

Campbell, Angus; Converse, P. E.; Miller, W. E.; and Stokes, D. E., *The American Voter, An Abridgment*, New York: Wiley, 1964.

Campbell, Donald T., "Ethnocentric and Other Altruistic Motives," in D. Levine (ed.), *Nebraska Symposium on Motivation*, Lincoln: University of Nebraska Press, 1965, pp. 283–311.(a)

————, "Variation and Selective Retention in Socio-cultural Evolution," in Barringer, Blanksten, and Mack (eds.), *Social Change in Developing Areas, Cambridge*, Mass.: Schenkman, 1965, pp. 19–49.(b)

Camus, Albert, *The Fall*, New York: Random House (Vintage Books), 1956.

Canetti, Elias, *Crowds and Power*, New York: Viking, 1962.

Cantril, Hadley, *Gauging Public Opinion*, Princeton, N.J.: Princeton University Press, 1944.

Cantril, Hadley; Gaudet, H.; and Herzog, H., *The Invasion from Mars*, Princeton, N.J.: Princeton University Press, 1940.

Caplow, T., "Rumors in War," *Social Forces*, vol. 25, 1947, p. 302.

Carden, Maren L., "Experimental Utopia in America," *Deadalus*, Spring 1965, pp. 403–418. (Also in Gusfield, 1970, pp. 419–435.)

Cargill, Oscar (ed.), *Henry D. Thoreau, Selected Writings on Nature and Liberty*, New York: Liberal Arts Press, 1952.

Carmichael, Stokely, and Hamilton, C. V., *Black Power—The Politics of Liberation*, New York: Random House, 1967.

Carpenter, C. R., *Naturalistic Behavior of Nonhuman Primates*, University Park: Pennsylvania State University Press, 1964.

Cartnal, Alan, "Poverty Making a Comeback in New Look," *Los Angeles Times*, June 21, 1970.

Cash, W. J., *The Mind of the South*, New York: Knopf, 1941.

Cassirer, Ernst, *An Essay on Man*, New Haven: Yale University Press, 1944.

————, *Language and Myth*, New York: Harper & Row, 1946. (Translated by Susanne K. Langer.)

Cattell, R. B., *Personality and Motivation, Structure and Measurement*, London: Harrap, 1957.

Chapin, F. Stuart, *Cultural Change*, New York: The Century Company, 1928.

Chaplin, J. P., *Rumor, Fear and the Madness of Crowds*, New York: Ballentine, 1959.

Chaplin, Ralph, *Wobbly, the Rough-and-Tumble Story of an American Radical*, Chicago: University of Chicago Press, 1948.

Chase, Stuart, *Tragedy of Waste*, New York: Macmillan, 1925.

Chauvin, Remy, *Animal Societies, From the Bee to the Gorilla*, New York: Hill and Wang, 1968. (Translated by George Ordish.)

Ciardi, John, "Miracles, More or Less," *Saturday Review*, Aug. 8, 1970, p. 6.

Clark, James V., *A Healthy Organization*, Los Angeles: University of California Institute of Industrial Relations, Reprint No. 114, 1962.

Clark, S. D., *Church and Sect in Canada*, Toronto: University of Toronto Press, 1948.

Cleaver, Eldridge, *Soul On Ice*, New York: McGraw-Hill, 1968.

Cleveland, Harlan, *The Overseas Americans*, New York: McGraw-Hill, 1960.

Clinard, Marshall, *The Black Market*, New York: Holt, Rinehart and Winston, 1952.

Cobliner, W. Godfrey, "Feminine Fashion as an Aspect of Group Psychology," *Journal of Social Psychology*, vol. 31, 1950, 283–289.

Cohen, Albert K., *Delinquent Boys, the Culture of the Gang*, New York: Free Press, 1955.

————, *Deviance and Control*, Englewood Cliffs, N.J.: Prentice-Hall, 1966.

Cohen, Jerry, and Murphy, W. S., "Burn, Baby, Burn," *Life*, July 15, 1966, pp. 36–42.

Cohn, Norman, *The Search for the Millennium*, London: Secker and Warburg, 1957.

Cohn-Bendit, Daniel and Gabriel, *Obsolete Communism: The Left-Wing Alternative*, New York: McGraw-Hill, 1969.

Colby, Benjamin N., "Behavioral Redundancy," *Behavioral Science*, vol. 3, 1958, pp. 317–322.

Coleman, James S., *The Adolescent Society, The Social Life of the Teenager and Its Impact on Education*, New York: Free Press, 1961.

Cooley, Charles H., *Social Process*, New York: Scribner, 1918.

————, *Human Nature and the Social Order*, New York: Scribner (1902), 1922.

————, *Social Organization, A Study of the Larger Mind*, New York: Scribner (1909), 1927.

Cooper, Eunice, and Jahoda, Marie, "The Evasion of Propaganda: How Prejudiced People Respond to Antiprejudice Propaganda," *Journal of Psychology*, vol. 23, 1947, pp. 15–25.

Coser, Lewis A., *Functions of Social Conflict*, New York: Free Press, 1956.

Cox, Harvey, *The Feast of Fools*, Cambridge: Harvard University Press, 1969.(a)

————, "In Praise of Festivity," *Saturday Review*, Oct. 25, 1969, pp. 25–28.(b)

Crain, Robert L.; Katz, Elihu; and Rosenthal, Donald B., *The Politics of Community Conflict: The Flouridation Decision*, Indianapolis: Bobbs-Merrill, 1969.

Crotty, William J.; Freeman, D. M.; and Gatlin, D. S. (eds.), *Political Parties and Political Behavior*, Boston: Allyn and Bacon, 1966.

Dahl, Robert A., *A Preface to Democratic Theory*, Chicago: University of Chicago Press, 1956.

Dance, Frank E. X. (ed.), *Human Communication Theory, Original Essays*, New York: Holt, Rinehart and Winston, 1967.

Daniels, Arlene K., "The Social Construction of Military Psychiatric Diagnoses." Paper delivered at the American Sociological Association Meeting, San Francisco, September 1969.

Davies, James C., "The J-Curve of Rising and Declining Satisfactions as a Cause of Some Great Revolutions and a Contained Rebellion," in Graham and Gurr, *Violence in America, Historical and Comparative Perspectives*, New York: New American Library, 1969, pp. 671–709.

Davis, Angela, Quoted in *Life*, Sept. 11, 1970.

Davis, Fred, "San Francisco's Mystique," *Trans-Action*, April 1970, pp. 75–80.

Davis, James H., *Group Performance*, Reading, Mass.: Addison-Wesley, 1969.

Dawson, Carl A., and Gettys, Warner E., *An Introduction to Sociology* (3d ed.), New York: Ronald Press, 1948.

DeFleur, Melvin, *Theories of Mass Communication*, New York: McKay, 1966.

Denney, Reuel, *The Astonished Muse*, Chicago: University of Chicago Press, 1957.

Dennis, Landt, "Firms Ride Astrology Bandwagon," *Christian Science Monitor*, Dec. 23, 1969.

———, "In Pace with the Universe," *Christian Science Monitor*, Aug. 1, 1970.

Denov, Louis, "Kolo Hoolyeh," *Viltis, a Folklore Magazine*, October–November 1954, pp. 10–11.

Dentler, Robert A., and Erikson, Kai T., "The Functions of Deviance in Groups," *Social Problems*, vol. 7, 1959, pp. 93–107.

Deutsch, Karl W., *Nationalism and Social Communication, An Inquiry into the Foundations of Nationality*, Cambridge, Mass.: The M.I.T. Press, 1953.

———, "On Social Communication and the Metropolis," *Daedalus*, vol. 90, 1961, pp. 99–110.

———, *The Nerves of Government, Models of Political Communication and Control*, New York: Free Press, 1966.

Deutsch, Karl W., and Foltz, William J. (eds.), *Nation-Building*, New York: Atherton, 1963.

Devereaux, Edward C., Jr., "Gambling and the Social Structure: A Sociological Study of Lotteries and Horse Racing in Contemporary America." Unpublished Ph.D. dissertation, Harvard University, 1950.

Dewey, John, *Human Nature and Conduct*, New York: Modern Library (1922), 1930.

Dexter, Lewis A. and White, David M. (eds.), *People, Society and Mass Communications*, New York: Free Press, 1964.

Douglas, Mary, *Purity and Danger, An Analysis of Concepts of Pollution and Taboo*, New York: Praeger, 1966.

Dube, S. C., "Communication, Innovation, and Planned Change in India," in Lerner and Schramm (eds.), *Communication and Change in the Developing Countries*, Honolulu: East-West Center Press, 1967.

Dubos, Rene, *So Human an Animal*, New York: Scribner, 1968.

Duijiker, H. C. J., and Frijda, N. H., *National Character and National Stereotypes*, Amsterdam: North Holland Publishing Company, 1960.

Duncan, Hugh D., *Language and Literature in Society: A Sociological Essay on Theory and Method in the Interpretation of Linguistic Symbols*, Chicago: University of Chicago Press, 1953.

————, *Communication and Social Order*, New York: Bedminster Press, 1962.

————, *Symbols in Society*, New York: Oxford University Press, 1968.

Du Nouy, Lecomte, *Human Destiny*, New York: Longmans, 1947.

Durkheim, Emile, *The Elementary Forms of Religious Life*, New York: Macmillan, 1915.

————, *The Rules of Sociological Method*, Chicago: University of Chicago Press (1895), 1938.

Dynes, Russell R., "Church-Sect Typology and Socio-Economic Status," *American Sociological Review*, vol. 20, October 1955, pp. 555–556.

Easton, David, *A Systems Analysis of Political Life*, New York: Wiley, 1965.

Ehrlich, Paul, *The Population Bomb*, New York: Ballentine, 1968.

Eiseley, Loren, *The Unexpected Universe*, New York: Harcourt, 1964.

Eisen, Jonathan (ed.), *The Age of Rock, Sounds of the American Cultural Revolution*, New York: Random House, 1969.

Eisenstadt, S. N., "Communication Processes Among Immigrants in Israel," *Public Opinion Quarterly*, vol. 16, 1952, pp. 42–58.

Eliade, Mircea, *Birth and Rebirth, The Religious Meanings of Initiation in Human Culture*, New York: Harper & Row, 1958.

————, *Shamanism, Archaic Techniques of Ecstasy*, New York: (Bollingen Foundation) Random House (Pantheon Books), 1964.

Elkin, Frederick, "Advertising in French Canada," in Zollschan and Hirsch (eds.), *Explorations in Social Change*, Boston: Houghton Mifflin, 1964, pp. 522–546.

Ellul, Jacques, *The Technological Society*, New York: Knopf, 1965.

Epstein, Brian, *A Cellar Full of Noise*, New York: Doubleday, 1964.

Erikson, Erik H., *Childhood and Society*, New York: Norton, 1963.

————, *Identity, Youth and Crisis*, New York: Norton, 1968.

————, *Gandhi's Truth, On the Origins of Militant Nonviolence*, New York: Norton, 1969.

Erikson, Kai T., *Wayward Puritans; A Study in the Sociology of Deviance*, New York: Wiley, 1966.

Essien-Udom, E. U., *Black Nationalism, A Search for Identity in America*, Chicago: University of Chicago Press, 1963. (Reprinted Dell Publishing, 1964.)

Etzioni, Amitai (ed.), *Complex Organizations*, New York: Holt, Rinehart and Winston, 1961.

Evans, Robert R. (ed.), *Readings in Collective Behavior*, Chicago: Rand McNally, 1969.

Evans-Pritchard, E. E., *Witchcraft, Ordeals and Magic Among the Azande*, Oxford: Clarendon Press, 1937.

Fabre, J. Henri, *The Life of the Caterpillar*, New York: Liveright, 1916.

Faris, Ellsworth, *Nature of Human Nature*, New York: McGraw-Hill, 1937.

Faris, Robert E. L. (ed.), *Handbook of Modern Sociology*, Chicago: Rand McNally, 1964.

Fauconnet, Paul, *La Responsabilite*, Paris: Alcan, 1920.

Feierabend, Ivo K., and Nesvold, Betty A.; with Feierabend, Rosalind L.,

"Social Change and Political Violence: Cross-National Patterns," in Graham and Gurr, *Violence in America, Historical and Comparative Perspectives*, New York: New American Library, 1969, pp. 606–668.

———, "Political Coerciveness and Turmoil: A Cross-National Inquiry," *Law and Society Review*, August 1970.

Feldman, Arnold S., *Public Opinion Quarterly*, vol. 19, pp. 124–139; reprinted in Evans (ed.), 1969, pp. 216–230.

Feshbach, Seymour, and Singer, Robert D., *Television and Aggression*, San Francisco: Jossey-Bass, 1970.

Festinger, Leon, *A Theory of Cognitive Dissonance*, New York: Harper & Row, 1957.

———, *Conflict, Decision and Dissonance*, Stanford: Stanford University Press, 1964.

Festinger, Leon; Cartwright, D.; Barber, K.; Fleischl, J.; Gottsdanker, J.; Keyson, A.; and Leavitt, G., "A Study of Rumor: Its Origin and Spread," *Human Relations*, vol. 1, 1948, pp. 464–486.

Festinger, Leon; Pepitone, A.; and Newcomb, T. M., "Some Consequences of De-Individuation in a Group," *Journal of Abnormal and Social Psychology*, vol. 47, 1952, pp. 382–389.

Festinger, Leon; Riecken, H. W.; and Schachter, S., *When Prophecy Fails*, Minneapolis: University of Minnesota Press, 1956.

Festinger, Leon; Schachter, S.; and Back, K., *Social Pressures in Informal Groups, A Study of Human Factors in Housing*, New York: Harper & Row, 1950.

Finerty, John F., *War-Path and Bivouac*, Chicago: copyright by JFF, printed by Donohue and Henneberry, 1890.

Finestone, Harold, "Cats, Kicks and Color," *Social Problems*, vol. 5, 1957, pp. 3–13.

Firth, Raymond, "Rumor in a Primitive Society," *Journal of Abnormal and Social Psychology*, vol. 53, 1956, pp. 122–132.

Fogel, Lawrence J., *Biotechnology: Concepts and Applications*, Englewood Cliffs, N.J.: Prentice-Hall, 1963.

Foote, Nelson N., and Hart, Clyde W., "Public Opinion and Collective Behavior," in Sherif and Wilson (eds.), *Group Relations at the Crossroads*, New York: Harper & Row, 1953, ch.13.

Form, William, and Nosow, Sigmund, *Community in Disaster*, New York: Harper & Row, 1958.

Forrester, Jay, *Urban Dynamics*, Cambridge, Mass.: The M.I.T. Press, 1969.

Fortune, Reo, *Sorcerers of Dobu*, London: Routledge, 1932.

Free (Abbie Hoffman), *Revolution for the Hell of It*, New York: Dial, 1968.

Freiden, Eliot (ed.), *The Hospital in Modern Society*, New York: Free Press, 1963.

French, John R. P., Jr., "The Disruption and Cohesion of Groups," *Journal of Abnormal and Social Psychology*, vol. 36, 1941, pp. 361–377.

Freud, Sigmund, *Group Psychology and the Analysis of the Ego*, London: International Psychoanalysis Press, 1922.

———, *The Future of an Illusion*, published by Horace Liveright and the Institute of Psychoanalysis, 1928.

Friedenberg, Edgar Z., *The Vanishing Adolescent*, Boston: Beacon, 1959.

————, *Coming of Age in America*, New York: Random House, 1963.

Fromm, Erich, *Escape from Freedom*, New York: Holt, Rinehart and Winston, 1941.

————, *The Sane Society*, New York: Holt, Rinehart and Winston, 1955.

Fuchs, Lawrence H., *Those Peculiar Americans, The Peace Corps and the American National Character*, New York: Meredith Press, 1967.

Fulop-Miller, Rene, *Leaders, Dreamers and Rebels, An Account of the Great Mass-Movements of History and of the Wish-Dreams that Inspired Them*, New York: Viking, 1935.

Fyfe, H., *The Illusion of National Character*, London: Watts, 1946.

Galdston, Iago, and Zetterberg, Hans (eds.), *Panic and Morale*, Conference Transactions, New York Academy of Medicine and the Josiah Macy Foundation, New York: International Universities' Press, 1958.

Gardner, Eric F., and Thompson, George G., *Social Relations and Morale in Small Groups*, New York: Appleton, 1956.

Gennep, Arnold Van, *Rites of Passage*, Chicago: University of Chicago Press (1909), 1960.

Gerard, R. W.; Kluckhohn, C.; and Rapoport, A., "Biological and Cultural Evolution," *Behavioral Science,* vol. 1, 1956, pp. 6–43.

Gerth, H. H., and Mills, C. W. (eds.), *From Max Weber, Essays in Sociology,* New York: Oxford University Press, 1958.

Giddings, Franklin H., *Principles of Sociology*, New York: Macmillan, 1896.

Gilchrist, J.; Shaw, M.; and Walker, L., "Some Effects of Unequal Distribution of Information in a Wheel Group Structure," *Journal of Abnormal and Social Psychology*, vol. 51, 1955, pp. 119–122.

Gittler, Joseph B. (ed.), *Review of Sociology, Analysis of a Decade*, New York: Wiley, 1957.

Gladstone, Arthur, "The Conception of the Enemy," *Conflict Resolution*, vol. III, June 1959, pp. 132–137.

Glaser, Barney G., and Strauss, A. L., *Awareness of Dying*, Chicago: Aldine, 1965.

————, *Time for Dying*, Chicago: Aldine, 1968.

Glazer, Nathan, and Moynihan, Daniel P., *Beyond the Melting Pot*, Cambridge, Mass.: The M.I.T. Press, 1963.

Goen, Prof. C. C., of Wesley Theological Seminary; quoted by D. L. Thrapp, *Los Angeles Times*, July 19, 1970:F–6.

Goffman, Erving, "On Face-Work: An Analysis of Ritual Elements in Social Interaction," *Psychiatry*, vol. 18, 1955, pp. 213–231.

————, *The Presentation of Self in Everyday Life*, Edinburgh: University of Edinburgh Social Sciences Research Centre, Monograph No., 2, 1958.

————, *Asylum*, New York: Doubleday (Anchor Books), 1961.

————, *Behavior in Public Places, Notes on the Organization of Gatherings*, New York: Free Press, 1963.(a)

————, *Stigma; Notes on the Management of Spoiled Identity*, Englewood Cliffs, N.J. Prentice-Hall, 1963.(b)

Goode, William J., "The Sociology of Morale," in Galdston and Zetterberg (eds.), *Panic and Morale*, Conference Transactions, New York Academy of Medicine and the Josiah Macy Foundation, New York: International Universities' Press, 1958, pp. 119–151.

————, "A Theory of Role Strain," *American Sociological Review*, vol. 25, 1960, pp. 483–496.

Goodman, Paul, *Growing Up Absurd, Problems of Youth in the Organized System*, New York: Random House, 1956.

Goodman, Paul and Percival, *Communitas, Means of Livelihood and Ways of Life*, New York: Random House (Vintage Books) (1947), 1960.

Gorden, Raymond L., "Attitude and the Definition of the Situation," *American Sociological Review*, vol. 17, 1952, pp. 50–58.

Gouldner, Alvin W., *Wildcat Strike: A Study in Worker-Management Relationships*, Yellow Springs, Ohio: Antioch Press, 1954. (Also, New York: Harper & Row.)

Graham, Hugh D., and Gurr, Ted R., *Violence in America, Historical and Comparative Perspectives*, New York: New American Library, 1969.

Graves, Ralph, "Look What's Happening at MY House," *Life*, Feb. 5, 1965.

Greenberg, Ira A., *Psychodrama and Audience Attitude Change*, Beverly Hills, Calif.: Behavioral Studies Press, 1969.

Gregory, Paul M., "An Economic Interpretation of Women's Fashions," *Southern Economic Journal*, vol. 14, 1947, pp. 148–162.

Gross, Bertram M., "Operation Basic: The Retrieval of Wasted Knowledge," in Dexter and White, *People, Society and Mass Communications*, New York: Free Press, 1964, pp. 457–475.

Gurr, Ted Robert, "A Comparative Study of Civil Strife," in Graham and Gurr, *Violence in America, Historical and Comparative Perspectives*, New York: New American Library, 1969, pp. 544–605.

Gusfield, Joseph R., *Symbolic Crusade, Status Politics and the American Temperance Movement*, Urbana: University of Illinois Press, 1963.

Gusfield, Joseph R. (ed.), *Protest, Reform and Revolt, A Reader in Social Movements*, New York: Wiley, 1970.

Haggerty, Sandra, "On Being Black," *San Diego Union*, June 29, 1970.

Halasz, Nicholas, *Captain Dreyfus, the Story of a Mass Hysteria*, New York: Grove (Evergreen Books), 1957. (Originally published 1955.)

Hall, Edward T., *The Silent Language*, New York: Doubleday, 1959.

Hallowell, Irving, "Aggression in Salteaux Society," *Psychiatry*, vol. 3, 1940, pp. 395–407.

Halsted, John B. (ed.), *Romanticism*, New York: Walker, 1969.

Halverson, Guy, "New Hit-and-Run Guerrilla Tactics," *Christian Science Monitor*, Oct. 11, 1969.

Hampden-Turner, Charles, *Radical Man, The Process of Psycho-Social Development*, Cambridge, Mass.: Schenkman, 1970.

Hansen, Chadwick, *Witchcraft at Salem*, New York: Braziller, 1969.

Hardin, Garrett, "The Cybernetics of Competition: A Biologist's View of Society," in Buckley (ed.), *Modern Systems Research for the Behavioral Sciences*, Chicago: Aldine, 1968, pp. 449–459.

Hare, A. Paul; Borgatta, E. F.; and Bales, R. F., *Small Groups, Studies in Social Interaction*, New York: Knopf, 1955.

Hausknecht, Murray, *The Joiners, A Sociological Description of Voluntary Association Membership in the United States*, New York: Bedminster Press, 1962.

Heberle, Rudolf, *Social Movements, An Introduction to Political Sociology*, New York: Appleton, 1951.

Hecker, J. F. C., *The Black Death and the Dancing Mania*, New York: Cassell, 1888. (Translated by B. C. Babington.)

Heidegger, Martin, *Discourse on Thinking*, New York: Harper & Row, 1966.

Henry, Jules, *Culture Against Man*, New York: Random House, 1963.

Heyen, William, "The Poet's Leap into Reality," *Saturday Review*, Aug. 1, 1970, pp. 21–22.

Higham, T. M., "Experimental Study of the Transmission of Rumor," *British Journal of Sociology*, vol. 42, 1951, pp. 42–55.

Hine, Robert V., *California's Utopian Colonies*, San Marino, Calif.: Huntington Library, 1953.

Hirsch, Paul M., "Processing Fads and Fashions: An Organization-Set Analysis of Cultural Industry Systems," *American Journal of Sociology*, vol. 77, 1972, pp. 639–659.

Hobsbawm, E. J., *Social Bandits and Primitive Rebels*, New York: Free Press, 1959.

Hocking, William E., *Morale and Its Enemies*, New Haven: Yale University Press, 1918.

Hoehling, A. A. and Mary, *The Last Voyage of the Lusitania*, New York: Holt, Rinehart and Winston, 1956.

Hoffer, Eric, *The True Believer; Thoughts on the Nature of Mass Movements*, New York: Harper & Row, 1951.

Hoffman, Abbie, *See* Free.

———, "Raps with Abbie," *Sunrise*, June 24, 1970.

Hoffman, Arthur S. (ed.), *International Communication and the New Diplomacy*, Bloomington: Indiana University Press, 1968.

Hoffman, L. R., and Maier, N. R. F., "Quality and Acceptance of Problem Solutions by Members of Homogeneous and Heterogeneous Groups," *Journal of Abnormal and Social Psychology*, vol. 62, 1961, pp. 401–407.

Hoffman, Stanley and Inge, "The Will to Grandeur: De Gaulle as Political Artist," *Daedalus, Philosophers and Kings: Studies in Leadership*, Summer 1968, pp. 829–887.

Hofstadter, Richard, *Social Darwinism in American Thought*, Philadelphia: University of Pennsylvania Press, 1944. (Also, Boston: Beacon Press, 1955.)

———, *The American Political Tradition*, New York: Random House, 1948.

———, *The Age of Reform*, New York: Random House, 1955.

———, *The Paranoid Style in American Politics and Other Essays*, New York: Knopf, 1966.

Holloway, Mark, *Heavens on Earth, Utopian Communities in America, 1680–1880*, London: Turnstile Press, 1951.

Holmstrom, David, "SDS: Unconventional Maybe, but Is It Leading a Conspiracy?" *Christian Science Monitor*, March 27, 1969.

Homans, George C., "Anxiety and Ritual," *American Anthropologist*, vol. XLIII, 1941, pp. 164–172.

———, *The Human Group*, New York: Harcourt, 1950.

Hopper, Rex D., "The Revolutionary Process," *Social Forces*, vol. 28, March 1950, pp. 270–279.

Horney, Karen, *The Neurotic Personality of Our Time*, New York: Norton, 1937.

Horton, Donald, and Strauss, A. L., "Interaction in Audience-Participation Shows," *American Journal of Sociology*, vol. LXII, May 1957, pp. 579–587.

Howard, Jane, *Please Touch*, New York: McGraw-Hill, 1970.

Hsu, Francis L. K., *Psychological Anthropology*, Homewood, Ill.: Dorsey Press, 1961.

Hughes, Helen M., *News and the Human Interest Story*, Chicago: University of Chicago Press, 1940.

Huizinga, Johan, *Homo Ludens, A Study of the Play Element in Culture*, Boston: Beacon (1950), 1955.

Hunter, Floyd, *Community Power Structure*, Chapel Hill: University of North Carolina Press, 1953.

———, *Top Leadership, U.S.A.*, Chapel Hill: University of North Carolina Press, 1959.

Huxley, Aldous, *Brave New World*, New York: Doubleday, 1932.

———, *Brave New World Revisited*, New York: Harper & Row, 1958.

———, *The Doors of Perception*, New York: Harper & Row, 1954.

———, *Island*, New York: Penguin, 1964.

Inkeles, Alex, and Bauer, Raymond A., "Keeping Up with the News," in Berelson and Janowitz (eds.), *Reader in Public Opinion and Communication*, New York: Free Press, 1966, pp. 569–570.

Inoguchi, Rikihei; Nakajima, T.; and Pineau, R., *The Divine Wind, Japan's Kamakaze Force in World War II*, Annapolis, Md.: U.S. Naval Institute, 1958. (Also, Bantam Books, 1960.)

Ionescu, Eugene, Interview, *Evergreen Review*; reprinted in *Intellectual Digest*, May/June 1971, pp. 61–69, 143–144.

Jacobs, Norman, "The Phantom Slasher of Taipei: Mass Hysteria in a Non-Western Society," *Social Problems*, vol. 12, 1965, pp. 318–328.

Jacobs, Paul, and Landau, Saul, *The New Radicals*, New York: Penguin (Vintage Books), 1966.

Jahoda, Marie, and Warren, Neil (eds.), *Attitudes*, New York: Penguin, 1966.

James, William, *Varieties of Religious Experience*, New York: Longmans, 1902.

Janis, I. L., and King, B. T., "Influence of Role-Playing on Opinion Change," *Journal of Abnormal and Social Psychology*, vol. 49, 1954, pp. 211–218.

Janis, Irving L., Hovland, C., et al., *Personality and Persuasibility*, New Haven: Yale University Press, 1959.

Janney, J. E., "Fads of College Women," *Journal of Abnormal and Social Psychology*, vol. 36, 1941, pp. 275–278.

Janowitz, Morris, *Social Control of Escalated Riots*, Chicago: University of Chicago Center for Policy Study, 1968.

———, "Patterns of Collective Racial Violence," in Graham and Gurr, *Violence in America, Historical and Comparative Perspective*, New York: New American Library, 1969, pp. 393–422.

Jeffries, Vincent; Turner, Ralph H.; and Morris, Richard T., "The Public Perception of the Watts Riot as Social Protest," *American Sociological Review*, vol. 36, 1971, pp. 443–451.

Jennings, Helen H., *Leadership and Isolation*, New York: Longmans, 1943.

Johnson, Alvin, "Short Change," *New Republic*, vol. 14, April 27, 1918, pp. 381–383.

Johnson, D. M., "The Phantom Anesthetist of Matoon: A Field Study of Mass Hysteria," *Journal of Abnormal and Social Psychology*, vol. 40, 1945, pp. 175–186.

Johnstone, John, and Katz, Elihu, "Youth and Popular Music: A Study in the Sociology of Taste," *American Journal of Sociology*, vol. 62, 1957, pp. 563–578.

Jones, N. G. Blurton, "An Ethological Study of Some Aspects of Social Behaviour in Nursery School," in Desmond Morris (ed.), *Primate Ethology*, Chicago: Aldine, 1967b, pp. 347–368.

Josephson, Eric and Mary (eds.), *Man Alone, Alienation in Modern Society*, New York: Dell, 1962.

Jourard, Sidney M., *The Transparent Self: Self Disclosure and Well-Being*, Princeton, N.J.: Van Nostrand, 1964.

Kahl, Joseph A., *The Measurement of Modernism, A Study of Values in Brazil and Mexico*, Austin: University of Texas Press, 1968.

Kahler, Erich, *The Tower and the Abyss, An Inquiry into the Transformation of the Individual*, New York: Braziller, 1957.

Kanter, Rosabeth M., "Commitment and Social Organization: a Study of Commitment Mechanisms in Utopian Communities," *American Sociological Review*, vol. 33, August 1968, pp. 499–517.

Katz, Elihu, "Diffusion of New Ideas and Practices," in Schramm (ed.), *The Science of Communication, New Directions and New Findings in Communication Research*, New York: Basic Books, 1963.

Katz, Elihu, and Lazarsfeld, Paul, *Personal Influence, The Part Played by People in the Flow of Mass Communications*, New York: Free Press, 1955.

Katz, Elihu; Levin, M.; and Hamilton, H., "Traditions of Research in the Diffusion of Innovation," *American Sociological Review*, vol. 28, 1963, pp. 237–252.

Kazantzakis, Nikos, *The Odyssey, A Modern Sequel*, New York: Simon and Schuster, 1958. (Translated by Kimon Friar.)

Keesing, Felix M. and Marie M., *Elite Communication in Samoa, a Study of Leadership*, Stanford, Calif.: Stanford University Press, 1956, pp. 91–129.

Kelley, H. H., "Salience of Membership and Resistance to Change of Group-Anchored Attitudes," *Human Relations*, vol. 8, 1955, pp. 275–289.

Kelley, H. H.; Thibaut, J. W.; Radloff, R.; and Mundy, O., "The Development of Cooperation in the 'Minimal Social Situation' ", *Psychological Monographs*, vol. 76, no. 19, 1962, Whole No. 538.

Kellogg, W. N., and Kellogg, L. A., *The Ape and the Child*, New York: Hafner, 1933.

Kelman, Herbert C. (ed.), *International Behavior, A Social-Psychological Analysis*, New York: Holt, Rinehart and Winston, 1966.

Keniston, Kenneth, "Alienation and the Decline of Utopia," in H. M. Ruitenbeek (ed.), *Varieties of Social Theory*, New York: Dutton, 1963, pp. 79–177.

Kennedy, John F., *Profiles in Courage*, New York: Harper & Row, 1964.

Kerckhoff, Alan C., and Back, Kurt W., *The June Bug: A Study of Hysterical Contagion*, New York: Appleton, 1968.

Kerner Commission, *Report of the National Advisory Commission on Civil Disorders*, Washington, D.C.: Government Printing Office, 1968.

Killian, Lewis M., "Social Movements," in Robert E. L. Faris (ed.), *Handbook of Modern Sociology*, Chicago: Rand McNally, 1964, pp. 426–455.

Kilpatrick, F. P., "Problems of Perception in Extreme Situations," *Human Organization*, vol. 16, 1957, pp. 20–22.

King, C. Wendell, *Social Movements in the United States*, New York: Random House, 1956.

Klapp, Orrin E., "Creation of Popular Heroes," *American Journal of Sociology*, vol. 54, 1948, pp. 135–141.

————, "The Fool as a Social Type," *American Journal of Sociology*, vol. LV, 1949, pp. 157–162.(a)

————, "Hero Worship in America," *American Sociological Review*, vol. XIV, February 1949, pp. 53–62.(b)

————, "The Clever Hero," *Journal of American Folklore*, vol. 67, 1954, pp. 21–34.

————, "The Concept of Consensus and Its Importance," *Sociology and Social Research*, vol. 41, 1957, pp. 336–342.

————, "Vilification as a Social Process," *Pacific Sociological Review*, vol. 2, 1959, pp. 71–76.

————, *Heroes, Villains and Fools; The Changing American Character*, Englewood Cliffs, N.J.: Prentice-Hall, 1962.

————, *Symbolic Leaders, Public Dramas and Public Men*, Chicago: Aldine, 1964.(a)

————, "Mexican Social Types," *American Journal of Sociology*, vol. LXIX, 1964, pp. 404–414.(b)

————, A survey of fashion-consciousness among university students, summarized in Klapp, 1969, p. 74.

————, *Collective Search for Identity*, New York: Holt, Rinehart and Winston, 1969.

Klapper, Joseph T., *The Effects of Mass Communication*, New York: Free Press, 1960.

Klineberg, Otto, *The Human Dimension in International Relations*, New York: Holt, Rinehart and Winston, 1964.

Kluckhohn, Clyde, *Navaho Witchcraft*, Boston: Beacon (1962), 1944.

Kluckhohn, Clyde, and Leighton, Dorothea, *The Navaho*, Cambridge: Harvard University Press, 1947.

Knapp, Robert H., "A Psychology of Rumor," *Public Opinion Quarterly*, vol. 8, 1944, pp. 25–26.

Komisar, Lucy, "The New Feminism," *Saturday Review*, Feb. 21, 1970, pp. 27–30, 55.

Kornhauser, William, *The Politics of Mass Society*, New York: Free Press, 1959.

Kriesberg, Martin, "Cross-Pressures and Attitudes: A Study of the Influence of Conflicting Propaganda on Opinions Regarding American-Soviet Relations," *Public Opinion Quarterly*, vol. 13, Spring 1949, pp. 5–16.

Krishnamurti, J., *Freedom from the Known*, New York: Harper & Row, 1969.

Kroeber, A. L., *Style and Civilizations*, New York: Cornell University Press, 1957.

Kummer, Hans, *Social Organization of Hamadryas Baboons, A Field Study*, Chicago: University of Chicago Press, 1968

La Barre, Weston, "Paralinguistics, Kinesics and Cultural Anthropology," in Matson and Montagu, *The Human Dialogue, Perspectives on Communication*, New York: Free Press, 1967, pp. 456–490.

Laing, R. D., *The Politics of Experience*, New York: Ballentine Books, 1967.

Lang, Kurt and Gladys, "Decisions for Christ. Billy Graham in New York," in Maurice R. Stein, et al. (eds.), *Identity and Anxiety, Survival of the Person in Mass Society*, New York: Free Press, 1960, pp. 416, 425–426.

————, *Collective Dynamics*, New York: Crowell, 1961.

————, "Collective Behavior Theory and the Escalated Riots of the Sixties," in Shibutani (ed.), *Human Nature and Collective Behavior, Papers in Honor of Herbert Blumer*, Englewood Cliffs, N.J.: Prentice-Hall, 1970, pp. 94–110.

Langer, Susanne K., *Philosophy in a New Key, A Study of the Symbolism of Reason, Rite, and Art*, New York: Penguin (1942), 1948, pp. 63–83.

Lanternari, Vittorio, *Religions of the Oppressed, A Study of Modern Messianic Cults*, New York: Knopf (Mentor Books), 1963.

LaPiere, Richard T., *Collective Behavior* (1st ed.), New York: McGraw-Hill, 1938.

Larrabee, Eric, and Meyersohn, Rolf (eds.), *Mass Leisure*, New York: Free Press, 1958.

Larsen, Otto N. (ed.), *Violence and the Mass Media*, New York: Harper & Row, 1968.

Lasch, Christopher, *The New Radicalism in America (1889–1963), The Intellectual as a Social Type*, New York: Knopf, 1965.

Laski, Marghanita, *Ecstasy, A Study of Some Secular and Religious Experiences*, London: Cresset Press, 1961.

Lasswell, Harold D., "The Climate of International Action," in Kelman (ed.), *International Behavior, A Social-Psychological Analysis*, New York: Holt, Rinehart and Winston, 1966, pp. 339–353.

Lauter, Paul, and Howe, Florence, "What Happened to the 'Free University'?" *Saturday Review*, June 20, 1970, pp. 80–82, 93.

Lazarsfeld, Paul, "The Election Is Over," *Public Opinion Quarterly*, vol. 8, Fall 1944, pp. 317–330.

Lazarsfeld, Paul F.; Berelson, Bernard; and Gaudet, Helen, *The People's Choice*, New York: Duell, Sloan and Pearce Meredith, 1944.

Lazarsfeld, Paul, and Merton, Robert K., "Friendship as a Social Process," in M. Berger, T. Abel, and C. Page, *Freedom and Control in Modern Society*, New York: Van Nostrand, 1954.

Leavitt, Harold J., "Some Effects of Certain Communication Patterns on Group Performance," *Journal of Abnormal and Social Psychology*, vol. 46, 1951, pp. 38–50.

Le Bon, Gustave, *The Crowd, A Study of the Popular Mind*, New York: Viking, 1960. (First published in 1895.)

Lee, A. M., and Humphrey, N. D., *Race Riot*, New York: Dryden, 1943.

Leighton, Alexander H., *The Governing of Men: General Principles and*

Recommendations Based on Experience at a Japanese Relocation Camp, Princeton: Princeton University Press, 1946.

Leighton, Alexander H. and Dorothea C., *The Navaho Door, An Introduction to Navaho Life*, New York: Russell & Russell, 1944.

Leites, Nathan, and Bernaut, Elsa, *Ritual of Liquidation, The Case of the Moscow Trials*, New York: Free Press, 1954.

Lemert, Edwin M., "Paranoia and the Dynamics of Exclusion," *Sociometry*, vol. 25, March 1962, pp. 2–19.

Lenin, V. I. (Nicolai), *State and Revolution*, New York: International (1918), 1932.

Lerbinger, Otto, and Sullivan, A. J. (eds.), *Information, Influence and Communication*, New York: Basic Books, 1965.

Lerner, Daniel, "Communication Systems and Social Systems," *Behavioral Science*, vol. 2, 1957, pp. 266–275. (Also, in Alfred G. Smith, *Communication and Culture, Readings in the Codes of Human Interaction*, New York: Holt, Rinehart and Winston, 1966, pp. 577–564.)

————, *The Passing of Traditional Society*, New York: Free Press, 1959.

Lerner, Daniel, and Schramm, Wilbur (eds.), *Communication and Change in the Developing Countries*, Honolulu: East-West Center Press, 1967.

Lesieur, Frederick G. (ed.), *The Scanlon Plan: A Frontier in Labor Management Cooperation*, Cambridge, Mass.: The M.I.T. Press, 1958.

Lever, Janet, "Soccer, the Opium of the Brazilian People," *Trans-Action*, December 1969, p. 34 ff.

Levine, D. (ed.), *Nebraska Symposium on Motivation*, Lincoln: University of Nebraska Press, 1965.

Levine, Gene N., and Modell, John, "American Public Opinion and the Fallout-Shelter Issue," *Public Opinion Quarterly*, vol. 29, 1965, pp. 270–279.

Lewin, Kurt, *Resolving Social Conflicts*, New York: Harper & Row, 1948.

Libo, Lester, *Measuring Group Cohesiveness*, Ann Arbor: University of Michigan, Research Center for Group Dynamics, Institute for Social Research, 1953.

Lincoln, C. Eric, *The Black Muslims of America*, Boston: Beacon, 1961.

Lindbergh, Charles, *We*, New York: Grosset & Dunlap, 1927.

Lindesmith, Alfred R., and Strauss, A. L., *Social Psychology* (3d ed.), New York: Holt, Rinehart and Winston, 1968.

————, *Readings in Social Psychology*, New York: Holt, Rinehart and Winston, 1969.

Linton, Ralph, "Nativistic Movements," *American Anthropologist*, vol. 45, 1943, pp. 230–240.

Lionberger, Herbert F., *Adoption of New Ideas and Practices*, Ames: Iowa State University Press, 1960.

Lippitt, Ronald; Watson, Jeanne; and Westley, Bruce, *The Dynamics of Planned Change: A Comparative Study of Principles and Methods*, New York: Harcourt, 1958.

Lippman, Walter, *Public Opinion*, New York: Free Press, 1965.

Lippman, Walter, *A Preface to Morals*, New York: Macmillan, 1929.

Lipset, Seymour M., *A Changing American Character?*, Berkeley: Institute of Industrial Relations, University of California, 1962, Reprint No. 180.

(Reprinted from S. M. Lipset and L. Lowenthal, *Culture and Social Character*, New York: Free Press, 1961.)

Lipset, Seymour M., and Raab, Earl, *The Politics of Unreason; Right-Wing Extremism in America, 1790–1970*, New York: Harper & Row, 1970.

Lipset, Seymour M., and Wolin, Sheldon S. (eds.), *The Berkeley Student Revolt*, New York: Doubleday, 1965.

Lipton, Lawrence, *The Holy Barbarians*, New York: Messner, 1959.

Lomax, Louis F., *The Negro Revolt*, New York: New American Library, 1962.

Loomis, Charles P., *Social Systems*, New York: Van Nostrand, 1960.

———, "In Praise of Conflict and Its Resolution," *American Sociological Review*, vol. 32, December 1967, pp. 875–890.

Loomis, Charles P., and McKinney, J. C., "Systemic Differences Between Latin-American Communities of Family Farms and Large Estates," *American Journal of Sociology*, vol. LXI, 1956, pp. 404–412.

Lorenz, Konrad, *On Aggression*, New York: Harcourt (Bantam Books), 1966.

Lowenthal, Leo, and Guterman, Norbert, *Prophets of Deceit, A Study of the Techniques of the American Agitator*, New York: Harper & Row, 1949.

Lyman, Stanford M., and Scott, Marvin B., *A Sociology of the Absurd*, New York: Appleton, 1970.

Lynes, Russell, *The Taste-Makers*, New York: Harper & Row (1949), 1954.

MacDonald, Julie, *Almost Human, the Baboon: Wild and Tame—in Fact and in Legend*, New York: Chilton, 1965.

Mackay, Charles, *Extraordinary Popular Delusions and the Madness of Crowds*, Boston: Page (1841, 1852), 1932.

Maddocks, Melvin, "We are Not Amused—and Why," *Time*, July 20, 1970, pp. 30–31.

———, "Underground Gropings, and a Past for the ex-Now Generation," *Christian Science Monitor*, March 26, 1971.

Malamud, Daniel I., and Machover, Solomon, *Toward Self-Understanding, Group Techniques in Self-Confrontation*, Springfield, Ill.: Charles C Thomas, 1965.

Maltz, Maxwell, *Psycho-Cybernetics*, New York: Simon and Schuster (Essandess), 1967. (Prentice-Hall, 1960.)

Mann, John, *Encounter, A Weekend with Intimate Strangers*, New York: Grossman, 1970.

Mann, W. E., *Sect, Cult and Church in Alberta*, Toronto: University of Toronto Press, 1955.

Mannheim, Karl, *Ideology and Utopia, An Introduction to the Sociology of Knowledge*, New York: Harcourt, 1936.

Manning, Robert, "International News Media," in Arthur S. Hoffman, *International Communication and the New Diplomacy*, Bloomington: Indiana University Press, 1968, pp. 158–163.

Marcus, Stanley, "Fashion Is My Business," *Atlantic*, June 1948, pp. 43–47.

Marcuse, Herbert, *One-Dimensional Man*, London: Routledge and Kegan Paul, 1964.

Marshall, Samuel L. A., *Men Against Fire*, New York: Morrow, 1947.

Martin, Everett Dean, *The Behavior of Crowds*, New York: Harper & Row, 1920.

Martindale, Don, "The Formation and Destruction of Communities," in

Zollschan and Hirsch (eds.), *Explorations in Social Change*, Boston: Houghton Mifflin, 1964, pp. 61–87.

Martinez, Thomas M., and La Franchi, Robert, "Why People Play Poker," *Trans-Action*, July 1969, pp. 30–35 ff.

Maruyama, Magoroh, "The Second Cybernetics: Deviance-Amplifying Mutual Causal Processes," in Buckley (ed.), *Modern Systems Research for the Behavioral Scientist*, Chicago: Aldine, 1968, pp. 304–313.

Maslow, Abraham, *Toward a Psychology of Being*, New York: Van Nostrand, 1962.

Mathison, Richard R., *Faiths, Cults and Sects of America, From Atheists to Zen*, Indianapolis: Bobbs-Merrill, 1960.

Matson, Floyd W., and Montagu, Ashley (eds.), *The Human Dialogue, Perspectives on Communication*, New York: Free Press, 1967.

Mayo, Elton, *The Human Problems of an Industrial Civilization*, Boston: Harvard University and Macmillan, 1933.

McCall, Michel, "Some Ecological Aspects of Negro Slum Riots (1968)," in Gusfield (ed.), *Protest, Reform and Revolt, A Reader in Social Movements*, New York: Wiley, 1970, pp. 345–362.

McCleery, Richard H., "Policy Change in Prison Management," in Etzioni (ed.), *Complex Organizations*, New York: Holt, Rinehart and Winston, 1961, pp. 376–400.

McClosky, Herbert, and Schaar, John H., "Psychological Dimensions of Anomy," *American Sociological Review*, vol. 30, 1965, pp. 14–40.

McCord, William; Howard, J.; Friedberg, B.; and Harwood, E., *Life Styles in the Black Ghetto*, New York: Norton, 1969.

McDougall, William, *The Group Mind*, New York: Putnam (1920), 1927.

McGill, William J., Quoted, *San Diego Evening Tribune*, June 30, 1970:B–6.

McGlashan, Alan, *The Savage and Beautiful Country*, Boston: Houghton Mifflin, 1967.

McHugh, Peter, *Defining the Situation, The Organization of Meaning in Social Interaction*, New York: Bobbs-Merrill, 1968.

McLeod, Jack M., "Contribution of Psychology to Communication Theory," in Dance (ed.), *Human Communication Theory, Original Essays*, New York: Holt, Rinehart and Winston, 1967, pp. 209–235.

McLuhan, Marshall, *Understanding Media: The Extensions of Man*, New York: McGraw-Hill, 1964. (Also *Understanding Media: The Extensions of Man*, New York: (McGraw-Hill, 1964), Signet Books, 1966.

————, Preface to Robert Wallis, *Time: Fourth Dimension of the Mind*, New York: Harcourt, 1968, p. vii.

McWilliams, Carey, *Witch Hunt, The Revival of Heresy*, Boston: Little, Brown, 1950.

Mead, George H., *Mind, Self and Society*, Chicago: University of Chicago Press, 1934.

————, *Philosophy of the Act*, Chicago: University of Chicago Press, 1938.

Mead, Margret, *Cooperation and Competition Among Primitive Peoples* (1st ed.), New York: McGraw-Hill, 1937.

————, "Some Cultural Approaches to Communication Problems," in Bryson (ed.), *The Communication of Ideas, A Series of Addresses*, New York: Cooper Square Publishers, 1964, pp. 9–26.

————, *Psychological Aspects of Foreign Policy, Hearings of Committee on Foreign Relations*, U.S. Senate, Washington, D.C.: Government Printing Office, 1969.(a)

————, *Symposium "Generation Gap"*, San Diego, Calif., June 2, 1969.(b)

————, *Culture and Commitment, A Study of the Generation Gap*, New York: Doubleday (Natural History Press), 1970.

Mecklin, John M., *The Passing of the Saint*, Chicago: University of Chicago Press, 1941.

Medalia, Nahum Z., and Larsen, O. N., "Diffusion and Belief in a Collective Delusion: The Seattle Windshield Pitting Epidemic," *American Sociological Review*, vol. 23, 1958, pp. 221–232.

Meerloo, Joost A. M., in Dance (ed.), *Human Communication Theory, Original Essays*, New York: Holt, Rinehart and Winston, 1967, p. 133.

Menninger, Karl, *The Crime of Punishment*, New York: Viking, 1968.(a)

————, "The Crime of Punishment," *Saturday Review*, Sept. 7, 1968, pp. 21–22.(b)

————, Statement of Committee on Foreign Relations, U.S. Senate, Ninety-First Congress, First Session, June 19, 1969.

Merei, Ferenc, "Group Leadership and Institutionalization," *Human Relations*, vol. 2, 1949, pp. 23–39.

Merritt, Richard L., *Symbols of American Community, 1735–1775*, New Haven: Yale University Press, 1966. (Also in Deutsch and Foltz (eds.), *Nation Building*, New York: Atherton, 1963, pp. 69–70.

Meryman, Richard, Interview with Paul McCartney, "I Felt the Split Was Coming," *Life*, April 16, 1971, p. 52.

Merton, Robert K., *Mass Persuasion*, New York: Harper & Row, 1947.

————, *Social Theory and Social Structure*, New York: Free Press, 1968.

Merton, R. K.; Broom, L.; and Cottrell, L. S., Jr. (eds.), *Sociology Today*, New York: Basic Books, 1958.

Merton, Thomas, Quoted in *Time*, April 11, 1949; quotation is from *Seeds of Contemplation*, 1949.

Messinger, Sheldon L., "Organizational Transformation: A Case Study of a Declining Social Movement," *American Sociological Review*, vol. 20, 1955, pp. 3–10. (Also in Turner and Killian, 1957, pp. 493–501.)

Meyers, John, Quoted on violence in professional football, *San Diego Union*, July 31, 1969.

Meyersohn, Rolf, and Katz, Elihu, "Notes on a National History of Fads," *American Journal of Sociology*, vol. 62, 1957, pp. 594–601.

Milgram, Stanley, "Behavioral Study of Obedience," *Journal of Abnormal and Social Psychology*, vol. 67, 1963, pp. 371–378.

Miller, George A., *Psychology of Communication, Seven Essays*, New York: Basic Books, 1967.

Miller, James G., "Information Input Overload and Psychopathology," *American Journal of Psychiatry*, vol. 111, February 1960, pp. 695–704.

————, "Living Systems," *Behavioral Science*, vol. 10, 1965, pp. 193–237, 337–411.

————, "Living Systems: The Group," *Behavioral Science*, vol. 16, 1971, pp. 277–398.

Miller, N. E., and Dollard, John, *Social Learning and Imitation*, New Haven: Yale University Press, 1941.

Millis, Walter, *Road to War: America 1914–17*, Boston: Houghton Mifflin, 1935.

Mills, C. Wright, *Whitecollar, The American Middle Classes*, New York: Oxford University Press, 1951.

———, *The Power Elite*, London: Oxford University Press, 1956.

———, *The Marxists*, New York: Dell Publishing Company, 1962.

Mills, Theodore M., "Power Relations in Three-Person Groups," *American Sociological Review*, vol. 18, 1953, pp. 351–357.

———, "Equilibrium and the Processes of Deviance and Control," *American Sociological Review*, vol. 24, 1959, pp. 671–679.

Miner, Horace, "Body Ritual Among the Nacirema," *American Anthropologist*, vol. LVIII, 1956, pp. 503–507.

Monane, Joseph H., *A Sociology of Human Systems*, New York: Appleton, 1967.

Moore, Shirley, *Biological Clocks and Patterns*, New York: Criterion Books, 1967.

Moreno, J. L., *Who Shall Survive?*, Boston: Beacon Press.

Morris, Desmond, *The Naked Ape*, New York: Dell, 1967.(a)

Morris, Desmond (ed.), *Primate Ethology*, Chicago: Aldine, 1967.(b)

Morris, Richard T., *The Two-Way Mirror, National Status in Foreign Students' Adjustment*, Minneapolis: University of Minnesota Press, 1960.

Moynihan, Daniel P., "The Professionalization of Reform," *The Public Interest*, vol. 1, Fall, 1965, pp. 6–10. (Also in Gusfield, 1970, pp. 245–258.)

Moynihan, M., "Communication in New World Primates," in Desmond Morris (ed.), *Primate Ethology*, Chicago: Aldine, 1967b, pp. 236–266.

Nash, Jay B., *Building Morale*, New York: Barnes and Noble, 1942.

National Commission on the Causes and Prevention of Violence, *Violence in America, Historical and Comparative Perspectives*, H. D. Graham and T. R. Gurr (eds.), New York: New American Library, 1969.

Needleman, Jacob, *The New Religions*, New York: Doubleday, 1970.

Nelson, Joan, "Migrants, Urban Poverty, and Instability in Developing Nations," *Foreign Service Journal*, March 1970, pp. 26–40.

Nettler, Gwynn, "A Measure of Alienation," *American Sociological Review*, vol. 22, 1957, p. 675.

Nevin, David, "Autocrat in the Action Arena," *Life*, Sept. 5, 1969, pp. 51–52.

———, " 'Powerless' Students," *McCall's*, July 1970, pp. 45 ff.

Newcomb, Theodore H., "The Study of Consensus," in Merton, Broom, and Cottrell (eds.), *Sociology Today*, New York: Basic Books, 1958.

Newcomb, Theodore M., "An Approach to the Study of Communicative Acts," *Psychological Review*, vol. 60, 1953, pp. 393–404.

Niebuhr, H. Richard, *Social Sources of Denominationalism*, New York: Living Age Books (1929), 1957.

Niebuhr, Reinhold, *Moral Man and Immoral Society, A Study in Ethics and Politics*, New York: Scribner, 1932.

Nisbet, Robert A., *The Quest for Community*, New York: Oxford, 1953.

———, *The Social Bond, An Introduction to the Study of Society*, New York: Knopf, 1970.

Nordhoff, Charles, *The Communistic Societies of the United States*, New York: Hillary House (1960), 1875.

Nordskog, John Eric, *Contemporary Reform Movements*, New York: Scribner, 1954.

Norman, E. Herbert, "Mass Hysteria In Japan," *Far Eastern Survey*, vol. 14, 1945, pp. 67–70. (Also in Turner and Killian, 1957, pp. 31–36.)

Ogburn, William Fielding, *Social Change* (Huebsch, 1922), New York: Viking, 1950.

Olson, Philip (ed.), *America as a Mass Society, Changing Community and Identity*, New York: Free Press, 1963.

Otto, Herbert A., "Has Monogamy Failed?," *Saturday Review*, April 25, 1970, pp. 23–25, 62.

Packard, Vance, *The Waste-Makers*, New York: McKay, 1960.

Park, Robert E., "Human Nature and Collective Behavior," *American Journal of Sociology*, vol. 32, 1927, pp. 733–741.

————, "Collective Behavior," *Encyclopedia of Social Science*, vol. 3, 1930, pp. 631–633.

————, *An Outline of the Principles of Sociology*, New York: Barnes and Noble, 1939.

————, "Morale and the News," *American Journal of Sociology*, vol. 47, 1941, pp. 360–377.

————, *Society; Collective Behavior, News and Opinion, Sociology and Modern Society*, New York: Free Press, 1955.

————, in Ralph H. Turner (ed.), *On Social Control and Collective Behavior*, Chicago: University of Chicago Press, 1967.

Park, Robert E., and Burgess, Ernest W., *Introduction to the Science of Sociology*, Chicago: University of Chicago Press, 1924.

Parker, Dorothy L., "The Fitzgerald that Might Have Been," *Christian Science Monitor*, June 18, 1970.

Parsons, Talcott, *The Social System*, New York: Free Press, 1951.

Peterson, Warren A., and Gist, Noel P., "Rumor and Public Opinion," *American Journal of Sociology*, vol. 57, 1951, pp. 159–167. (Also in Turner and Killian, 1957, pp. 68–79.)

Polanyi, Karl, *The Great Transformation*, New York: Holt, Rinehart and Winston, 1944.

Pope, Liston, *Millhands and Preachers*, New Haven: Yale University Press, 1942.

Popper, K. R., *The Open Society and Its Enemies*, London: Routledge and Kegan Paul, 1952.

Proshansky, Harold, and Seidenberg, B. (eds.), *Basic Studies in Social Psychology*, New York: Holt, Rinehart and Winston, 1965.

Pye, Lucian W., *Politics, Personality and Nation-Building, Burma's Search for Identity*, New Haven: Yale University Press, 1962.

————, *Communications and Political Development*, Princeton, N.J.: Princeton University Press, 1963.

Quarantelli, Enrico, "The Behavior of Panic Participants," *Sociology and Social Research*, vol. 41, 1957, pp. 187–194.

————, "Emergent Accommodation Groups: Beyond Current Collective Behavior Typologies," in Shibutani (ed.), *Human Nature and Collective Behavior*, Englewood Cliffs, N.J.: Prentice-Hall, 1970, pp. 111–123.

Quarantelli, Enrico, and Hundley, James R., Jr., "A Test of Some Propositions About Crowd Formation and Behavior," in Evans (ed.), *Readings
in Collective Behavior*, Chicago: Rand McNally, 1969, pp. 538–554.

Quastler, H., and Wulff, V. J., "Human Performance in Information Transmission," *Control System Laboratory Report R-62*, University of Illinois.
(See Fogel, 1963, p. 362.)

Rabin, Albert I., *Growing Up in the Kibbutz*, New York: Springer, 1965.

Rabinowitz, L.; Kelley, H. H.; and Rosenblatt, R. M., "Effects of Different
Types of Interdependence and Response Conditions in the Minimal
Social Situation," *Journal of Experimental Social Psychology*, vol. 2, pp.
169–197.

Ragni, Gerome, and Rado, James, *Hair, The American Tribal Love-Rock
Musical*, New York: Simon and Schuster (Pocket Books), 1969.

Rand, Ayn, *The Romantic Manifesto, A Philosophy of Literature*, New York:
New American Library, 1971.

Rapoport, Anatol, "What is Information?" *ETC*, vol. 10, 1953, pp. 247–260.
(Also in Alfred G. Smith, *Communication and Culture, Readings in the
Codes of Human Interaction*, New York: Holt, Rinehart and Winston,
1966, pp. 41–55.)

Raymond, R. C., "Betting on the New Technologies," in Bright (ed.), *Technological Planning at the Corporate Level*, Boston: Division of Research,
Harvard School of Business, 1962.

———, "Communication, Entropy and Life," in Buckley (ed.), *Modern
Systems Research for the Behavioral Scientist*, Chicago: Aldine, 1968,
pp. 157–160.

Reda, Mario; Fappiano, Eugene; and Czikowsky, Leon (eds.), *Systems and
Processes, Collected Works in Sociology*, New Haven: College and
University Press, 1968.

Redfield, Robert, "The Folk Society," *American Journal of Sociology*, vol.
LII, 1947, pp. 293–308.

———, *The Little Community and Peasant Society and Culture*, Chicago:
University of Chicago Press, 1960.

Redl, Fritz, and Wineman, David, *Children Who Hate*, New York: Free Press,
1951.

Reed, John, *Ten Days that Shook the World* (Foreword by N. Lenin), New
York: International, 1967.

Reich, Charles A., *The Greening of America*, New York: Random House,
1970.

Riddle, Donald W., *The Martyrs, A Study in Social Control*, Chicago: University of Chicago Press, 1931.

Rienow, Robert and Leona Train, "Should People Be Dragged to the Polls?",
Saturday Review, July 30, 1960, pp. 8–9.

Riesman, David; with Glazer, Nathan, and Denney, Reuel, *The Lonely Crowd*,
New Haven: Yale University Press, 1950.

Rimmer, Robert H., *The Harrad Experiment*, New York: Bantam, 1966.

Roethlisberger, Fritz J., *Management and Morale*, Cambridge: Harvard University Press, 1941.

Rogers, Carl R., *On Becoming a Person*, Boston: Houghton Mifflin, 1970.

Rogers, Everett M., *Diffusion of Innovations*, New York: Free Press, 1962.

Rogers, John G., "What Life at Cape Kennedy Does to Marriage," *Parade*, July 6, 1969, pp. 12–13.

Rohrer, J. H., and Sherif, M. (eds.), *Social Psychology at the Crossroads* New York: Harper & Row, 1951.

Rokeach, Milton, "Open and Closed Mind," *Trans-Action*, January–February, 1965, p. 10.

Roper, Elmo, Study reported in *Saturday Review*, Aug. 9, 1969, p. 41.

Rose, Arnold M., *Theory and Method in the Social Sciences*, Minneapolis: University of Minnesota Press, 1954.

————, *The Power Structure, Political Process in American Society*, New York: Oxford, 1967.

Rosenau, James N., *Public Opinion and Foreign Policy*, New York: Random House, 1961.

Rosenberg, Bernard, and White, David H., *Mass Culture; The Popular Arts in America*, New York: Free Press, 1957.

Rosenberg, Stuart E., *The Search for Jewish Identity*, New York: Doubleday, 1965.

Rosman, Anraham, and Rubel, Paula G., *Feasting with Mine Enemy, Rank and Exchange among Northwest Coast Societies*, New York: Columbia University Press, 1971.

Ross, Edward A., *Social Psychology*, New York: Macmillan, 1908.

Ross, Irwin, *The Image Merchants; the Fabulous World of Public Relations*, New York: Doubleday, 1959.

Roszak, Theodore, *The Making of a Counter Culture; Reflections on the Technocratic Society and Its Youthful Opposition*, New York: Doubleday, 1969.

Rovere, Richard H., *Senator Joe McCarthy*, New York: Harcourt, 1959.

Rude, George, *The Crowd in History*, New York: Wiley, 1964.

Rudwin, Maximilian, *The Devil in Legend and Literature*, Chicago: Open Court, 1931.

Ruesch, Jurgen, and Kees, Weldon, *Nonverbal Communication, Notes on the Visual Perception of Human Relations*, Los Angeles: University of California Press, 1956.

Ruitenbeek, Hendrik M., *The Individual and the Crowd, A Study of Identity in America*, New York: New American Library, 1964.

Saikowski, Charlotte, "What Do Russians Really Think About?," *Christian Science Monitor*, Jan. 30, 1970.

Salk, Jonas, "The World We Will Live In," address to National Association of Manufacturers, The Annual Congress of American Industry, New York, Dec. 4, 1969.

Sander, Ellen, "John and Yoko Ono Lennon: Give Peace a Chance," *Saturday Review*, June 28, 1969.(a)

————, "The Stones Keep Rolling," *Saturday Review*, Nov. 29, 1969, pp. 67–68.(b)

Sanford, F. H., *Authoritarianism and Leadership*, Philadelphia: Institute for Research in Human Relations, 1950.

Sann, Paul, *Fads, Follies and Delusions of the American People*, New York: Crown, 1967.

Sapir, Edward, "Fashion," *Encyclopedia of Social Science*, vol. 6, 1931, pp. 139–144.

———, *Culture, Language and Personality*, Berkeley: University of California Press (1949), 1957.

Sarvis, B. C., "An Experimental Study of Rhythms," *Psychology Monographs*, vol. 44, 1933, pp. 207–232.

Schachter, Stanley, and Burdick, H., "A Field Experiment on Rumor Transmission and Distortion," *Journal of Abnormal and Social Psychology*, vol. 50, 1955, pp. 363–371.

Schatzman, Leonard, and Bucher, Rue, "Negotiating a Division of Labor Among Professionals in the State Mental Hospital," *Psychiatry*, vol. 27, 1964, pp. 266–277.

Scheff, Thomas J., "Toward a Sociological Model of Consensus," *American Sociological Review*, vol. 32, 1967, pp. 32–46.

Schoeck, Helmut, "The Evil Eye: Forms and Dynamics of a Universal Superstition," *Emory University Quarterly*, vol. XI, October 1955, pp. 153–160.

Schramm, Wilbur, *The Process and Effects of Mass Communication*, Urbana: University of Illinois Press, 1954.

———, *Mass Communications, A Book of Readings*, Urbana: University of Illinois Press, 1960.

Schramm, Wilbur (ed.), *The Science of Human Communication, New Directions and New Findings in Communication Research*, New York: Basic Books, 1963.

———, *Mass Media and National Development, the Role of Information in the Developing Countries*, Stanford, Calif.: Stanford University Press, 1964.

———, "Communication and Change," in Lerner and Schramm (eds.), *Communication and Change in the Developing Countries*, Honolulu: East-West Center Press, 1967, pp. 11–15.

Schultz, Duane P. (ed.), *Panic Behavior, Discussion and Readings*, New York: Random House, 1964.

Schutz, Alfred, *The Phenomenology of the Social World*, Evanston, Ill.: Northwestern University Press, 1967. (Translated by C. Walsh and F. Lehnhert.)

Schwartz, Mildred A., *Public Opinion and Canadian Identity*, Berkeley: University of California Press, 1967.

Schwartz, Robert L., "New Hope for the Dull," *Life*, June 12, 1970, p. 16.

Scott, Jerome F., and Homans, George C., "Reflections on the Wildcat Strikes," *American Sociological Review*, vol. 12, 1947, pp. 278–287.

Scott, John C., Jr., "Membership and Participation in Voluntary Associations," *American Sociological Review*, vol. 22, 1957, pp. 315–326.

Scott, Marvin B., *The Racing Game*, Chicago: Aldine, 1968.

Scott, Marvin B., and Lyman, Stanford M., "Accounts," *American Sociological Review*, vol. 33, 1968, pp. 46–62.

Seeman, Melvin, "On the Meaning of Alienation," *American Sociological Review*, vol. 24, 1959, pp. 783–791.

Sellers, Charles, "The Equilibrium Cycle in Two-Party Politics," *Public Opinion Quarterly*, vol. 29, 1965, pp. 16–37.

Sennett, Richard, *The Uses of Disorder: Personal Identity and City Life*, New York: Knopf, 1970.(a)

———, "Sex, Censorship and Society's Psyche," *Medical World News*, Oct. 2, 1970, pp. 20–28.(b)

Shannon, Claude E., and Weaver, Warren, *The Mathematical Theory of Communication*, Urbana: University of Illinois Press, 1949.

Shapiro, David, Quoted in *Time*, June 7, 1968, p. 44.

Shaw, Marjorie E., "A Comparison of Individuals and Small Groups in the Rational Solution of Complex Problems," *American Journal of Psychology*, vol. XLIV, 1932, pp. 491–504.

Shearer, Lloyd, "Intelligence Report," *Parade*, June 1970, p. 4.

Shellow, Robert, and Roemer, D. V., "The Riot that Didn't Happen," in Evans (ed.), *Readings in Collective Behavior*, Chicago: Rand McNally, 1969, pp. 523–536.

Shepard, Martin, and Lee, Marjorie, *Marathon 16*, New York: Putnam, 1970.

Sherif, Muzafer, *The Psychology of Social Norms*, New York: Harper & Row, 1936.

———, "Superordinate Goals in the Reduction of Intergroup Conflict," *American Journal of Sociology*, vol. 63, 1958, pp. 349–356.

Sherif, Muzafer and Carolyn W., *Groups in Harmony and Tension; An Integration of Studies on Intergroup Relations*, New York: Harper & Row, 1953.

———, *Reference Groups, Exploration into Conformity and Deviation of Adolescents*, New York: Harper & Row, 1964.

Sherif, Muzafer, and Harvey, O. J., "A Study in Ego-Functioning: Elimination of Stable Anchorages in Individual and Group Situations," *Sociometry*, vol. 15, 1952, pp. 272–305.

Sherif, Muzafer, and Wilson, M. O. (eds.), *Group Relations at the Crossroads*, New York: Harper & Row, 1953.

Shibutani, Tamotsu, *Society and Personality: An Interactionist Approach to Social Psychology*, Englewood Cliffs, N.J.: Prentice-Hall, 1961.

———, "Reference Groups and Social Control," in Arnold Rose (ed.), *Human Behavior and Social Processes*, Boston: Houghton Mifflin, 1962.

———, *Improvised News, a Sociological Study of Rumor*, Indianapolis: Bobbs-Merrill, 1966.

Shibutani, Tamotsu (ed.), *Human Nature and Collective Behavior, Papers in Honor of Herbert Blumer*, Englewood Cliffs, N.J.: Prentice-Hall, 1970.

Shils, Edward, and Janowitz, Morris, "Cohesion and Disintegration in the Wehrmacht in World War II," *Public Opinion Quarterly*, vol. 12, 1948, pp. 280–315.

Sidey, Hugh, "The Presidency: Making Points with Civility," *Life*, April 10, 1970, p. 4.

Silberman, Charles E., *Crisis in the Classroom, The Remaking of American Education*, New York: Random House, 1970.

Simmel, Georg, *The Sociology of Georg Simmel*, New York: Free Press, 1950. (Translated by Kurt H. Wolff.)

———, "Fashion," *American Journal of Sociology*, vol. LXII, 1957, pp. 541–558.

Simmons, J. L., and Winograd, Barry, *It's Happening*, New York: Rand McNally, 1968.

Singer, George, *Morale Factors in Industrial Management, The Examination of a Concept*, New York: Exposition Press, 1961.

Sitomer, Curtis J., "Wave of Good Samaritanism Sweeps Over Los Angeles," *Christian Science Monitor*, Feb. 16, 1971.

Smelser, Neil J., *Theory of Collective Behavior*, New York: Free Press, 1962.

Smith, Alfred G., *Communication and Culture, Readings in the Codes of Human Interaction*, New York: Holt, Rinehart and Winston, 1966.

Smith, Ernest A., *American Youth Culture Group Life in Teenage Society*, New York: Free Press, 1962.

Smith, Henry Nash, *Virgin Lands*, New York: Random House (Vintage Books), 1957.

Snyder, Louis L., *The New Nationalism*, Ithaca, N.Y.: Cornell University Press, 1968.

Sorel, Georges, *Reflections on Violence*, New York: Huebsch (1906), 1912.

Southwick, Charles H. (ed.), *Primate Social Behavior*, Princeton, N.J.: Van Nostrand, 1963.

Spicer, Edward, "Persistent Cultural Systems," *Science*, vol. 174, November 1971, pp. 795–800.

Stanford, Neal, "Flood of Scientific Data Rises," *Christian Science Monitor*, January 23, 1971.

Starkey, Marion L., *The Devil in Massachusetts*, New York: Knopf, 1949.

Stein, Judy, "Passionate Feminists," *McCall's*, July 1970, pp. 53, 113.

Stein, Maurice R.; Vidich, A. J.; and White, D. M. (eds.), *Identity and Anxiety, Survival of the Person in Mass Society*, New York: Free Press, 1960.

Steiner, Ivan D., and Fishbein, Martin (eds.), *Current Studies in Social Psychology*, New York: Holt, Rinehart and Winston, 1965.

Stephenson, William, *The Play Theory of Mass Communication*, Chicago: University of Chicago Press, 1967.

Sternhell, Carol Ruth, "A Harbinger," *McCall's*, January 1970, p. 36.

Stone, Gregory P., "Appearance and the Self," in Arnold M. Rose (ed.), *Human Behavior and Social Processes*, Boston: Houghton Mifflin, 1962, pp. 86–118.

Strauss, Anselm L., *Mirrors and Masks; The Quest for Identity*, New York: Free Press, 1959.

Strauss, Anselm L., et al., "The Hospital and Its Negotiated Order," in Eliot Freiden, *The Hospital in Modern Society*, New York: Free Press, 1963, pp. 148, 162.

Strecker, Edward A., *Beyond the Clinical Frontiers*, New York: Norton, 1940.

Stringer, William H., "Patrol by Grizzlies," *Christian Science Monitor*, March 25, 1971.

Sumner, W. G., *Folkways*, New York: Ginn, 1906.

Swanson, Guy E., "A Preliminary Laboratory Study of the Acting Crowd," *American Sociological Review*, vol. 18, 1953, pp. 522–533.

———, "Toward Corporate Action: A Reconstruction of Elementary Collective Processes," in Shibutani (ed.), *Human Nature and Collective Behavior, Papers in Honor of Herbert Blumer*, Englewood Cliffs, N.J.: Prentice-Hall, 1970, pp. 124–144.

Talmon, Yonina, "Pursuit of the Millennium: The Relation Between Religious and Social Change," in Gusfield (ed.), *Protest, Reform and Revolt: A Reader in Social Movements and Collective Action*, New York: Wiley, 1969, pp. 436–452. (Abridged from *The European Journal of Sociology*, vol. II, 1962, pp. 130–144.)

Tarde, Gabriel, *The Laws of Imitation*, New York: Holt, Rinehart and Winston, 1903.

Tawney, Richard H., *The Acquisitive Society*, New York: Harcourt, 1920.

Tec, Nechama, *Gambling in Sweden*, Totowa, N.J.: Bedminster Press, 1964.

Thayer, Lee, "Communication and Organization Theory," in Dance (ed.), *Human Communication Theory*, New York: Holt, Rinehart and Winston, 1967, pp. 70–115.

Thibaut, John W., and Coules, John, "Role of Communication in Reduction of Interpersonal Hostility," *Journal of Abnormal and Social Psychology*, vol. 47, 1952, pp. 770–777. (Also in Barnlund (ed.), *Interpersonal Communication: Survey and Studies*, Boston: Houghton Mifflin, 1968, pp. 497–508.

Thomas, W. I., and Zuarriechi, Florian, *The Polish Peasant in Europe and America*, Chicago: University of Chicago Press, 1918.

Thoreau, Henry David, in Cargill, *Henry D. Thoreau, Selected Writings on Nature and Liberty*, New York: Liberal Arts Press, 1952, pp. 108–139. (Originally, "Walking," *Atlantic Monthly*, June 1862.)

Toch, Hans, *Social Psychology of Social Movements*, Indianapolis: Bobbs-Merrill, 1965.

Toffler, Alvin, *Future Shock*, New York: Random House, 1970.

Tonnies, Ferdinand, *Fundamental Concepts of Sociology*, New York: American Book Company. (Translated by Charles P. Loomis.), 1940.

Townsend, Edward, "Drugs Bite at Business," *Christian Science Monitor*, Aug. 5, 1970.

Triandis, Harry C., and Vassiliou, Vasso, *A Comparative Analysis of Subjective Culture*, Technical Report Number 55 (67–11), October 1967, Urbana: Group Effectiveness Research Laboratory, University of Illinois.

Troeltsch, Ernst, *The Social Teaching of the Christian Churches*, New York: Macmillan, 1932.

Trotter, W., *Instincts of the Herd in Peace and War*, New York: Macmillan, 1917.

Tumin, Melvin M., and Feldman, Arnold S., "The Miracle at Sabana Grande," *Public Opinion Quarterly*, vol. 19, 1955, pp. 124–139.

Turner, Ralph H., "Role-Taking: Process Versus Conformity," in Rose (ed.), *Human Behavior and Social Processes*, Boston: Houghton Mifflin, 1962, chap. 2.

———, "New Theoretical Frameworks," *Sociological Quarterly*, April 1964, pp. 122–132. (Also in Evans (ed.), *Readings in Collective Behavior*, Chicago: Rand McNally, 1969, pp. 95–104.)

Turner, Ralph H. (ed.), Robert E. Park, *On Social Control and Collective Behavior*, Chicago: University of Chicago Press, 1967.

————, "The Public Perception of Protest," *American Sociological Review*, vol. 34, 1969, pp. 815–831.

Turner, Ralph H., and Killian, Lewis M., *Collective Behavior*, Englewood Cliffs, N.J.: Prentice-Hall, 1957.

Turner, Ralph H., and Surao, Samuel J., "Zoot-Suiters and Mexicans: Symbols in Crowd Behavior," *American Journal of Sociology*, vol. 62, 1956, pp. 14–20. (Also in Turner and Killian, 1957, pp. 122–129.)

Turner, Victor W., *The Forest of Symbols, Aspects of Ndembu Ritual*, Ithaca, N.Y.: Cornell University Press, 1967.

————, *The Ritual Process, Structure and Anti-Structure*, Chicago: Aldine, 1969.

Veblen, Thorstein, *The Theory of the Leisure Class: An Economic Study of Institutions*, New York: Modern Library (1899), 1934.

Veltfort, Helene R., and Lee, George E., "The Cocoanut Grove Fire: A Study in Scapegoating," *Journal of Abnormal and Social Psychology*, vol. 38, Clinical Supplement, 1943, pp. 138–154. (Also in Turner and Killian, 1957, pp. 197–207.)

Verveer, E. M.; Barry, J.; and Bousfield, W., "Change in Affectivity with Repetition," *American Journal of Psychology*, vol. 45, 1933, pp. 30–34.

Vickers, Geoffrey, "Is Adaptability Enough?," in Buckley (ed.), *Modern Systems Research for the Behavioral Scientist*, Chicago: Aldine, 1968, pp. 469–470.

Von Frisch, K., *The Dancing Bees*, New York: Harcourt, 1955.

————, "Dialects in the Language of the Bees," *Scientific American*, vol. 207, August 1962, pp. 79–87.

Wallace, Anthony C., "Revitalization Movements," *American Anthropologist*, vol. 58, 1956, pp. 264–281.

Wallace, Robert, "The Rugged Basis of American Protestantism," *Life*, Dec. 25, 1955, pp. 71 ff.

Waller, Willard, "The Rating and Dating Complex," *American Sociological Review*, October 1937, pp. 727–735.

Warner, W. Lloyd, *A Black Civilization, A Social Study of an Australian Tribe*, New York: Harper & Row, 1937.

————, *American Life, Dream and Reality*, Chicago: University of Chicago Press, 1953.

————, *The Living and the Dead, A Study of the Symbolic Life of Americans*, New Haven: Yale University Press, 1959.

Warner, W. Lloyd, and Henry, William E., "The Radio Day-Time Serial: A Symbolic Analysis," *Genetic Psychology Monographs*, vol. 37, 1948, pp. 7–13, 55–64.

Warriner, Charles K., "Groups Are Real: A Reaffirmation," *American Sociological Review*, October 1956, pp. 549–554.

Wax, Murray, "Cosmetics and Grooming," *American Journal of Sociology*, vol. LXII, 1957, pp. 588–593.

Webb, G. E. C., *Gypsies, The Secret People*, London: Herbert Jenkins, 1960.

Webber, Everett, *Escape to Utopia: The Communal Movement in America*, New York: Hastings, 1959.

Weber, Max, *Theory of Social and Economic Organization*, New York: Free

Press, 1957; originally pub. 1922. (Translated by A. M. Henderson and Talcott Parsons.)

———, *From Max Weber, Essays in Sociology*, H. H. Gerth and C. Wright Mills (eds.), New York: Oxford (1946), 1958.

Wecter, Dixon, *The Hero in America, A Chronicle of Hero Worship*, New York: Scribner, 1941.

Weick, Karl E., *The Social Psychology of Organizing*, Reading, Mass.: Addison-Wesley, 1969.

Westbrook, Robert, *The Magic Garden of Stanley Sweetheart*, New York: Crown Publishers, 1969.

Wheelis, Allen, *The Quest for Identity*, New York: Norton, 1958.

White, David M., "The Gatekeeper, A Case Study in the Diffusion of News," in L. A. Dexter and D. M. White (eds.), *People, Society, and Mass Communication*, New York: Free Press, 1964.

Whorf, Benjamin L., *Language, Thought and Reality* (New York: Wiley, 1956), M.I.T. Press, 1967.

Whyte, William H., *The Organization Man*, New York: Simon and Schuster, 1956.

Wiebe, Gerhart, "The Effect of Radio Plugging on Students' Opinions of Popular Songs," *Journal of Applied Psychology*, vol. 24, 1940, pp. 721–727.

Wiener, Norbert, *The Human Use of Human Beings, Cybernetics and Society*, Boston: Houghton Mifflin, 1950.

———, *Cybernetics, or Control and Communication in the Animal and the Machine* (2d ed.), Cambridge, Mass.: The M.I.T. Press (1948, 1961), 1965.

Wilensky, H. L., "Mass Society and Mass Culture," *American Sociological Review*, vol. 29, 1964, pp. 173–197.

Wilkins, Leslie T., *Social Deviance: Social Policy, Action and Research*, Englewood Cliffs, N.J.: Prentice-Hall, 1965.

Williams, Leonard, *Man and Monkey*, Philadelphia: Lippincott, 1968.

Wilson, Bryan R., "An Analysis of Sect Development," *American Sociological Review*, vol. 24, February 1959, pp. 3–15.

———, *Sects and Society: A Sociological Study of the Elim Tabernacle, Christian Science, and Christadelphians*, Berkeley: University of California Press, 1961.

Wilson, William, "Should New York Roadshow Have Stopped Here?," *Los Angeles Times*, June 21, 1970.

Winick, Charles E., *The New People, Desexualization in American Life*, New York: Western Publishing (Pegasus), 1968.

Wirth, Louis, Preface to Karl Mannheim, *Ideology and Utopia*, New York: Harcourt, 1936, pp. xiii–xxxi.

———, "Consensus and Mass Communications," *American Sociological Review*, vol. 13, February 1948, pp. 1–15.

Wohl, Paul, "Anti-intellectuals vs. Dropouts," *Christian Science Monitor*, Aug. 29, 1970.

Wolfe, Tom, *The Electric Kool-Aid Acid Test*, New York: Farrar, Straus, 1968.

Wolfenstein, Martha, and Leites, Nathan, *Movies, A Psychological Study*, New York: Free Press, 1950.

Wong, Herman, "Disneyland: Can It Top 15 Years of Success?," *Los Angeles Times*, July 12, 1970.

Woodstock, Songs and Photos, New York: Warner Brothers, 1970.

Wright, Charles R., *Mass Communication: A Sociological Perspective*, New York: Random House, 1959.

———, "Functional Analysis and Mass Communication," in Lerbinger and Sullivan (eds.), *Information, Influence and Communication*, New York: Basic Books, 1965.

Yoors, Jan, *The Gypsies*, New York: Simon and Schuster, 1967.

Young, Frank W., *Initiation Ceremonies, A Cross-Cultural Study of Status Dramatization*, Indianapolis: Bobbs-Merrill, 1965.

Young, Kimball, *Social Psychology*, New York: Appleton, 1956.

Zajonc, Robert B., "The Concepts of Balance, Congruity and Dissonance," *Public Opinion Quarterly*, vol. 24, 1960, pp. 280–296. (Also in Steiner and Fishbein (eds.), *Current Studies in Social Psychology*, New York: Holt, Rinehart and Winston, 1965, pp. 27–41; and in Jahoda and Warren (eds.), *Attitudes*, New York: Penguin, 1966.)

Zald, Mayer N., and Ash, Roberta, "Social Movement Organizations: Growth, Decay and Change," *Social Forces*, vol. 44, March 1966, pp. 327–340. (Reprinted in Gusfield, 1970, pp. 516–537.)

Zetterberg, Hans, "Some General Problems . . . Definition, and Dimensions of Morale," in Galdston and Zetterberg (eds.), *Panic and Morale*, Conference Transactions, New York Academy of Medicine and Josiah Macy Foundation, New York: International Universities Press, 1958, pp. 227–319.

Zollschan, George K., and Hirsch, Walter (eds.), *Explorations in Social Change*, Boston: Houghton Mifflin, 1964.

Zorbaugh, Harvey, *The Gold Coast and the Slum*, Chicago: University of Chicago Press, 1929.

Zuckerman, S., *The Social Life of Monkeys and Apes*, London: Kegan Paul, Trench, Trubner, 1932.

Index